EUROPEAN JEWRY AND THE FIRST CRUSADE

EUROPEAN JEWRY
AND THE
FIRST CRUSADE

Robert Chazan

UNIVERSITY OF CALIFORNIA PRESS
Berkeley   Los Angeles   London

University of California Press
Berkeley and Los Angeles, California

University of California Press, Ltd.
London, England

Copyright © 1987 by The Regents of the University of California

First Paperback Printing 1996

Library of Congress Cataloging-in-Publication Data

Chazan, Robert.
European Jewry and the First Crusade.

Bibliography: p.
Includes index.
1. Jews—Germany—History—1096–1147. 2. Jews—
Germany—Persecutions. 3. Crusades—First, 1096–1099—
Jews—Germany. 4. Germany—Ethnic relations.
I. Title.
DS135.G31C45 1987   943'.004924   86-6938
ISBN 0-520-20506-5

Printed in the United States of America

1 2 3 4 5 6 7 8 9

Contents

v

Preface

This book has been in the works for a number of years.
The formal project was stimulated by an invitation to
spend the academic year 1977–78 at the Institute for Advanced Studies of the Hebrew University. As I had recently
completed a prior project, the anticipated year of research
moved me to identify my next major study. In many ways,
however, my research into the experience of the Jews in
Europe during the First Crusade began at least a decade
earlier, when I took part in a stimulating doctoral seminar
at Columbia University under the direction of Professor
Gerson D. Cohen. That seminar whetted my interest in
Jewish historiography in general and in the remarkable
Hebrew First-Crusade chronicles in particular. I subsequently published a series of studies on the Hebrew
chronicles of the First, Second, and Third Crusades. My
decision to do a full-length study of Jewish fate during the
First Crusade meant in essence moving from an interest
restricted to Jewish historiography to a broader concern
with the general history of that turbulent but creative
period. Little did I know that the project would prove so
time-consuming and difficult. In fact, I complete this book
feeling that, had I the requisite patience, the study could
be carried even further: I regularly find new insights into
this material, on which I have already worked for so long.
Surely the time has come to draw this project to a close
and to proceed on to new ones.

There are a number of people and institutions to whom
I owe a serious debt of gratitude. I have already mentioned

Professor Gerson D. Cohen, who kindled my interest in
Jewish historiography and in the First-Crusade chronicles.
I must also thank the Institute for Advanced Study, which
offered me release from normal teaching duties, provided
a gracious environment for research and writing, and afforded the stimulating company of a distinguished group
of colleagues chaired by Professor Ephraim E. Urbach, to
whom I owe special thanks. My colleagues and friends
Professor David Berger and Professor Michael A. Signer
have read the manuscript and offered illuminating and
helpful suggestions. Since coming to New York, I have
greatly benefited in my work on a series of historical issues
from the stimulation of a number of gifted colleagues and
friends. I would like to note in particular Professors Steven
M. Cohen and Samuel C. Heilman, from whom I have
learned much and whose influence is undoubtedly reflected in this study.

Because the manuscript has been in the works for such
a long time, members of the secretarial staffs of both the
Department of History at Ohio State University and the
Word Processing Centers of Queens College have done
substantial typing of an ever-changing manuscript, always
carefully and cheerfully. It was Professor Arnold J. Band
who first discussed with me the possibility of submitting
the study to the University of California Press, and he has
remained helpful throughout. A number of people at the
University of California Press have been extremely helpful.
John R. Miles, Stanley Holwitz, and Matthew Lee Jaffe
have been most solicitous and kind. Genise Schnitman did
careful and exacting copy editing, and Shirley Warren saw
the book through the various phases of production with
concern and consideration.

These notes of appreciation must conclude with special
mention of my family. This book has accompanied us
through a period of significant transitions. Our stay at the
Institute for Advanced Studies imposed some difficulty on
my children and caused serious interruption of my wife's
busy work schedule. The later stages of this study saw us
move from Ohio to Israel to New York; at the same time,

our children were venturing out on their own into college and beyond. Such transitions are never easy, and the capacity of my wife and children to endure them, mature through them, and all the while support this ongoing project puts me deeply in their debt. To my wife in particular, who sacrificed much in her own professional development for this and other projects, I express gratitude and to her I offer the fruits of our joint efforts.

Introduction

The First Crusade was an intense and explosive outburst of religious exhilaration that culminated in a remarkable military achievement. Pope Urban II, in his call to the crusade at Clermont in late 1095, touched a nerve in western Christendom, unleashing forces that far exceeded his anticipations and proved impossible to control. Motivations both noble and base impelled armies of crusaders to journey to the East. Despite formidable obstacles, many of these military forces succeeded in reaching the Holy Land; in mid-1099 they breached the walls of Jerusalem and in a paroxysm of frenzy conquered the Holy City.

This extraordinary religious and military venture has long fascinated historians. To the Christian chroniclers of the late eleventh and early twelfth century, it represented the saga of religious dedication and zeal rewarded by God's miraculous interventions on behalf of his loyal servants. The remarkable success of this audacious effort, capped by the conquest of Jerusalem during the summer months of 1099, reinforced this religious and romantic view of the great military campaign as a divinely supported undertaking on the part of an army of devoted Christian warriors. To be sure, the Christian foothold established in the Near East crumbled quickly, and subsequent crusading efforts never duplicated the brilliant achievements of the 1090s. As setbacks mounted, the historical sources began to reflect doubt and disillusionment where there had been simple admiration on the part of the earlier crusade historians. Modern skepticism has taken the revisionism fur-

1

ther. The result is a set of crusade accounts that present an increasingly unsavory picture of the enterprise, emphasizing the cupidity that sent many crusaders into the Levant in quest of temporal gains and pointing to the fanatic cruelties that sprang from the initial religious exhilaration. Another line of investigation has focused on the attempts of the papacy to regain control of the movement it had launched, to define the movement more clearly, and to administer it more effectively. In the twentieth century, historians have sought to understand the wellsprings of this dynamic movement. Deeply aware of the innovative aspects of crusading behavior and ideology, these contemporary historians have sought to identify key elements in crusading theory and practice, to discover their origins in eleventh-century European life, and to discern their impact upon the rapidly developing civilization of twelfth-century western Christendom. The result of all this is a mosaic of diverse views of the First Crusade; there have been pious, perjorative, institutional, social, and spiritual perspectives and explanations.

A dramatic by-product of the religious fervor associated with the First Crusade was a series of devastating attacks on Jewish communities in northern Europe. Certain crusading bands interpreted the papal initiative as a call to overcome *all* infidelity and chose to begin their mission with an assault on the infidels immediately at hand, the Jews. These attacks were both cruel and thorough, resulting in the total destruction of a number of important Jewish settlements. The response of the besieged Jews reflects a level of religious fervor as intense as that of the attacking crusaders. In a variety of ways these Jews remained firm in their faith and militantly fought off the challenge of Christianity, in most instances at the cost of their lives. Crusader persecution of the Jews and consequent Jewish martyrdom have long been known to historians of the crusades and to historians of the Jews alike. The Christian chroniclers of the late eleventh and early twelfth century showed little interest in the anti-Jewish violence of 1096; their modern counterparts have dealt with it more extensively, generally using these assaults to highlight some of the negative aspects of the crusading venture.[1] To Jewish historians the events of 1096 have held far greater meaning. Following the catastrophe, observers preserved recollections of these incidents. These recollections were eventually fused into two unusual and innovative Hebrew chronicles, both devoted to celebrating the martyrdom of the Jews under assault. The pious attitudes of the twelfth-century Jewish chroniclers have by and large been adopted by their nineteenth- and twentieth-century successors, although modern Jewish experience has led to some critical perspectives on medieval Jewish martyrdom. Jewish sources and commentators through the years have generally concurred in interpreting the events of 1096 as an instance of remarkable Jewish heroism and as a disastrous turning point in the course of medieval Jewish history.[2]

This study began with my conviction that the anti-Jewish violence associated with the First Crusade deserves and requires full analysis. No one has isolated the phenomenon and made it the focus of detailed scrutiny before now. The first step in such an analysis would be a careful examination of the available sources, followed by an evaluation of their reliability. It quickly becomes apparent that the key to a study of Jewish fate in 1096 lay in the two original Hebrew chronicles. Extended examination of these unusual and innovative sources indicates that they are in fact relatively reliable. They were composed fairly close in time to the events depicted, are based on first-hand testimony, are committed to a portrayal of a variety of patterns of Christian and Jewish behavior, and are written in a plain and unadorned style. On examination, these unusual Hebrew chronicles reveal, besides their reliability, a striking stylistic parallel with the corresponding Christian accounts of the First Crusade. This concurrence shows that northern European Jews at these early stages formed a community that shared the spiritual environment of the Christian world in which it was embedded.

What are my findings from the careful study of these valuable records? For the anthropologically oriented, the events of 1096 would seem intrinsically interesting as instances of unusual group behavior—both the radical violence of the Christians and the equally radical martyrdom chosen in response by the Jews. In depicting these fascinating behaviors, I have often quoted the language of the sources because I felt that paraphrasing would diminish the powerful impact of the medieval portrayal. While attempting to convey some of the intrinsic power of the medieval accounts, I have also tried to remain aloof of their seductive appeal. These sources—especially the extensive Jewish records—seek to leave an impression of overall Christian bestiality and Jewish heroism. In fact, however, they provide sufficient detail to indicate that the reality was more complex and nuanced. For one thing, not all Christians were united in hostility to the Jews; even the Christian burghers of the Rhineland cities, usually excoriated by the Jewish chroniclers as aligned monolithically with the popular crusading bands, are nonetheless depicted as displaying a wide variety of behaviors, ranging from full collaboration with the attacking crusaders to vigorous efforts to protect their Jewish neighbors. Nor should the Jews who were affected by the events of 1096 be depicted simplistically as having responded uniformly to adversity. They reacted to their persecution in a number of ways. Even those who opted for martyrdom did so in ways that followed a variety of patterns. In the depiction of violence on the part of Christians toward Jews, and the response of their victims, the *diversity* of behavior will be emphasized. In addition, unlike the medieval chroniclers, I have chosen to do more than depict. I have attempted also to explain the development of these behaviors, finding the sources of the violence in some of the essential motives of the crusade and in some of its organizational shortcomings, while discerning the roots of Jewish martyrdom in both the Jewish tradition and in the vibrant spirituality of late eleventh-century northern Europe.

The events of 1096 are striking and significant for more

than their intrinsic fascination. They tell us much about general facets of the First Crusade and its aftermath—the exhilaration and frenzy of the masses, the loss of control by the papacy, and the resolute efforts on the part of the Church to regain and maintain effective leadership during the ensuing crusading ventures. To be sure, these aspects of the First Crusade and its aftermath are well documented elsewhere and have been carefully analyzed by modern historians. Nonetheless, the perspective afforded by examining the anti-Jewish assaults is important for a general understanding of aspects of the crusading experience.

More significant still is the light shed on the early development of Ashkenazic (i.e., northern European) Jewry by the events of 1096. This fledgling Jewish community began to emerge as a cohesive force in Jewish life during the eleventh century; it survived through the centuries and held a place of leadership on the modern Jewish scene. Given the importance of this community and the paucity of evidence related to the early stages in its development, the data provided by the incidents of 1096 are of great import.

Scholars interested in early Ashkenazic Jewry have tended to see this vibrant young community as socially and spiritually isolated from its immediate environment. General medievalists usually neglect this Jewish community when investigating major social and spiritual trends of the eleventh and twelfth centuries. Specialists in Jewish history have by and large remained insouciant of general tendencies of this creative epoch. Careful study of the events of 1096, however, has convinced me that early Ashkenazic Jewry was far better integrated into its environment than is generally assumed.

This integration can first be seen with regard to social interaction. Despite the largely negative view of Christians expressed in the post-1096 Hebrew records, it is clear that many Jews during the crisis period itself saw their Christian neighbors—both those in positions of power and the common burghers as well—as genuinely well disposed. There is no other way to explain the widely noted tendency of Jews to seek refuge with their Christian neighbors. No amount of after-the-fact disillusionment can gainsay the expectation on the part of the Jews of 1096 that they could count on the support and protection of segments of the Christian populace.

A second—and more striking—reflection of the integration of the Jews into their milieu is the pattern of Jewish martyrdom at this time. Granted that pre-1096 Jewish experience afforded some precedents, the martyrdom of 1096 took startling new forms. As this study proceeded, I came to feel that both the extreme behavior of the attacking crusaders and that of the besieged Jews must be seen within the context of the eleventh-century propensity for new and innovative interpretations of prior traditions. This after all was the hallmark of the eleventh century in Europe, characterizing a creative upsurge felt throughout western Christendom. The new-style papacy and its demands constitute a major example of this tendency toward innovation, disguised always as reassertion of the old and true. Crusading itself constituted a radical departure in Christian practice, although both the calls to crusade and the chronicles of the period were couched in terminology that obscures its novelty. In much the same way, a segment of those committed to the crusade—and a small segment at that—created its own pathbreaking and destructive exegesis on prior Christian doctrine concerning the place of the Jews in Christendom and its own radical interpretation of the notion of the crusade. Out of these novel interpretations emerged the devastating assaults on Rhineland Jewry. Likewise the Jews under attack constructed their own innovative and extreme interpretation of earlier Jewish teachings on how to respond to religious persecution, leading them to a radical manner of manifesting their rejection of the crusader call to conversion. In the process, these Jews significantly enriched the historic Jewish legacy of *kiddush ha-Shem* (martyrdom), thereby enshrining themselves in the annals of Jewish heroism.

For too long, those studying medieval Ashkenazic Jewry have tended to see this vibrant young community as spiritually isolated from its immediate environment. My study of Rhineland Jewry in 1096 convinced me that both the anti-Jewish assaults and the remarkable Jewish responses must be seen against the backdrop of intense late eleventh-century spirituality, in both its positive and negative aspects. Treating this young Jewry in isolation from its ambiance can yield only unresolved questions and outright distortions; studying early Ashkenazic Jewry in its temporal context affords a much richer understanding of its remarkable efflorescence. The late eleventh century in Europe was a period of unusual creativity and innovation; new ideas, always masked as restatements of the old and valued, abounded. The events to be presented here—both the aggressions of the popular crusaders and the zealous reactions of the beleaguered Jews—can, at their core, be comprehended only against the backdrop of this volatile spirituality.

A third index of the degree of integration of late eleventh-century Ashkenazic Jewry into its environment is the special style of history writing that emerged in the wake of the disaster. Once again, Jewish tradition provided historiographic precedents, yet a new style of history writing was forged out of the intense Jewish response to the events of 1096. This new style shows striking similarities to the historiographic tendencies in late eleventh- and early twelfth-century northern Europe, suggesting once more that the Jews of this area were influenced far more by the general patterns of spiritual and intellectual creativity than heretofore recognized. The examination of this limited set of events and reactions thus opens the way for a better appreciation of key characteristics of early Ashkenazic Jewry, and should be of interest both to general medievalists and to specialists in the history of the Jews.

Besides demonstrating that the events of 1096 illustrate important features of crusading history and of the history of early Ashkenazic Jewry, this study also raises the question of the place of 1096 within the overall development of medieval Ashkenazic Jewry. The results negate a widely held assumption: It has been a commonplace of modern historiography that 1096 serves as a decisive and disastrous watershed in medieval Jewish history. This extended investigation of the events of 1096 concludes that the tangible impact of crusader violence on European Jewry was quite limited. While the violence was aimed at and resulted in the destruction of three of its leading communities, the bulk of early Ashkenazic Jewry emerged from the crisis unscathed and in fact its rapid development continued with little impediment. This conclusion led inexorably to further questioning of the broadly accepted thesis that 1096 served as a disastrous turning point and eventually to its rejection. The thirteenth-century decline of western Ashkenazic Jewry must be associated with other, and less dramatic, developments on the European scene.

While I have come to reject the notion of 1096 as marking a sharp turn in medieval Jewish history, I do believe that the events of that year serve to introduce us to new developments that were to prove central to twelfth- and thirteenth-century Ashkenazic Jewish experience. Some of these developments were decidedly negative. The perception of the Jew as enemy of Christendom, which lay at the heart of the popular anti-Jewish violence in 1096, intensified during the twelfth century, culminating in the series of destructive slanders that were to plague European Jewry down through the ages. There are positive indicators in the events of 1096 as well. In particular the responses of the beleaguered Rhineland Jews serve as a harbinger of the intense and creative spirit that distinguishes Ashkenazic Jewry of the twelfth and thirteenth centuries. Much of the creativity expressed by the Tosafists and German Pietists is foreshadowed in the Rhineland Jews' remarkable readiness for martyrdom in 1096, and in the evocative symbols that aroused and sustained this attitude.

This study concludes by examining the events of 1096 from the broad perspective of Jewish history in its entirety. This wide focus suggests that these events introduced into the history of the Jews a new-style persecution and a new-style response to persecution. This new-style persecution, repudiated though it was by the ecclesiastical authorities, constitutes a disturbing precedent for later medieval and modern projects to eradicate the Jews. The radical behavior of the Jewish martyrs of 1096 was likewise precedent-setting. To be sure, later Jewish tradition tended to efface some of the radical quality of this behavior, in effect domesticating it into a confirmation of older styles of Jewish martyrdom. My analysis, however, emphasizes the unique and innovative aspects of the Jewish martyrdom of 1096.

In many respects then, the events of 1096 merit our consideration and study: They are intrinsically interesting and significant; they point beyond themselves to important aspects of eleventh-century Christian and Jewish life and to striking new developments on the twelfth- and thirteenth-century scene; and they highlight important new elements—both negative and positive—in the long and complex history of the Jews. When I began this study, I had no clear idea where the analysis of the events of 1096 would lead. As it has concluded, I am convinced that, as so often happens, the close scrutiny of a limited set of events has provided broader and more revealing perspectives on medieval western Christendom and its Jews than one could have guessed at the start.

I

The Background

The Awakening of Northern Europe

The development of the First Crusade, as well as the state of late eleventh-century northern European Jewry, can be understood only against the background of a broad material and spiritual revival throughout western Christendom during the tenth and eleventh centuries, which had particularly pronounced impact in the heretofore backward areas of northern Europe. The precise starting point, the causes, and the stages of this revival are shrouded in obscurity and are consequently debated by modern historians. What is remarkable, however, is the level of agreement in present-day research concerning the fact of this upsurge. Students of demography and economics, social organization, urban development, and intellectual life all describe a new vitality in European life during these poorly documented centuries.[1]

This revival seems to have proceeded on a number of fronts simultaneously. It is impossible to pinpoint a single causative factor and to attribute developments in other sectors to its impact. Instead, the scholarly consensus suggests that demographic growth, economic vitalization, political maturation, and intellectual renewal took place side by side. To be sure, these developments were interrelated and reinforced one another. There is widespread agreement that the demographic curve rose from the late tenth century on, although no clear data to prove this population growth are available. The widely shared impression of demographic expansion is based on evidence of city development, land reclamation, and outward migration. Such population growth was supported by improvements in the economic and political spheres and contributed in turn to economic and political betterment. Advances in the economic sphere are even more palpable than in the demographic. Much as it is true that the raids of the Norsemen, widely lamented in the literature of the ninth and early tenth century, were devastating to segments of European society, recent historians have emphasized that these attacks also had certain positive effect. New trade routes were opened and precious metals and goods flowed more freely. Particularly affected by these developments were northern areas, which had been on the peripheries of the Carolingian Empire. These include England, Flanders, and sections of western and northern Germany.

Related to demographic growth and economic revival is an improvement in forms of political organization. This improvement flowed in part from the demographic and economic advances; in part it accelerated them. As the period of anarchy began to recede, increasingly large and cohesive political units developed. Perhaps most impressive were the counties and duchies of western France, which were eventually responsible for the conquest of England and the establishment of an empire on both sides of the English Channel. The Capetian monarchy controlled a small area in a modest but effective way; there was little to suggest that the groundwork was being laid for one of Europe's most stable kingdoms. At this early point, the largest political unit in western Christendom was the revived Holy Roman Empire, which stretched across Germany into Italy. The extent of imperial holdings and the pomp of the imperial court have not blinded modern historians to fundamental and fatal flaws in this incarnation of the empire. By the late twelfth century, as the English and French monarchies were reaping the benefits of patient building, Germany had begun its long and irreversible decline.

Of special significance is the growth of urban centers, by which is meant both the enlargement of already existing urban nuclei and the establishment of new settlements. Both occurred widely throughout western Europe, during this time again most noticeably in the areas involved in the newly expanding trade. In some instances, vigorous new townships developed alongside the ruins of Roman cities, while in others entirely new urban nuclei were established. These expanding urban centers served both the commercial purposes of the burgeoning trade of northern Europe and the administrative purposes of the maturing political administrations. Jews are mentioned often in the documentation related to this urbanization and it is obvious that this urbanization was a major factor in the rapid development of Jewish life in the area.[2]

The same broad pattern of revival affected the Church. It expressed itself at every level: in the enhanced efficiency of ecclesiastical organization, in the reforming of ecclesiastical discipline, and in the dynamically expanding Cluniac movement. The spearhead of this process and its most visible symbol was the reformed papacy, exemplified in the reign of Pope Gregory VII. Particularly significant was the new vigor of the monasteries, with the Cluniacs taking the lead. Monastic practices were scrutinized and regularized, with efforts made to ensure adherence to proper standards. The monasteries became centers for the creative advances of the late tenth and eleventh century.

These creative advances were expressed in the institutional changes just noted; the real focus, however, was the hearts and minds of individuals. A growing number of men and women began to devote themselves to exploring fundamental issues of faith and, once this force of inquiry was unleashed, it very quickly came to absorb the talents and time of gifted teachers and students. It has often been suggested that the Jews, by their very presence, afforded some measure of stimulation to this intellectual renewal.

Likewise, the general intellectual vigor of the wider society had its impact upon the Jews of northern Europe.[3] This spirit of questioning and intellectual vigor extended beyond the formal school structure and the established curriculum. It filtered down into society at large, occasionally evoking new religious ideas and ideals. Some of the most exciting and innovative research of the past half century has been devoted to identifying and understanding the new spirit that emerged in western Europe in the last decades of the eleventh century and the first decades of the twelfth. Its impact was felt everywhere—in religious life, in education, in the relation of the individual to society and in the very notion of individual identity itself, in every branch of the sciences and the arts. There is a general sense among contemporary scholars that the predominance of European civilization on the world scene down through the twentieth century is rooted largely in the creative and fruitful new lines of thought spawned during the epoch under consideration.[4] In some instances the new ideas and ideals were absorbed into normative ecclesiastical thinking; in other cases their adherents were viewed as heretical dissenters and persecuted as such. It is no accident that the new creativity went hand-in-hand with the first serious outbreak of northern European heresy.[5]

So far I have emphasized the positive developments of the tenth and eleventh centuries. It is clear, however, that such periods of dynamic growth are never free of the conflict and tension that rapid change inevitably produces. Although both secular and ecclesiastical governments matured rapidly, neither was able to cope fully with the internal conflicts generated by widespread change. In part the atmosphere of dynamic growth encouraged the bold to aggrandizement at the expense of their neighbors. In part the changes left many, particularly at the lower levels of society, frustrated and dissatisfied. Conflict extended from the highest stratum of society to the lowest.

The conflict at the highest levels is epitomized by the struggle for power between church and state, dubbed by subsequent historians the Investiture Controversy. The seed of this controversy lay in the changes that had upset the old order and opened new possibilities for power and control. Within lay ranks the lust for greater power occasioned a series of extended conflicts. The stakes were high and the victors, for example the Norman dukes and the Angevin counts, emerged as the foremost political leaders in Europe. Less romantic and more pervasive was the daily violence endemic to the period. Everyday violence, both organized and spontaneous, was a fearsome reality. At the beginning of the eleventh century, the bishop of Worms gave a compelling description of the widespread mayhem: "Every day, murders in the manner of wild beasts are committed among the dependents of St. Peter's. They attack each other through drunkenness, through pride, or for no reason at all. In the course of one year thirty-five serfs of St. Peter's, completely innocent people, have been killed by other serfs of the church; and the murderers, far from repenting, glory in their crime."[6] The violence thus described plays a central role in the story I set out here. An effort to direct the "given" violence of the society into legitimate channels is widely cited as one factor among many in the call to the crusade. Moreover, the Jews, a weak and exposed element in European society, probably suffered disproportionately from the general lawlessness of the period. Finally, one element in the massacre of the Jews in 1096 was precisely the general tendency toward bestiality depicted above.

The period that preceded 1096—and that succeeded it as well—is thus revealed as an epoch of dramatic change and growth. A brilliant young civilization was beginning to emerge in northern Europe. The upsurge manifested itself in every sphere of societal activity and lent a new attractiveness to a heretofore backward area. Among those particularly responsive to the appeal of this newly developing area were the Jews. Indeed the attraction was mutual; the farsighted leaders of northern Europe were interested in attracting Jews and Jews were prepared to take the risks involved in migration. At the same time, dangers manifested themselves almost immediately. In part, these dangers were general—the violence often spawned by the aggressiveness and the frustrations of a period of rapid change; in part, they were particularly threatening for the Jews, as newcomers and as dissenters from the central religious faith that united most inhabitants of the area.

The major characteristic of eleventh-century northern Europe seems to have been vitality. Out of this vitality emerged budding new urban centers, along with small but significant Jewish settlements, and the physical and spiritual vigor that engendered the First Crusade developed with them. Unfortunately every such period of growth has its victims as well, and the Jews who had been attracted to this rapidly developing area were destined to suffer from the crusading fervor that sprang from eleventh-century vitality.

The Growth and Development of Northern European Jewry

Jewish life benefited enormously from tenth- and eleventh-century change, and Jewish communities expanded rapidly, while the Jews in turn made their own contribution to general growth and development. By the end of the eleventh century, Jewish settlements could be found throughout Europe. The oldest of these were in the southern areas: Italy, southern France, and the sections of northern Spain under Christian control. A whole set of newer Jewish communities had also sprung up north of the Loire, stretching from England in the west all the way across to eastern Europe. It was these northern (Ashkenazic) communities that were most dramatically affected by the remarkable growth spurt of the late tenth and eleventh century, just as it was these settlements that were destined to suffer most grievously from some of the dangerous side effects of this rapid change.[7]

The general revival of the tenth and eleventh centuries did not leave historians much in the way of primary sources, and the same is true for Jewish history at this period as well. It is widely agreed that this period brought to Ashkenazic Jewry an intellectual ferment parallel to that in the surrounding majority society, albeit in somewhat different form, yet few direct products of this creativity have reached us.[8] Much of the source material has been preserved in volumes written or edited in the twelfth or thirteenth century. Diverse genres of literary creativity are reflected in the few fragments that have survived. They include Jewish law, in the forms of practical responsa,[9] commentaries on classical texts,[10] and compilations;[11] biblical study, where the extensive commentary of Rabbi Solomon ben Isaac of Troyes (also known as Rashi) is an early work, one quickly elevated to the status of an accepted and authoritative formulation;[12] original poetry;[13] and occasional prose chronicles, which are as useful and informative as they are rare.[14] The diversity of genres further complicates the work of the modern historian. It necessitates an awareness of the problems in using these various literary types. The paucity of texts combined with the diversity of literary genres has made the task of reconstructing tenth- and eleventh-century northern European Jewish history difficult and has occasioned some serious scholarly disagreement. In general, students of Jewish history have tended to see the Jewish experience as an extension of the general developments noted above— demographic growth, economic development, and intellectual vitality. The extent to which these Jews suffered from the general disorder of the period has not been sufficiently recognized.[15]

The Jewish population of northern Europe, like the general population, showed both flux and growth during the tenth and eleventh centuries. Jews moved regularly from town to town as required by their commercial enterprises.[16] In some instances the distances traversed were considerable, taking Jewish traders, for example, from the Rhineland eastward into Hungary and back.[17] The long Hebrew First-Crusade chronicle, in describing the destruction of the Jewish community of Cologne, depicts the periodic gatherings at the fair in Cologne of Jewish leaders from a variety of communities.[18] The well-known and important disputation written by Gilbert Crispin portrays a confrontation between the abbot of Westminister and a Jew from Mainz whose business brought him to England.[19] Trade was not the only motivation for travel. As in the Christian world at the time, the intellectual revival brought to the fore gifted teachers whose schools attracted students from near and far. The most widely noted instance of travel for the sake of learning concerns the distinguished Rabbi Solomon ben Isaac of Troyes (Rashi). The fame of the Rhineland academies, particularly those of Worms and Mainz, attracted the young Solomon of Troyes to study at these academies for an extended period. Upon his return to Troyes, he became the central figure in a school that was likewise destined to attract students from a variety of areas.[20] The instance of Rabbi Solomon is just one well-known example of a widespread phenomenon.

Two additional sources reflecting extensive movements are worth citing. A late tenth-century Hebrew letter written in celebration of the miraculous deliverance of Le Mans Jewry from potential catastrophe describes the peregrinations of a curious character named Sehok ben Esther. Born in Blois, this renegade from Jewish life traveled throughout northwestern France, visiting a number of Jewish communities and eventually settling in Le Mans.[21] Perhaps the most striking instance of wide-ranging movement is afforded by the biographical sketch of a prominent Jewish leader, given credit for extricating northern European Jewry from serious peril at the end of the first decade of the eleventh century. Probably born in Lorraine, Jacob ben Yekutiel found himself in Normandy at the outbreak of the persecution, spent four years in Rome in a successful effort to enlist papal aid for his endangered fellow Jews, returned to Lorraine for a twelve-year period, and then accepted the invitation extended by Baldwin of Flanders to settle in Arras.[22]

These last two sources document movement that resulted in permanent relocation to a new area, that is, migration, instead of short-term travel associated with business or with learning. In the case of Sehok ben Esther, his wanderings led him to Le Mans, the site of an established Jewish community. The story of Jacob ben Yekutiel, in contrast, reflects the establishment of a new Jewish settlement. At the conclusion of his successful intervention at the papal court, Jacob returned to Lorraine, where he eventually received an invitation to settle in Flanders. Jacob and thirty fellow Jews accepted the invitation. Jacob unfortunately died only three months later. While the settlement in Flanders never took root, the Jews moved across the English Channel in precisely the same way at the invitation of the Norman conquerors of England. This Jewish community did strike roots, growing and flourishing for over two centuries until the expulsion of the Jews from England in 1290.

The clearest and fullest information available for the establishment of a new Jewish enclave comes from the community of Speyer, founded in 1084. By fortuitous circumstance, valuable sources from both the Jewish and Christian sides have been preserved. The Jewish recollections are embedded in a communal memoir, probably composed in the 1170s.[23] It depicts a disastrous fire in the Jewish neighborhood of Mainz and how some of the Jews, fearful of burgher animosity, decided to go to Speyer to seek a safer haven, where they received a warm welcome from the bishop of that town. The charter of invitation granted by Bishop Rudiger of Speyer has happily survived, corroborating the Jewish account and offering fuller information on the details of Jewish settlement.[24] The concurrence of these two valuable sources argues powerfully for their authenticity. A wealth of evidence is thereby provided for understanding the process by which new Jewish settlements were established.

The motivations of both sides are clear. The Jews leaving Mainz sought safer quarters. It seems likely that, in most such instances, hopes for economic betterment played an equal or greater role in the Jewish desire to establish a new settlement. Even more interesting is the bishop's motivation. The invitation to the Jews is pre-

sented as part of an extensive effort to improve the status
of Speyer. The bishop obviously perceived the Jews as
useful contributors to this effort at urban development. To
be sure, the bishop's views were not necessarily accepted
by the burghers of Speyer. That the bishop built a wall
around the Jewish quarters reflects the background of tensions in Mainz; it also presupposes the emergence of similar tensions in Speyer as well.

The historical evidence portrays a high degree of geographic mobility among tenth- and eleventh-century
Ashkenazic Jews; they traveled short and long distances,
settling in established Jewish communities and founding
new centers of Jewish life. It also points to—though it
cannot prove—Jewish population growth during this
period. As is the case for the general rise in population
believed to have occurred during the same period, no
satisfactory data can be adduced. The explanations for
this demographic growth are inevitably vague and general, centering on biological factors and the immigration
that would naturally result from developing economic
opportunities.

Perhaps the most interesting question to pose—and
the most difficult to answer—concerns the origins of those
Jews who were truly immigrants, that is to say those who
made their way to northern Europe from elsewhere. Simple good sense suggests that they came from the Mediterranean region. One would like to have corroborating data;
unfortunately few are available. Many scholars feel that
northern France was a source of Jewish settlers, who
fanned out into the areas that developed later, meaning
northern Germany, Normandy, and England. This impression is conveyed by information on random individuals
and by the apparently widespread use of French as a
vernacular among German and English Jews. This would
make northern France a conduit through which southern
Jews passed northward, fanning out into Germany, northwestern France, and England. A second route taken by
some Jews went directly from Italy to Germany, into the
cities of the Rhineland in particular. There are a number

of individual scholars in the Rhineland cities whose Italian origins are certain. The most famous of these are the descendants of the Kalonymide family, supposed to have been transplanted from Lucca to Mainz by "Emperor Charles." The process of inviting Jewish settlers is so well established for the eleventh century that there is no reason to question the possibility of such a transfer. However, the sources that document this specific transfer are highly suspect and, despite major efforts to discover the "grain of historical truth" in the later sources, one may skeptically regard such efforts as futile.[25] Details aside, however, there can be no serious doubt that there did exist an Italy-Rhineland route of Jewish immigration into northern Europe.

The charter mentioned earlier, extended by Bishop Rudiger to the Jews settling in Speyer in 1084, is useful in reconstructing a number of major characteristics of this early Ashkenazic community. Since the privilege was intended to attract Jews by providing better conditions than those available elsewhere; it had perforce to address itself to the economic and social realities of Jewish life and to afford inducements related directly to those realities. A close look at the economic stipulations in the charter reveals a Jewish community in which the key economic activity is trade. All the economic boons conferred by the bishop involve trade; this is clearly the Jews' major occupation. Jewish sources reveal that this trade took place on a variety of levels. As already noted, Jews were involved in long-distance trade, with its opportunities for high profits and its attendant high risks. Other Jews occupied themselves with more moderate business carried on within a narrow radius of their home town itself. The data available are too limited to permit clear delineation of the kinds of goods that Jews bought and sold, although one gleans a general sense of broadly ranging interests; there are references in the sources to pelts, clothes, vessels, animals, fish, and grapes.

The most suggestive indication of the centrality of business in Jewish economic life of the period is contained in a question posed by the Jewish community of Troyes to

the early eleventh-century rabbinic authority, Rabbi Joseph
Tov-Elem. In the community of Troyes a dispute had broken out over taxation. While everyone agreed to the general principle that each household pay a certain percentage
of its possessions as tax, members of the community
disagreed over what precisely constituted these taxable
possessions. According to some, all profitable possessions—merchandise, money, and vineyards—should be
considered in assessing taxes. A woman in the community
who possessed several vineyards argued that her vineyards should be exempt because of the precarious nature
of the profits which she derived therefrom. The response
of Rabbi Joseph is striking.

> If the matter is as written, it seems to me that Leah
> [the woman who owned the vineyards] is correct and
> her claim is valid. Her work is not as simple as trading
> and her profit is not as readily available as that of
> usury. . . . How then can one compare an occupation
> where the labor is difficult and the profit small to an
> occupation where the labor is easy and the profit is
> large.[26]

While Rabbi Joseph's statement on the safety and security
of business seems a bit exaggerated, his stand on the taxation issue reflects a community increasingly rooted in
business affairs.

Since business involves catering to perceived lacks and
needs, it makes sense that potential customers would
sometimes need credit to complete transactions before
they had available the necessary capital.[27] It should be
noted that in the sources of this period the Jews appear
both as borrowers and lenders. Extensive involvement in
moneylending on the part of Jews did not develop fully
until the twelfth century, when the Catholic church began
to vigorously enforce its legal proscription against Christians collecting interest from other Christians.[28] Most of
the lending reflected in the sources is of a relatively simple
variety, with return of the borrowed sums usually guaran-

teed by the deposit of a pledge. There are occasional indications of more sophisticated arrangements as well.

It is likewise not surprising that business affairs involved the Jews in the complications of monetary exchange. An eleventh-century responsum refers, for example, to the practice of lending a pound, containing twelve ounces of silver, in Cologne and receiving in repayment thirteen ounces in coin in Mainz or Worms.[29] Similar involvement in the complexities of exchange are recurrently reflected in the rabbinic sources of the period.

While trade seemed to have been the Jews' primary occupation, there are occasional indications in rabbinic texts of other economic activities as well, including bread baking, cheesemaking, grape-growing and wine-making, and handiwork associated with ritual objects. Although individual Jews certainly supported themselves in these ways, these services were apparently offered within the Jewish community. Bread, cheese, wine, and meat all involved ritual requirements that necessitated preparation by Jews. There were undoubtedly additional members of the community who supported themselves and their families by providing necessary services within the community. The viability of the community as a whole, however, rested on the general contributions it could make to the burgeoning European economy, and that contribution lay in the area of trade. Trade—and thereby the Jews, who were needed for the crucial role they played in it—was the cornerstone of the community's economic viability and, thus, of its political security as well.

The general picture is fairly clear—small communities of Jews contributed to and benefited from the expansion of the trade that was a major factor in the economic recovery of the tenth and eleventh centuries. These Jews possessed a number of qualifications that prepared them for their special role in European society. They came to northern Europe as an already urbanized group, hence familiar with business, which was obviously concentrated in the cities. It is likely that they brought with them advanced business techniques, more sophisticated than those developing slowly in northern Europe. These techniques stemmed partially from the Mediterranean milieu out of which they had come and partly from their intimate familiarity with talmudic texts that preserved recollections of an earlier period of more advanced business methods.

Turning once more to Bishop Rudiger's invitation to the Mainz Jews settling in Speyer, we discern clear recognition of the Jews' right to self-government. The formulation of this right is striking: "Just as the mayor of the city serves among the burghers, so too shall the Jewish leader adjudicate any quarrel which might arise among them or against them."[30] The Jews are in effect treated as a second municipality within the physical boundaries of Speyer. Like the Christian municipality of Speyer, it is subject ultimately to the authority of the episcopal suzerain. The motivations and reactions of all three interested parties are not difficult to identify. The bishop gained a valuable independent ally within the city, thereby reducing the autonomy of the burghers' municipal institutions. Likewise, the Jews had a number of reasons for desiring autonomy. Aware of religious, social, and economic antipathy toward them on the part of the burghers, the Jews had little or no confidence that they would receive equitable treatment in the municipal courts; they much preferred the more paternal treatment they expected from the bishop. They were motivated by more than fear alone. They were heirs to a well-developed set of regulations for conducting communal and judicial affairs. Autonomy of the kind extended by Bishop Rudiger afforded the Jews an opportunity to conduct community business in accordance with the dictates of Jewish law. Finally, it does not take much imagination to guess the reactions of the burghers of Speyer. The arrangement concluded between the bishop and the Jews represented a blow to the burghers' interests and an infringement on their power—serious resentment seems inevitable. In fact, one senses strongly a vicious cycle. Fearful of subjugation to the burghers and their institutions, the Jews preferred to maintain parallel autonomous institutions directly answerable only to the bishop. This preference, readily understandable as it is, only widened the gulf between the Jews and their resentful burgher neighbors.

Normally the Jews lived in physically separate quarters or neighborhoods. We have already noted, in mentioning the fire that devastated it, that in 1084 Mainz had a Jewish quarter, and that the Mainz émigrés went to Speyer to establish a new Jewish quarter. This incident reveals one of the major motivations for a separate Jewish neighborhood, namely, physical security. The erection of a wall around the Jewish quarter of Speyer seems to have been an unusual step, reflecting the special circumstances of 1084. Even in calmer times, however, the Jews tended to congregate together for social, psychological, and religious reasons. There is, at this early point, no evidence of legally enforced segregation—this would not come until some time later. It is not clear precisely how Jewish the Jewish quarter was during the tenth and eleventh centuries. References to Jews and Christians living in close proximity would seem to suggest that the Jewish neighborhood was identifiably or even preponderantly Jewish; it does not seem to have been exclusively Jewish.

During the poorly documented late tenth and eleventh century, Ashkenazic Jewry successfully adapted earlier Jewish traditions of self-rule, reflected in the Talmud, to the new circumstances of northern Europe. The well-organized Jewish community carried on negotiations with the larger society around it, raised the moneys needed for externally imposed levies and for its own internal needs, enforced discipline upon its members, and provided an extensive set of social, religious, and educational services. It truly operated as a parallel formation to the Christian municipality. Like the Christian municipality, its power was highly localized, resting in the local Jewish settlement itself.[31]

Perhaps the most impressive achievement of these young Jewish settlements was their intellectual vigor. Here again the parallel to Christian society is noteworthy. While many of the achievements of this period reflect the newness of Jewish intellectual activity in northern Europe, it is remarkable how quickly the scholarship of this community developed.[32]

One of the key achievements attributed to the first great intellectual leader of Ashkenazic Jewry, Rabbi Gershom ben Judah of Mainz, is the copying of the text of the Talmud and the establishment thereby of an authoritative basis for textual study. This was a necessary first step in the development of a foundation for text-centered study. The second giant of this community's early history, Rabbi Solomon ben Isaac of Troyes, also expended considerable effort to establish proper textual readings. The major achievement of Rabbi Solomon was his authorship of an extensive introductory commentary to the talmudic text. His commentary consists of short observations on numerous words and phrases. The cumulative effect is to provide a running guide to the intricate arguments of the talmudic text. The rapidity with which the work became a classic, used extensively down to the present day, should not obscure the fact that it originated in a community still in the early stages of forging an intellectual tradition.

While study of rabbinic texts reflects one aspect of the intimate connections between academic life and community affairs, these links led to the development of other branches of intellectual activity as well. Clearly the Bible was widely read and studied. Biblical selections after all constituted a major segment of the liturgy, and biblical passages were often adduced in discussions of Jewish law. But beyond this the Bible formed a basis for the Jewish weltanschauung and was studied in this way. This is reflected in the great commentary of Rabbi Solomon ben Isaac on the Bible. As many observers have noted, Rabbi Solomon makes the biblical text the foundation of a total educational framework, deducing from it the laws, ethics, folklore, and broad attitudes that were intended to guide the community and establish its goals. The extent to which this effort to integrate fully the Bible into Jewish thinking was successful is reflected in the random historical texts that have come to us. They are suffused with biblical quotations woven inextricably into the fabric of the story they attempt to tell. One rarely senses conscious striving for effect; rather the Bible so permeated the consciousness of these Jews that they could not fail to see contemporary events as conforming to well-established and well-known biblical stories and motifs, as indeed was the case among their Christian neighbors as well.

The centers of the rapidly developing intellectual life of Ashkenazic Jewry were concentrated in the Rhineland and especially in the two great communities of Mainz and Worms.[33] Students traveled substantial distances to study at the schools of Mainz and Worms. Like their Christian counterparts, the Jewish schools were loosely structured and their reputations depended primarily on the presence of a gifted teacher or set of teachers. The eulogies written in the wake of the destruction of those great centers of learning and religious life at Worms and Mainz were not exaggerated. These were young but extraordinarily vibrant new centers of Jewish creativity. Perhaps a measure of their vitality is the fact that the physical destruction associated with the First Crusade could not stamp out the sparks of creativity. The early vigor of the Rhineland communities was carried to other areas of northern Europe and there continued to bear fruit.

In sum, the Jewish communities of northern Europe show a vitality that parallels that of the larger Christian environment. The Jews were attracted by the vigorous young society developing in northern Europe, contributed to the growth of that society, and benefited from its dynamism. Inevitably, however, there were tensions and problems. Nonetheless, the rapidly expanding urban centers of northern Europe seem overall to have accommodated and accepted a small but useful Jewish minority.

CHRISTIAN-JEWISH RELATIONS

So far I have looked at the rapid development of Ashkenazic Jewry in northern Europe, mentioning its interactions with the non-Jewish world only in passing. From these random references it is already clear that Jewish life was powerfully conditioned by the achievements, needs, and antipathies of the non-Jewish world that surrounded it. Northern European towns of the tenth and eleventh centuries were small and their Jewish populations tiny. As a result, substantial interaction between Jews and non-Jews was inevitable.[34]

In this newly developing area, there was only one inherited tradition that defined the stance of majority society toward the Jewish minority, and that was the legacy of the Roman Catholic Church. This legacy, already well formulated by the period under discussion, was inherently complex and problematic. It revolved around three central elements: theological negation, political toleration, and practical limitation. The theological negation involved more than the simple assertion that the Jews were in error (the Jews, for their part, would have said precisely the same of their Christian neighbors). Church doctrine asserted that the Jews had once in fact possessed the truth of revelation, misread it, and thereby forfeited their covenental relationship with the Deity (whereas the Jews would see the Christians as errant followers of a false messiah). From the perspective of the Christians the Jews might be seen as superior to all other non-Christians—for they had once possessed the truth—or equally as inferior to all others—it being more reprehensible to have had the truth and given it up than to have simply never known it. This negative assessment of the Jews was deepened by the imputation to them of guilt for the crucifixion of the messiah, whom they should—according to the Christians—have accepted. These strongly negative opinions regarding the Jews were not limited to esoteric theological circles; they were graphically embodied in central rituals of the Church, which assured widespread dissemination to broad segments of the Christian populace. Despite its negative outlook on Judaism, the Church formally called for toleration of Jewish life within Christendom. It was a Pyrrhic sort of toleration, buttressed by several theological rationales, most of which reinforced negative stereotypes of the Jews. The essential fact remained, however, that Jews were to be permitted to exist within Christian society and to fulfill their religious obligations as Jews. The toleration of Jewish existence was circumscribed in ways meant to obviate perceived risks to Christians or Christendom. Social contact, for example, was to be limited, so that Jews would have no serious opportunity to influence the religious beliefs of their Christian neighbors. These then were the key elements governing how the dominant institution of the time handled its relations with the Jews. These elements constituted a complex doctrine, and therein lay grave danger. In untroubled times, to negate Judaism while tolerating Jews was perhaps feasible; in periods of agitation and stress, the complex and contradictory doctrine was apt to disintegrate. The early months of the First Crusade were not untroubled times—they were tumultuous. .

Jewish life in northern Europe was thus conditioned by social realities and by a complex doctrinal legacy. Some evidence of normal and tranquil Jewish-Christian relations survives, although the sources—as always—tend to highlight disruption rather than tranquility and normalcy. There were inevitably extensive transactions between the Jews of northern Europe and their neighbors: The Jews employed Christian laborers in a variety of domestic activities, entered various kinds of partnerships with Christians, bought from and sold to their non-Jewish neighbors, borrowed from and lent to their fellow townsmen. Several passages in the sources reflect cordial relationships. Rabbi Solomon ben Isaac of Troyes, for example, discusses the ritual complications entailed by a gift he received from a non-Jew on the last day of Passover.[35] Christians are on occasion depicted as assisting Jewish neighbors at moments of crisis.[36] Thus, when the renegade Sehok ben Esther arranged the assassination of a Jew in Le Mans, the cries of the dying Jew aroused the townspeople. They carried him to his home and tried to identify his assassins.[37]

Jewish relations with the authorities were particularly

warm. As noted earlier, the relationship was symbiotic. The suzerains gained allies within the often hostile urban enclaves, as well as valuable revenues; the Jews gained physical security and economic support. Christian sources preserve a number of references to cordial relations between the Jews and the bishops of various German cities.[38] The Jews of twelfth-century Speyer remembered the kindness extended by Bishop Rudiger at the time of the founding of the community in 1084.[39] As I have already indicated, this cordiality in some ways fostered ill will between the Jews and their burgher neighbors; it was a mixed blessing.

Perhaps the most striking index of extensive interaction is the copious evidence documenting conversion from Judaism to Christianity and to a lesser extent, vice versa. Such movement from camp to camp is understandable against the background of young and small Christian and Jewish societies, with extensive intergroup contacts. Evidence of Christian conversion to Judaism is limited and the phenomenon was probably limited as well; nonetheless incidents are known.[40] More widely documented—and probably more widespread—is conversion from the minority faith to the religion of the majority. Some of these conversions were the result of violence and force; others, however, were not.[41] Conversion from Judaism to Christianity occurred at every level of Jewish society. While details are not available, widely reported traditions speak of the apostasy of sons of Rabbi Simon ben Isaac and Rabbi Gershom ben Judah of Mainz, two of the foremost figures of early eleventh-century Ashkenazic Jewry.[42]

While, on the one hand, the immaturity of northern European society facilitated contact between Jews and Christians, fostered some degree of cordial relations, and encouraged some crossing of religious lines, there is also evidence of antipathy in the relations between the two groups and occasional violence on the part of the majority against the minority.[43] To some extent, the animosity from which the Jews suffered had little or nothing to do with Jewish-Christian relations per se. In many instances the

Jews were rather the victims of the violence that was endemic to northern European society of the period. A remarkable responsum captures the anarchy of this epoch. The question addressed to Rabbi Gershom of Mainz concerns a Jewish trader who bought from and sold to the overlords of the towns in his vicinity. He would often sell on credit

> or exchange goods with them, taking the cattle that they had plundered. He would buy them cheaply, bring them home and sell them at a high price, and thus profit. He followed this practice for six or seven years. He was despised by the plundered villagers and by their overlords, the barons, who said: "This Jew incites our enemies against us, since he is always prepared to buy up the plunder. Therefore they are accustomed to assault us and proceed securely." Moreover, many of the overlords [with whom the Jew dealt] quarreled with him on a number of occasions concerning the pledges entrusted to him and concerning the interest which he charged. They would continually threaten him. . . . A number of times they took him in custody and held him for ransom, but he was saved. A number of times other Jews were taken for ransom and thus lost money on his account. On another occasion some of his children were taken, but were saved. . . . He thus continued to come and go, he and the others, until a time when the king of France came with his troops, along with the duke of Burgundy, and placed under siege a town a half day's journey from that of the Jew. His fellow townsmen were accustomed to go there among the soldiers, to sell to them their needs and to buy from them the plunder. This Reuben went there, to that area, as was his custom. The army remained there about three months. Soldiers from the army would plunder all that they could. Those near to their towns would send their booty home, and, when they left the king, they carried much booty with them. Many of these plundering barons hated Reuben. Prior

to the withdrawal of the barons, a rumor spread in his city that he had been imprisoned—that his enemies had found him and led him off. Others came and said that he was held captive in a far-off place, for his far-off enemies had also been involved in the siege. It was further said that he had been killed. Subsequently men came and said to his relatives: "I know the place where Reuben is imprisoned." Others said: "I know the place where Reuben was killed. Choose someone to accompany me and give me recompense and I shall show him the corpse." Yet others say: "Everything that these people say—that they will reveal him to your agents—is a lie. It is only said in order to take your money. You know that no trace of Reuben will ever be found in this kingdom."[44]

This is a remarkable portrait of a violent age. The violence heavily involves the ruling class—the lords who are described in a general way and the rulers of France and Burgundy who are noted specifically. It is violence from which many suffer and which some exploit. The Jewish trader at the center of the query is one of a class of people who enriched themselves from the rampant anarchy. The game such people played was a dangerous one. He had a series of narrow escapes. Seemingly the last set of incidents described indicate the death of this adventurer. It must be emphasized, however, that his Jewishness seems to play no special role either in his attraction to such dangerous business nor his ultimate downfall. There is no hint that his demise stemmed from his Jewishness but rather from his involvement in risky and illicit business.

The same sense of a violent society in which Jews were occasionally caught up in the general anarchy is afforded by the Hebrew letter from Le Mans. According to this report, Sehok ben Esther was arrogant, highhanded, and immoral. Eventually he fell into a serious dispute with a Jewish neighbor, hired assassins from his former hometown to kill him, and eventually refused to pay the wages of these hired assassins, precipitating further problems and violence for the entire citizenry of Le Mans.[45] Again violence is pervasive, engulfing Jew and Christian alike. It is the violence of an open age that favors the aggressive and the assertive. The governing authorities remain remote, perhaps incapable of quelling the strife. Once more there is no sense of violence directed against a Jew qua Jew. The killing of the Jew seems merely a part of the general anarchy of this early stage of northern European history.

Although the violence I have described thus far is not directed specifically against the Jews as Jews, it is clear that their involvement in trade with its necessary supplies of goods and capital made the Jews particularly tempting targets for the marauders of this period. Robbery from Jewish homes is mentioned frequently in the responsa of the period, as are attacks upon traveling merchants. In some cases these merchants were stripped of their goods; in other cases they were forced to redeem themselves by the payment of ransom money. The businessman's sense of uncertainty is conveyed in a responsum that describes a traveling Jewish trader in a strange town entrusting his funds to a local Jew, from whom they were eventually stolen.[46] This merchant enlisted the help of fellow Jews to minimize the risks associated with trading in a strange town. He obviously anticipated problems stemming from the lawlessness of the period, took steps to safeguard his funds, and was robbed anyway.

All the foregoing reflects general violence and lawlessness as it impinged upon the small Jewish enclaves of northern Europe, a violence that affected Christians also. Although the Jews in these incidents were not singled out by their Jewishness, other incidents *were* sparked by specifically anti-Jewish animus. Jews and Christians were heirs to ancient traditions that contained much material derisive of the sister faith and its adherents. Naturally such legacies had an impact on the thinking and the actions of Jews and Christians in tenth- and eleventh-century northern Europe.

The Jewish view of Christianity and Christian society

is harsh and critical. The narrative sources that have survived are filled with uncomplimentary epithets. While it
may be argued that these literary sources stem from
periods of tension and persecution and are thus understandably derisive, the responsa literature, reflecting
calmer issues and problems, shows a similar antipathy
toward Christianity and Christians. It is certainly assumed
that Christianity is, in technical terms, polytheistic. This
is the basis for abstaining from wine touched by Christians.[47] To be sure, this Jewish antipathy could not serve as
the prelude to the outbreak of anti-Christian violence,
since the Jews constituted a weak and exposed minority
group.

Anti-Jewish stereotypes were more firmly entrenched
in Christian society, as we have already seen.[48] An obvious
reflection of popular anti-Jewish sentiment is to be found
in the Le Mans incident of 992. I have argued that the
tension between Sehok ben Esther, who converted from
Judaism to Christianity, and his Jewish neighbors was not
religious. I have suggested that it was rooted in the general
lawlessness of the period. It is clear, at the same time, that
Sehok based his anti-Jewish agitation upon broadly shared
anti-Jewish attitudes and that his efforts stimulated an
outbreak of anti-Jewish animus. Specifically our Jewish
source informs us that Sehok fashioned a wooden image
in the likeness of a man and secretly placed it in the ark
of the synagogue of Le Mans. He then alleged to the count
that the Jews had made a figurine of their ruler and pierced
it regularly in an effort to destroy him. Sehok further
suggested that the Jews should be killed for their crime
and their wealth confiscated. Such action would win for
the count riches, popular approbation, and wide fame.[49]

The appeal by Sehok, as described by this Jewish
source, is exceedingly clever. He played on the fears of the
count, on his appetite for money, on his desire for popular
approval, and on his hopes for general fame. All this was
based, however, on the assumption that the count would
be prepared to accept the notion of Jewish malevolence,
Jewish enmity toward Christendom, and Jewish familiarity

with magical techniques that could produce great harm. There seems to be reference both to an earlier incident, possibly involving alleged desecration of Christian images, and to the prototype of Jewish malevolence and enmity, the supposed responsibility of the Jews for the crucifixion of Jesus. Sehok clearly assumed the count's readiness to believe the worst about Jews.

These anti-Jewish stereotypes are reflected not only in Sehok's assumption of their existence and in the count's actual reaction but also indicated in the broad popular response, once the incident was under way. Popular animosity burst forth against the Jews, fanned by the incendiary preaching of a clergyman. Again a basic stereotype of Jewish malevolence is involved. The Jewish author or authors plainly assume underlying Christian hatred of Jews. They see in the persecution of 992 a sense in Christian society that the moment for revenge had arrived.[50]

Of particular significance for my argument is a set of incidents that took place in the period between 1007 and 1012.[51] A number of sources describe a series of persecutions that took place across northern Europe during these years. These sources depict ecclesiastical and political leaders making strenuous efforts to convert the Jews. Often these efforts meant forcing Jews to choose between conversion and expulsion. According to one source, the choice offered conversion or death. A variety of figures are involved in these efforts; those mentioned specifically include the bishop of Limoges, the king of France, the duke of Normandy, and the German emperor. I have suggested that these persecutions were related to the initial outbreaks of heresy among Christians in northern Europe. Frightened by signs of religious schism, major ecclesiastical and political figures lashed out against another group of dissidents, the Jews. This affords an illustration of the general observation made earlier. Under the pressure of incipient heresy, the complex Christian doctrine of negation cum toleration unraveled, giving way to persecution of the Jews, who were perceived as a hostile threat. To be sure, the incidents were short-lived. According to one of our Jewish sources, a prominent Jew traveled to Rome and elicited from the pope an edict of protection that bears a striking similarity to the later *Constitutio pro Judeis*. In any case, Jewish life quickly reverted to the status quo ante, but inherent dangers were made manifest.

Thus the Jews suffered partially from the general lawlessness and partially from the anti-Jewish stereotypes that pervaded Christian society. There seems to have been still one more factor contributing to anti-Jewish animosity, although the evidence is not explicit. As noted, the Jews appeared in the developing urban centers of northern Europe as clients of the lords of these towns, infringing the autonomy of the burghers. Anti-Jewish hostility may well have flowed in part from these political complications. It will be recalled that the new Jewish community of Speyer was formed from a nucleus of Jews who left Mainz after a catastrophic fire. "The entire Jewish quarter and their street burned down, and we greatly feared the burghers."[52] Likewise, the first provision of the charter extended by Bishop Rudiger was a walled enclave "in order that they not be easily disturbed by the violence of the mob." While it is possible to argue that this burgher hostility is simply the general violence of the period and the occasional religious animosity already exhibited, it is more likely that we see here a reflection of specifically urban tensions, both in Mainz and in Speyer. Bishop Rudiger knew that the very act of settling Jews in Speyer would arouse the Christian burghers and hence immediately offered the Jews the enhanced security of a walled-in quarter.

Thus the most obvious feature of Christian-Jewish relations during the late tenth and eleventh century was the inevitability of extensive contact. Given the small size of the European towns, the miniscule size of most Jewish communities, and the Jewish tendency toward economic specialization, the situation could not have been otherwise. Such extensive contact fostered often cordial relations. Sometimes relations were strained and tense. When violence broke out, it was sometimes simply a derivative of the general tendency toward lawlessness noted earlier.

Often, however, such violence reflected specific anti-Jewish religious motifs or resentment of separate and special Jewish political status. Under normal circumstances the authorities made themselves responsible for Jewish safety and security, although on occasion they themselves became the offenders. When this happened, it sometimes represented normal baronial depredation, occasionally indicated a sharing of popular anti-Jewish views, and in rare instances reflected a responsible effort to protect Christian society against alleged dangers. The Jews were only somewhat less secure than their Christian contemporaries; given the tenor of the time, however, one can hardly depict pre-1096 Jewry as safe and untroubled.

II

The Sources and Their Reliability

THE CHRISTIAN SOURCES

The First Crusade was an exhilarating social and spiritual experience for late eleventh-century Christian Europe. It profoundly impressed those who lived through it and continued to fascinate a number of subsequent generations. As a result, historical sources that stem from this complex movement abound. There are public documentary records; private and personal epistles; contemporaneous narratives, composed by participants in the grand venture; chronicles written a little later by authors who used both written sources and the oral testimony of eyewitness observers; and later accounts, composed during the following generations and based upon a combination of earlier written materials and the emergent mythology of the First Crusade.[1]

Christian sources that discuss the First Crusade focus on the piety and valor of the crusaders and on heroic incidents in the conquest of the Holy Land. Scant mention is made of the shortcomings of the enterprise and little concern is shown for its victims. As a result, despite the copious data available for reconstructing most aspects of the crusading experience, Christian material that sheds light on the related persecution of European Jewry is scarce. This dearth of evidence can be readily explained. In the first place, little attention is paid to the popular crusading bands largely responsible for the anti-Jewish violence. These forces were not part of the victorious enter-

38

prise and were therefore of meager interest to contemporary observers and to subsequent chroniclers. Indeed these
unruly bands were something of an embarrassment; they
were seen as having sullied the holy campaign with their
extremism and their ignominious failure. Anti-Jewish activity was likewise of minimal interest. The grand crusading project included no formal anti-Jewish objective. While
there was much latent anti-Jewish sentiment in the Christendom of this epoch, most participants and almost all
observers saw in the crusade no basis for attacks upon the
Jews and no reason for subsequent glorification for any
such assaults. Thus neither the violence nor its perpetrators were of great concern to those who left us records of the momentous events of the late 1090s. At best
these incidents were useful in distinguishing what they
would have viewed as the pious and hence successful
crusaders from the perverse and therefore unsuccessful
crusading bands. It is only in this connection that the
anti-Jewish violence was of any interest to Christian
crusade chroniclers.

   Most modern historians of the First Crusade have re-
lied heavily on accounts written by crusade participants:
the anonymous *Gesta Francorum*, Fulcher of Chartres' *Historia Hierosolymitana*, and Raymond of Aguiler's *Historia
Francorum*.[2] None of these three valuable works refers to
the German bands or to their assaults on the Jews. The
only crusade chroniclers who mention the bands that
devastated a number of northern European Jewish communities were Ekkehard of Aura and Albert of Aix. Ekkehard joined the crusade of 1101 and was one of those
who succeeded in reaching the Near East. His chronicle is
based on a combination of written materials and oral reports and shows keen interest in the fate of the various
popular crusading bands. It is in this connection that he
includes a brief depiction of the 1096 attacks upon the
Jews.[3] Albert of Aix never journeyed east. He compiled his
record of the First Crusade and the early history of the
Kingdom of Jerusalem from a combination of written and
oral sources. Like Ekkehard, Albert was interested in the

fate of the German crusading bands and he too describes, in a bit more detail, their assaults on the Jews.[4] Neither account is extensive, but both are useful in the effort to reconstruct the anti-Jewish violence that occurred during the spring months of 1096.

A number of local Christian chronicles also preserve recollections of the assaults on European Jewry. These records are of varying significance. Many are late and cursory; a few are detailed and offer much help reconstructing the attacks and the Jewish response.[5] Again, however, when viewed broadly, the extensive local reporting of the events of the First Crusade evinces little interest in the anti-Jewish episodes. In general, Christian sources for the anti-Jewish outbursts of 1096 and for the Christian and Jewish responses are of limited quantity and limited value. At best they provide corroborative evidence for information supplied in the Jewish sources, which depict much more fully the assaults of 1096 and the responses they evoked.

THE JEWISH SOURCES

Just as the First Crusade excited the imagination of Christian observers, so too did it attract the interest of Jews, albeit for different reasons and in very different ways. This fascination is reflected in a variety of materials. There are detailed lists of Jews who perished in the attacks, elegies to be recited in memory of the victims of crusader fury, legal discussions of persecution-related issues, and moralistic tales designed to hold up examples of proper Jewish behavior. Once more, however, historical narratives are the most valuable sources for reconstructing the realities of the First Crusade. Three unusual Hebrew chronicles preserve, along with some interesting reflections of general aspects of the First Crusade, lengthy and detailed depictions of the attacks and the attackers, of the reactions of a variety of elements in Christian society, of the efforts at self-defense within the Jewish community, and of the mass martyrdoms where all else failed.[6] These chronicles constitute a rich historical record, represent a breakthrough in medieval Jewish historiography, and pose complex problems to the modern reader. The evidence they provide forms the backbone of this study, and they must therefore be scrutinized in an effort to assess their reliability. We must examine the structure of these historical narratives, attempt to identify and evaluate the sources at the disposal of the chroniclers, and—most important of all—seek to fathom the essential content, the purposes, and the resultant style of these unusual records.

Before examining the individual chronicles, it is necessary to look briefly at the three together and to make some observations concerning the relationship or relationships among them.[7] It has long been recognized that the three Hebrew chronicles share significant passages, raising the question as to whether we are in fact provided with three independent testimonies to the events of 1096—or only two, or one. A number of possibilities have been proposed to explain the relationships among the three Hebrew narratives: (1) an original lost text is the source of all three; (2) one of the three is the source of the other two; (3) one of the three is the source of a second, with the third relatively independent.[8] Before the issue of relationships can be taken up, two key points must be asserted: (1) The precise beginning and conclusion of the three chronicles must be carefully delineated. This means, in effect, eliminating from consideration introductory and interpolated comments made by later copyists.[9] (2) Inasmuch as it is obvious that no single person could have been an eyewitness to all events depicted and that oral and written reports were used extensively by the chroniclers, the most revealing sections of the chronicles are the opening and closing portions and the broad framework established by the author. Accepting these two principles, I suggested some time ago that the brief, anonymous Hebrew chronicle and the lengthier account sometimes attributed to Solomon ben Simson are essentially independent of each other, and that they use common written reports for their depiction of the assaults upon Mainz Jewry.[10] The Hebrew chronicle generally attributed to Rabbi Eliezer ben Nathan is in all likelihood a shortened version of the lengthy Hebrew narrative, embellished with the author's own poetic dirges.[11]

The best and probably also the earliest of the three extant Hebrew narratives is the truncated account that was designated by a medieval copyist as "The Account of the Former Persecution." It has been called by modern scholars "The Mainz Anonymous" and will be identified throughout this study as S, that is, the *short* narrative. S, in its present form, covers only the early development of the crusade and the assaults on the Jewish communities of Speyer, Worms, and Mainz. The loss of the remainder of S is lamentable, for its author was an intelligent narrator of events, and its materials were skillfully knit into a coherent and moving depiction of the variety of attacks and responses on the part of the victims.[12]

The longest Hebrew chronicle extant is that often attributed to Solomon ben Simson. I shall follow the published version of this text, which presents it as a cohesive unit, and shall designate it as L, that is, the *lengthy* narrative. While this designation is convenient, it is by no means certain that we are dealing with a unified text. In order to understand L more clearly, we must begin by seeing it in its manuscript context. The narration or narrations of the events of 1096 are embedded in a composite communal chronicle composed in the Jewish community of Speyer, probably sometime in the 1170s.[13] Two possibilities suggest themselves: The first is that a Speyer Jewish author of the 1170s combined the following elements into a historical mélange comprising: (1) a full description now lost, of the tragedy of 1096 in Speyer and Worms; (2) a cohesive account of the catastrophe in Speyer, Worms, and Mainz; (3) a narrative of the Cologne disaster; (4) brief and random reports of additional persecutions in 1096; (5) praise for the "insincere converts" to Christianity (who remained steadfastly loyal to their Jewish faith); (6) a somewhat garbled version of the demise of some of the popular crusading bands; (7) a series of reports on the tragedy of 1171; (8) a closing statement on the reconstruction of the Speyer synagogue and the ongoing use of it down through the 1170s. There is a second possibility, which posits an additional intermediate editor. More specifically, according to this view, elements 2 through 6 listed above were organized by a prior editor into a lengthy account of Jewish fate during the First Crusade, composed perhaps in 1140. Thus the Speyer chronicler had an extensive account of Jewish suffering in 1096 available to incorporate into the historical mélange.[14] I can find no justification, at present, to favor either alternative. For convenience, the 1096 material will be treated here as a unit; whether it is in fact a unit or simply a set of disparate sources gathered together by the later Speyer editor remains open to question.

Yet a third source, one merely a derivative of the second, exists. It consists of an abridgment of L, embellished by the original elegiac poetry of the well-known Rabbi Eliezer bar Nathan. Probably because of the renown of Rabbi Eliezer, this account is the most widely copied and used of the three.[15] To the modern historian, however, it has the least interest.

The two original Hebrew chronicles are thus very much like the Latin narratives of Peter Tudebod, Baldric of Dol, Robert the Monk, Guibert of Nogent, Ekkehard of Aura, and Albert of Aix: they were written by authors at some remove from the events themselves. No Jew could possibly have moved from one assaulted Jewish community to the next, compiling a running account of events along the way. Rather, these Jewish narratives must have been based upon oral testimony and upon prior written sources. There are a number of references in the text of L to oral evidence: (1) near the end of the Mainz section reference is made to the testimony of "those few remaining who were forcibly converted, who heard with their ears and saw with their eyes that which these pious ones did when they killed them and what they said at the moment of their death, slaughter and killing;"[16] (2) in the Cologne section, at the end of the depiction of events in the fourth of the seven refuges in which Cologne Jewry has been installed we find; "I, Solomon ben Simson, wrote down this incident in Mainz. There I asked the elders the entire episode. From their mouths I arranged each detail properly. They told me of this act of sanctification";[17] (3) a bit later in the Cologne section, the author reports the moving exhortation of Moses the *cohen*, showing how he had embellished the regular grace after meal with original entreaties, "because of the edict hanging over them, as my ancestors and the rest of the elders occupied with the labor have told me."[18] These brief references to oral testimony reflect two different types of evidence; the first supplied by eyewitness survivors and the second by those looking back on the events sometime later. Modern-day students of the extant Hebrew First-Crusade chronicles generally agree that the recurrence of identical material in the two independent narratives of S and L indicates the existence of early local letters or records, which were subsequently utilized by the later chroniclers.[19] Thus the author-editors of both S and L had at their disposal both oral and written evidence. The key questions are: (1) how reliable was this evidence; (2) what were the channels of transmission of this evidence to the later composers of the extant narratives; (3) what biases and distortions might the later narrators have imposed upon the earlier materials.

There is no foolproof method available for establishing the reliability of the sources from which S and L drew. These sources are surely rooted in eyewitness observation, but this is in itself no guarantee of accuracy. The most striking characteristic of these sources, it seems to me, is their commitment to detail and diversity. Rather than portraying a stereotyped and repetitive set of behaviors, both Christian and Jewish, they focus on a variety of actions and reactions. The uniqueness of specific circumstances, groups, and individuals is highlighted. To cite one very important example, Christian behaviors—as we shall see— are not depicted as uniform. The sources express awareness of and distaste for the bloodthirsty attitudes of some of the crusaders and their burgher allies. Nonetheless, they offer numerous examples of Christian burghers assisting Jews and political authorities defending zealously their Jewish subjects. The variety of Jewish behaviors portrayed is even wider: conversion, negotiation, flight, passive acceptance of death at crusader hands, activist martyrdom. The diversity of behavior depicted is the best index available of the reliability of the original sources used by S and L. While there may have been exaggeration of some aspects of Christian or Jewish behavior, both wholesale suppression of key tendencies and widespread fabrication of actions and attitudes are unlikely.

The question of transmission is relatively simple. The time elapsed between the events and the composition of the later narratives was generally quite brief and, at most, only four or five decades separated an event from the report. In cases where the materials came from written sources, the degree of similarity in corresponding passages in S and L can be taken as evidence that the two chroniclers accurately reproduced information from the earlier written sources. Where the sources were oral, the narrators apparently heard firsthand from survivors of the tumultuous events. The transmission of earlier source material to the later narrators does not seem to entail complications that would diminish the reliability of the chronicles.

The third issue concerns the possible distortion of materials by the later narrators. The two original Hebrew chronicles are clearly tendentious in nature. They were written in the wake of the catastrophe in order to address pressing theological and spiritual issues and to allay gnawing doubts. They are meant to reassure the Jewish reader and, at the same time, to present Jewish supplications to the Deity. These are clearly interpretative efforts, focusing heavily on the valor of the Jewish martyrs as both a consolation for the human audience and a foundation for the prayers directed at the divine auditor.[20] Given such a focus, the chronicles could understandably have become highly distorted. However, in fashioning these texts of consolation and supplication, the narrators of S and L seem to have retained the strong sense of the specific, the unique, and the diverse that is the hallmark of their sources. While there is an obvious desire—as was the case with their sources as well—to highlight bestiality on the part of the crusaders and heroism on the part of the Jews, the diversity of actions and reactions that had occurred in actuality is well reported in the S and L narratives. The range of behavior displayed by both Christians and Jews as depicted in these narratives is remarkably broad.[21]

This attitude of respect for historical reality seems to me to derive from several directions. The first is the narrators' reverence for the actual behavior of the martyrs of 1096. Just as the Christian chronicles of the First Crusade generally told their story in a relatively straightforward and unadorned style, so too the Jewish chroniclers seem to have felt that the best way they could convey the meaning of 1096 was to let Jewish actions speak for themselves. To be sure, the actions—both the martyrdoms described by the Jewish narrators and the crusades narrated in the Christian sources—had a message, but the message could best be conveyed to God and man by retelling the events as fully and accurately as possible. This tendency of crusading and martyrological historiography is closely related, I believe, to the growing concern, during this period, for historical realities in general. In his admirable study of the growing literacy of the twelfth and thirteenth centuries and its implications, Brian Stock draws attention to a new commitment to accuracy of detail, expressed in many areas of material and spiritual life, including the depiction of contemporary events.[22] In the most extensive recent examination of medieval historiography, Bernard Guénée emphasizes the growth of commitment to accurate reporting.[23] A concern for accuracy is evident in these Hebrew chronicles. In addition to citing sources, they refer on occasion to conflicting testimony. For example, three differing versions with regard to the death of Kalonymous of Mainz are presented, and two divergent reports on the rumors that led Isaac ben David and his friend Uri ben Joseph to burn down the synagogue of Mainz.[24] Thus a tendency to accuracy in historical detail in the Hebrew narratives is in fact parallel to broad crusading historiography and to general intellectual trends of the early twelfth century.

Two further arguments for the reliability of the Hebrew chronicles may be made. The first concerns the correspondence between the Christian sources and the Jewish records for the events of 1096. Of course the Christian sources are far skimpier. Also, the events of 1096 are evaluated in markedly different ways in the two sets of sources. Nonetheless the data supplied corroborate one another strikingly. To cite but one key example, both sets of sources agree on the predominant Jewish reaction of activist martyrdom. While this correspondence cannot be used to argue the absolute accuracy of details that do not appear in the Christian narratives, it does suggest a tendency toward careful depiction of actualities. Likewise the broad agreement between the two independent Jewish sources suggests faithful rendering of the events themselves. There are certainly stylistic differences between the two. As I have suggested, S is far better organized and it gives a fuller depiction of the early development of the crusade. As will be evident presently, L is richer in theological expression. Despite these stylistic differences, the general tenor of the details provided in S and L is remarkably consistent, indicating once more a commitment to faithful depiction of historical events.

All these arguments for the reliability for S and L afford, it seems to me, probability and not certainty. The level of probability seems fairly high, given the limited resources at our disposal. Of course, the specific issues under discussion must always be borne in mind. Only minimal uncertainty is entailed in discussing the patterns of Christian and Jewish behavior—the evidence on those topics seems fairly conclusive. As regards questions of motivation in these historical events, however, the potential for distortion—especially as the sources become more remote from the events they describe—increases and the certainty of our findings correspondingly diminishes. The available data are far from foolproof, but the S and L narratives do seem to constitute efforts at an accurate rendition of complex and diverse behavior on both sides, Christian and Jewish. They afford a foundation for the reliable reconstruction of this important chapter in crusading and Jewish history. The fullest argument for the trustworthiness of the Jewish sources is provided by the analysis undertaken in the following chapters. The evidence for varied patterns of Christian and Jewish behavior in 1096 persuades one that the Jewish narrators were committed to provide a record as full and accurate as possible of the events depicted. These chroniclers, committed to highlighting Christian cruelty, will supply numerous accounts of Christian justice and decency; these same authors, who emphasize Jewish heroism and martyrdom, also describe unabashedly instances of the abandonment of Judaism. As appeared among their Christian contemporaries, there appeared likewise among the Rhineland Jews of the late eleventh and early twelfth century a new spirit of accurate depiction of landmark historical events.

Having examined a number of technical issues associated with the reliability of the Hebrew First-Crusade chronicles, I shall conclude by discussing briefly more theoretical concerns. Literary critics, anthropologists, and psychoanalysts have increasingly alerted us to the extent to which the human mind imposes form and pattern upon an inchoate reality, rather than extracting from it some sort of preexistent order. One of the major techniques through which such order is appealingly and convincingly perceived and then transmitted is the narrative. There is much concern over the relation of the appealingly coherent narrative to the less structured and more chaotic underlying reality. This study assumes that the reality was a good deal more complex and amorphous than the Hebrew (and Latin) narratives would suggest. It takes the chaotic nature of the Christian and Jewish behaviors and motivations in 1096 for granted.

Nonetheless the focus of this study is inevitably upon discernible patterns. My essential argument is that, beyond the chaos of individualized actions, there were identifiable patterns of behavior and thought. These patterns are particularly striking to the extent that they represent departures from prior modes of Christian and Jewish behavior and thought. I carry, in all this, no intention to deny the amorphous quality of the underlying reality. At the same time, I acknowledge the historian's sense that, when all is said and done, not all amorphous realities are the same; differing patterns *can* be discerned and these patterns (not an imposed perception of them) constitute the essence of the movement of history.

The crucial question for historians in search of identifiable patterns of behavior and thought is whether the sources at their disposal afford a reliable basis for discerning these patterns. My examination of the data available for the events of 1096 persuades me that the combined Hebrew and Latin sources—while neither copious nor problem-free—do indeed provide a relatively trustworthy foundation for reconstructing significant aspects of the anti-Jewish violence associated with the First Crusade and the innovative Jewish responses to that unanticipated violence.

III

The Violence of 1096

VARIETIES OF VIOLENCE

The vigorous development of eleventh-century northern European society was powerfully expressed in the First Crusade. The stimulus to the First Crusade ostensibly lay in a series of deleterious changes in the eastern Mediterranean. In truth, however, the most important changes had taken place in the West.[1] Western Christendom now had the material strength and the spiritual will to do battle against its Muslim enemies. While the physical capacities were important, far more significant was the militant new spirit palpable in western Christendom. In fact, this new militance had already begun to reveal itself in the 1060s in the expansion of Christian power in Spain and Italy. In the late 1090s the newfound power of European society manifested itself far more dramatically in the ambitious plan to assault Muslim forces located far from the base of Christian attackers. The call to the crusade was rooted also in the internal evils fostered by the rapid growth of the eleventh century. The violence endemic to the eleventh century was perceived by many contemporary observers as one of the major factors in the papal call.

It was the growing power, complexity, and militance of European society that spawned the ambitious program of the First Crusade. Its inchoate yearnings were galvanized into action by the call of Pope Urban II in Clermont. One question that has bedeviled modern crusade studies is the precise content of this papal appeal. A

50

number of versions of this appeal are extant, some of them written by eyewitnesses. As a result of the rapid expansion of the original call and its remarkable success, these versions differ substantially one from another, resulting in an ongoing scholarly debate. Was Jerusalem central to the papal initiative or not? How much emphasis was there on the Byzantine empire and its travails and how much hope for a significant expansion of papal authority?[2] Fortunately these serious and important questions need not detain us. Jewish fate was affected by the complex crusading movement that far exceeded the appeal and expectations of Urban II, whatever these might have been.

One element in the papal call that has been satisfactorily identified is the nature of the movement that Urban hoped to set in motion. A variety of sources clearly show that the pope intended to launch a carefully organized military force unified under ecclesiastical control. In order to achieve this, Urban first of all limited participation in the enterprise, excluding the elderly, the feeble, and women, among others. Papal measures to keep the expedition well controlled extended beyond limiting participation. There was, in addition, emphasis on clerical leadership, in the person of the bishop of Le Puy, and on a unified fighting force, which would prepare itself carefully and depart in mid-August 1096.

Every aspect of this papal plan was nullified. A series of armies sprang up, most of them under the direct leadership of important feudal lords. Despite the general respect for Bishop Adhemar and the role of other clerics, there was neither unity nor clerical control. More significant yet, the efforts to control participation failed. The old and feeble, the destitute, a large number of women and children— all were galvanized by the call to crusading and the promise of reward. To some extent, Pope Urban II set in motion these unanticipated developments by initiating a preaching program that inevitably escaped close scrutiny and control. To some extent, he was the unwitting victim of ideas and slogans whose power he failed to recognize. In any case, the expansion of the First Crusade from the relatively restricted base envisioned by the pope to the mass movement that actually developed held enormous significance. It meant that there was little or no control over crusading theory and practice. It is important to emphasize both elements. Because of the diverse composition of the crusading armies, the lack of unity, and the lack of clerical control, it was impossible, first of all, to control interpretations of the ideology of the crusade. There was the possibility—and indeed the reality—of bizarre and unwarranted extension of the call to the crusade. Beyond this, there was additional difficulty in controlling the day-to-day behavior of large and unruly groups. Hungry crusaders often embarked on programs of pillage and devastation. The eyewitness accounts of the First Crusade are replete with evidence for loss of control of both theory and practice. Both developments were of momentous significance for European Jewry.

Most modern histories of the First Crusade identify diverse sets of forces that embarked on the journey east.[3] The most important consisted of the organized armies of major baronial figures such as Raymond of Saint-Gilles, Bohemond of Taranto, Hugh of Vermandois, Robert of Normandy, Stephen of Blois, Robert of Flanders, Godfrey of Bouillon, and his brothers Eustace and Baldwin. Often ill disciplined, and occasionally at odds with one another, these were nonetheless trained and capable armed forces. In a remarkable way they succeeded in reaching the East and in the middle of July 1099 breached the walls of Jerusalem and conquered the Holy City. These relatively organized armies prepared themselves with some care, most of them departing eastward in late summer 1096 or thereabout.

The Christian chroniclers of the First Crusade focus extensively on these baronial armies but cite no instances of anti-Jewish activity within their ranks on European soil. The Hebrew chronicles are less clear. Particularly in the early stages of their description, they speak vaguely and loosely of crusaders and their anti-Jewish actions in Germany. It is obvious, however, that almost none of this anti-Jewish activity in Germany can be attributed to the baronial armies, for almost none of them traversed Germany. The armies of Raymond of Toulouse and Bohemond of Taranto originated in southern Europe and proceeded east from there. Most of the northern French barons—Hugh of Vermandois, Robert of Flanders, Robert of Normandy, and Stephen of Blois—traveled east via Italy, thus avoiding Germany. Only Godfrey of Bouillon and his brother Baldwin traveled up the Rhine River, and they did so some time *after* the initial anti-Jewish tensions and the terrible massacres. In fact there is only one clear-cut instance of anti-Jewish action on the part of the baronial forces. According to L, "a duke arose, Godfrey by name—may his bones be ground up—harsh in spirit. A fickle spirit moved him to go with those journeying to their idolatrous shrine. He swore wickedly that he would not depart on his journey without avenging the blood of the Crucified with the blood of Israel and that he would not leave a remnant or residue among those bearing the name Jew." After rapid Jewish intercession with Emperor Henry IV, a charter ordering protection of the Jews was elicited. At this juncture, "the wicked duke swore that it had never occurred to him to do them any harm. Nonetheless, we bribed him in Cologne with five hundred silver *zekukim*. They likewise bribed him in Mainz."[4] In sum, the baronial armies seem to have caused no damage to European Jewry, with only Godfrey of Bouillon exploiting Jewish fears in order to extort funds for his journey.

The baronial armies that eventually conquered Jerusalem represented something of a deviation from papal plans. Even further from papal intentions was the less professional force that crystallized around the charismatic figure of Peter the Hermit.[5] One of a number of popular preachers of the crusade, Peter was by far the most successful, attracting to himself a large and heterogeneous army of followers. Winning adherents throughout northern France, Peter crossed into the Rhineland in the spring of 1096, preached briefly and effectively, and moved on eastward to Constantinople. Once Peter's forces entered

Muslim territory, they were quickly set upon and annihilated. It seems likely that some of the anti-Jewish agitation in France and Germany is to be attributed to Peter's followers. Once again the Christian sources that depict Peter's army say nothing of anti-Jewish incitement or violence. The Jewish sources, generally vague in their usage of the term "crusader," mention a number of developments that seem to be associated with Peter's followers. S, which is fuller than L in its depiction of the emergence of anti-Jewish violence, indicates that the crusaders in France "taunted us from every direction. They took counsel, ordering that either we turn to their abominable faith or they would destroy us from infant to suckling."[6] The Jews of France were deeply distressed and sent off letters to their Rhineland brethren, warning of the danger and requesting prayers on their behalf. Given the slow mobilization of the baronial armies and the early date of this agitation, attributing it to the followers of Peter the Hermit seems warranted. To be sure, the Jewish chroniclers know of no overt violence in France. Only Guibert of Nogent depicts an incident in Rouen that claimed a number of Jewish lives. The incident was rather spontaneous and did not involve a full-blown military force.[7] It is tempting to associate this attack with some of Peter's followers but, since Guibert supplies no date or names, such a link remains speculative.

As Peter's forces passed into Germany, they brought with them the threat of injury to the Jews. The danger took two forms, the first being random anti-Jewish violence. "The crusaders with their insignia came, with their standards before our houses. When they saw one of us, they ran after him and pierced him with a spear, to the point that we were afraid even to cross our thresholds."[8] A second form of anti-Jewish behavior was financial exploitation of Jewish anxieties. The crusaders demanded money for provisions and the Jews, out of fear, complied. In one passage, L explicitly associates this kind of extortion with the forces of Peter the Hermit.

It came to pass on the fifteenth of the month of Nisan, on the first day of Passover, there arrived an emissary to the crusaders from France, an emissary of Jesus, named Peter. He was a priest and was called Peter the prelate. When he arrived there in Trier—he and the very many men with him—on his pilgrimage to Jerusalem, he brought with him a letter from France, from the Jews, [indicating] that, in all places where his foot would tread and he would encounter Jews, they should give him provisions for the way. He would then speak well on behalf of Israel, for he was a priest and his words were heeded. . . . We gave [funds] to the priest Peter and they went on their way.[9]

Thus the forces associated with Peter the Hermit, not surprisingly, showed anti-Jewish tendencies. Specifically, this manifested itself in sporadic violence and the economic exploitation of Jewish anxieties. To be sure, had the First Crusade consisted only of the baronial armies and of Peter the Hermit's forces, European Jewry would have been spared serious calamity.

In fact, however, Peter's preaching in Germany elicited a new set of military bands and new dangers to the Jews. Peter reached Cologne on Saturday, April 12, 1096. By this time, it was becoming increasingly difficult for Peter to control his large and unwieldy army. Peter began preaching immediately and it is not unlikely that the exhilaration of Easter Sunday added to the success of this preaching. New adherents to the sacred mission were gained, but Peter in the process saw thousands of his troops depart the following Tuesday under the leadership of Walter Sans-Avoir. Peter himself headed east on April 20. He had brought the message of the crusade into the Rhineland, had won important new followers, and had stimulated the formation of a number of additional crusading bands. These bands were destined for an even less auspicious fate than that of Peter's army. They were to prove incapable of reaching Muslim territory. Falling into conflict with the

authorities in Hungary, they were wiped out while still
within the confines of Christendom.

Out of these popular German crusading bands, inspired by the preaching of Peter the Hermit, evolved the
serious assaults on European Jewry, in particular on the
major Jewish communities of the Rhineland. Again the
danger took a variety of forms. As had been the case
among Peter's own followers, there were instances of
spontaneous violence. A graphic and revealing portrait of
one such incident is provided in the Hebrew chronicles.

> It came to pass on a certain day that a gentile woman
> came and brought with her a goose which she had
> raised since it was a gosling. This goose went
> everywhere that the gentile woman went. She said to
> all passersby: "Behold this goose understands that I
> intend to go on the crusade and wishes to go with
> me." Then the crusaders and burghers gathered
> against us, saying to us: "Where is your source of
> trust? How will you be saved? Behold the wonders
> that the Crucified does for us!" Then all of them came
> with swords and spears to destroy us. Some of the
> burghers came and would not allow them [to do so].
> At that time they stood . . . and killed along the Rhine
> River, until they killed one of the crusaders. Then they
> said: "All these things the Jews have caused." Then
> they almost gathered [against us]. When the saintly
> ones saw all these things, their hearts melted.[10]

The description clearly indicates random violence, touched
off by the supposedly miraculous behavior of the goose.
Burgher opposition to this violence reflects its limited
proportions. Indeed the Jewish chronicler suggests an es-
calation of the violence—when a crusader is killed, a new
anti-Jewish unanimity is achieved.

Similar unpremeditated violence is apparently reflected in the account of the initial assault in Worms. The
Jewish community of Worms, upon learning of prior violence in Speyer, divided into two groups. Some of the Jews

elected to stay in their homes, while others sought refuge in the bishop's palace.

> It came to pass on the tenth of Iyyar, on Sunday, they plotted craftily against them. They took a trampled corpse of theirs, that had been buried thirty days previously and carried it through the city, saying: "Behold what the Jews have done to our comrade. They took a gentile and boiled him in water. They then poured the water into our wells in order to kill us." When the crusaders and burghers heard this, they cried out and gathered—all who bore and unsheathed [a sword], from great to small—saying: "Behold the time has come to avenge him who was crucified, whom their ancestors slew. Now let not a remnant or a residue escape, even an infant or a suckling in the cradle." They then came and struck those who had remained in their houses—comely young men and comely and lovely young women along with elders. All of them stretched forth their necks. Even manumitted servingmen and servingwomen were killed along with them for the sanctification of the Name which is awesome and sublime, . . . who rules above and below, who was and will be. Indeed the Lord of Hosts is his Name."[11]

The small group that hatched the plot intended to arouse violence against the Jews. Most of the perpetrators of this violence, however, were galvanized into action by the accusation hurled against the Jews.

The next level of violence involved premeditated assaults upon Jews, carried out by a combination of burghers and crusaders, singly or in groups, within a given city. This type of attack is described by S:

> It came to pass on the eighth of the month of Iyyar, on the sabbath, the measure of justice began to manifest itself against us. The crusaders and burghers arose first against the saintly ones, the pious of the Almighty

in Speyer. They took counsel against them, [planning]
to seize them together in the synagogue. But it was
revealed to them and they arose [early] on the sabbath
morning and prayed rapidly and left the synagogue.
When they [the crusaders and burghers] saw that their
plan for seizing them together was foiled, they rose
against them [the Jews] and killed eleven of them.[12]

Similar violence is described in the account in S of the
second attack in Worms. While the first assault had been
activated by the parading of a Christian corpse through
the city and the accusation that Jews had poisoned wells,
the second attack was far from spontaneous.

It came to pass on the twenty-fifth of Iyyar that the
crusaders and the burghers said: "Behold those who
remain in the courtyard of the bishop and in his chambers. Let us take vengeance on them as well." They
gathered from all the villages in the vicinity, along
with the crusaders and the burghers; they besieged
them [the Jews]; and they did battle against them.
There took place a very great battle, one side against
the other, until they seized the chambers in which the
children of the sacred covenant were. When they saw
the battle raging to and fro, the decree of the King of
kings, then they accepted divine judgment and expressed faith in their Creator and offered up true
sacrifices.[13]

This planned assault was carried out by crusaders located
within the city, by burghers, and by neighboring villagers.
The result was the devastation of the remaining segment
of Worms Jewry.

The fiercest anti-Jewish violence was carried out by
organized armies in military fashion. In Mainz, the Hebrew chronicles highlight the arrival of Emicho's army at
the gates of the city and its encampment outside these
gates. On the third of Sivan, Emicho's army swept into
Mainz and besieged the Jews who had gathered in the

archbishop's palace. The Hebrew chronicle depicts an organized military assault.

> It came to pass at midday that the wicked Emicho—
> may his bones be ground up—he and all his army—
> came, and the burghers opened up to him the gates.
> Then the enemies of the Lord said one to another:
> "Behold the gates have been opened by themselves.
> All this the Crucified has done for us, so that we
> might avenge his blood on the Jews." They came with
> their standards to the archbishop's gate, where the
> children of the sacred covenant were—an army as
> numerous as the sands on the seashore. When the
> saintly and God-fearing saw the huge multitude, they
> trusted in and cleaved to their Creator. They donned
> armor and strapped on weapons—great and small—
> with R. Kalony-mous ben Meshullam at their head.[14]

Every aspect of the account points to a situation of organized warfare: the arrival at Mainz, the movement into the city, the siege at the palace, and the Jewish response.

After the victory at the gate of the palace and the destruction of the Jews who had sought refuge there, the army moved to a new scene of battle.

> Then the crusaders began to exult in the name of the
> Crucified. They lifted their standards and came to the
> remnant of the community, to the courtyard of the
> nobleman, the burgrave. They besieged them as well
> and did battle against them.[15]

This is once again a description of an organized military effort.

The testimony of the Jewish sources is corroborated by Albert of Aix. In his account of the decimation of the Jewish community of Mainz, Albert indicates that it was not the result of random violence. After describing the flight of the Jews to the archbishop's quarter, Albert adds: "But Emicho and the rest of his band held a council and, after sunrise, attacked the Jews in the hall with arrows and lances."[16] The attack was a planned and organized military venture; it was not a haphazard outbreak of violence.

The same is true of the destruction of the Jewish community of Cologne. Threatened by burgher violence, these Jews had been dispersed, for their own safety, into a number of outlying towns. During a brief five-day period, most of these refuges were attacked and the Jews gathered in them were almost totally wiped out. Although the Jewish author responsible for the extant description of this disaster was relatively uninterested in identifying the attackers, there can be no doubt that a particular crusading band systematically hunted down these Jews and destroyed them.[17] An extensive series of attacks of this nature cannot reflect incidental violence; the nearly successful effort to destroy Cologne Jewry was deliberate. In fact the crusading army responsible for this series of attacks does appear in the account of events in Moers. The description leaves no doubt as to the presence of a formal military force:

> On Sunday, the seventh of the month of Tammuz, the enemy of the Lord arose against the pious of God [in Moers] to obliterate them from the world. They besieged the city—a multitude as large as the sand on the seashore. The mayor of the city came and went out to meet them in a field and requested them to wait till dawn.[18]

It was this kind of attack that was most terrifying and caused the greatest number of Jewish casualties.

The anti-Jewish violence that accompanied the First Crusade, then, was linked with the followers of Peter the Hermit and the bands galvanized into action by his preaching. The range of anti-Jewish activity was broad, extending from limited, spontaneous violence to full-scale military attacks on the Jewish communities of Mainz and Cologne. A fuller analysis of the devastating assaults follows.

THE DEVASTATING ASSAULTS:
A CLOSER LOOK

The first question to pose in regard to the anti-Jewish violence associated with the First Crusade concerns its scope: How many Jewish communities were affected and how extensive was the damage inflicted?

In attempting to answer this fundamental question, we immediately encounter a serious discrepancy in the sources. On the one hand, there are claims of wide-ranging massacres of Jews. Ekkehard of Aura, in describing the movement of Count Emicho's followers through the areas of Rhine, the Main, and the Danube, states that these crusaders either slaughtered or conquered the Jews "wherever they found them."[19] Albert of Aix speaks similarly of wide-ranging slaughter "throughout all the cities."[20] In the Hebrew chronicles there are two statements that reflect extensive violence against the Jews. Both come in the context of arguments advanced by powerless political authorities claiming they could no longer protect their Jews. The first of these speeches is attributed to the bishop of Trier, depicted as "a stranger in the city, without a relative or acquaintance." Feeling incapable of withstanding any longer the pressures brought to bear against the Jews, the bishop posed the following query: "What do you wish to do? Indeed you see that from every side the Jews have already been killed. It was my desire and it was proper to keep my pledge to you, as I had promised you, up to that time which I had specified to you—until there remained no [Jewish] community in Lorraine. Behold now the crusaders have risen against me, to kill me."[21] The bishop is clearly not suggesting that all the Jewish communities of Lorraine had been destroyed. To the contrary, he indicates explicitly that this has not happened. He had promised to protect his Jews until no Jewish community remained in Lorraine; the Jews of Lorraine had not been wiped out; nonetheless he could no longer protect his Jews because of fear of the crusaders. In any case there is vague reference to the Jews being killed all about. A more explicit statement is attributed to the head of the municipality of Moers, caught in much the same helpless predicament: "In truth, at the outset I promised to protect you and to maintain you until there remain no Jew in the world. But I have fulfilled this condition. Henceforth I cannot save you from all these people."[22] Thus this leader claims that in fact all the Jews had, by the end of June 1096, been destroyed.

Ranged against this evidence of widespread destruction, on the other hand, is the general testimony of the Hebrew chronicles. Nowhere do the Hebrew chroniclers claim that there was generalized destruction. They lament in profound terms the fate of the great Jewish centers of Worms, Mainz, and Cologne, but they do not suggest that a similar fate befell scores of additional communities. To the contrary, the Jewish chroniclers were obviously eager to buttress their claims of Jewish suffering and heroism by adducing as much specific evidence as possible. It is hardly credible that these chroniclers knew of further suffering and declined to mention it or that they were, several years after the events, unaware of significant instances of crusader violence.[23] The testimony of the Hebrew chronicles indicates quite clearly that the anti-Jewish violence was limited and restricted.

In weighing the two sets of evidence one against the other, there can be, to my mind, little serious doubt that the latter testimony outweighs the former. The purpose of the Jewish chroniclers was, after all, to marshal evidence of Jewish suffering and heroism. In such an effort no stone would be left unturned. Against this, the general observation of Ekkehard and Albert and the tendentious claims of the mayor of Moers pale into insignificance. The First Crusade did spawn a measure of anti-Jewish sentiment. Among the baronial armies, this sentiment seems to have resulted in little overt persecution. In the large force that crystallized around the charismatic figure of Peter the Hermit, there was occasional random violence and some economic exploitation. The German armies drawn into the crusade by the preaching of Peter, engaged in sporadic violence and worse. These groups were responsible for the major attacks against the three most important early Ashkenazic communities—Worms, Mainz, and Cologne. The annihilation of these three centers constituted a serious blow to this nascent Jewry, but the assaults were nonetheless limited in scope and impact. Beyond these three major assaults we have evidence for the following incidents only: an attack on the Jews of Rouen, with some casualties; on the Jews of Trier, with some casualties; on the Jews of Metz, with twenty-two casualties; on the Jews of Speyer, with eleven casualties; and one on the Jews of Regensburg, with no reported casualties.[24] As lamentable as the major violence of 1096 was, it was neither general nor wide-ranging.[25] The bulk of northern European Jewry emerged from the crisis months shaken but unscathed.

The really devastating assaults on Jewish communities in the Rhineland must be investigated in detail, for it was there that the crusading potential for anti-Jewish violence was actualized and it was there also that powerful and important responses were generated.

In order to properly understand these major attacks, it is necessary to discuss first the nature of the German crusading bands stirred up by the preaching of Peter the Hermit. Modern historians have tended to see these forces as loose, amorphous, and utterly undisciplined, basing their assessment primarily on the fact that these bands were destroyed when they confronted the troops of the Hungarian monarchy. These popular armies, it is widely thought, were thoroughly undisciplined from the outset, their weaknesses culminating in and exposed by their rout at the hands of the Hungarians. It should be noted, however, that both Christian and Jewish sources see the popular bands as military forces to be reckoned with. Albert, Ekkehard, and the two Jewish chroniclers all depict the followers of Count Emicho as a full-fledged army. It seems to me an error to overlook this important testimony. None of the crusading armies could boast effective discipline. Instances of loss of control abound. On some occasions, this loss of control was generated by fear and anxiety; in some instances by cupidity; in some, by the distortion of central ideas. The German crusading bands may have been particularly prone to the breakdown of internal discipline; the proportion of trained professional soldiers may have been lower than among the other baronial armies; and religious idiosyncrasies may have been more pronounced among them. Nonetheless these bands should not be seen as qualitatively different from the other armies.[26] They organized themselves in military fashion; they were led by trained knights; they were broadly committed to the exalted goals of the crusade. What made these bands significant for the history of medieval European Jewry was not a spillover of incidental anti-Jewish violence within their ranks. They are important because they developed— in an unusual but understandable way—an anti-Jewish component in their crusading goals, resulting in *organized* efforts to destroy major Jewish communities before their departure for the East.

To the extent that modern historians have dealt with the factors leading to the anti-Jewish outbreak of 1096, they have often seen it as an expression of socioeconomic animosity masked by feigned crusading zeal.[27] To be sure, there are occasional instances in which this was the case, for example the burgher violence in the city of Cologne, with pillage clearly the goal. However, neither the Christian sources nor the Jewish sources specify cupidity as the reason for the assaults of 1096. While these sources refer to pillage in the wake of the attacks, the overwhelming impression they convey is one of violence inspired primarily by ideas and ideals. I believe that these destructive anti-Jewish ideals represent yet another late eleventh-century radical reinterpretation of received tradition. Such radical reinterpretation of received tradition was a prime characteristic of the dynamic creativity of this turbulent period. Some of these innovations were absorbed into the normative teaching of the Church; others were condemned as heretical. Given the inherent complexity of the received tradition vis-à-vis the Jews as well as the explosive implications of the new crusading doctrine, it is, in a sense, not altogether surprising that in certain sectors of the crusading camp—the least normative sectors at that—a dissident reading of crusading doctrine emerged.[28]

Indeed both the Christian and Jewish chroniclers are aware of a tendency to ideational extremism among the German crusading bands, in particular the one that coalesced around the figure of Count Emicho of Leiningen.[29] According to Ekkehard, Emicho saw himself called by divine revelation, as a kind of latter-day Saul, to lead his troops to victory.[30] Albert of Aix preserves a much more negative depiction, claiming that the German crusaders "asserted that a certain goose was imbued with the divine spirit and that a goat was no less filled with the same spirit. These they made guides for themselves for the holy journey to Jerusalem, and they worshiped them fulsomely."[31] Albert's description should probably not be taken too literally. It represents an effort to discredit totally Emicho and his followers, to distinguish sharply between them and the true crusaders, and to preserve thereby the honor of the crusading enterprise. We are justified, however, in extracting from Albert's account a sense of radical beliefs and convictions broadly held among the German bands. The Hebrew chronicle L echoes Ekkehard's report, depicting Emicho as having claimed heavenly revelation and that he had been promised eventual divine coronation.[32] These bands were thus hotbeds of radical interpretation of a generally loose and fluid crusading doctrine. The unusual anti-Jewish teachings of these bands must be seen against the backdrop of this discernible tendency to ideational extremism.

The two Christian historians who accord attention to the popular crusading bands and to the anti-Jewish assaults—Albert of Aix and Ekkehard of Aura—assert that these attacks arose out of anti-Jewish principles. According to Albert, these crusaders "arose in a spirit of cruelty against the Jewish people scattered throughout all the cities and slaughtered them cruelly, especially in the kingdom of Lorraine, *asserting it to be the beginning of their expedi-*

tion and of their duty against the enemies of the Christian faith."[33]
Albert's testimony has not been taken seriously enough
by modern historians. He claims that the destruction of
the Jews was seen by those crusading bands as an integral
part of their sacred task. The same view is reflected in the
briefer comments of Ekkehard of Aura. He indicates that
the German crusaders, "likewise in this matter zealously
devoted to the Christian faith, took pains to destroy utterly
the execrable Jewish people wherever they found them or
to force them into the bosom of the Church."[34] Again,
there was a commitment in principle to eliminate the Jews.

The Jewish chroniclers share this perception of doctrinally grounded hatreds. S, which is generally more
trustworthy in its depiction of the early development of
the crusade, describes the roots of the anti-Jewish animosity in the very call to the crusade itself.

> It came to pass in the year one thousand twenty-eight
> after the destruction of the Temple that this evil befell
> Israel. There first arose the princes and nobles and
> common folk in France, who took counsel and set
> plans to ascend and to rise up like eagles and to do
> battle and to clear the way for journeying to Jerusalem,
> the Holy City, and for reaching the sepulcher of the
> Crucified, a trampled corpse who cannot profit and
> cannot save for he is worthless. They said to one
> another: "Behold we travel to a distant land to do
> battle with the kings of that land. We take our souls
> in our hands in order to kill and to subjugate all those
> kingdoms which do not believe in the Crucified. How
> much more so [should we kill and subjugate] the Jews,
> who killed and crucified him."[35]

According to S, the anti-Jewish hostility is thus related to
an understanding of the essential mission of the crusade.
In a sense, of course, the Jewish chroniclers were wrong.
As we have seen, the bulk of the crusaders departed for
the East without inferring from the call to the crusade an
imperative to destroy the Jews. These Jewish chroniclers

were correct, however, in perceiving such an inference among the doctrinally extreme German crusading bands.

A similar perception is reflected in L. While the opening segment of L differs somewhat from that in S and preserves some interesting variations in general depiction of the crusade and in the specifics of the anti-Jewish slogans, it gives a comparable broad sense of anti-Jewish principles.

It came to pass in the year 4856, the year 1028 of our exile, in the eleventh year of the two hundred and fifty-sixth cycle, during which we had hoped for salvation and comfort according to the prophecy of the prophet Jeremiah: "Cry out in joy for Jacob, shout at the crossroads of the nations!" Instead it was turned into agony and sighing, weeping and crying. Many evils designated in all the [passages of] rebuke—written and unwritten— passed over us. For then rose up initially the arrogant, the barbaric, a fierce and impetuous people, both French and German. They set their hearts to journey to the Holy City, which had been defiled by a ruffian people, in order to seek there the sepulcher of the crucified bastard and to drive out the Muslims who dwell in the land and to conquer the land. They put on their insignia and placed an idolatrous sign on their clothing—the cross—all the men and women whose hearts impelled them to undertake the pilgrimage to the sepulcher of their messiah, to the point where they exceeded the locusts on the land— men, women, and children. With regard to them it is said: "The locusts have no king."

It came to pass that, when they traversed towns where there were Jews, they said to one another: "Behold we journey a long way to seek the idolatrous shrine and to take vengeance upon the Muslims. But here are the Jews dwelling among us, whose ancestors killed him and crucified him groundlessly. Let us take vengeance first upon them. Let us wipe them out as a nation; Israel's name will be mentioned no more. Or else let them be like us and acknowledge the son born of menstruation."[36]

L, which is less well organized than S, introduces early in its depiction of the tragedy at Mainz yet another introductory passage, which includes the only Jewish reference to papal initiative as being behind the call to the First Crusade.

Then Satan also came—the pope of wicked Rome—and circulated a pronouncement among all the gentiles who believe in the offshoot of adultery, the children of Seir, that they congregate together and ascend to Jerusalem and conquer the city on a way built up for pilgrims and that they go to the sepulcher [of him] . . . whom they accepted as a deity over them. Satan came and mingled among the nations. They all gathered as one man to fulfill the commandment. They came as the sand on the seashore, with a noise like the rumbling of a storm or a tempest. It came to pass that, when the embittered and poor had gathered, they took evil counsel against the people of God. They said: "Why are they occupied with doing battle against the Muslims in the vicinity of Jerusalem? Indeed among them is a people which does not acknowledge their deity. What is more, their ancestors crucified their god. Why should we let them live? Why should they dwell among us? Let our swords begin with their heads. After that we shall go on the way of our pilgrimage."[37]

The detailed description of the crusader attacks further indicate the ideational roots of the assaults. The goal of the attacks was certainly not plunder. Plundering by the crusaders manifested itself after the fact, as a kind of spoils of war. The attacks also reflect much more than social hatreds of the Jews. Rather the catastrophic assaults in such Jewish communities as Worms, Mainz, and Cologne reflect a doctrinal commitment to the elimination of the Jews, either through conversion or through death.[38]

A number of reports of crusading slogans emphasize the total nature of the war to be waged against the Jews.

> Let us take vengeance first upon them. Let us wipe them out as a nation; Israel's name will be mentioned no more. Or else let them be like us and acknowledge the son born of menstruation.[39]

In S's description of the opening assault on Worms Jewry, the notion of total elimination of the Jews recurs:

> They cried out and gathered—all who bore and unsheathed [a sword], from great to small, saying: "Behold the time has come to avenge him who was crucified, whom their ancestors slew. Now let not a remnant or residue escape, even an infant or suckling in the cradle."[40]

The Jewish description of the hated Emicho emphasizes the last point in the previous quotation, the totality of the slaughter:

> It came to pass on the new moon of Sivan that the wicked Emicho—may his bones be ground up on iron millstones—came with a large army outside the city, with crusaders and common folk. For he also said: "It is my desire to go on the crusade." He was our chief persecutor. He had no mercy on the elderly, on young men and young women, on infants and sucklings, nor on the ill. He made the people of the Lord like dust to be trampled. Their young men he put to the sword and their pregnant women he ripped open.[41]

The graphic portrayal of specific incidents shows that the complete annihilation of the Jews was intended. Albert of Aix reports two major crusader assaults. The first developed in the aftermath of violence in Cologne:

When they [the Jews] saw this cruelty, approximately
two hundred took flight by boat in the silence of the
night to Neuss. The crusaders, discovering them, inflicted upon them a similar slaughter and despoiled all
their goods *leaving not even one alive.*[42]

Albert's description of the massacre in Mainz is even more
revealing.

Emicho and the rest of his band held a council and,
after sunrise, attacked the Jews in the courtyard with
arrows and lances. When the bolts and doors had been
forced and the Jews had been overcome, they killed
seven hundred of them, who in vain resisted the attack
and assault of so many thousands. They slaughtered
the women also and with the point of their swords
pierced young children of whatever age and sex. The
Jews, seeing that their Christian enemies were attacking them and their children and were sparing no
age, fell upon one another—brothers, children, wives,
mothers and sisters—and slaughtered one another.
Horrible to say, mothers cut the throats of nursing
children with knives and stabbed others, preferring to
perish thus by their own hands rather than be killed
by the weapons of the uncircumcised.[43]

The scene depicted is appalling—no one would be
spared, not even women or children.[44] The Jews, according
to Albert, clearly perceived this. They therefore made the
horrible decision to take their own lives.[45]

The Jewish sources preserve even more striking evidence of the thoroughness with which the program of
destruction was carried out. They too note the fact that
all normal constraints were abandoned and that those
normally considered harmless—the elderly, women, and
children—were not spared. Thus, L's description of the
crusader assault on the archbishop's palace in Mainz includes the following:

After the children of the holy covenant who were in the [archbishop's] chambers were killed, the crusaders came upon them, to strip the corpses and to remove them from the chambers. They threw them naked to the ground through the windows—heap upon heap, mound upon mound, until they formed a high heap. Many were still alive as they threw them. Their souls were still attached to their bodies and they still had a bit of life. They signaled to them with their fingers: "Give us a bit of water that we might drink." When the crusaders saw them, that there was still life in them, they asked them: "Do you wish to sully yourselves? Then we shall give you water to drink and you will still be able to be saved." They shook their heads and looked to their Father in heaven, saying: "No." They pointed with their fingers to the Holy One blessed be he, but could not utter a word from their mouths as a result of the many wounds which had been inflicted upon them. They continued to smite them mightily, beyond those [earlier] blows, until they killed them a second time.[46]

Reflected here is a cruel thoroughness that goes beyond ordinary military behavior. L. portrays concerted efforts to wipe out the Jewish community of Mainz, either spiritually or physically.

The Cologne section shows the same phenomenon. The author of this segment of L was relatively uninterested in depicting the attackers, their motivation, or their behavior. The author did make it clear, however, in the course of the account that the attacks were carried out by an organized military force and that the number of survivors was negligible. At the end of almost each report on the seven refuges, the author carefully notes the number of survivors: For Neuss and Wevelinghofen, "two young men and two infants";[47] for אילנא, "there remained of them only a few";[48] for the second אילנא, "there remained no one, for all of them died for the purity for the sanctification of the unique Name";[49] for Xantes, "there remained no one except those who were wounded and writhing in blood among the dead";[50] in Moers the bulk of the community was converted.[51] Only in Kerpen were the Jews unharmed.[52] Again, the report shows the nearly total destruction of most of these segments of Cologne Jewry.

In the wake of these terrible assaults, observers often reported a sense that there was complete annihilation. Thus in Mainz, after destroying the Jewish refugees in the episcopal palace and in the burgrave's palace, the crusaders fell upon David ben Nathaniel the *gabbai*, who had hidden himself and his family in a priest's courtyard. This friendly cleric tried to persuade him to accept baptism, with the following argument:

> Behold, there remains in the courtyard of the bishop and in the courtyard of the burgrave neither a remnant nor a residue. They have all been killed, cast out, and trampled, in the streets, with the exception of a few whom they baptized. Do likewise and you will be able to be saved—you and your wealth and all the members of your household—from the hands of the crusaders.[53]

While the impression of total destruction was not altogether accurate, it does reflect an awareness of the intentions of those responsible for the assaults.

Thus the accounts of both crusader attitudes and crusader behavior reflect the ideational roots of the devastating assaults on the Jews. Out of these doctrinal foundations emerged the effort to obliterate segments of European Jewry.[54] The sources cited indicate that destruction of the Jews could take place in one of two ways—either spiritually or physically. To cite once more the Hebrew report of the crusaders' slogan: "'Let us wipe them out as a nation; Israel's name will be mentioned no more.' Or else let them be like us and acknowledge the son born of menstruation."[55] Clearly, of these two alternatives the second was preferred. Given the traditional preference for the spirit over the flesh, a victory of the spirit was far preferable to a victory of the flesh. In fact, while the conversion of the Jews was perceived as a victory of the spirit, physical annihilation of the Jews was ambiguous. It could be seen as punishment and purge—a victory for the forces of good in the world. At the same time, in a certain sense it was defeat. The refusal of the Jews to convert made the Christians uneasy, forcing them to confront the possible validity of the faith for which Jews were willing to die. The unsettling residue of ambiguity left when the Jews were physically annihilated was important. It explains why the Christians preferred to convert the Jews instead of resorting to slaughtering them and also helps to explain the remarkable Jewish readiness for martyrdom during this frenzied period.[56]

Evidence of the preference for conversion over slaughter abounds. The passage quoted earlier describing the treatment meted out to the wounded remnants of Mainz Jewry was adduced to illustrate the effort to destroy totally the Jewish community of Mainz. It records repeated attempts to persuade the wounded Jews to save themselves by accepting baptism. The crusaders who handled the corpses of slaughtered Jews so viciously somehow still wished, above all else, to bring the surviving Jews to conversion. I quoted also the efforts to convert David the *gabbai*, who had survived the main attacks in Mainz by hiding out in the house of a friendly priest. He feigned acquiescence, eliciting this reaction from the priest and the crusaders:

> When the priest heard the words of David the *gabbai*, he was very happy over his words, for he thought: "This distinguished Jew has agreed to heed us." He ran to meet them and told them the words of the saintly one. They likewise were very happy. They gathered around the house by the thousands and the ten thousands.[57]

Although many more instances of the unremitting effort to convert groups and individuals could be adduced, one more example will suffice—the protracted and eventually successful efforts to convert the group of Cologne Jews who had found refuge at Moers. The crusading band that had already destroyed a series of Jewish refuges appeared at Moers and besieged the town. The head of the municipality then committed himself to an effort to save his city by bringing those Jews to baptism.

> The mayor of the city came and went out to meet them in a field and requested them to wait till dawn. Thus he said to them: "Perhaps I shall convince the Jews and they will listen to me out of fear and do my will." The suggestion was acceptable to them. The mayor returned to the city, to the Jews, immediately and ordered that they be called and brought before him. Thus he said to them: "In truth, at the outset I promised to protect you and to maintain you until there remain no Jew in the world. But I have fulfilled this condition. Henceforth I cannot save you from all these people. Now decide what you wish to do. Know that, if you do not do thus and so, then the city will surely be destroyed. It is better for me to turn you over to them, so that they not come upon us·in siege and destroy the fortress." They all—from small to great— said in unison: "We are prepared and wish to stretch forth our necks for the fear of our Creator and for the unity of his Name." When the minister saw that he could not overcome them, he immediately made a different plan, in order to impose upon them the fear of the crusaders so that they do their will and be baptized—to lead them out of the city to a place where the crusaders were camped. All of this was unavailing, for they said: "we are not moved by fear of the crusaders." Thus they all responded. When they saw that what they had done was unavailing, they returned them to the city, seized them, and put them in custody, each one separately, till the morrow, so that they not harm themselves for they heard that the others had harmed themselves. . . . On the morrow they seized them

against their will and gave them to the crusaders. They [the Jews] left the town in urgent haste. They killed some of them. Those whom they left alive they baptized against their will. They did with them as they wished.[58]

It is of course not surprising that the townspeople should have wished to avoid violence by bringing the Jews to baptism. What is striking is the willingness of the crusaders to allow the townspeople ample time and opportunity to convert these Jews. The incidents at Moers illustrates once more the powerful desire to covert the Jews if at all possible.

Thus the serious anti-Jewish violence was grounded in a destructive distortion of ideas and involved efforts to convert the Jews if possible or, if necessary, to exterminate them. In identifying the motives of the crusaders as essentially ideational, I do not mean to imply the existence of a carefully worked-out doctrine, merely a simplistic distortion of a preexistent and complex set of teachings. I have noted already the Church's complicated policy toward the Jews—simultaneous denigration and toleration; I have also suggested that this complicated combination was likely to unravel under strain, as indeed seems to have happened during the early reactions to incipient heresy in northern Europe. Now, under the far more intense pressures of crusading propaganda and exhilaration, the breakdown of the traditional doctrine was far more serious. Again, in most crusading circles the traditional teachings remained in force; in the ideologically extreme ambiance of the German crusading bands they gave way, replaced by an ideal that demanded the utter elimination of the Jews.[59]

What ideas generated within the crusading movement afforded the basis for the doctrinal distortions I have identified? Modern research has suggested two major concepts that together informed the First Crusade: holy war and pilgrimage.[60] No matter what the precise nature of Urban's intentions, it is clear that both notions played decisive roles in the crusading movement. Indeed much of the force of the movement stemmed from the explosive combination of these two powerful ideas. The notion of holy war in particular had dangerous implications for the Jews, while the concept of pilgrimage in its own way served to deepen noticeably the identification of the Jews as the enemies of Christendom.

While the call to do battle against the external foes of Christendom occasionally evoked a strong sense of the Jews as internal enemies,[61] it was only among the popular German bands that this perception of the Jews as enemies crystallized in such a way as to undo the traditional precarious balance between denigration and toleration of the Jews. The simple notion of the Jews as an enemy people is clearly articulated in Guibert of Nogent's version of the crusader slogan: "We wish to attack the enemies of God in the East, after travelling great distances. However, before our very eyes are the Jews, and no people is more hostile to God than they are. Such an arrangement is absurd."[62] We find here a number of distortions of the papal message. Despite the gaps in our knowledge of Pope Urban's call to the First Crusade, it is obvious that he did not preach a simple message of warfare against the Muslims as "enemies of God," although such a theme was certainly part of crusader ideology. It is likewise certain that Pope Urban never uttered nor endorsed the disastrous a fortiori argument just noted. Rather the complex call to the crusade was simplistically and erroneously interpreted in some of the popular bands, with the misinterpretation serving as the basis—or rationale—for anti-Jewish hostility and violence. A somewhat fuller expression of this line of thought is preserved in L's vague account of the papal call to the crusade. The crusader slogan reported deserves a close second look:

> They said: "Why are they occupied with doing battle against the Muslims in the vicinity of Jerusalem? Indeed among them is a people which does not acknowledge their deity. What is more, their ancestors crucified their god. Why should we let them live? Why

should they dwell among us? Let our swords begin with their heads. After that we shall go on the way of our pilgrimage."[63]

The crusaders are here depicted as setting out for a holy war against the Muslims in the vicinity of Jerusalem. The basis for the battle seems to lie in the fact that the Muslims do not acknowledge Jesus. At this point the a fortiori argument is made more precise: If war is waged against the Muslim nonbelievers, then the worst of the nonbelievers—the Jews, because of the sin of deicide attributed to them—should be the first target.

The most extreme distortion of the holy war theme is found in a passage in S. The crusaders' anti-Jewish slogan reported at the outset of S was formulated in the following terms:

Behold we travel to a distant land to do battle with the kings of that land. We take our souls in our hands in order to kill and to subjugate all those kingdoms which do not believe in the Crucified. How much more so [should we kill and subjugate] the Jews, who killed and crucified him.[64]

According to this report, the crusading appeal was even more radically distorted. Holy war is understood as the effort "to kill and to subjugate *all* those kingdoms which do not believe in the Crucified." This formulation goes far beyond the papal initiative. At most, Urban called for liberation of certain areas from Muslim domination. The notion of subjugating all infidels constitutes the most radical expansion of the papal concept of holy war. Onto this distortion the already noted a fortiori argument was grafted.

This notion of destruction of the Jews as a correlative of the general call to battle against the enemies of God and Christendom may be reflected in the terminology that the Jewish sources use for the crusaders. The most neutral term utilized is מסומנים, "those bearing insignia." More widely used is the term תועים, which is a perjorative distortion of the Latin "perigrini." The Hebrew connotes wandering *in error*. Another widely used term is אויבים or אויבי השם, "the enemy or the enemies of the Lord." This may reflect awareness on the part of the Jews that the crusaders perceived them as the enemies of Christendom, indeed the enemies of the Christian deity.

The essential notion of Jewish enmity is deepened by the emphasis on misdeeds of which the Jews are accused. Not only are the Jews perceived as denying the message of Christianity but are portrayed as having committed violence against its messiah and deity. Thus many versions of the distorted crusading slogans include, beyond a simple call for battle against the Jewish infidel, the even more inflammatory call for vengeance against the sacrilegious Jews. According to L, the crusader slogan was as follows:

> Behold we journey a long way to seek the idolatrous shrine and to take vengeance upon the Muslims. But here are the Jews dwelling among us, whose ancestors killed him and crucified him groundlessly. Let us take vengeance first upon them. Let us wipe them out as a nation; Israel's name will be mentioned no more. Or else let them be like us and acknowledge the son born of menstruation.[65]

The crusade did not aim at generalized holy war but rather the liberation of the Holy Sepulcher and revenge against the Muslims who had held it and defiled it. Once again attention is turned on the Jews: If the Muslims must be punished for desecration of the Holy Sepulcher, then the Jews all the more—for they were said to be guilty of the sin that first made the Holy Sepulcher a sacred shrine. It is in this connection that the second major stimulus to the First Crusade—the notion of pilgrimage—had its impact. The emphasis on the sacred shrines of Christendom, preeminently the Holy Sepulcher, focused attention on the allegation of deicide, deepened the sense of Jewish enmity, and fed the vengeance motif among the popular crusading bands.[66]

This theme of vengeance recurs more frequently than does the notion of generalized holy war; S reports it a number of times. In describing the first outbreak of violence in Worms, S depicts the allegation of well poisoning and the following response:

> They said: "Behold the time has come to avenge him who was crucified, whom their ancestors slew. Now let not a remnant nor a residue escape, even an infant and a suckling in the cradle."[67]

The same theme is sounded by S in the accounts of the second assault in Worms:

> The crusaders and burghers said: "Behold those who remain in the courtyard of the bishop and in his chambers. Let us take vengeance upon them as well."[68]

As Emicho and his troops invaded the city of Mainz, with the aid of burgher collaboration, the S narrative again emphasized the notion of vengeance:

> The enemies of the Lord said to one another: "Behold—the gates have been opened by themselves. All this the Crucified has done for us, so that we might avenge his blood upon the Jews."[69]

The power of the vengeance motif within crusader mentality should not be minimized. It is widely reported that the conquest of Jerusalem in early July of 1099 was accompanied by acts of unusual cruelty. The *Gesta Francorum* reports that "there was such a massacre that our men were wading up to their ankles in enemy blood." Later on, in describing the aftermath of the conquest, the *Gesta* adds:

> So the surviving Saracens dragged the dead ones out in front of the gates and piled them up in mounds as big as houses. No one had ever seen or heard of such

a slaughter of pagans, for they were burned on pyres like pyramids, and no one save God alone knows how many there were.[70]

Some modern historians have explained these excesses as the result of crusader exhilaration at the conquest of the Holy City. Perhaps, equally influential was the desire for vengeance on the Muslims who had allegedly desecrated the sacred shrine of Christianity. The savagery manifested against the Jews of western Europe and the massacre in Jerusalem may both reflect the thirst for vengeance among the masses of crusaders.

I maintain, then, that the ideas at the core of the First Crusade bore the potential for disrupting the fine balance between negation and toleration in the traditional Church doctrine vis-à-vis the Jews. In most crusader circles, these notions only enhanced a preexisting animosity toward the Jews; in the radical German bands they triggered murderous assaults on them. At this juncture it may be objected that the foregoing analysis of crusader behavior and crusader attitudes leans too heavily and directly upon sources that were likely to exaggerate ideals and minimize the influence of more mundane factors. The Jewish sources, it may be argued, would tend to emphasize the religious ideals of the attackers in order to accentuate the martyrdom of the Jewish victims. Even the Christian sources were so accustomed to framing the crusade in terms of religious zeal that they could see the behavior of the radical bands only in terms of misguided ideals, when in fact this behavior represented mere marauding despoliation on the part of poor, hungry, and envious crusaders. I would certainly not wish to minimize the complexity of crusader motivation in the anti-Jewish violence. A measure of envy and want undoubtedly had a role in motivating these assaults. I would assert, however, that the Christian and Jewish sources are accurate in identifying crusade-related zeal as the *essential* ingredient in the anti-Jewish violence.

Whereas other antipathies may have been activated by

the crusading ideals, the key factor in the outbreak of violence in 1096 was the call to the crusade, the potential it held for anti-Jewish distortion, and the actualization of that potential in the radical German bands. Indeed, at that point in the development of the German crusading bands, there is no evidence that they suffered desperate want and hunger. There were, to be sure, instances of violence triggered by desperation later in the journey east; at that point, however, there are no reports of such tendencies. Moreover, had the crusaders merely been expressing desperate want or socioeconomic hostilities, they would have been unlikely to be so extreme in their behaviors. Finally, had the Jews seen these attacks as mere depredation, their reaction of massive martyrdom would make no sense. For all these reasons, I prefer to follow the lead of the sources themselves in emphasizing the role of crusading fervor in triggering the anti-Jewish violence of 1096. That economic want or envy may well have exacerbated the essentially doctrinal animus is of course a perfectly reasonable notion; human motivations are complex in all ages.

Indeed, the Jewish sources themselves suggest that crusading zeal activated one other major source of anti-Jewish animosity. I have already adduced the existence of substantial hostility on the part of the burghers of the Rhineland cities against their Jewish neighbors, a hostility perhaps rooted in theology but buttressed by economic and political tensions. Burgher collusion in the devastating assaults is clearly reflected in both Christian and Jewish sources. S, in describing the early stages of the crusader movement eastward, stresses the general phenomenon of burgher involvement in the anti-Jewish violence: "The burghers in every city to which the crusaders came were hostile to us, for their [the burghers] hands were also with them [the crusaders] to destroy vine and stock all along the way to Jerusalem."[71] Both S and L claim that the city gates of Mainz were opened to Count Emicho by burgher collaborators. In general, S (and less systematically L) insists that the burghers were consistently involved in every anti-Jewish outbreak. There is surely an element of overstatement in all this: some of the burghers of the Rhineland cities were quite friendly to the Jews. Both S and L recount burgher opposition to early and sporadic anti-Jewish violence in Mainz. Moreover the common Jewish tendency to seek refuge with helpful burghers indicates that a segment of Christian urban populace was sympathetic to the Jews.[72] What must be concluded, therefore, is that the young and rapidly growing Rhineland cities—rife with tension and violence—included elements both friendly to and hostile to the Jews.[73] For the hostile burghers, the distorted crusading ideology of Emicho and his followers provided legitimation for preexistent anti-Jewish animus. For the crusaders, the burghers fanned the antipathies already widespread in their ranks and, on occasion, burghers hostile to the Jews provided useful assistance, as when they opened the barred gates to the city of Mainz. The combination of crusader and burgher opposition was deadlier than either element would have been in isolation.

In assessing the devastating assaults on the Rhineland communities of Worms, Mainz, and Cologne, yet a third factor must be taken into consideration. Unfortunately for the Jews, the general political circumstances in Germany allowed significant leeway for the expression of both distorted ideology and individual depravity. In one sense of course, Germany was the most advanced political state in western Christendom at this period. It was large and centralized, with heavy emphasis on its connections with earlier epochs of imperial Roman power. The bureaucracy necessary to maintain central rule over such a vast area, however, had simply not yet developed. Thus in practice much of the empire was under the de facto authority of local magnates, both ecclesiastical and lay.[74] The barons of southern and northern France were more capable of maintaining discipline and stability during a period of upheaval than were the surrogates of imperial authority in Germany. The general political weakness in Germany was further exacerbated by the anti-imperial bent of many crusaders who were after all responding to the papal call—and hence almost automatically hostile to the emperor and his followers.

As the radical popular bands began to form and to sweep across the areas of Germany, the danger they represented for the Jews was compounded by the absence of the emperor and the weakness of his surrogates. The Jewish sources point out several times the significance of the emperor's absence. Thus, in the early stages of danger, when threatened by Duke Godfrey, the Jews quickly—and successfully—solicited imperial protection. A major Jewish leader "sent an emissary to Emperor Henry in the Kingdom of Apulia, where he had tarried for nine years. He told him of all these events. The anger of the emperor was aroused, and he sent letters throughout all the provinces of his empire, to the princes and bishops, to the nobles and to Duke Godfrey—messages of peace and [orders] with regard to the Jews that they protect them so that no one harm them physically and that they provide aid and refuge to them."[75] The imperial order—reinforced by the payment of bribes by Jews—was successful in thwarting the violence threatened by Duke Godfrey. Such orders, however, could have no real impact on a raging army of crusaders bent on doing violence to the Jews. In the account of the fate met by the Jews of Trier, the emperor is mentioned a second time. The bishop, attempting to explain to the Jews why he could no longer afford them the protection he had promised, admitted utter powerlessness. Not only could he not protect the Jews but he felt endangered himself! "The community answered and said: 'Did you not specify at a time in your pledge—that you would support us until the emperor arrived in the kingdom?' The bishop answered and said: 'The emperor himself could not save you from the crusaders. Be converted or accept upon yourself the judgment of heaven.'"[76] The passage reflects the weakness of the local authorities, the Jewish yearning for imperial intervention, and the contention (justified or not) that even the emperor could not stem crusader violence. Despite the last claim, it does seem likely that an imperial presence might well have reduced the anti-Jewish violence in Trier. The weakness of the local authorities, as the Trier instance shows, is manifested throughout the Hebrew chronicles.

In sum, the kernel of the disaster that befell Rhineland Jewry lay in the potential for distortion inherent in the very call to the crusade, in the interpretation of that call among the forces of Peter the Hermit, and in the radical distortion spun out among the German crusading bands. Like all catastrophes, this one too was complex, complicated by longstanding tensions between the Jews and their urban neighbors and by the grave weakness of the political order in Germany. This disastrous combination gave rise to the annihilation of the three major communities of nascent Ashkenzic Jewry.

IV

The Patterns of Response

In meeting the variety of threats posed by the crusaders and their burgher collaborators, a number of groups pooled their efforts: a segment of the burgher population, the local authorities, the central authorities and, most of all, the Jews themselves. Various techniques were tried; under given circumstances one or another of these techniques proved successful; in a small number of important instances, all efforts failed.

The first and apparently best line of defense was to establish direct contact with the crusaders, initiating steps to forestall the outbreak of violence. The Jews made serious attempts to deal directly with the crusaders. S, which gives the fuller description of early anti-Jewish agitation, offers the best broad depiction of Jewish efforts to stem crusader violence before it broke out. "When the crusaders began to reach this land, they sought funds with which to purchase bread. We gave them, considering ourselves to be fulfilling the verse: 'Serve the king of Babylon and live.'"[1] For the Jews, such expenditures were eminently sensible. For the crusaders, the money realized helped solve the difficult problem of provisioning an ill-equipped army. It may well be—although there is no specific documentation—that there was some deliberate crusader intention to exploit the Jewish "enemy" in preparation for battle against the Muslim "enemy."[2]

Three specific crusading groups are named as recipients of Jewish funds. In one instance, that of Peter the Hermit, the fact that it was thought appropriate that the Jews contribute to the expenses of the crusade is mentioned explicitly. According to L, Peter "brought with him a letter from France, from the Jews, [indicating] that, in all the places where his foot would tread and he would encounter Jews, they should give him provisions for the way. He would then speak well on behalf of Israel."[3] The Jewish community of Trier did in fact give Peter funds and his troops passed through without incident.

The second instance involved important baronial figures. S and L give parallel descriptions of the incident, the former identifying the baron as Ditmar and the latter as Godfrey.[4] According to the latter—and somewhat fuller—version Duke Godfrey warned that he would not depart on the crusade "without avenging the blood of the Crucified with the blood of Israel." Kalonymous the *parnas* of Mainz elicited an imperial letter enjoining special protection for the Jews. Nonetheless, "the Jews in Cologne bribed him [Godfrey] with five hundred silver marks and the Jews of Mainz bribed him likewise." In this case no explicit relationship is drawn between Jewish funds and crusader provisions. Whether such a relationship existed in the mind of Duke Godfrey or of the Jews is open to speculation. More important is the success of payment of bribes in forestalling attacks in these two cases.

In the third recorded incident, the strategy failed. When Count Emicho appeared before Mainz, the Jews attempted precisely the technique that had proved successful with Peter the Hermit and Duke Godfrey. After securing promises of protection from the local authorities, they turned directly to the aggressor. Their thinking is reflected in L's report: "For this purpose we have disbursed our moneys, giving the archbishop and his ministers and his servants and the burghers approximately four hundred silver *zekukim*. We gave the wicked Emicho seven gold pounds so that he might assist us. It was of no avail."[5] Their miscalculation was reasonable, but tragic. They were simply not prepared for the radical ideologies that inspired Emicho and his followers. The approach that had worked with Peter the Hermit and a few of the potentially dangerous barons were inappropriate in these unusual circumstances.

A second line of defense for the endangered German Jews was to turn to their burgher neighbors for assistance. While in retrospect the Jewish chroniclers denigrated the ineffective burghers, it is quite clear that the Jews of the Rhineland, during the early stages of the violence, perceived their neighbors as willing and capable protectors. This is surely the only way to understand the tendency of the Jews in such places as Worms, Mainz, and Cologne to seek out the protection of their burgher neighbors. This is particularly striking in Worms, where

> the community divided itself into two groups. Some of them fled to the bishop in his towers; some of them remained in their homes, for the burghers promised them vainly and cunningly. They are splintered reeds, for evil and not for good, for their hand was with the crusaders in order to destroy our name and remnant. They gave us vain and meaningless encouragement, [saying]: "Do not fear them, for anyone who kills one of you—his soul will be forfeit for yours." They [the burghers] did not give them [the Jews] anywhere to flee, for the Jews deposited all their money in their [the burghers'] hands. Therefore they surrendered them.[6]

The after-the-fact recriminations of the chronicler do not obscure the fact that they had expected assistance. The same assumption is reflected in the initial reaction of Cologne Jewry when threatened:

> When they heard that the [Jewish] communities had been killed, they all fled to gentile acquaintances. They remained there for the two days of Shavuot.[7]

While some of the burghers joined the crusaders in attacking the Jews, others were reported to remain staunchly committed to the maintenance of law and order. To be sure, as the magnitude of the danger increased, even the best intentioned of the well-disposed burghers proved ineffective in protecting the Rhineland Jews.

As the dimensions of the threat became clearer, the most significant line of defense lay in the intercession of the established political authorities.[8] The most powerful of these was of course the emperor. When, according to L, Duke Godfrey announced that he would not leave for Jerusalem without taking vengeance upon the Jews, strenuous efforts were made to thwart him. In addition to bribing Duke Godfrey, the Jews turned to the emperor and received from him a letter of protection. Emperor Henry addressed, inter alia, the duke directly, warning him against anti-Jewish actions. The willingness of the emperor to respond quickly and decisively to Jewish entreaties is not at all surprising or difficult to understand. Emperor Henry was interested in maintaining internal peace and security in general and in protecting his Jewish subjects in particular. More important, the imperial missive, together with bribes paid by Jews, apparently convinced Duke Godfrey to leave the Jews in peace. According to L, the duke responded to the imperial epistle by disavowing any such intentions: "The wicked duke swore that it had never occurred to him to do them any harm."[9] Like bribes, imperial warnings could be and were successful with the well organized and capably led crusader forces. Like bribes, they were also not successful in restraining the popular crusading bands, moved as they were by radical anti-Jewish doctrine. It will be recalled that, during the negotiations between the Jews and the bishop of Trier, the Jews reminded the bishop that he had promised them protection until the emperor would reach Germany. To this the bishop replied: "The emperor himself could not save you from the crusaders."[10]

Because of the unfortunate absence of the emperor, a heavy burden fell on the agents of imperial authority in Germany. According to L, when informed of the threat to the Jews, the emperor responded with anger, sending charters "throughout all the provinces of his empire to the barons, the bishops, and the nobles," ordering that protection and aid be extended to the endangered Jews. The emperor, as a result of his absence, had done all he could do; the Jews themselves and the burghers were relatively powerless. The essential burden had to be borne by the available authorities—the bishops and the secular lords.

To be sure, the Jews played a role in securing the aid of these authorities, as they had done with the emperor. In fact, our information on the negotiations between the Jews and these authorities is much fuller than it is for the negotiations with Emperor Henry. There are, for example, references to contact between the leadership of the Jewish community of Mainz and the archbishop of that town in both Christian and Jewish sources. Albert of Aix gives the following account:

> The Jews of this city, knowing of the slaughter of their brethren and that they themselves could not escape the hands of so many, fled in hope of safety to Bishop Ruthard. They put an infinite treasure in his custody and trust, having much faith in his protection, because he was bishop of the city.[11]

L gives a somewhat fuller account that agrees in its essentials with Albert.

> The notables of Israel gathered together to give them good counsel, so that they might be able to be saved. They said to one another: "Let us choose of our elders and let us decide what we shall do, for this great evil will swallow us up." They agreed on the counsel of redeeming their souls by spending their moneys and bribing the princes and officers and bishops and burghers. The leaders of the community, notable in the eyes of the archbishop, then rose and came to the archbishop and to his ministers and servants to speak with them. They said to them: "What shall we do about the report which we have heard concerning

our brethren in Speyer and in Worms who have been killed?" They said to them: "Listen to our advice and bring all your moneys to our treasury. Then you, your wives, your sons and daughters, and all that you have bring into the chamber of the archbishop until these bands pass by. Thus will you be able to be saved from the crusaders."[12]

A number of factors made the political authorities responsive to such Jewish overtures. In the first place, there was the imperial order just noted. Beyond this, the bishops and barons, like the emperor, were committed to general preservation of law and order and specifically to protection of Jews. Many of them, like the bishop of Speyer, had undertaken obligations to their Jews. Moreover, the bishops were surely aware of the distortion involved in the anti-Jewish slogans and concerned to maintain the normative Church stance of physical protection for the Jews in Christendom. There may have been humanitarian motives as well. What is not clear is the role of "bribery" or payment for protection. In his report on the fate of Speyer Jewry, S notes specifically that the Jews were saved by Bishop John, "for the Lord inclined his heart to sustain them without bribe."[13] According to Albert of Aix, Archbishop Ruthard of Mainz was careful to set aside the money of the Jews, apparently in order to protect it. According to L, however, the archbishop was heavily bribed to secure his aid. It seems likely in some cases bribes were given, whereas in others they were not.

The effectiveness of the protection provided by the local political authorities was commensurate with the seriousness of the threat posed. Where the anti-Jewish violence was sporadic and poorly organized, the authorities could save their Jews. Indeed the most impressive instance of protection of Jews occurred in the city of Speyer, where the violence was relatively unorganized. When this violence broke forth Bishop John reacted quickly and decisively:

When Bishop John heard, he came with a large force and helped the [Jewish] community wholeheartedly and brought them indoors and saved them from their [the crusaders and burghers] hands. He seized some of the burghers and cut off their hands.[14]

Without detracting from the Jewish chronicler's admiration for Bishop John, it is clear that the military threat which he faced at this early point was far less imposing than that faced, for example, by the prelates of Worms and Mainz. To be sure, Bishop John was subsequently successful in protecting the Jews in his area from the crusading bands. His decisive intervention at the beginning of May, however, was undertaken against a far less formidable foe.

I have also noted sporadic, incipient violence in Mainz and in Cologne; in both cases, the burghers intervened effectively at the outset. It seems highly likely that in both cities the bishops could have successfully protected the Jews against such violence. The strategy of the archbishop of Cologne—removing the Jews from Cologne—would probably have been quite successful, had this sporadic violence been the only threat to Jewish life.

While the local authorities could deal effectively with sporadic and unorganized violence, they were hardly equipped to withstand the assaults of popular crusading armies that numbered in the thousands and perhaps tens of thousands. The Jewish authors, deeply upset by the magnitude of the calamity that had struck German Jewry, sometimes questioned in retrospect the sincerity of these local authorities. Yet, even after the fact, the narrators of the Jewish chronicles seem convinced that the bishops and barons were genuine in their efforts to save the Jews. L, for example, at one moment denigrates the efforts by the archbishop of Mainz by suggesting that the advice to gather up Jewish goods and to bring all the Jews into the archbishop's palace was simply a ploy designed to despoil the Jews. Yet, in the next breath, the chronicler acknowledges that the archbishop did intend to save Mainz

Jewry: "The archbishop gathered his ministers and his servants—exalted ministers, nobles—in order to assist us. For at the outset it was his desire to save us with all his strength. Indeed we gave him great bribes to this end, along with his ministers and servants, since they intended to save us. Ultimately all the bribery and all the diplomacy did not avail in protecting us on the day of wrath from catastrophe."[15]

The seriousness of the archbishop's intentions is clearly indicated by L further on in his account. After failing to save the bulk of the Jewish community, Archbishop Ruthard fled the city. Even at this point, however, he remained committed to honor his obligations toward the group led by Kalonymous, the *parnas*, which had been spared during the massacre in Mainz. L describes this sense of ongoing commitment in touching terms.

> In the middle of the night the archbishop sent someone to the window of the storehouse, to R. Kalonymous the *parnas*. He called to him and said: "Listen to me, Kalonymous. Behold the archbishop has sent me to you to learn whether you are still alive. He commanded me to save you and all those with you. Come out to me. Behold with him are three hundred warriors, armed with swords and dressed in armor. Our persons are pledged for yours, even to death. If you do not believe me, then I shall take an oath. For thus my lord the archbishop commanded me. He is not in the city, for he went to the village of Rüdesheim. He sent us here to save the remnant of you that remains. He wishes to assist you." They did not believe until he took an oath. Then R. Kalonymous and his band went out to him. The minister placed them in boats and ferried them across the Rhine River and brought them at night to the place where the archbishop was, in the village of Rüdesheim. The archbishop was exceedingly happy over R. Kalonymous, that he was still alive, and intended to save him and the men that were with them.[16]

This report leaves little room to doubt the sincerity of Archbishop Ruthard. Even after the massive failure in Mainz, he remained committed to saving the remnant of Mainz Jewry. This brief account also points to the major reason for failure. Three hundred armed warriors, well equipped as they might have been, were hardly a match for the twelve thousand crusaders Count Emicho was said to have under command.

The first sensible step available to the local authorities for warding off the violence of the popular crusading bands was to deny them entrance into the city. This was done at Mainz, where Emicho and his troops remained outside the city for two full days until the gates were opened to them, and at Moers, where the local authority begged the crusaders to remain outside the town, allowing him to try and convince the Jews to convert and thus to avoid violence for both the Jews and the town.[17] While sensible, this could hardly be an effective ploy. The town walls were simply too extensive and the defensive forces too limited to create any prolonged barrier against the crusaders. According to S, the gates of Mainz did not even have to be stormed; they were opened by sympathetic burghers.

The sources refer to two efforts to protect the Jews by moving them temporarily from the central city to neighboring locales. In both cases—Speyer and Cologne—the initial violence seems to have been sporadic, rather than massive. The technique of taking the Jews out of main urban centers would seem to have been a sensible measure for protecting them from the popular crusading bands also (these bands were likely to make their way through the major cities, bypassing smaller locales). According to S, the Jews of Speyer were indeed threatened by the crusading bands. "They remained there [in the fortresses], fasting and weeping and mourning. They despaired deeply, for every day the crusaders and the gentiles and Emicho—may his bones be ground up—and the common folk gathered against them, to seize them and to destroy them."[18] These dangers notwithstanding, the fortifications held and the dispersed

Jews of Speyer were saved. The experience of Cologne
Jewry was the opposite. The effort to save them by removing them from the city failed miserably. As we have seen,
the crusading forces hunted down Cologne Jewry and
virtually wiped it out.[19]

The more usual strategy was to discourage the crusaders by gathering the Jews with their possessions in the
most formidable strongholds in the city, to discourage the
crusaders from attacking, and to make defense possible if
they attacked anyway. L's description of the negotiations between the Jews and Archbishop Ruthard shows
the archbishop giving precisely this advice. Albert of Aix
corroborates:

> Then that excellent bishop of the city cautiously set
> aside the incredible amount of money received from
> them. He placed the Jews in the very spacious hall of
> his own castle, out of the sight of Count Emicho and
> his followers, that they might remain safe and sound
> in a very secure and strong place.[20]

The plan, though sane and sensible, misjudged both the
depth of the crusaders' commitment to destroying the Jews
and the military power of their forces.

The ultimate failure of these preventive measures is
reflected in the slaughter of the Jewish communities of
Worms, Mainz, and Cologne. In a few instances the authorities themselves realized that they were powerless in
the face of the crusader forces, a conclusion with which
even the Jews agreed. L preserves a series of statements
by important local authorities in which they avow utter
powerlessness. The archbishop of Mainz, for example,
though committed to saving the remnant of Mainz Jewry,
even after the massacre of the bulk of the community,
eventually admitted—or claimed—total inability to withstand the crusaders, and the reply of Kalonymous the
parnas is revealing:

He called to R. Kalonymous and said: "I cannot save
you. Your God has abandoned you; he does not wish
to leave you a remnant and a residue. I no longer have
sufficient strength to save you or to assist you henceforth. Therefore know what you must do—you and
your band that stands with you. Either believe in our
deity or bear the sins of your ancestors." R. Kalonymous the pious answered him and cried out in anguish: "It is true that our God does not wish to save us.
Therefore your words are true and correct, that you no
longer have the power to assist. Now give me time till
tomorrow to respond to your words."[21]

Similar statements of powerlessness—in all likelihood
similarly accurate—are attributed by L to the bishop of
Trier and to the municipal authority at Moers.[22]

By the time the authorities recognized their powerlessness, there still remained the possibility of removing the
essential "reason" for the crusader assaults by bringing the
Jews, in one way or another, to baptism. According to the
Gesta Treverorum, this was done by the bishop of Trier. The
chronicle reports a lengthy conversionist address by the
bishop to the Jews assembled in the episcopal palace and
indicates that these Jews accepted baptism, albeit by and
large insincerely.[23]

L gives a somewhat different report, alleging forced
conversion at the hands of the bishop and his men. According to L, the bishop, after exposing himself to considerable danger by attempting to protect the Jews, finally
gave up these efforts. He informed the Jews that he could
no longer save them from the crusaders and advised them
either to convert—thus ending the threat of violence—or
leave his palace, likewise ending the threat of violence
against the bishop and his followers. In order to frighten
the bulk of the Jews into converting, he sent a small
number of Jews to meet their death at the hands of the
crusaders. When this failed, the bishop's followers forcibly
converted the Jews:

After these were killed, the enemy saw those remaining in the palace—that they were as firm in their faith
as at the outset and that their hands had not been
weakened by what had been done to these first [mar-
tyrs]. They said to one another: "All this the women
do—they incite their husbands, strengthening their
hands to rebel. . . . " Then all the ministers came and
each grasped forcefully the hands of the women, smiting and wounding them, and led them to the church
in order to baptize them. Afterwards they sent and
took forcefully children from the bosoms of their
mothers and took them with them, to fulfill what is
said: "Your sons and daughters shall be delivered to
another people." The women raised their voices and
wept. Three days prior to informing them of this forced
conversion, the ministers came to the palace and closed
the pit in which water was held in the palace, for they
feared lest they throw their children there to kill them.
They did not permit them to ascend the wall, so that
they not throw themselves from the wall. All night
they guarded them that they not kill one another, until
dawn. All this they planned because they did not wish
to kill them—rather they labored to seize them and to
forcibly convert them.[24]

This account ends with the stories of a few women who
thwarted their captors and martyred themselves.

A similar report, somewhat less clear, is given for
Regensburg.

The community in Regensburg was forcibly converted
in its entirety, for they saw that they could not be
saved. Indeed those who were in the city, when the
crusaders and the common folk gathered against them,
pressed them against their will and brought them into
a certain river. They made the evil sign in the water,
the cross, and baptized them all simultaneously in that
river.[25]

The account is not fully detailed, and there is ambiguity concerning the Jewish willingness for baptism. Nonetheless the effort to avoid violence against the Jews by forcing them to accept baptism is once again evident.

An even more radical method of saving the town and its Christian populace is reflected in L's depiction of the incident at Moers. Here too the authorities came to the conclusion that they were powerless in the face of the crusaders and decided to save the town. The speech of the local municipal authority is remarkably explicit, indicating his own sense that the alternatives were destruction of Moers or accession to the demands of the crusaders. The latter of the choices, much preferable to the townspeople, involved either the conversion of the Jews or their surrender to the crusaders. As at Trier, an effort was made to terrorize the Jews into conversion. When the efforts at frightening the Jews into baptism failed, the authorities at Moers simply turned the Jews over to the crusaders.[26]

The last alternative was self-defense, an option that was exercised frequently. It is not altogether clear if the Jews who donned armor in order to do battle against the crusaders did so in hopes of saving themselves and their community, or if this inclination to battle simply represents a form of martyrdom. While no definite answer is possible, it does seem that the Jewish warriors undertook military operations in the hope of holding back the crusaders and saving their fellow Jews.

The first major instance of self-defense took place at the bishop's palace in Worms. The initial attack on Worms Jewry was directed at those who had chosen to remain in their houses. Two weeks later a more organized assault took place on the bishop's palace, and the Jews defended themselves vigorously.

It came to pass on the twenty-fifth of Iyyar that the crusaders and the burghers said: "Behold those who remain in the courtyard of the bishop and in his chambers. Let us take vengeance on them as well." They

> gathered from all the villages in the vicinity, along
> with the crusaders and the burghers; they beseiged
> them [the Jews]; and they did battle against them.
> There took place a very great battle, one side against
> the other, until they seized the chambers in which the
> children of the sacred convenant were.[27]

The battle that took place at the archbishop's palace in
Mainz was apparently even fiercer:

> They came with their standards to the archbishop's
> gate, where the children of the sacred covenant were—
> an army as numerous as sands on the seashore. When
> the saintly and God-fearing saw the huge multitude,
> they trusted in and cleaved to their Creator. They
> donned armor and stripped on weapons—great and
> small—with R. Kalonymous ben Meshullam at their
> head.[28]

A description of hostilities at the burgrave's palace conveys
a similar sense of a small force battling against overwhelming odds, with no real hope of success.

One poorly documented case attests to successful
military activity by Jews. Although the report is somewhat
suspect, the incident is nonetheless worthy of mention.
After the extensive description of the fate of the major
Jewish communities along the Rhine—Speyer, Worms,
Mainz, and Cologne—L adds a series of briefer accounts
of additional persecution—Trier, Metz, Regensburg, and
שלא. The account for Trier is detailed and seems relatively
reliable; the other three reports are short and sketchy. The
last one is particularly problematic. The narrative begins
with the usual set of alternatives—conversion or death:

> They exacted from the crusaders and their fellow
> townsmen three days' time and reported the matter to
> their lord by means of emissary. For those three days
> they declared a fast and beseeched the living God with
> fasting and weeping and crying out. Their prayer was

accepted and the merciful God saved them. The lord
strengthened their hand during the three-day period
and sent them a duke and with him a thousand caval-
rymen, girded with sword, along with the Jews living
in the city of . . . five hundred young men, armed
with swords and men of war, who never retreat before
an enemy. They came upon the city confidently and
smote greatly the crusaders and the townspeople. Of
the Jews only six were killed.[29]

The best that can be suggested is that rumors of effective Jewish military opposition in central Europe circulated
in the wake of the First Crusade. The one conclusion that
is solidly established is that Jews surely did resort to arms
in certain situations, generally in the face of overwhelming
odds.

Thus the efforts to save the lives and property of Jews
were many and varied. Where the threat was minimal,
these efforts were usually successful. Where the threat
was overwhelming, neither the Jews nor the authorities
were capable of meeting the challenge. Appeals based on
reason, accepted norms, or material blandishments failed
with the ideologically motivated crusading bands. When
force was marshaled against force, the crusaders generally
emerged with the military victory.

CONVERSION OR MARTYRDOM

The radical anti-Jewish ideology that permeated the popular crusading bands called for the utter destruction of the
Jews. This meant one of two alternatives: conversion or
death. When the effort to preserve Jewish life and property
failed, the Jews faced the extreme choice set for them by
the crusaders. It should be emphasized that the basic alternatives open to the Jews were defined by the Christian
attackers; in this sense the Jews were powerless. Both
alternatives, however—conversion and death—were far
from simple. Each encompassed a range of options, which

posed for the Jews choices and decisions and gave them a measure of control over their destiny, even under these extremely oppressive circumstances.

We have already noted that, of the two alternative modes of destroying Jewishness, the crusaders much preferred conversion, which they made extensive efforts to secure.[30] Both Jewish and Christian sources note instances of conversion; both agree that the number of converts was far exceeded by the number of martyrs. The Jewish sources nowhere make this claim explicitly—one senses that, for the Jewish chroniclers, such an assertion would be unnecessary and demeaning. The Hebrew narratives, by focusing on the heroism of the martyrs, certainly convey a distinct impression of the preponderant acceptance of death at the moment of crisis. The Christian sources concur. Albert of Aix, for example, after describing the horrible slaughter at Mainz, notes: "A few [Jews] escaped; and a few, because of fear, rather than because of love of the Christian faith, were baptized."[31]

There are further points of agreement between the Jewish and Christian sources. Both indicate that these conversions were the result of duress, were generally insincere, and were normally short-lived. While the two sets of sources agreed on the objective reality, they naturally disagree totally in their evaluations of this reality. For the Jews the insincerity of conversion and the continued loyalty to Judaism was a great virtue. L makes such observations in one of the final segments of the chronicle:

Now it is fitting to tell the praise of those forcibly converted. For all that they ate and drank they mortally endangered themselves. They slaughtered meat and removed from it the fat. They examined the meat according to the regulations of the sages. They did not drink wine of libation. They did not go to church except occasionally. Every time they went, they went out of great duress and fear. They went reluctantly. The gentiles themselves knew that they had not converted wholeheartedly, but only out of fear of the crusaders, and that they did not believe in their deity, but that rather they clung to the fear of the Lord and held fast to the sublime God, creator of heaven and earth. In the sight of the gentiles they observed the Sabbath properly and observed the Torah of the Lord secretly. Anyone who speaks ill of them insults the countenance of the Divine Presence.[32]

This is lavish praise for the insincerity of the converts. As the Jewish chronicler claims, this insincerity was obvious and was known to Christian observers. Albert of Aix, in noting the conversion of some Jews in Mainz, says that it took place "because of fear, rather than because of love of the Christian faith," a comment almost parallel to that of L. Albert is rather mild in his formulation. Other Christian chroniclers were far harsher in denouncing insincere conversion and backsliding to Judaism.[33]

The phenomenon of conversion took a number of different forms. In some cases it involved brutal physical coercion. This seems to have been the case at Moers, where L reports the handing over of the Jews to the crusaders and concludes: "They killed some of them. Those whom they left alive they baptized against their will. They did with them as they wished."[34] In some instances it was the authorities, anxious to save themselves and their Christian subjects—and perhaps the Jews as well—who executed such acts of physical conversion. Thus the burghers of Regensburg apparently forced the Jews of that city into the river and carried out a formal act of baptism in order to save the Jews and themselves.[35]

A second—and only slightly less coercive—mode of converting Jews was to threaten them with immediate death should they reject conversion. As I have noted, such threats were made against the dying survivors of the massacre at Mainz.[36] The Jewish sources do not specify instances in which these threats were successful, although it is highly likely that some forced conversions did occur in this way.

A third mode of converting Jews was to point to the

backdrop of death and destruction as an argument for the wisdom of abandoning Judaism. A particularly striking version of this argument is found in S's account of the massacre at Worms. After the Jews gathered in the bishop's palace had been slaughtered, the townsmen found a highly placed woman who had remained hidden outside of the city. In what seems to have been a genuine effort to save her life, the burghers pleaded with her:

> All the men of the city gathered and said to her: "Behold you are a capable woman. Know and see that God does not wish to save you, for they lie naked at the corner of every street, unburied. Sully yourself [with the waters of baptism]." They fell before her to the ground, for they did not wish to kill her. Her reputation was widely known; for all the notables of the city and the princes of the land were found in her circle.[37]

The Jewish sources report no instance of Jewish conversion on the basis of this argument, while the Christian author of the *Gesta Trevorum* describes a Jewish leader who converted out of hopelessness:

> One of these Jews, a scholar whose name was Micah, said: "Indeed what you have said is true. It is better that we join the Christian faith than to suffer daily danger to our persons and property."[38]

It is interesting that, according to this report, this was the only one of those converted in Trier who became and remained a loyal Christian.

We have seen so far three different modes of converting Jews, with the Jewish sources reporting only instances of conversion through overt physical coercion. There is a fourth mode mentioned in the Jewish sources only: temporary acceptance of Christianity for ulterior purposes. The following report concludes S's account of the first massacre at Worms:

There were those of them who said: "Let us do their will for the time being, and let us go and bury our brethren and save our children from them." For they had seized the children that remained, "a small number," saying that perhaps they would remain in their pseudo-faith. They [the Jews who converted] did not desert their Creator, nor did their hearts incline after the Crucified. Rather they cleaved to the God on high. Moreover, the rest of the community, those who remained in the chambers of the bishop, sent garments with which to clothe those who had been killed through those who had been saved. For they were charitable.[39]

In sum, it seems clear that, in addition to minimizing the number of converts and emphasizing the insincerity of conversion, the Jewish chroniclers present as motivation for the act of conversion only direct physical coercion and ulterior concerns. While the Jewish sources knew of other kinds of efforts, they did not know of—or declined to relate—instances of Jews succumbing to these other pressures.

On occasion the act of conversion, particularly when brought about by physical coercion, could have powerful psychological impact on the convert. One of the most striking stories in the Hebrew narratives concerns a prominent Jew in Mainz, Isaac ben David the *parnas*, who converted and quickly repented of his action. He accepted baptism on the third of Sivan, the day of the terrible massacre, and decided almost immediately that his act had been ill conceived:

He thought: "I shall do penitence and be faithful and perfect with the Lord God of Israel, to the point where I commend to him my soul. In his hand shall I fall. Perhaps he will do according to his loving-kindness and I shall still join my comrades and come with them to their circle, to the great light. It is revealed and known before the examiner of the heart that I did not

accede to the enemy except in order to save my children from the hands of the wicked and so that they
not remain in their pseudo-faith. For they are young
and cannot distinguish between good and evil."[40] He
went to the house of his ancestors and hired workers.
They restored the doors of the house which the enemy
had broken down. When they finished restoring the
doors, on Thursday, the eve of Shavuot, he came to
his mother and told her what he intended to do. He
said to her: "Woe my mother, my lady! I have decided
to offer a sin-offering to the God on high, so that I may
thus find atonement." When his mother heard the
words of her son and that he feared the Lord, she
adjured him not to do this thing, for her mercies
toward him had been aroused. Indeed he alone remained of all her beloved ones. His saintly wife had
been killed—Scholaster—who was the daughter of
R. Samuel the great. His mother herself was confined
to bed, for the enemy struck her a number of blows.
This son of hers, Isaac, saved her from death without
baptism after he had already been baptized. Isaac the
pious, her son, did not attend to her words and did
not listen to her. He came and closed the doors of the
house upon himself and his children and his mother
from all sides. The pious one asked his children: "Do
you wish that I sacrifice you to our God?" They said:
"Do what you will with us." The saintly one responded
and said: "My children, my children, our God is the
true God and there is no other." Isaac the saintly one
took his two children, his son and his daughter, and
led them through the courtyard at midnight and
brought them to the synagogue, before the holy ark,
and slaughtered them there for the sanctification of the
great Name, the sublime and exalted God, who commanded us never to deny his awe . . . and to cleave
to his holy Torah with all our heart and with all our
soul. He spilled their blood on the pillars of the holy
ark, so that they would come as a memorial before the
unique and everlasting King and before the throne of

his glory. [He said:] "May this blood serve me as atonement for all my sins." The pious one returned through the courtyard to the house of his ancestors and set fire to the house at its four corners. His mother remained in the house and was consumed by fire for the sanctification of the [Divine] Name. The pious Isaac returned a second time to burn the synagogue. He lit the fire at all the entrances. The pious one went from corner to corner with his palms spread heavenward, to his Father in heaven. He prayed to the Lord from the midst of the fire in a loud and lovely voice. The enemy called out to him through the windows: "Wicked man! Escape the fire! You can still be saved!" They extended to him a staff with which to pull him out of the fire, but the saintly one did not wish it. The blameless, upright, God-fearing man was there consumed by fire. His soul is hidden in the portion of the saintly in paradise.[41]

This portrait is one of the most vivid that has survived from this intense period. It is the portrait of a man maddened by suffering, pain, and guilt and consumed by a powerful drive for repentance and atonement. The act of conversion shattered Isaac, leaving him possessed by the desire to undo the sin which he felt he had committed.

Isaac of Mainz affords us an appropriate transition from conversion to martyrdom for several reasons: simply because he did both; because his story in all its detail indicates how central the phenomenon of martyrdom is to the Jewish chroniclers; and because his tale immediately reveals how intense the phenomenon is and how rich it is in evocative religious and emotional symbols. The tales of martyrdom form the heart of the Hebrew crusade chronicles. To the extent that these narratives are addressed to human beings, martyrdom is the central lesson the authors wished to teach; to the extent that these records are addressed to God, martyrdom is the basis for beseeching redemption for the Jews and vengeance upon their enemies.[42]

Lest it be suggested that the Jewish chroniclers exaggerated the phenomenon as a result of these various concerns, we should note that the Christian records concur in the centrality of martyrdom among the beleaguered Jews. They too highlight Jewish rejection of the alternative of conversion. Once more the objective fact gave rise to radically divergent evaluations. Whereas for the Jews rejection of Christianity and acceptance of death represent the highest human heroism and ultimate proof of the truth of Judaism, for Christian observers these actions were savage and barbarous. Albert of Aix notes a variety of Jewish behaviors during the massacre at Mainz. He indicates the wide range of victims slain by the attacking crusaders—men, women, and children—and goes on to describe Jews who took their own lives:

> The Jews, seeing that their Christian enemies were attacking them and their children, and were sparing no age, fell upon one another—brothers, children, wives, mothers, and sisters—and slaughtered one another. Horrible to say, mothers cut the throats of nursing children with knives and stabbed others, preferring them to perish thus by their own hands rather than be killed by the weapons of the uncircumcised.[43]

Albert's account is quite close to that of the Jewish source both in highlighting the acceptance of death by the Jews and in emphasizing its active—even frenzied—quality. He of course differs in his evaluation. The willingness to slaughter one's children—which the Jewish observers count the very highest heroism—Albert can see only as a horror. In any case, both Jewish and Christian sources concur in the centrality of this powerful Jewish response.[44]

The passage in Albert of Aix reveals that the alternative of death—like the alternative of conversion—came in a number of forms. The Hebrew sources, which view each Jewish death as an instance of martyrdom, show an even wider variety of forms of Jewish acceptance of the alternative of death. As we have already indicated, the attacks

on the Jews took varied forms. It is therefore to be expected
that the Jews relinquished their lives in varied ways also.
For example there was the sporadic nonideological violence, including the first outburst in Cologne—which I
identified as an instance of incidental burgher violence—
that claimed three Jewish lives. One such incident is described in some detail:

> They also found a notable woman there, named Re-
> becca, as she left her house. The enemy accosted her
> laden down with objects of gold and silver in her
> sleeves. She wished to carry them to her husband
> R. Solomon, for he had already left his house and was
> in the house of his Christian acquaintance. They took
> the money from her and killed her. There the saintly
> one died in sanctity.[45]

The attack was an incidental one, aimed primarily—it
would seem—at robbery. Nonetheless it cost this woman
her life and earned her the crown of martyrdom in the
eyes of her fellow Jews.

The doctrinally inspired assaults produced many more
casualties and more genuine examples of Jewish martyrdom. In some cases the victims rejected baptism and accepted death at the hands of the attackers. A striking
instance of this occurred after the conquest of the gate to
the archbishop's palace in Mainz. Inside the courtyard the
crusaders found a group of Jews awaiting their fate.

> The enemy, immediately upon entering the courtyard,
> found there some of the perfectly pious with Rabbi
> Isaac ben R. Moses, the dialectician. He stretched forth
> his neck and they cut off his head immediately. They
> had clothed themselves in their fringed garments and
> had seated themselves in the midst of the courtyard in
> order to do speedily the will of their Creator. They did
> not wish to flee. They stuck down all those whom
> they found there, with blows of sword, death, and
> destruction.[46]

Here baptism is rejected quietly and death at the hands of the crusaders accepted quiescently.

Some Jews chose to accept death at the hands of their enemies in a more active way. In a number of cases, Jews who were confronted with the alternatives of conversion or death responded by ostensibly accepting the former. When a Christian crowd had gathered to celebrate this achievement, the Jew then took the opportunity to revile Christianity and exalt Judaism. This of course meant instant death. In the process, however, Jews like these had vigorously and forcefully met the Christian challenge, dying actively as martyrs to the truth of their faith. The story of David the *gabbai* is one instance of such martyrdom. After Emicho's army had stormed both the archbishop's palace and the burgrave's palace and totally destroyed all the Jews gathered there, the effort to wipe out Mainz Jewry in its entirety continued. A prominent Jew, David the *gabbai*, was discovered in the courtyard of a priest. Feigning readiness to convert, David requested the assembling of the crusaders and their burgher accomplices.

> They gathered around the house by the thousands and ten thousands. When the saintly one saw them, he trusted in his Creator and called to them saying: "Lo you are the children of lust. You believe in one who was born of lust. But I believe in the God who lives forever, who dwells in the highest heaven. In him I have trusted to this day, to the point of death. If you kill me, my soul will repose in paradise, in the light of life. But you will descend to the nethermost pit, to everlasting abhorrence, to hell, where you will be judged along with your deity, who was a child of lust and was crucified." When they heard the pious one, they were enraged. They raised their standards and camped about the house and began to call and shout in the name of the Crucified. They assaulted him and killed him and his saintly wife and his children and his son-in-law and all the members of his household

and his maidservant. All were killed there for the sanctification of the [Divine] Name. There fell the saintly one and the members of his household.[47]

This was an aggressive and active response to the challenge presented by the crusaders. It breathes a martial air—it is a warlike answer to the Christian attackers.[48]

Even more radical was the decision made by many Jews to die at their own hands. Like the Jews who flaunted their hatred of Christianity openly, these Jews also exhibited aggressiveness and activism. The form, however, differed. Instead of directly assaulting Christian sensitivities and dying as a result at Christian hands, these Jews chose to perish at their own hands. Albert of Aix, a Christian, was struck by this phenomenon. In the selection quoted above, Albert highlights the Jews' decision to take their own lives and expresses his own horror at this behavior. To the Jewish observers, this form of death represents the very highest level of heroism and martyrdom. The most vivid and moving stories in their narratives are devoted to such acts of active martyrdom.

In some of these instances, Jews took their own lives. There are, for example, several reports of Jews throwing themselves into the Rhine. In the town of Wevelinghofen a number of Jews took this action.

When the enemy came before the town, then some of the pious ones ascended the tower and threw themselves into the Rhine River that flows around the town and drowned themselves in the river and all died.[49]

Christians were fully aware of this tendency among the Jews. Thus in L's report on Trier there is reference to a number of steps taken to obviate suicide by the Jews. One was to prevent the Jewish women from ascending the wall, so that they could not throw themselves from it.[50]

The most radical manifestation of Jewish readiness for martyrdom was the willingness of Jews to take one another's lives. To take one's own life was an awesome responsibility; to take the lives of others was even more overwhelming. Yet the intense atmosphere of 1096 aroused such willingness among the beleaguered Jews. In some cases a measure of organization was associated with these acts.

> On the fourth day of the month of Tammuz, on Thursday, the enemy gathered together against the saintly ones of . . . in order to torture them with great and terrible tortures until they agree to baptism. The matter became known to the pious ones. They confessed before their Creator and they volunteered and chose for themselves five pious and saintly ones, men of good heart and God-fearing, who would slaughter all the others.[51]

In other cases decisions were made on the spur of the frenzied moment. One of the most shattering descriptions in the entire literature of the period concerns two young Wevelinghofen men, who were unable to drown themselves:

> Subsequently those [Jews] that remained in the town, who did not go up on the tower, came and saw the others who had drowned. They found there the two good friends, totally saintly, clasped together. When the pious Samuel saw his son Yehiel who had thrown himself in the water but had still not died—he was a comely young man, as majestic as Lebanon—he cried out: "Yehiel, my son, my son! Stretch out your neck before your father and I shall offer you up as a sacrifice before the Lord. . . . I shall make the benediction for slaughtering and you shall respond amen." R. Samuel the pious did so and slaughtered his son with sword in the water. When R. Samuel the bridegroom ben R. Gedaliah heard that his friend Yehiel the saintly had acceded to his father, that he slaughter him in the water, then he decided to do the same. He called to Menachem who was the sexton in the synagogue of

Cologne and said to him: "By your life, take your sharp
sword and examine it carefully that it have no defect
and slaughter me likewise, so that I not see the death
of my friend. Make the benediction for slaughtering
and I shall respond amen." These pious ones did thus.
When they were slaughtered together, prior to death,
they clasped one another by the hand and died together in the river. They fulfilled the verse: "They
were never parted in death."[52]

Subsequently the bereaved father enjoined the sexton to
slaughter him, and, as a final act in this dreadful sequence,
the sexton took his own life.

A special issue in this phenomenon involved children.
There was a deep fear of youngsters falling into Christian
hands, being forcibly converted, and passing completely
into the Christian camp.[53] The killing of youngsters, which
obviously required the most radical suppression of normal
human feelings, must have been based on the most powerful fears. It will be recalled that, for Albert of Aix, the
most horrifying aspect of the Jewish response to the attacks
of 1096 was the slaughter of innocent children. For him,
of course, such slaughter was an act of unspeakable barbar-
ity, because it was after all done in the name of a faith that
was, in his view, false.[54] For the Jewish observers, however, the readiness to suppress normal tenderness and
love constituted the very highest level of self-sacrifice on
behalf of the divine. Probably the most shattering single
episode in the Hebrew chronicles is the account of Rachel
of Mainz and her four children.

Who has seen anything like this; who has heard anything like that which the saintly and pious woman,
Rachel daughter of R. Isaac ben R. Asher, wife of
R. Judah, did? She said to her companions: "I have
four children. On them as well have no mercy, lest
these uncircumcised come and seize them alive and
they remain in their pseudo-faith. With them as well
you must sanctify the Name of the holy God." One of

her companions came and took the knife to slaughter her son. When the mother of the children saw the knife, she shouted loudly and bitterly and smote her face and breast and said: "Where is your steadfast love, O Lord?" Then the woman said to her companions in her bitterness: "Do not slaughter Isaac before his brother Aaron, so that he not see the death of his brother and take flight." The women took the lad and slaughtered him—he was small and exceedingly comely. The mother spread her sleeve to receive the blood; she received the blood in her sleeves instead of in the [Temple] vessel for blood. The lad Aaron, when he saw that his brother had been slaughtered, cried out: "Mother, do not slaughter me!" He went and hid under a bureau. She still had two daughters, Bella and Matrona, comely and beautiful young women, the daughters of R. Judah her husband. The girls took the knife and sharpened it, so that it not be defective. They stretched forth their necks and she sacrificed them to the Lord God of Hosts, who commanded us not to renounce pure awe of him and to remain faithful to him, as it is written: "You must be wholehearted with the Lord your God." When the saintly one completed sacrificing her three children before the Creator, then she raised her voice and called to her son: "Aaron, Aaron, where are you? I shall not have mercy nor pity on you as well." She pulled him by the leg from under the bureau where he was hidden and she sacrificed him before the sublime and exalted God. She placed them under her two sleeves, two on each side, near her heart. They convulsed near her, until the enemy seized the chamber and found her sitting and mourning them. They said to her: "Show us the moneys which you have in your sleeves." When they saw the children and saw that they were slaughtered, they smote her and killed her along with them. With regard to her it is said: "Mothers and babes were dashed to death together." She [died] with her four children as did the saintly woman with her seven sons. With regard to them it is said: "The mother of the children is happy."[55]

The description is horrifying—and it is meant to be. The Jewish author wanted to convey the anguish, in order to highlight what he saw as the mother's incredible heroism.

It is striking that, while the persecutors of the Jews apparently came only from the lower classes and the popular leaders of the German crusading bands, the Jews who chose martyrdom encompassed entire communities, and the action was both sanctioned and led by distinguished rabbinic authorities. The descriptions of mass martyrdom emphasize the involvement of all elements in the community and all age groups: "When the children of the sacred covenant [the Jews of Mainz gathered in the archbishop's palace] saw that the decree had been issued and that the enemy had overcome them, they all cried out—young men and old men, young women and children, menservants and maidservants—and wept for themselves and their lives."[56] It is sometimes noted in medieval sources that those with little to lose, such as the aged and the poor, were particularly prepared to sacrifice their lives.[57] To be sure, many of the martyrs of 1096 were elderly and indigent. Indeed, one of the martyrs singled out for description is Jacob ben Sulam, who calls out cuttingly to his fellow Jews: "All the days of my life, till now, you have despised me. Now I shall slaughter myself."[58] The acts of self-sacrifice in 1096, however, were not limited to those with little to lose. The wealthiest members of the community willingly gave themselves up to death as did those in the very flower of youth.

The young women and the brides and the bridegrooms looked out through the windows and called out loudly, saying: "Look and see, God, what we do for the sanctification of your great Name."[59] Only two young men did not die in the water—R. Samuel the bride-groom-to-be ben R. Gedaliah and Yehiel ben R. Samuel. . . . They said: "Woe for our youth, for we have not been

deemed worthy to see seed go forth from us or to reach
old age. Nonetheless, let us fall into the hands of the
Lord. He is a steadfast and merciful God and King."[60]

Youngsters are often portrayed as anxious to join in the
acts of martyrdom.[61] Over all these actions presided the
leaders of these distinguished Jewish communities. Note,
for example, the description of Judah ben Abraham, one
of the Cologne Jews who found temporary refuge and
subsequent death.

> There was the *parnas*, the head of them all [all the
> leaders of Cologne Jewry], the most outstanding of
> the aristocrats, the leading spokesman, Judah ben
> R. Abraham, the counselor and sage and respected
> one. When all the communities came to Cologne to the
> fairs three times a year, he was the one who spoke
> before them all in the synagogue, and they sat silently
> before him and listened to his words.[62]

Perhaps most striking is the involvement of the intellectual
luminaries who made Mainz and Worms the first great
centers of Ashkenazic spiritual life. In his fine study of
these eleventh-century centers, Abraham Grossman notes
the death of most of the intellectual elite in 1096.[63] The
actions of a number of these teachers are indicated
explicitly in the Hebrew chronicles. Their behaviors ran
the entire range of martyrdom styles which we have depicted, from the quiescent acceptance of death at the hands
of the crusaders by Rabbi Isaac ben Moses to the slaughter
of a son by Kalonymous ben Meshullam the *parnas*. Thus
every level of Rhineland Jewry is portrayed as committed
to martyrdom—poor and wealthy, old and young, little
known and widely respected.

Having established a variety of forms of martyrdom
and a diversity among the martyrs, I will now turn to the
wellsprings of this remarkable willingness to accept martyrdom. Obviously a clearly reasoned and carefully articulated stance on the part of the Jewish martyrs of 1096

should not be expected. These people were caught up in unanticipated violence and reacted spontaneously to the frightening circumstances in which they found themselves. That is not to say that the actions of these Jewish martyrs were blind and instinctive; rather, they were founded upon important concepts and symbols from the Jewish past and were further influenced by the intense spirituality of the closing decade of the eleventh century. My present task is to assay a reconstruction of this complex of concepts and symbols that led so many Jews to choose death for the sake of their faith and their God.[64]

Our best sources for this investigation are the speeches of the martyrs as reported by the Jewish chroniclers. Clearly these speeches cannot be taken as literal transcriptions of addresses delivered during the frenzied moments of martyrdom; they are rather part of the long tradition of soliloquies reconstructed or invented by historians as a means of presenting ideas current in the circles they were attempting to portray.[65] Thus the crucial question is whether the ideas and symbols found in these speeches were in fact current among the beleaguered Rhineland Jews of 1096. The reliability of the chroniclers' reports on the attitudes of the Jewish martyrs is necessarily lower than that of the more prosaic information they provide. In reconstructing the attitudes of the martyrs, the Jewish chroniclers would have been far more prone to introduce their own views and perceptions. Nonetheless two considerations mitigate somewhat doubts one might have about the reliability of these data. The first is the existence of earlier written records from which the chroniclers drew. Many of the speeches attributed to the martyrs of Mainz appear in identical form in both S and L, suggesting that neither chronicler attempted to tinker with preexisting materials. Second, the chroniclers themselves emphasize somewhat different themes as they wrestle with the theological problems posed by the catastrophe. This disparity leaves the impression that there was little alteration of reports earlier circulated. If the later chroniclers did not create the symbols reflected in the soliloquies attributed to the martyrs, then at worst these symbols were spawned by the eyewitness observers whose oral and written testimony forms the backbone of S and L. If, however, such symbols were already on the scene in the 1090s and if the radical Jewish behaviors are a certainty, it seems to me simplest to suggest that the potent symbols in question did in fact circulate within the ranks of the martyrs themselves. In view of all this, I shall utilize the recorded speeches of the martyrs of 1096, recognizing that the reliability of my conclusions must be open to some measure of doubt.

The chroniclers—Christian and Jewish—were not interested in the broad range of human motivations involved in the martyrdoms. They occasionally reveal awareness of such social considerations as the desire of lowly members of the community to prove themselves through heroic behavior. Motives of this kind were of minimal interest to the chroniclers. What mattered to them was the thought system of the martyrs, the set of concepts and symbols that sustained these Ashkenazic Jews and made possible their remarkable acts. My analysis will follow the lead of the medieval chroniclers in focusing on ideas and symbols. I shall assume that normal human motivations played their accustomed role, but what is unique were the concepts and symbols spawned during the intense spring months of 1096.

The Rhineland Jews of 1096, faced with an ideologically motivated assault on their faith, were deeply rooted in the rich and varied legacy of talmudic Judaism. This legacy provided some limited guidance to Jews faced with the difficult alternatives of conversion or death.[66] I shall attempt to analyze the normative talmudic tradition and its impact on the Rhineland Jews of 1096 and shall then proceed to note the ways in which these Jews expanded and altered this talmudic legacy under the influence of the intense spirituality of the late eleventh century.

The halachic requirements for those faced with the choice between conversion or death are only minimally addressed in the Talmud. The Mishnah says nothing on

the matter, and the talmudic discussion, which is appended to the Mishnaic law prohibiting the killing of a Jew
about to commit idolatry, is hardly extensive.[67] The basic
requirement is formulated in the decision taken by a group
of second-century rabbis at Lod that, in all cases of a choice
between death and transgression, a Jew should transgress,
except in the case of three special demands, namely,
idolatry, sexual misconduct, and murder. In these three
instances only, a Jew is required to allow himself or herself
to be killed rather than transgress. Thus the essential
halachic demand imposed upon the Jews of 1096 was that
they allow themselves to be put to death rather than accept
Christianity.[68] It should be noted that the Talmud introduces a dissenting view, that of Rabbi Ishmael, who says
directly that, given the choice between idolatry and death,
a Jew should submit to idolatrous worship. The Talmud
concludes that there was indeed a difference of opinion
between important rabbis with Rabbi Ishmael ruling in
favor of submission to idolatry and Rabbi Eliezer opposing
such submission, and that the rabbis assembled in Lod
chose the view of Rabbi Eliezer over the view of Rabbi
Ishmael. It is important for our purposes to indicate that
the view of Rabbi Eliezer is based on a key biblical verse
and commandment: "You must love the Lord your God
with all your heart and with all your soul and with all your
might."[69] Thus the commandment underlying the requirement of death is the basic *mizvah* (commandment) to love
God with all of one's faculties. The commandment of *kiddush ha-Shem* (sanctification of the Divine Name), more
widely cited in reference to the behaviors of 1096 and
similar instances, does make an appearance in this talmudic discussion, but only in a secondary role. In assessing the view of Rabbi Ishmael, a distinction is drawn between a demand for idolatrous behavior made in private,
to which the Jew may (or should) submit, and a public
demand, which even according to Rabbi Ishmael must be
resisted. The basis for such rejection of the public demand
is the commandment to sanctify God's Divine Name.

Beyond this basic legal requirement, the Talmud also

bequeathed a number of hero-figures, whose exploits are depicted briefly and who were obviously intended to serve as models for subsequent Jewish behavior. The most ancient of these hero-figures are the biblical Hananiah, Mishael, and Azariah. The full story of these three young men is found in the book of Daniel, and they are mentioned in passing in the Talmud. The reference in the Talmud is pertinent here, since it raises the question of the basis for the young men's refusal to bow down before the royal image and their acceptance of the resultant punishment.

> Why were Hananiah, Mishael, and Azariah willing to give up their lives for the sanctification of the Divine Name? They reasoned comparatively from the frogs [in the account of the second plague]. If in regard to frogs who are not commanded to sanctify the Divine Name it is written: "And they shall come up and enter your palace, your bedchamber and your bed, the houses of your courtiers and your people, and your ovens and your kneading bowls,"[70] . . . then we who are commanded to sanctify the Divine Name all the more so.[71]

The underlying rationale here for the behavior of the three hero-figures is the commandment to sanctify God's Name.

Further guidelines to Jewish behavior are provided by the actions of the woman and her seven sons.[72] The story, found originally in II Maccabees, is transferred in its talmudic version to the period of Roman persecution. In this story also there is substantial concern with the bases for rejection of idolatry and acceptance of death. The bases for such actions are reflected in the responses given by each of the seven sons to the demands of the emperor. These include: (1) "I am the Lord your God who brought you out of the land of Egypt, the house of bondage."[73] (2) "You shall have no other gods beside me."[74] (3) "Whoever sacrifices to a god other than the Lord alone shall be proscribed."[75] (4) "You must not worship any other god."[76] (5)

"Hear, O Israel! The Lord is our God, the Lord is one."[77]
(6) "Know therefore this day and keep in mind that the
Lord alone is God in heaven above and on earth below."[78]
(7) "You have affirmed this day that the Lord is your God,
that you will walk in his ways, that you will observe his
laws and commandments and norms, and that you will
obey him. And the Lord affirmed this day that you are, as
he promised you, his treasured people which shall observe
all his commandments."[79] The last (and youngest) son is
said to have added this comment to the verse he quoted:
"We have already sworn to the Holy One blessed be he
that we shall never exchange him for another god; he
likewise swore to us that he will not exchange us for
another people."[80] In this account the key theme is the
biblical demand for unswerving loyalty to God, couched
in both positive and negative terms. The seven sons see
themselves in a positive sense as enjoined to affirm the
uniqueness of their God as the only true God and negatively as prohibited from worshiping any other deity.

The final set of major hero-figures—in particular Rabbi
Akiba and Rabbi Haninah ben Teradion—come from the
period of the Hadrianic decrees. To be sure, the circumstances of these two figures diverge somewhat from the
simple halachic injunction and from the precedents of the
three young men and the woman and her seven sons.
Rabbi Akiba and Rabbi Haninah ben Teradion are not
confronted with the alternatives of idolatry or death; they
are rather ordered to cease teaching Torah and refuse to
do so. Nonetheless the issues are close enough to accord
them a place in the company of the other resisters. At the
point of his death, Rabbi Akiba, according to the Talmud,
introduced two of the themes pointed out in other instances I have given. In response to his students, who
marvel at his fortitude and ask how he sustains it, he
explains that he had waited all his life to fulfill the commandment of loving the Lord with all his soul. At the same
time, the theme of declaration of God's unity is also central. While tortured, Rabbi Akiba recited the key verse,
which declares God's unity, and he expired pronouncing

its final word, "one."[81] The stories of Rabbi Haninah ben Teradion are complex. For my purposes, it is interesting to note the lack of any reference to the grounds for his actions. These accounts leave only the behavior itself as a guide; there is no internal justification offered for this behavior.[82]

To review, the body of Jewish tradition, in response to persecution of the kind that challenged the Rhineland Jews in 1096, included straightforward halachic injunction, a series of hero-figures who fulfill the basic injunction, and a number of rationales for such stalwart behavior. These rationales include: (1) the commandment to proclaim the unity and uniqueness of God; (2) the concomitant prohibition against worshiping any other deity; (3) the commandment to love the Lord with all of one's faculties; (4) the commandment to sanctify God's Divine Name.

Interestingly, the halachic injunction is nowhere reflected in the Hebrew chronicles. There is no reference to the decision of the rabbis at Lod, nor is the halachic language of "being killed and not transgressing" even mentioned. There are a number of possible explanations for this significant absence. It may be that the entire context of the halachic decree is too minimalist for the intense circumstances of 1096; the rabbinic decision at Lod affirms the requirement to transgress rather than die *except* under the three special circumstances noted. Perhaps recollection of this context would serve to weaken, rather than to strengthen the resolve of those committing themselves to death. Moreover, the tone of the talmudic passage, with its citation of the opposing view of Rabbi Ishmael and its intellectualized proposal of a series of issues and possibilities, would also hardly buttress the commitment of those facing the frightful alternatives of conversion or death. Guidelines simpler, firmer, and more exhilarating were required and these were found rather in the aggadic precedents.

All three of the sets of figures I have presented appear, recurrently, in the Hebrew chronicles. Sometimes they are mentioned in the speeches of the Jews under assault; more often, they are cited by the chroniclers as precedents for the worthy behaviors which they were memorializing in their narratives. To take one example, L's lengthy depiction of the events in Mainz concludes with the following:

> All these things were done by those whom we have singled out by name. That which they did . . . The rest of the community and the notables of the congregation, for whom we have not detailed their activities and their piety, they did all the more. The activities which they undertook in order to proclaim the unity of the Name of the King of kings, the Holy One blessed be he, [were] like those of R. Akiba and his associates, and they stood the test like Hananiah, Mishael, and Azariah.[83]

Most striking is the invocation of the image of the woman and her seven sons, introduced at the close of the dramatic description of the death of Rachel, the daughter of Isaac ben Asher, and her four children. The horrifying portrayal of the slaughter of the four youngsters by Jewish hands and the subsequent death of the mother at the hands of the crusaders concludes:

> She died with them, as did that [earlier] saintly one with her seven sons. With regard to her it is said: "The mother of the child is happy."[84]

Yet more significant than the invocation of these hero-figures is the more consistent recourse to the commandments that underlay both the halachic injunction and the aggadic precedents. These commandments are constantly proclaimed as the basis for Jewish resistance to crusader demands. I have identified four of these fundamental commandments, three of which loom large in the speeches of the Jews under attack, and the fourth appears recurrently in the third-person depictions of the chroniclers. The first of these four, it will be recalled, was the obligation to proclaim the unity and uniqueness of God. The Jews of

Mainz, for example, urged by Menahem ben David the *levi*
to martyr themselves, responded by calling out "loudly:
'Hear O Israel! The Lord is our God, the Lord is one.'"[85]
Likewise Moses the *cohen* concludes his remarkable exhor-
tation to the Cologne Jews who had sought refuge in
Xantes and now faced death in the following manner:

> When they rose from the table, the pious one said to
> them: "You are the children of the living God. Recite
> loudly and in unison: 'Hear O Israel! The Lord is our
> God, the Lord is one.'" They did so.[86]

Similarly the determination to refuse to recognize any
other deity is widely reflected in the speeches of the martyrs. Thus, Isaac ben Daniel of Worms, when asked to
convert, responded: "Heaven forfend that I deny him; in
him shall I trust. Thus shall I commend to him my soul."[87]
In similar fashion, Minna of Worms declared: "Heaven
forfend that I deny the God on high. For him and his holy
Torah kill me and do not tarry any longer."[88] So too the
mizvah of *kiddush ha-Shem* is invoked repeatedly. The Jews
of Mainz called out in their agony: "Look and see, God,
what we do for the sanctification of your great Name!"[89]
The chronicler points in awe to the unique behavior of
these Rhineland Jews:

> Behold, has such a thing ever happened before? For
> they jostled one another, saying: "I shall sanctify first
> the Name of the King of kings."[90]

The commandment of love of God does not appear in the
speeches of the martyrs themselves, but these martyrs are
frequently depicted as sanctifying the Divine Name "with
all their heart and with all their soul and with all their
might." In sum, it is clear that the web of *mizvot* which I
have identified in the talmudic legacy played a central role
in the remarkable Jewish behaviors of 1096.

As we have already seen, these behaviors of 1096 went
far beyond the norms prescribed in the halachic discussion

and presented in the major aggadic precedents. Jews did far more than simply allow themselves to be killed; they took their own lives and, in many instances, the lives of family and friends. A basis for some of these actions may be found in the talmudic story of the four hundred youths who chose to drown themselves rather than submit to sexual defilement. According to the talmudic account, knowing the nature of their fate, these young people raised the question: "If we drown in the sea, will we reach the life of the world to come?" The story continues:

> The senior among them explained: "'The Lord said, I will retrieve from Bashan, I will retrieve from the depths of the sea.'[91] 'I will retrieve from Bashan'—from out of the teeth of lions; 'I will retrieve from the depths of the sea'—those who drown in the sea." When the girls heard this, they all jumped and fell into the sea. The boys reasoned further concerning themselves: "If this is the response of those for whom such acts are natural, for us, for whom such acts are unnatural, all the more so." They likewise jumped into the sea. In regard to these youngsters Scriptures says: "It is for your sake that we are slain all day long."[92]

While these four hundred young martyrs are not mentioned explicitly in the Hebrew First-Crusade chronicles, they do seem to play a role in the thinking of the chroniclers, certainly, and perhaps of the members of the persecuted communities. In a number of cases, Jews are portrayed as taking their lives by drowning and the key verse from the talmudic tale is cited with regard to such martyrs. It seems likely that this precedent may well have been borne in the minds of some of the activist martyrs.

Looking back, I have discerned three styles of martyrdom during the tumultuous months of 1096: some allowed themselves to be slain at the hands of the crusaders, some took their own lives, and some took the lives of other Jews. The acts of the first group were securely rooted in both halachah and aggadah; the acts of the second group had no overt halachic grounding, but could appeal to the aggadic precedent of the four hundred young people; the acts of the third group lacked both halachic and aggadic foundations. Given this disparity between accumulated Jewish tradition and the Jewish behaviors of 1096, how are we to explain the unusual forms of martyrdom associated with the First Crusade? My answer is to suggest that the Jewish behaviors of 1096 reflect both the accumulated weight of Jewish tradition and the remarkable spiritual milieu of the late eleventh century. The exhilarated religiosity of this intense and turbulent period led the Rhineland Jews of 1096 to appropriate old Jewish symbols and adapt them creatively to the needs of the difficult circumstances in which they found themselves.[93] The best introduction to the compelling new symbolism that sustained the activist martyrs can be found in the major exhortations included in the Hebrew chronicles. One of the richest of these is that attributed to Moses the *cohen* of Cologne. The Cologne Jews who had sought refuge in Xantes had barely seated themselves at the Sabbath table on Friday, June 27, when the tumult of the approaching crusaders reached their ears. Moses the *cohen* was accorded the honor of addressing his fellow Jews:

> Then the pious and faithful one—the priest who stood above his brethren—said to the congregation seated around him at the table: "Let us recite the grace to the living God and to our Father in heaven. For the table is set before us in place of the altar. Now let us rise up and ascend to the house of the Lord and do speedily the will of our Creator. For the enemy has come upon us today. We must slaughter on the Sabbath sons, daughters, and brothers, so that he bestow upon us this day a blessing. Let no one have mercy—neither on himself nor on his companions. The last one remaining shall slaughter himself by the throat with his knife or pierce his belly with his sword, so that the impure and the hand of evil ones not sully us with their abominations. Let us offer ourselves up as a sac-

rifice to the Lord, like a whole burnt offering to the Most High offered on the altar of the Lord. We shall exist in a world that is entirely daylight, in paradise, in the shining light. We shall see him eye to eye, in his glory and in his majesty. Each one shall receive a golden crown on his head, in which are set precious stones and pearls. We shall be seated there among the pillars of the universe and shall eat as part of the society of the saintly in paradise. We shall be part of the company of R. Akiba and his associates. We shall be seated on a golden throne under the Tree of Life. Each of us shall point to him by finger and say: 'This is our God; we trusted in him [and he delivered us. This is the Lord, in whom we trusted;] let us rejoice and exult in his deliverance.' There we shall observe the Sabbath [properly], for here, in this world of darkness, we cannot rest and observe it properly." They all responded loudly, with one mouth and one heart: "Amen. So may it be and so may it be his will." The pious Rabbi Moses began to recite the grace, for he was a priest of Almighty God. He intoned: "Let us bless our God of whose bounty we have eaten." They responded: "Blessed is our God of whose bounty we have eaten and through whose goodness we exist." He intoned: "May the Merciful avenge during the days of those who remain after us and in their sight the blood of your servants which has been spilled and which is yet to be spilled. May the Merciful save us from evil men and from conversion and from idolatry and from the impurity of the nations and from their abominations." He further intoned many benedictions related to the event at hand, because of the edict hanging over them.[94]

This is the lengthiest of the speeches preserved in the Hebrew chronicles, and it presents the major theme associated with the innovative and activist forms of Jewish martyrdom.

Surely the major image in this style of martyrdom is

the Temple and the sacrificial system, which resonate widely throughout the Hebrew narratives.[95] Jews about to commit a radical act found for themselves symbols that would provide justification and encouragement for the extreme action they would undertake. In evoking the imagery of the Temple these Jews moved far beyond the traditional demands of resistance to idolatry and into the realm of activist self-sacrifice, tapping in the process themes in earlier Jewish lore. In a number of ways, these themes in earlier Jewish thought were activated by the crusader exhilaration of 1096. Jerusalem, as we have seen, was central to the crusade. For the Christian crusaders this meant especially the Holy Sepulcher; Jews, fully aware of Jerusalem as the goal of the Christian expedition, probably found that recollections of Jerusalem and its Jewish sacred sites were triggered. Moreover, in all the crusading propaganda there is heavy emphasis on imitating Jesus and his suffering:

> The lord pope also said: "Brothers, you must suffer for the name of Christ many things, wretchedness, poverty, nakedness, persecution, need, sickness, hunger, thirst, and other such troubles, for the Lord says to his disciples, 'You must suffer many things for my name,' and 'Be not ashamed to speak before men, for I will give you what you shall say.' But afterward 'Great will be your reward.'"[96]

For Jews, the notion of imitating a suffering deity was anathema. A ritual of sacrifice, however, does capture the same sense of intense commitment, even unto death. Furthermore, the invocation of Temple imagery reinforces the feeling of the cosmic significance of the acts to be undertaken. Fulcher of Chartres was moved to compare the Christian crusaders to the great heroes of the past on behalf of whom God had intervened in history.[97] The Jewish martyrs likewise saw themselves as attaining a uniquely high level of historical import—they were resuming the long-suspended Temple cult, indeed in a remarkably personal and original manner. The stance is audacious, but fully consonant with the spirit of those turbulent times.

The Jews of 1096 were further sustained by the related imagery of Abraham's near-sacrifice of his son Isaac.[98] In Jewish tradition, this key biblical incident served as a precursor to the sacrificial system. The site of Isaac's binding was associated with the Temple mount and the surrogate offering of a ram with the later cult; in Christian thought the same incident foreshadowed Jesus and Golgotha. Although the tale of the binding of Isaac was usually seen as a repudiation of the ancient notion of human sacrifice, under the unusual circumstances of 1096 it served to sanction martyrdom that was activist, associated with Jerusalem, and cosmic in significance. In view of the fact that many of the activist Jewish martyrs slaughtered their own children, the Abraham-Isaac imagery is particularly poignant. The very first activist martyrdom recorded in the Hebrew chronicles, that of Isaac the son of Meshullam of Worms, highlights the *aqedah* (the near-sacrifice of Isaac) theme.

> There was a certain young man, named R. Meshullam ben R. Isaac. He called out loudly to all those standing there and to Zipporah his helpmate: "Listen to me both great and small. This son God gave me. My wife Zipporah bore him in her old age and his name is Isaac. Now I shall offer him up as did our ancestor Abraham with his son Isaac." Zipporah replied: "My lord, my lord. Wait a bit. Do not stretch forth your hand against the lad whom I have raised and brought up and whom I bore in my old age. Slaughter me first, so that I not witness the death of the child." He then replied: "I shall not delay even a moment. He who gave him to us will take him as his portion. He will place him in the bosom of Abraham our ancestor." He then bound Isaac his son and took in his hand the knife with which to slaughter his son and made the benediction for slaughtering. The lad answered amen.

> He then slaughtered the lad. He took his screaming
> wife. The two of them departed together from the
> chamber and the crusaders killed them.[99]

The biblical image serves as justification of and goad to
activist martyrdom.[100]

In these cases of activist martyrdom, the gruesome
acts are joined with traditional ritual practices. Repeatedly,
individuals check their instruments of death in order to
make certain that they are unblemished, in accordance
with the requirements for ritually-proper slaughtering of
animals; blessings are recurrently intoned; Moses the *cohen*
weaves the required grace after meal into his exhortation to martyrdom.[101] All this is designed to reinforce the
sense of propriety of the extraordinary acts to be undertaken. The appropriation of traditional rituals reinforces
the central conviction that Jewish martyrdom represents
the highest level of fulfillment of the weighty divine commandments to proclaim God's unity, to exhibit wholehearted love for God, and to sanctify his Name.

There are thus a variety of positive bases for the acts
of martyrdom in 1096. For some of the Jewish martyrs, the
old tradition of resistance to religious coercion sufficed; for
others, the act of accepting death at the hands of persecutors was embellished with an impassioned denunciation
of Christianity; yet others went beyond acceptance of
death and took their own lives and the lives of fellow Jews,
stimulated by the intense religiosity of the period and by
an innovative invocation of earlier Jewish symbols. In addition to these positive commitments, there were powerful
negative feelings toward Christianity engendered by the
crisis of 1096. These negative attitudes reflect in heightened form broadly held Jewish critiques of medieval Christianity.[102] To be sure, not all the themes of Jewish anti-
Christian polemic are embodied in the Hebrew First-
Crusade chronicles, but those that are present are expressed vituperatively. The extreme emotions of 1096
allow us, in some senses, to identify the most basic elements in the medieval Jewish critique of Christianity.

It is not surprising that the two common Jewish criticisms of Christianity expressed in the Hebrew records for 1096 revolve about the perception of polytheism in the Christian doctrine of the Trinity and the intellectual and moral recoil from the notion of Incarnation. The Jewish martyrs of 1096 are described repeatedly as "declaring the unity of the [Divine] Name," in effect emphasizing the unity of the Jewish deity as opposed to what is perceived as the multiplicity of Christian divinities. The recurrent recitation of Deuteronomy 6:4 is a traditional demand of Jewish law; at the same time these words—"Hear O Israel! The Lord is our God; the Lord is one."—reaffirm the commitment to a pure monotheism as contrasted with what the Jews perceived as the adulterated monotheism or even outright polytheism of their Christian attackers. Yet more deeply repugnant to medieval Jews was the notion of Incarnation of the deity in human form, further complicated by the details of the birth and death of Jesus. Medieval Jewish polemics hammered at this issue and the rhetoric of these polemical thrusts reflect both intellectual disagreement and moral outrage.[103] Under the intense circumstances of 1096, these objections took on explosive force, as manifested in the rhetoric quoted in the narrative's depiction of an incident in Mainz:

> The young women and the brides and the bridegrooms looked through the windows and cried out loudly and said: "Look and see, God, what we do for the sanctification of your great Name, rather than to abandon your divinity for a crucified one, a trampled and wretched and abominable offshoot . . . , a bastard and a child of menstruation and lust."[104]

The generally held Jewish objections to the notion of the deity incarnate, to the questionable birth of the messiah-deity, and to his inglorious demise on the cross find potent expression in the soliloquies of the Hebrew First-Crusade chronicles and in the third-person comments of the chroniclers.

The Jewish martyrs of 1096 saw in their behavior actions that would surely win divine approbation, both on the group and individual levels. For the group, this would mean corporate salvation; for the individual, it would mean an immediate and richly endowed afterlife. It is not surprising that the focus was on individual afterlife. There was an overwhelming sense among the Jewish martyrs that their rejection of Christianity, their wholehearted devotion to the God of Israel, and their radical fulfillment of the commandment of *kiddush ha-Shem* would certainly earn them immediate and wondrous eternal reward.[105] This notion is palpable throughout the speeches attributed to these martyrs. Let us recall the extraordinary soliloquy of Moses the *cohen*, which assures the martyrs that they would find themselves "in a world that is entirely daylight, in paradise, in the shining light"; see God "eye to eye, in his splendor and majesty"; and sit "among the pillars of the universe, in the company of the righteous in paradise."[106]

Such descriptions abound. The conviction of rich and endless reward for the martyrs is constantly contrasted with meanness and transitoriness of this-worldly existence, which the Rhineland Jews were prepared to abandon.

> Blessed are we if we do his will and blessed are all those who are killed and slaughtered and die for the unity of his Name. Not only are they privileged to enter the world-to-come [*'olam ha-ba*] and sit in the circle of the saintly pillars of the universe. What is more, they exchange a world of darkness for a world of light, a world of pain for a world of happiness, a transitory world for one that is eternal and everlasting.[107]

There is a second contrast drawn as well, between the ultimate rewards of the Jewish martyrs and the eventual punishment of their oppressors. In a fierce denunciation of Christianity, David the *gabbai* concludes:

If you kill me, my soul will repose in paradise in the light of life. But you will descend to the nethermost pit, to everlasting abhorrence, to hell, where you will be judged along with your deity, who was a child of lust and was crucified.[108]

Sacrifice of one's own life and the readiness to take the lives of others required a sure sense of the rewards for such extreme acts. The martyrs of 1096 were powerfully imbued with just such a sense.

While graphic descriptions of the rewards of afterlife abound, the conviction of corporate reward for the entire Jewish people is also apparent. We have noted that the call to destruction of the Jews and Judaism involved either physical obliteration or spiritual conquest. As already indicated, the Christian attackers preferred the victory of conversion over the victory of annihilation. While the end result was the same—destruction of the Jews and Judaism—conversion of the Jews represented an unsullied success, whereas Jewish obstinacy and martyrdom left nagging doubts and questions. Looking at the same issue from the Jewish perspective, we can identify large-scale conversion as total defeat. More important, resistance and martyrdom were seen by the Jews as an ultimate victory. To be sure, lives were lost on a large scale. Nonetheless, there was moral and religious triumph in Jewish loyalty to their faith. There was in fact a sense of proving the truth of Judaism to all humankind by the public display of readiness for martyrdom. The triumph was more than simply spiritual—there was a profound conviction that the Jewish willingness for martyrdom constituted a powerful case for divine intervention in the process of history, specifically for punishment of those guilty of persecuting the Jews and redemption of those who had proved beyond all conceivable doubt their unflagging devotion and loyalty.

The Rhineland Jews of 1096 were influenced in their remarkable behavior from two directions—from their Jewish past and from the intense environment in which they lived. Prior Jewish experience, while perhaps not so recurrently beset by persecution as is sometimes assumed, had bequeathed to these eleventh-century Jews a major halachic injunction regarding resistance to forced conversion, a set of hero figures to further guide Jewish behavior, and a web of fundamental biblical commandments that firmly buttressed the tendency to resist. Beyond these normative materials, the Jewish past had also handed down a rich and diverse legacy of symbols that could, under the proper circumstances, afford support for unusual and innovative behaviors. Under the extraordinary conditions of 1096 the potential of these rich and evocative symbols was actualized.

These Rhineland Jews were of course fully aware of the exalted goals of the crusaders, which can be discerned behind the scornful distortions of the Hebrew sources. They were cognizant of the frenzy that had gripped their neighbors and of the certainty in crusader ranks of the highest rewards for commitment to the great enterprise. In many senses, Jewish behavior during the limited but violent persecutions of 1096 constituted a "counter-crusade," a militant Jewish response to the aggression of Christendom. Like their Christian neighbors, the Jews felt themselves caught up in a struggle of cosmic proportions; like their neighbors they felt a responsibility to exhibit the highest possible devotion to their cause; like their neighbors they were eager to make the profoundest sacrifice possible, in some instances expanding the dictates of Jewish law and exceeding the precedents of the past; like their neighbors they were certain of eternal celestial reward for their heroism. In other words, the Jews show much of the same religious frenzy that swept European society at the end of the eleventh century. When, in certain limited quarters, this general frenzy degenerated into anti-Jewish violence, the Jews under attack responded with much the same militance and readiness for self-sacrifice out of which the crusading movement had been spawned.[109]

To be sure, the attacks on the Jews engendered by the First Crusade aroused violent Jewish antipathy to Christianity in general and to the crusade in particular. For these Jews, Jewish and Christian exhilarations were poles apart—one devoted to the eternal and true God and the other frittered away on vanity and emptiness. These Jews would never have seen themselves as inspired by a general wave of religious zeal that had aroused both Christians and Jews alike. There is therefore no conscious suggestion of such influences in the sources of the period. Nonetheless, the modern historian is permitted to suggest that a broad zeitgeist existed, which had profound impact in opposing camps.

Indeed the sense of a broad zeitgeist exerting influence upon Rhineland Jewry of 1096 extends beyond the immediate circumstances of the First Crusade. Both the Christian crusaders and the Jewish counter-crusaders were part of a civilization caught up in dramatic new creativity. Over the past few decades, this stunning creativity has been subjected to careful scholarly analysis. While this inquiry will undoubtedly continue, much has already been achieved in delineating the major features of this new creativity, and the results indicate a set of innovative values clearly reflected in the Jewish behaviors of 1096.[110]

A number of features characterize the new civilization of the late eleventh and twelfth century. One of the most striking is the imaginative reinterpretation of older codes of religious behavior and symbol systems. Static ideals were transformed into something more active and penetrating. Surely the Jewish martyrs of 1096 illustrate this pervasive new style. As we have seen, they act out of the matrix of an older tradition of behavioral demands, popular hero figures, and religious ideals. Most important in my analysis, however, is the extent to which these Jews pushed beyond the prior legacy, taking it in novel and radical directions. As one reads, for example, R. W. Southern's analysis of many of the major innovations of the period between 1050 and 1150, one is struck by the parallels in the Jewish behaviors of 1096, with the specifics of Jewish creativity differing inevitably, owing to the divergence of the Christian and Jewish legacies.[111]

To flesh out these generalizations, let us look briefly

at two specific aspects of this new European sensibility
and creativity. The first is a growing inwardness and emphasis on intentionality, which a number of recent observers have discerned.[112] To cite the summary statement
of Caroline Walker Bynum:

> For Robert Hanning, Colin Morris, and other scholars
> who have given the phrase [the discovery of the indi-
> vidual] currency, it refers to the emphasis placed by
> thinkers of the late eleventh and twelfth centuries on
> inner motivation, on the emotions, on psychological
> development. To begin with the most frequently cited
> example, Abelard's *Ethics* locates the ethical value of
> an act in the actor's intention, not in the outward deed.
> And other twelfth-century thinkers who do not go as
> far (including Abelard's opponent Bernard) frequently
> couch their discussions of particular matters as if in
> agreement with this theory. Twelfth-century theories
> of penance locate remission of sin in contrition, not
> oral confession, although the requirement of confes-
> sion is not removed.[113]

Looking back at the Jewish materials I have presented
here, we find a parallel concern with intentionality. It is
not enough to die for the unity of the Divine Name; one
must articulate a full awareness of the sacrifice to be made
and then undertake it with a full heart. Even children are
enjoined to give their full assent to their own demise.
Thus, Isaac ben David the *parnas*, whose saga is recounted
in the narratives at length, asked his children: "Do you
wish that I sacrifice you to our God?"[114] In the same way,
Moses ben Helbo of Mainz addressed his children:

> My sons Helbo and Simon. At this moment, both hell
> and heaven are open [before you]. Into which do you
> wish to enter?[115]

Throughout the speeches of the martyrs, there is a heavy
emphasis on full awareness and on the profound intention

of serving God totally, both deeply characteristic of the new spirit of the late eleventh and early twelfth century.

A second specific index of the sensibilities reflected among the martyrs of 1096 is afforded by the emergence of the individual. This issue has been widely explored of late, with a perceptive and useful summary provided again by Caroline Walker Bynum.

> My argument about the twelfth century is not merely a reiteration of its diversity nor a plea that historians broaden the number of items to which they give attention. It is also an effort to give a more specific definition of the concerns for self and community by locating each in the context of the other. Just as the discovery of self is not a twentieth-century awareness of personality, so the emphasis on models, types, and ways of affiliating with groups cannot be the modern sense of personal lifestyle. Not only is it possible to specify something of the particular nature of twelfth-century culture by the phrase "discovery of self"; it is possible to delineate the period even more precisely when "discovery of self" is coupled with and understood in the context of "discovery of model for behavior" and "discovery of consciously chosen community."[116]

Once again the characteristics identified in the study of majority society are seen among the Jews of the period. The emergence of the individual in the Hebrew crusade chronicles is a stunning phenomenon, given the earlier Jewish tradition of personal anonymity. The newly emergent figures show highly individuated traits of gender, age, class, and community standing; they are shown to be motivated by powerful personal emotions and commitments. They are not, however, the individuals of the modern period; rather they are enmeshed in their community and its web of relationships and their strivings are outlined by model figures from a rich past, which they attempt to emulate and sometimes even to surpass.

Thus in sum the events of 1096 enable us to see late

eleventh-century Rhineland Jewry affected by both the accumulated legacy of its rich Jewish past and by the striking new creativity of the larger society within which it found itself. Through the latter, these Jews—like their Christian counterparts—forged new directions for the religious and social thinking of their tradition.[117]

V

Subsequent Jewish Reactions

THE RETURN TO NORMALCY

By early summer of 1096, the brief and limited explosion of anti-Jewish violence had abated. While this disastrous episode is often treated as a major watershed in the history of medieval Ashkenazic Jewry, there is in fact no real evidence to support such a view.[1] As we have seen, the bulk of Ashkenazic Jewry survived the dangerous summer months unscathed; it is therefore not surprising that these events had relatively little impact on the majority of the new Ashkenazic communities. Even in those areas which suffered devastation and where the calamity was suitably memorialized, there was a strong tendency to begin immediately the rebuilding process. It is to this movement toward normalcy that I now turn.

Nothing is known of the immediate Jewish reaction following the departure of the German crusading bands eastward. The only activity specifically mentioned is the intercession of Moses the *parnas* of Speyer with Emperor Henry IV, successfully seeking permission for those forcibly converted to return to the Jewish faith.[2] This early post-1096 response shows us—in fragmentary fashion to be sure—a continuation of some of the pre-1096 patterns of Jewish political activity. That these earlier patterns continued is not at all surprising. In fact there was simply no alternative. The old alliance with the established political authorities was the only feasible means for ensuring Jewish safety in northern Europe. The breakdown of political authority in the Rhineland area had resulted in calamity, but such a breakdown was assumed to be anomalous. The status quo ante had resumed; the old authorities were once more in the saddle; and Jewish political activity had begun again.[3]

The resumption of these traditional patterns was demonstrated in Jewish behavior during the crisis periods occasioned by the major twelfth-century crusades. The Church leadership, responsible for initiating and directing these later crusades, was of course aware of the potential for anti-Jewish sentiment and violence and, beginning with the Second Crusade, exerted strenuous efforts aimed at obviating anti-Jewish assaults, efforts that were fully appreciated by the Jews.[4] Rabbi Ephraim of Bonn indicates that the Jews themselves also undertook a series of protective measures. In particular, they used the device that had proved successful in preserving the Jewish community of Speyer in 1096—that is, relocation out of the central cities to neighboring fortifications. Despite the failure of this technique to save the Jews of Cologne, the post-1096 evaluation of this ploy seems to have been quite positive. According to Rabbi Ephraim, in August of 1146, at the time of the arrival of the monk Ralph in the Rhineland, a few threats of violence frightened the Jews deeply.

> At that point the Jews were very frightened. They lifted their eyes to the hills and the fortifications. Then all the Jews asked their Christian acquaintances—any who had a tower or a fortress—to take them in, so that they might come into the cleft of the rocks and hide there until the period of wrath would pass over. After the holiday of Sukkot, 4906 [late September 1146] everyone left his city and turned to the fortified towns. The bulk of the community of Cologne gave the archbishop of Cologne large sums, so that he might turn over to them the fortress of Wolkenburg, which is unmatched in Lorraine. They removed from there by means of many gifts the baron in charge of the fortress. It was given over to the Jews alone, and Christians did

> not pass among them. . . . From the point at which
> word spread among the Christians that Wolkenburg
> had been turned over to the Jews and in it all the Jews
> had been gathered, they ceased pursuing them and
> respite was achieved for all the rest of the Jews who
> were fleeing to the towers.[5]

Reflected here is the Jews' full awareness of the danger
associated with the new crusade and careful preparations
to remove themselves from the centers of agitation and to
afford themselves the best possible circumstances for self-
defense. The lessons of 1096 had been carefully learned
by Rhineland Jewry. Ephraim considers this preparedness
a critical element in determining Jewish fate during the
Second Crusade.

The same technique was also used in 1188, as the Third
Crusade assembled. Jewish delight over crusader misfor-
tunes was tempered by fears of renewed persecution. The
Jewish fears were not at all unfounded. Violence did break
out in Mainz, spurred by anger over the catastrophe in the
East and the preaching of the new crusade. Fortunately,
the authorities were committed to protecting the Jews in
their jurisdiction.

> On Friday, the twenty-eighth of the month of . . . ,
> 4948 [late 1187 or early 1188], the Christians gathered
> to kill us and came into the Jews' street. The Jews then
> shut themselves up in their houses. The Christians
> broke through one of the Jews' roofs. Finally heavenly
> forces had pity upon us, and the chamberlain's men
> came and drove the Christians off. Thus our Creator—
> may he be blessed—saved us from all our enemies.[6]

As the new crusade began to take shape, with Mainz
the hub of crusading activity, the Jews of that key city
decided that it would be wise for them to follow well-established precedent and find refuge in fortified places. Rabbi
Elazar ben Judah of Worms, in a valuable account, indi-

cates that a number of Jewish communities made the same
decision.

> Meanwhile the Christians were taking the sign of the
> cross by the hundreds, by the thousands, and by the
> ten thousands, double and treble the number of those
> leaving Egypt, and were continually threatening to kill
> us. . . . All the Jews were in deep distress. Finally we
> decided to flee to fortifications—all the Jews of Mainz,
> Speyer, Strasburg, Worms, Wurzburg, and all the
> neighboring areas where Jews lived. We the Jews of
> Mainz left Torah scrolls, our beloved treasures, along
> with books and all our wealth, with the ravenous
> wolves, the burghers, in order to make it easier to flee
> for our lives. In the year 4948 [1188], during the month
> of Adar II, we fled to Munzenberg. Everywhere the
> Jews divided themselves up, fleeing to four villages or
> to five fortifications.[7]

The memoir of Rabbi Elazar, or more precisely the
letter of his brother-in-law embedded in Rabbi Elazar's
memoir, shows us another line of Jewish activity, again
not without precedent during the First Crusade.[8] Aware
that the German army was assembling in Mainz, a small
band of Jews chose to eschew the safety of flight and to
remain in the city in order to negotiate with the leaders of
the crusade. The dangers braved by this band of Jews were
formidable. Anti-Jewish passions ran high but, fortunately
for these Jews and their peers, the imperial authorities
were resolute in protecting them. The height of the danger
came on Saturday, March 26, the day before the mass
ceremony of taking the cross.

> On the Sabbath prior to the month of Nisan [March
> 26], the crusaders gathered in our street to assault us
> and to attack us. One arose, with a sword in his
> hand, and attempted to smite a Jew. Then the marshal
> came . . .[9] and seized him by the hair, pulling it, and
> smote him with a staff until his blood spilled to the

ground. The rest fled to the marketplace and told their fellow crusaders what had been done to them on account of the Jews. They all gathered, by the thousands and ten thousands, and wished to take a standard and advance upon our street. The matter was revealed to the marshal; with a staff in his hand, he took his servants with him and smote the crusaders and beat them, until they had all dispersed. We were in grave trouble—almost fatal—from Friday until Tuesday. Blessed is the Lord and may his memory be exalted forever, for he provided relief prior to the blow.[10]

According to the Jewish observer, the imperial actions had a telling effect on the barons of the realm. "The barons understood clearly the implications of these acts, saying: 'How beloved are the Jews in the eyes of the emperor!'" This, however, was not the goal of the Jews who had remained in Mainz. They worked for—and succeeded in eliciting—formal guarantees of Jewish safety.

On Tuesday, the emperor extended peace to the Jews, announcing: "Anyone who harms a Jew and causes an injury, his hand shall be cut off. Anyone who kills a Jew shall be killed." The bishops then excommunicated all who lift their hands to kill a Jew. The king further ordered an edict circulated both written and oral, that the Jews be protected carefully, even more than had been done heretofore. All of this was paid for fully.[11]

This is a remarkably cursory depiction of a number of highly significant actions. The first is an imperial edict outlawing violence against the Jews and specifying the penalties for such violence. The second is the ecclesiastical backing for this edict, removing any special privileges that might normally protect crusaders. Finally, the imperial edict was communicated to the network of officials who would bear responsibility for enforcing it. Looking back to the First Crusade, one is struck by the difference made by the presence of a strong emperor. To be sure, the anti-

Jewish pressures may have been considerably weaker, but the firm imperial stand is impressive nonetheless, as is the dedication of those Jews who endangered themselves in order to elicit Frederick's aid. The entire effort was successful; Rabbi Elazar ben Judah indicates that by late April the Jews of the Rhineland were able to return to their homes.

Thus, in addition to ecclesiastical leadership prepared for and opposed to anti-Jewish violence, we also see that the Jewish community was fully aware of the potential dangers and prepared to meet them. While the protective measures adopted—flight to rural fortifications and negotiations with the political authorities—are by no means new and innovative, combined with more effective ecclesiastical control of the late crusades and stronger secular governance, they were successful in securing a relatively high level of safety and security.

I have focused thus far on Jewish political activity, arguing that the events of 1096 do not seem to have altered prior patterns of Jewish behavior. It may be suggested, however, that, while patterns of political activity remained unchanged, Jewish perceptions shifted, with significant loss of a sense of security and well-being. While such a view has often been proposed, little evidence is available to support it.[12] There had been aspects of insecurity in pre-1096 Ashkenazic life, as I have already shown; there is really no greater sense of insecurity after 1096. Pre-1096 Ashkenazic views of Christianity and Christendom are resoundingly negative; there is no sense that hostility deepened after 1096. Perhaps the best indicator of post-1096 Jewish attitudes comes from the murky area of population movement. Did Jews massively leave northern Europe in general or the affected areas specifically? Despite the lack of statistical evidence, the answer is clearly no. To the contrary, all data point to enhanced Jewish migration into northern Europe during the twelfth and thirteenth centuries. Indeed, the very areas devastated were quickly resettled, hardly supporting the notion that the attitudes of Jews altered permanently. Post-1096 actions and attitudes imply a continuously developing Jewish community that had not reassessed in any fundamental fashion its place in northern European society.

Even when we turn from practical matters to spiritual issues, the same sense of a return to normalcy obtains. Ashkenazic thinking is far from obsessed with the events of 1096 and the related issues of martyrdom. The two original Hebrew chronicles were not widely copied or known. Medieval and early-modern Jewish histories give scant attention to the events of 1096.[13] The martyrs of 1096 are lamented in the traditional dirges recited on the Ninth of Av, though they in no way dominate the sad memories of the annual fast day. Halachic writers likewise do not devote much attention to the issues related to martyrdom. The commentaries on the relevant talmudic passages are hardly extensive, and the codes reflect minimal concern with the issue of martyrdom. Even German-Jewish Pietism, a major spiritual development with significant links to the martyrdom of 1096, demonstrated little awareness of the events I have described. While it has often been claimed that *Hasidut Ashkenaz* flowed directly from the persecutions of 1096, recent investigations have indicated very few reflections of these persecutions in the writings of the Pietists.[14] In fact, the *Sefer Hasidim* makes but one overt reference to crusaders and that single reference shows no real awareness of the nature of the catastrophe associated with the First Crusade. The story in *Sefer Hasidim* is as follows:

> An incident took place concerning a bishop who decreed in Mainz that the Jews should either be killed or converted. He sent for the crusaders and said: "Be extremely careful that you not touch the money of the Jews, but only their persons. Anyone who does not convert should be killed." But the matter was told to the Jews. Immediately upon hearing this, the Jews closed up their homes and threw into the street all their silver and gold and clothing. While the crusaders were occupied with plundering, many of the Jews fled through the courtyards to the homes of the burghers

and were saved. The bishop heard and sent for the crusaders. He then commanded them: "Do not harm the Jews." The crusaders returned and said: "Why did you permit harming the Jews initially, and now you forbid it?" He said to them: "Initially [I permitted it because,] so long as they had money, it would have been painful for them to lose large sums of money along with their lives and therefore they would have converted under duress. Now that the money is gone and they are already fearful for their lives, they will be killed before they transgress their law. Moreover, if you had not plundered but had immediately begun killing, you would have found them all—old and young men and young women. Since some of these would have converted under duress, others would have as well. Now, while you were occupied with plunder, the young men and the wealthy and the young women have fled. Only the old men and the old women and the very best remain. These will certainly allow themselves to be killed.[15]

This curious tale bears no relationship to the realities of 1096. The constellation of pro- and anti-Jewish forces is totally distorted. The author of this story was of course not interested in the historical realities; he was interested in the complexities of the response to persecution, particularly the influence of material possession and of age on a person's willingness to accept martyrdom. In any case it is striking that, in *Sefer Hasidim*, there remains no accurate recollection of the First Crusade. It should be added that the numerous references to persecutions are even more ahistorical, focusing completely on Jewish resistance or submission. We must take care not to exaggerate the impact of the events of 1096 on subsequent Jewish thinking.

To the extent that the martyrdom of 1096 did affect later Jewish thought, it tended to strengthen the traditional norms. The radical Jewish behaviors of 1096 were assimilated into the mainstream of traditional Jewish thinking. The martyrdom of 1096 served to reinforce the normative patterns of *kiddush ha-Shem*. The radical behaviors were eventually effaced, stripped of their uniqueness and extremism. There are a number of indices of the impact of the events of 1096 in strengthening the traditional notion of Jewish martyrdom. Perhaps the single most effective vehicle for perpetuating the memory of the martyrs of 1096 and enshrining their heroism was the inclusion of a prayer to their memory in the standard Ashkenazic liturgy. Rabbi Ephraim of Bonn in the twelfth century was the first to mention the following prayer as part of the Sabbath liturgy.[16]

May the Merciful Father, who dwells in heaven, in his abundant mercies remember compassionately the pious and righteous and pure, the sacred communities, who sacrificed themselves for the sanctification of the Divine Name. "Beloved and cherished in life, they were not parted in death."[17] They were swifter than eagles and stronger than lions in doing the will of their Creator and the desire of their Protector. May God remember them beneficently along with the other righteous of history. May he avenge the blood of his servants which has been spilled, as is written in the Torah of Moses, the man of God: "O nations, acclaim his people! For he will avenge the blood of his servants, wreak vengeance on his foes, and cleanse the land of his people."[18] By your servants the prophets it has been written: "When I establish innocence, I shall not excuse the shedding of their blood, and the Lord shall dwell in Zion."[19] In the Writings it is said: "Why should the nations say: 'Where is their God?' Before our eyes let it be known among the nations that you avenge the spilled blood of your servants."[20] It is likewise said: "For he does not ignore the cry of the afflicted; he who requites bloodshed is mindful of them."[21] It is likewise said: "He works judgment upon the nations, heaping up bodies, crushing heads far and wide. He drinks from the stream on his way; therefore he holds his head high."[22]

To be sure, the martyrs of 1096 are not specifically designated in this prayer. Given its place of origin, however,
and the similarity of its language to the Hebrew chronicles,
there can be little doubt that it refers especially to the
martyrs I have been discussing. However, the specific
identity of the martyrs of 1096 has been effaced; moreover,
lost also is the specificity of the actions they undertook. In
effect, this prayer serves to memorialize the martyrs in the
most general way and to reinforce normative thinking concerning martyrdom. The dramatic innovation in the radical
style of martyrdom in 1096 has been glossed over.

A similar tendency can be discerned among the legalists. The old injunctions are reinforced among Ashkenazic
Jews through the behavior of the Rhineland martyrs. Any
alternative to accepting death in the face of persecution is
unthinkable. Thus, as perceptively noted by Jacob Katz,
the Tosafists (twelfth- and thirteenth-century commentators on the Talmud) respond to the view of Rabbi Ishmael,
which permits acceptance of idolatry rather than requiring
death, with passionate negation, a tribute to the impact of
the heroic martyrdoms of 1096.[23] The Ashkenazic codes,
while not obsessed with *kiddush ha-Shem*, do consistently
emphasize the requirement to accept death rather than
submit to religious compulsion. Moreover, unlike Mai-
monides, they judge one who accepts death when not
required to do so as praiseworthy, not as in error.[24] Yet
neither the commentaries nor the codes deal at great
length with the radical forms of behavior noted in 1096.
Out of the trauma emerges a buttressing—but not an
extension—of the normative, in effect deradicalizing the
behavior of 1096. All the martyrs—traditional and untra-
ditional alike—are viewed from a traditionalist perspective. The normative is reinforced by behaviors both normative and extreme.

The Pietists took the same approach. While accurate
recollections of 1096 are not preserved, resistance to external pressure constitutes an important theme in *Sefer
Ḥasidim*. In those instances involving the choice between
forced conversion and martyrdom, *Sefer Ḥasidim* strongly

condemns those forcibly converted, as the interesting account that follows shows:

> There were two brothers who were apostates. The sage investigated their ancestors to learn what had brought this about. When the catastrophe struck, the Jewish community had said: "What shall we do?" The rabbi replied: "Watch me and do the same."[25] He took a cross and carried it so that the Christians not kill him. They forcibly converted him along with the other Jews of his town. Therefore his descendants had apostasized.[26]

To resist such conversion by force, even lying was permissible:

> An incident occurred during the period of forced conversion. The bishop said to the Jewish community in his town: "Send a Jew to a nearby town, for it has a bishop and Jews. You see what that Jewish community will do and do likewise. What that bishop will do to the Jewish community in his town I shall do to you." They sent a good Jew and he saw that the Jews were forcibly converted. When he returned, they asked him what he had seen. He said: "They were killed for the unity of the Divine Name." For if he had told them [what they actually did], they would have done likewise. Therefore he said this, so that they would be killed for sanctification of the Divine Name and would gain a place in the world to come.[27]

Once more the range of behaviors encountered in 1096 has been effaced, with the effect of reinforcing the established norms.

Thus the bulk of Ashkenazic Jewry resumed its patterns of living after the events of 1096. For most Ashkenazic Jews these dolorous incidents at most sharpened their perception of potential danger and reinforced traditional norms of resistance to non-Jewish religious coercion.

At least a century and a half of continued vitality lay ahead for this nascent Jewish community after the crusading armies had posed their threat and done their damage.

MEMORIALIZATION, RATIONALIZATION, AND EXPLANATION

Returning to prior patterns of Jewish living after 1096 was the norm. For some Jews, however, particularly those from the affected areas, such a resumption of everyday life was impossible. These Jews felt the impact of the events of 1096 profoundly. The dead had to be memorialized, their behaviors had to be rationalized, and difficult theological questions had to be answered. Once more one senses innovation and creativity coming into play as these issues were confronted and new directions assayed.

Veneration of the martyrs of 1096 meant memorialization and the survivors devised new memorial forms and techniques. In the later *Memorbuchen* (memorial books) which contain detailed lists of Jewish martyrs associated with specific incidents and dates, the earliest of the records are from 1096. It is not surprising that the persecutions of 1096 generated a new style of memorialization. More impressive, however, than the new ritual techniques was the equally innovative style of historical writing, which served even more effectively to enshrine the greatness of the fallen martyrs. Persecution in itself does not guarantee profound and moving commemoration. Works of the caliber of the Hebrew First-Crusade chronicles do not come about without both significant events and a literary style suited to their enshrinement. Clearly the events associated with the First Crusade were remarkable enough to evoke inspired history writing, and the Ashkenazic Jews of the late eleventh and early twelfth century developed a style suitable to convey the heroism of the Rhineland Jews of 1096. While this historiographic style may actually have resulted simply from the genius of an individual, it is reasonable to search for the literary antecedents of these exceptional Hebrew narratives.[28]

What were the historiographic models available to the anonymous authors of the early local records and to the composers of S and L? While the Hebrew Bible includes large and significant historical works, in style these historical sections bear little or no resemblance to the Hebrew First-Crusade chronicles. In one sense, the biblical narrative is far grander than the Ashkenazic records—it deals after all with an ongoing encounter between God and man. However, the biblical stories are in a way far less epic and heroic than our medieval accounts. In the Bible the overwhelmingly dominant figure is God; individual humans are not presented in the mold of the heroes of 1096.[29] Rabbinic midrash often embellishes the biblical narrative to flesh out the attenuated features of the key personalities in early Israelite history. These embellishments, however, are disqualified by their lack of continuity from any stylistic impact on the historical writings of the Rhineland Jews of the eleventh and twelfth centuries.[30] Among these Ashkenazic Jews, postbiblical history was known primarily through an important and widely read Hebrew work called the *Book of Josippon*.[31] It is certain that this opus was extensively copied and broadly disseminated among eleventh-century Ashkenazic Jews.[32] A sweeping history of the Jews from biblical times through the destruction of the Second Temple, the *Book of Josippon* is worlds away from the mood and style of our chronicles. In one respect, nonetheless, *Josippon* may well have exerted influence on the Hebrew crusade accounts. On occasion the large-scale saga in *Josippon* gives way to the depiction of individual heroes, their actions, and their utterances. These well-known incidents, such as those involving the aged priest Elazar, the woman and her seven sons, and the martyrs of Masada, may well have served as a model for some of the depictions in our Hebrew records.[33]

Besides this earlier Jewish literature, the Ashkenazic Jews of the eleventh and twelfth centuries were somewhat familiar with a second literary tradition, that of their non-Jewish environment. At precisely that point in time, oral stories in this milieu were coalescing into the written cycles of national epics known as the *chansons de geste*, and numerous chroniclers were portraying the glories and heroism of the First Crusade.[34] Both of these sets of Christian literature were produced out of an intensive spiritual exhilaration characteristic of the late eleventh and early twelfth century. It was, in many ways, the remarkably vibrant atmosphere of late eleventh- and early twelfth-century northern Europe that produced this impressive breakthrough in Jewish historiography.[35]

What did the Hebrew First Crusade chronicles set out to recount and why were they composed? Unfortunately none of the Hebrew narratives supplies a self-conscious introductory statement that lays bare the intentions of the author or editor. An extensive introduction to the chronicle of Fulcher of Chartres supplies some useful suggestions, which can then be carefully checked out in the Hebrew texts. Fulcher informs us, first of all, that his chronicle will focus on two essential items: (1) "the illustrious deeds of the Franks" and (2) "God's miracles which often occurred among them." A narrative that highlights human deeds and divine miracles is intended to serve a number of important purposes: (1) the recollection of the heroic deeds of the deceased, it was thought, would move the living to recall and to bless the souls of the departed; (2) the depiction of the piety of these Christian warriors would inspire the reader or listener to greater commitment and religious enthusiasm; (3) the portrayal of divine intervention would arouse feelings of thanksgiving among the audience.[36]

How well does this outline, which certainly depicts accurately most of the Christian First-Crusade chronicles, fit the Hebrew narratives? In their essential content, the Hebrew records focus on only one of the two areas of Fulcher's interest. Because the Hebrew narratives depict events that constitute military defeat, they convey no sense of God's miracles and no suggestion of divine intervention.[37] The reality of a military defeat, however, in no way detracts from the human heroism or reduces its impressiveness. A fitting title for these Hebrew chronicles would be something like:

מעשי קהלות אשכנז והיאך
קירשו שמו המיוחד והנשגב

The Deeds of the Jewish Communities of Ashkenaz and the Way in Which They Sanctified the Unique Divine Name, a parallel to the *Gesta Francorum et Aliorum Hierosolimitanorum*.[38] These Hebrew reports are not histories of the First Crusade nor even histories of the persecution of Rhineland Jewry; they are rather tales of the heroism of the Jews who, under assault, remained courageously steadfast in their commitment to the God of Israel. The purposes of these tales of Jewish heroism are precisely those indicated by Fulcher: the recollection of the dead and the construction of paradigms of proper behavior for the living.

Indeed these tales of heroism belong to a genre that literary historians and folklorists have come to call "the epic of defeat."[39] These Hebrew narratives show many of the classic characteristics of the epic of defeat: in them small forces are hopelessly outnumbered; the members of a higher civilization are overwhelmed by inferiors; there is a confrontation in which the smaller and superior group's way of life manages to survive; and there is an ultimate victory that transcends the immediate defeat.[40] Like many of the epics of defeat, the Hebrew chronicles are profoundly inspirational and moving.

The reality of physical defeat and the lack of divine intervention mean that the second of Fulcher's interests—the depiction of God's miracles—and the third of his objectives—the arousal of feelings of thanksgiving—can scarcely appear in the Hebrew texts. In place of the recital of divine miracles, there are expressions of deeply held convictions of future redemption; instead of thanksgiving, there are in these records justification and petition. In part these chronicles are intended to assure their Jewish readers that the persecution and the resultant losses were not without meaning, that they had a divine purpose and would, especially as a result of Jewish heroism and martyr-dom, eventuate ultimately in redemption. In part the message of the chronicles was directed at a divine audience, begging God to be mindful of Jewish commitment and readiness for self-sacrifice and thus to bring about the rewards that such heroism plainly merited.

The focus on human heroism limits the historical perceptions of the Jewish chroniclers but also intensifies them. The chroniclers show no real awareness of a broad historical span or of complex historical causation. The key ingredient in the Jewish chroniclers' view of history is the element of will, both human and divine. In the dramas they depict, the decisive factor is human will, seen as vicious and destructive in the Christian attackers and as heroic and constructive in the beleaguered Jewish martyrs. Whereas modern historians have been aware of a complex political and doctrinal background to the First Crusade, the Jewish narrators tell a story stripped of all complications and focused on human volition. Thus the inception of the crusade is simplistically depicted in the following terms:

> For then rose up initially the arrogant, the barbaric, a fierce and impetuous people, both French and German. They set their hearts to journey to the Holy City, which had been defiled by a ruffian people, in order to seek there the sepulcher of the crucified bastard and to drive out the Muslims who dwell in the land and to conquer the land.[41]

Christian animosity toward the Jews is described solely in terms of elemental religious hatred, while the Jewish response is likewise seen as a direct and sublime exercise in human will. Thus these Hebrew narratives present a series of heroic figures moving across the stage of events. Of course the Jewish figures are not heroic in the normal military sense—far from achieving stunning victories, they suffer crushing defeat. Spiritually, however—and the spiritual plane is surely the level of ultimate significance—they are truly remarkable, their will developed enough to subordinate every normal human fear and to transcend all vestiges of self-concern.

The extraordinary use of the passionate soliloquy by the authors of the Hebrew First-Crusade chronicles reflects their concern with human will and motivation. Although one might loosely argue that the technique is an old one and that these authors are part of a well-established tradition, these soliloquies in fact break new ground in Jewish historiography. They move beyond the soliloquy style of both the Bible and midrashic literature. Even the impassioned speeches of Josephus and *Josippon* are not truly mirrored in the hortatory expositions of the Hebrew crusade chronicles. What is different is precisely the emphasis on the arousal of human will to do the divine will. The famous exhortations in Josephus and *Josippon* sound much like legal briefs, arguing for the reasonableness of a given course of action; the speeches of the martyrs of 1096 in contrast are pleas to the heart, seeking to rouse unusual self-sacrifice by presenting a set of compelling symbols. The result is an innovative style in hortatory address.

The focus on human will and heroism produces an emphasis on specific actions. A set of individuals—Meshullam ben Isaac; David the *gabbai*; Isaac ben David the *parnas*; Rachel, the daughter of Isaac; and others—are graphically depicted. Though surely not portrayed in all their complexity, they are presented as specific human beings, of definite age, sex, and station in life. Their acts of martyrdom are similarly presented with a high degree of specificity. This is particularly striking in view of the general anonymity of the major Jewish figures of the period. The intellectual giants of this early period in Ashkenazic Jewish history remain vague and shadowy, while the heroes of 1096 have been given unusually specific human dimensions by the Jewish chroniclers.[42] This quality of specificity reflects the heroic mold in which these compositions are cast. Even more important than the individuation of specific characters is the recognition of the variety of modes of behavior displayed by both the attackers and the attacked. There is no attempt on the part of these authors to make events fit a simple mold. The assaults are portrayed in all their diversity; a variety of Jewish responses to these attacks is depicted; and even the noblest Jewish response—martyrdom—appears in diverse forms. The underlying concern with human will and heroism quickens the historian's impulse to describe the world in its complexity.

The delineation of specific heroic figures in the Hebrew chronicles contrasts sharply with the poetic facelessness one finds in the elegies composed in memory of the martyrs of 1096.[43] These dirges are abstract and stereotypic in their presentation. The disaster is depicted and the readers' emotions evoked by allusion to classical texts and to past happenings. The prose chronicles, by contrast, depict tragedy and evoke emotion by attacking directly the sensibilities of the reader. Death is portrayed in gruesome detail; blood gushes forth; the unbearable suffering of human hearts is highlighted.[44] The contrast described extends to the mode of presentation as well. The poetic dirges are highly contrived compositions; they utilize complex patterns of meter and rhyme and are rich in mind-teasing allusions. By contrast the prose chronicles seem artless in their directness. To be sure, signs of learnedness and allusion are by no means absent. However, poetic meter, rhyme, and excessive allusion are eschewed. It seems that the narrators were convinced that the story is so powerful that artful contrivance would detract rather than enhance. It is in this regard that the Hebrew (and Latin) chronicles diverge from the *chansons de geste*, which had such a marked impact upon them. Convinced that contemporary events reveal a heroism beyond that of the past, the crusade chroniclers attempt to portray this heroism in direct and simple terms, implying that the events speak best for themselves. The heroism of Roland, Oliver, and Archbishop Turpin were augmented by the storytelling capacities of the minstrels who sang of them. The valor of the crusade heroes needed no such external aids; their deeds were in themselves superbly eloquent.

Once again we are made aware of the extent to which these early Ashkenazic Jews were firmly rooted in the general spiritual and intellectual environment of northern Europe. Just as the responses of the martyrs reveal the profound influence of this vibrant environment, so too does the subsequent Jewish memorialization of the disaster. Once again the encounter between the Ashkenazic Jews with their traditions and the stimulating external environment produced an innovative set of responses.

The Hebrew First-Crusade chronicles thus constitute a remarkable new way of enshrining the memory of those who had given up their lives for the sanctity of the Divine Name. Yet another task that faced the survivors of the disaster was to reconcile the behaviors of the martyrs of 1096 with the norms of halachic and aggadic teaching. As we have already seen, to accept death at the hand of the crusaders fell well within the bounds of halachic injunction and aggadic precedent. Taking one's own life was somewhat more problematic; taking the lives of others highly problematic. While subsequent legalists do not deal at great length with these issues, efforts to provide a rationale for the problematic behaviors were made occasionally.

As noted already, the most common concern of the later Ashkenazic legalists was to buttress the traditional view that Jews should forfeit their lives when confronted with the alternatives of conversion or death. The Tosafists, as I have shown, went even further, rejecting any mitigation of this injunction. The more problematic issue of taking one's own life is addressed only occasionally. In the absence of clear halachic injunction, three aggadic precedents inform the discussion of this difficult issue: the biblical case of Saul, who took his own life; the talmudic story of the four hundred young people, who drowned themselves; and the talmudic report that criticized Rabbi Haninah ben Teradion for hastening his own death.[45]

The biblical figure of Saul, who took his life under duress, was interpreted by some as sanctioning suicide in that kind of situation, although others denied the propriety of his action. This difference in opinion is reflected in a passage in a biblical commentary that stems from Tosafist circles. In one view, Genesis 9:5 and an early rabbinic commentary on it are to be read as sanctioning the taking of one's own life out of fear of unbearable torture and to avoid transgressing; in another view, the biblical passage and its rabbinic exegesis are to be seen as a rejection of this notion. Proponents of this reading suggested that "one may under no circumstances harm himself and Saul behaved without rabbinic authorization."[46]

A second reflection of this concern is found in the talmudic commentary of the Tosafists. There the commentators note the seeming disparity between condemnation for Rabbi Haninah ben Teradion, who hastened his own death, and commendation for the four hundred youngsters, who drowned themselves. Rabbi Jacob Tam, one of the major figures in twelfth-century Ashkenazic intellectual life, connected the commendation for the four hundred young people with the issue of forced conversion, suggesting that, "when they [Jews in danger] fear that the gentiles will bring them to transgression, for example through unbearable torture, then it is a *mizvah* to harm oneself, as in the case found in *Gittin* with regard to the youngsters who were taken captive for immoral purposes and threw themselves into the sea."[47] In an interesting further note, a later Tosafist quoted Rabbi Jacob Tam and disagreed with his connection of the incident of the four hundred drowned youths with the issue of forced conversion. It is, however, striking that this authority, disagreeing as he did with the grounds of his predecessor's conclusion, accepted the conclusion itself. "Even though from that incident there is not convincing proof . . . . nonetheless it is reasonable that such behavior [the taking of one's own life out of fear of conversion] is permissible and it is a *mizvah*."[48] In effect this second Tosafist, Rabbi Elhanan, dismisses the prooftext but remains convinced of the conclusion. The great thirteenth-century rabbinic authority, Rabbi Meir ben Baruch of Rothenburg, in an important responsum took the position that taking of one's own life under the threat of persecution and the danger of conversion is certainly permissible, with the precedents of Saul, the four hundred youths, and the mother of the seven sons adduced as evidence.[49]

I have already noted that this behavior was seen as problematic and this after-the-fact uncertainty surely reinforces this analysis. To be sure, the criticism of this behavior implied in the treatment of the story of Saul seems to represent the less normative view. The general tendency seems to be to commend those who took their lives and to accept that behavior as laudable, while tacitly recognizing that precise grounding for the propriety of such behavior might not be available.

The taking of the lives of others was of course all the more problematic. Again the rabbinic sources of the twelfth and thirteenth centuries do not treat this issue in great detail. Once more difference of opinion is notable. The same passage in the biblical commentary just now noted extends the discussion of suicide to the taking of the lives of others, particularly children. A striking story is told:

> There is a report of certain rabbi who slaughtered many infants during a period of forced conversion, because he feared that they [the gentiles] would convert them. There was another rabbi with him, who was exceedingly angry with him and called him a murderer. But he [the first rabbi] did not waver. The [second] rabbi said: "If I am correct, let that rabbi be killed in an unusual way." Thus it was . . . . Subsequently the persecution subsided. If he had not slaughtered those infants, they would have been saved."[50]

Here the legitimacy of taking the lives of others is disputed; the view that this is not acceptable is endorsed.

The general tendency, however, points in the opposite direction: The taking of life is endorsed under the unusual circumstances of religious persecution. One post-1096 northern European source puts the matter this way: "On the following they based themselves in slaughtering, during the period of persecution, children who cannot distinguish between good and evil. For we fear lest such children be assimilated bodily among the gentiles as they mature. It is better that they die in innocence than that they later die in guilt. "[51] Perhaps the most striking statement of such thinking is contained in the aforecited responsum by Rabbi Meir ben Baruch of Rothenburg. In this responsum Rabbi Meir replied to the question raised by a Jew who had slain his wife and children in the midst of persecution. The key points in the responsum are: (1) the assertion that taking one's own life under circumstances of religious persecution is certainly permitted; (2) the suggestion that the taking of the lives of others is somewhat problematic; (3) the assertion that such behavior must be permissible in view of the fact that many respected figures had in fact done so; (4) an original reading of the passage in Genesis 9 to buttress the argument that such behavior is permissible.[52] As noted recently by David Berger, the style of reasoning advanced in this fourth and final point is, to put it mildly, highly unusual. It lacks the kind of halachic foundation usually adduced in argumentation of this sort.[53] Once more the overall sense is general acceptance of this extreme behavior, with little solid evidence advanced for such acceptance. In truth the most powerful argument for the validity of such behavior is that it was exhibited by people deemed worthy of respect and emulation.

A curious reflection of this positive view of taking the lives of others under extreme circumstances is the suggestion occasionally advanced that Abraham, the ancestor of the Jews and the exemplar of religious commitment, was more than prepared to sacrifice his beloved son Isaac—that in fact he did slaughter his son, who was then miraculously returned to life. This unusual view, brilliantly analyzed by Shalom Spiegel, is captured in the following stanzas of a liturgical poem written by Rabbi Ephraim of Bonn.

> He [Abraham] made haste, he pinned him down with his knees,

He made his two arms strong.
With steady hands he slaughtered him according to
    the rite,
Full right was the slaughter.
Down upon him fell the resurrecting dew, and he
    revived.
(The father) seized him (then) to slaughter him once
    more.
Scripture, bear witness! Well-grounded is the fact:
"And the Lord called Abraham, even a second time
from heaven."[54]

The notion that Isaac *was* actually slaughtered serves to buttress the argument that taking human life under certain dire circumstances can be acceptable. While the precise circumstances surrounding the Abraham-Isaac incident did not involve religious persecution, these commentators saw sufficient similarity to adduce Abraham's readiness to take Isaac's life as precedent and justification for the actions of 1096.

The events and actions of 1096 thus evoked interpretations that enshrined the memory of the martyrs while exploring the issues presented by their extreme behaviors. There was a third task as well. The chroniclers had to wrestle at the same time with difficult religious and theological questions. What was the meaning of the catastrophe? Why had God permitted such suffering on the part of an unusually righteous community of Jews?

Questions like these were posed by Christian observers of the persecutions of 1096. For example, in pleading with a wealthy Jewish woman from Worms to convert, the Christian burghers of that city argued: "Know and see that God does not wish to save you. For they lie naked at the corner of every street, unburied."[55] This argument is repeated by the desperate archbishop of Mainz to the remnant of the Jewish community that had fled across the Rhine to Rüdesheim: "I cannot save you. Your God has abandoned you; he does not wish to leave you a remnant and a residue."[56] Even the Jews themselves occasionally expressed a sense of abandonment. The Jews of Mainz, on hearing of the attacks in Speyer and Worms, reportedly cried out to the Lord and said:

> "Ah Lord God of Israel! Are you wiping out the remnant of Israel? Where are all your wondrous deeds about which our ancestors told us, saying: 'Truly the Lord brought you up from Egypt.' But now you have abandoned us, delivering us into the hands of the gentiles for destruction."[57]

Likewise Abraham ben Yom Tov of Triers, facing death, raised his voice and wept, saying:

> "Woe, O Lord God! Why have you abandoned your people Israel to calumny, plunder, and shame, destroying us through the hands of a people as impure as the pig which they eat. [Why have you done this] to us, the people that you chose to be your special people among all peoples. You have raised them up from the earth to heaven and now 'you have thrown down from heaven to earth the glory of Israel.' You have multiplied our corpses."[58]

To be sure, a sense of abandonment does not dominate reaction of the Jews under assault. Nonetheless, the issue of the meaning of the catastrophe remained and had perforce to be confronted.

In a preceding section I made heavy use of the speeches set in the mouths of the martyrs in order to identify the major motivations for these acts of heroism. In this section I shall focus on the comments and observations of the editors, as they attempt to present and make sense of the disaster that had befallen their community.[59] At this juncture note that I make a curious reversal in my use of the two original Hebrew narratives, designated S and L. While I have contended that S is the earlier of the two and shows better historical awareness and have therefore tended to rely on it more fully than on L, the latter provides more and richer theological wrestlings and editorial comments and observations. Thus, in the attempt to analyze the subsequent theological response to the crisis of 1096, I will make much more extensive use of L.

By the end of the eleventh century, a host of theological solutions to the problem of physical suffering was readily available to the Rhineland Jews. By this time, the most common explanation for catastrophe was the pattern of sin and punishment. Catastrophe was generally seen as a divine response to human sinfulness. This common view is recurrently reflected in the Hebrew First-Crusade chronicles: "Our sins brought it about that the burghers in every town to which the crusaders came were hostile to us."[60] "Our sins brought it about that the enemy overcame them and captured the gate."[61] "Indeed God did with us as he had said, for we sinned before him."[62] Despite these repeated references to Jewish sin and divine anger, such an explanation of the disaster of 1096 was immediately perceived as problematic. In a rambling consideration of the issue, the editor of L questions the sin-punishment paradigm. While in this passage he concludes by affirming the paradigm, the problems are keenly felt even here.

> But God who truly makes peace turned away from them and hid his eyes from his people and consigned them to the sword. No prophet or seer nor any man of wisdom or understanding can fathom the essential issue—how could the sin of the innumerable people be so heavy and how could the souls of these saintly communities be so destructive, as though shedding blood. Except that surely [God] is a just judge and we bear the shortcomings.[63]

This is a striking passage, and the affirmative conclusion, based on an absolute conviction of God's goodness, does not obscure the deep-seated doubts concerning the sin-punishment paradigm.[64]

Despite the familiar invocation of the sin-punishment pattern, nowhere in the chronicles are any failings on the part of the Jews of 1096 specified. To the contrary, the

afflicted Jews are never really depicted as sinful; they are
unfailingly portrayed in the most glowing terms, both during the period of crisis and prior to it. The great Jewish
community of Mainz is described in the following manner:

> Gone from Zion are all that were her glory, namely
> Mainz. The sound of the lords of the flock ceased,
> along with the sound of the valorous who repel at-
> tacks, who lead the many to righteousness. The glori-
> ous city, the citadel of joy, which had distributed un-
> told sums to the poor. One could not write with an
> iron stylus on a whole book the multitude of good
> deeds that were done in it of yore. In one place
> [were found] Torah and power and wealth and honor
> and wisdom and humility and good deeds, taking in-
> numerable precautions against transgression. But now
> their wisdom has been swallowed up and turned in-
> to destruction, like the children of Jerusalem in their
> destruction.[65]

This is hardly a description of a sinful community. The
glory of Rhineland Jewry prior to its destruction and its
heroism during the catastrophic months of 1096 necessitated an alternative theory to the sin-punishment paradigm. In place of sin and punishment, the Hebrew crusade
chronicles, particularly L, highlight a striking and radical
alternative—the view that the persecutions accompanying
the First Crusade were actually a test imposed upon a
uniquely worthy generation, a test in which these heroic
Jews triumphantly succeeded:

> The precious children of Zion, the children of Mainz,
> were tested ten times, like our ancestor Abraham and
> like Hananiah, Mishael, and Azariah. They offered up
> their children as did Abraham with his son Isaac. They
> accepted upon themselves the yoke of the fear of
> heaven, of the King of kings, the Holy One, blessed
> be he, willingly. They did not wish to deny the awe
> of our King or to exchange it for [that of] a loathesome

offshoot, a bastard born of menstruation and lust. They stretched forth their necks for the slaughter and commended their pure souls to their Father in heaven. The saintly and pious women stretched forth their necks one to another, to be sacrificed for the unity of the [Divine] Name. Likewise men to their children and brothers, brothers to sisters, women to their sons and daughters, and neighbor to neighbor and friend, bridegroom to bride, and betrothed to his betrothed. They sacrificed each other until the blood flowed together. The blood of husbands mingled with that of their wives, the blood of parents with that of their children, the blood of brothers with that of their sisters, the blood of teachers with that of their students, the blood of bridegrooms with that of their brides, the blood of cantors with that of their scribes, the blood of infants and sucklings with that of their mothers. They were killed and slaughtered for the unity of the revered and awesome Name.[66]

The testing theme is sounded here clearly and is widely repeated. There is, however, more here than abstract theory. In order to convey the anguish evoked by the divine challenge, the author is purposefully graphic. Mention is made of fathers and sons, of mothers and children, of brothers and sisters, of teachers and students, in an effort to awaken the reader's sense of the reality of human pain and sacrifice. The lengthy description of intermingling blood is intended to shock and to sicken and to emphasize thereby the monumental heroism that the victims displayed.

There is repeated identification of those tested of 1096 with the great Jewish figures of antiquity who were similarly subjected to painful testing—Rabbi Akiba and his associates, the three young men of the book of Daniel, and above all Abraham, the tested figure par excellence. Precisely because the consummate challenge to Abraham involved the offering up of his son as a sacrifice, the Rhineland Jews were seen by their chroniclers as repeating this

highest act of Jewish heroism. Indeed in many ways the
Jews tested in 1096 exceeded the mettle of Abraham. Abraham was only asked to sacrifice one son and that son
was ultimately spared. The Rhineland Jews were called
upon to sacrifice many sons and daughters and in actuality
did so.

> At such reports the ears of those who hear surely
> tingle. For who has heard the like? Who has ever wit-
> nessed such events? Ask and see. Were there ever so
> many sacrifices like these from the days of Adam?
> Were there ever a thousand one hundred sacrifices on
> one day, all of them like the sacrifice of Isaac the son
> of Abraham?[67]

The Jews of the Rhineland were chosen for the test because
of their unique qualities; their response to the divine
challenge accords them, in the eyes of their chroniclers,
an unparalleled place in the annals of human history.[68]
The crusading armies, for all their size and splendor, are
ultimately of merely terrestrial significance; the battles
they won or lost would be forgotten. The martyrdom of
the Rhineland Jewish communities stood, for the Jewish
chroniclers, on a different plane. It constituted one of a
select few significant encounters between man and God.
God had chosen this special generation of Jews, subjected
them to an excruciating test, and found them unfailingly
loyal.

Indeed so important were the actions of these Jewish
martyrs that the chroniclers see cosmic import in the
events. Thus L continues the above-cited passage in the
following fashion:

> For one [such act of self-sacrifice] the world shook,
> when he was offered up on Mount Moriah, as is said:
> "Hark! The angels cried aloud!" The heavens dark-
> ened. What has been done [this time]? Why did the
> heavens not darken? Why did the stars not with-
> draw their brightness? . . . and light—why did they

not darken in their cloud cover, when one thousand one hundred holy souls were killed and slaughtered on one day, on the third day of Sivan, a Tuesday.[69]

The acts of martyrdom in 1096 were seen as unique in human history and took on cosmic significance to those who wrestled with the implications of the tragedy in the following generation.

One advantage of the view that the persecutions had been a divinely ordained test was that such a view is consistent with the very positive self-image of Rhineland Jewry both before and after the assaults. A second advantage was that this perspective provided an optimistic sense of the inevitable aftermath to these painful events. When Abraham demonstrated absolute willingness to heed the divine call, God's message had been unequivocal: "Because you have done this and have not withheld your son, your favored one, I will bestow my blessings upon you and make your descendants as numerous as the stars of heaven and the sands on the seashore; and your descendants shall capture the gates of their enemies. All the nations of the earth shall bless themselves by your descendants, because you have obeyed my command."[70] For actions that had exceeded the heroism of Abraham and Isaac surely God would and could do no less. Thus emphasizing a divine test successfully met bears a positive message of divine redemption. This is the message of consolation and hope offered by the Jewish chroniclers: the losses had been grievous and painful; the heroism and commitment had been awesome; the divine reward would be inevitable. The chroniclers make supplications for divine reward and express their conviction that it would be forthcoming. The sense of divine response to the remarkable faithfulness of the martyrs involves two distinct elements: retribution against those who had perpetrated the violence and reward for those who had suffered it.

Seek of them the blood of your servants that has been given upon a bare rock. "Land—cover not their blood, and let there not be a place for our cries." May he give us our vengeance in our hands. "Before our eyes let it be known among the nations that you avenge the spilled blood of your servants" speedily, for your great Name by which we are called. Let all creatures know and understand their sin and their guilt for what they did to us. Requite their deeds upon them as they did to us. Then shall they know and understand and take to heart that for vanity they have thrown down our corpses to the ground and for foolishness they have killed our pious and for a foul corpse they have spilled the blood of saintly women and for the words of an enticer and beguiler they have spilled the blood of infants and sucklings. It is vanity—they do [not] recognize the [God] who created them and do not go on a good and straight path. They have not understood or taken to heart who made the sea and the land. In all their actions they have been foolish; they have lost their wisdom. [In vanity] they have placed their trust. They have not recognized or recollected the Name of the living God, who is the King of the universe and who is everlasting. May the blood of his pious ones serve for us as merit and atonement for succeeding generations and for all our descendants forever, like the binding of our ancestor Isaac, when our ancestor Abraham bound him on the altar. . . . May their virtue and their saintliness and their piety and their purity and their sacrifice serve us as an intercessor and as an advocate before the Almighty. May he deliver us from this exile under wicked Edom speedily in our days. May our true messiah arrive. Amen—speedily in our days.[71]

The heroism of the Jewish martyrs is seen as leading ineluctably to punishment of the erring Christians and to salvation for the faithful Jews. The chronicles are meant to bring this message to their Jewish readers, and at the same time to intone such a supplication before their divine audience.

Thus the problems posed by the persecution of 1096 were keenly felt, but the theological stance adopted was overwhelmingly affirmative. The disaster of 1096 reflected negatively upon neither God nor Israel. It was not a sign of divine weakness or of divine abandonment of the Jews. It was not even an indication of God's chastisement. It was rather a heavenly test imposed upon a generation uniquely fit for such testing. Thus, in a complex way, the disaster itself became a source of comfort and hope. The heroic Jewish response infused the losses with meaning and afforded the promise of better times to come. The painful depictions of martyrdom represent paradoxically a form of consolation: the pain is presented as theologically meaningful and as constituting a prelude to redemption.

Indeed the challenge to post-1096 Jewry went beyond the immediate events that occurred in the Rhineland. During the summer of 1099, the crusading armies took Jerusalem, eliciting a wave of euphoria in western Christendom. The Christian crusade chronicles, as we have already seen, reveal a sense of the unique relationship of God's people—Christendom—and God himself. The picture given in the text by Fulcher of Chartres, showing Christian warriors valiantly sacrificing themselves for their deity and a deity who in turn performed signs and wonders on their behalf, presented the Jews of western Christendom—from which the expedition had set forth and to which the joyous tidings were brought—with additional religious problems and issues.

The response of the Jewish chroniclers was to present their own historical depiction of the turbulent crusading period. Many of the characteristics claimed by the Christian chroniclers for their warrior-heroes are appropriated in the Hebrew narratives for the Jewish warrior-heroes. These Jewish heroes distinguish themselves by the depth of their commitment; they have earned the martyr's crown; they are God's elect, the true spiritual heir to biblical Israel. To be sure, God had not yet rewarded them with an earthly victory; but that he will ultimately do so is confidently assumed.

Thus, in this special kind of historical saga, apparent defeat is turned into ultimate victory, while the apparent victory of the Christian armies is stripped of all meaning. This is epic history with a profoundly important theological message for Ashkenazic Jewry, which had to wrestle with both its own losses and the stunning victory achieved by its antagonists.

VI

The Church, The Jews, And The Later Crusades

THE ASSERTION OF EFFECTIVE CONTROL OVER CRUSADING

The events of 1096 were injurious first and foremost to the Jewish victims, and I have examined Jewish responses during and after the calamity. The same events were problematic also—albeit in a different way—to the Church. It was the ecclesiastical leadership after all that had initiated the crusade and had attempted to direct it; it was therefore the Church that had to assume the burden of guilt for a variety of evils that had manifested themselves during the course of the enterprise. These included the murderous assaults on Rhineland Jewry and the deviant thinking on which these attacks were predicated. There is no evidence available of immediate ecclesiastical efforts to redress the ills inflicted upon the Rhineland Jews. Considerable information, however, is available regarding successful strategies to prevent further violence during the subsequent crusades initiated and directed by the Church leadership.[1]

The announcement of new crusades regularly risked stimulating anti-Jewish animus. Our major Jewish source for the Second Crusade, the chronicle of Rabbi Ephraim of Bonn, indicates that, almost immediately after the call to the new crusade, anti-Jewish preaching was initiated by the monk Ralph. The anti-Jewish themes invoked by Ralph precisely parallel those noted for the First Crusade.

169

Ephraim reports him as preaching the following message: "Avenge the Crucified upon his enemies who dwell among you, and subsequently you shall go forth to battle against the Muslims."[2] Embodied in this report are the two key motifs of the earlier anti-Jewish hostility: alleged Jewish enmity toward Christians and Christianity and the resultant need to take vengeance upon the Jews, with an emphasis on the latter. Otto of Freising in his account emphasizes the former: "He [Ralph] heedlessly included in his preaching that the Jews living scattered about in the cities and towns should be slain as foes of the Christian religion."[3] In my analysis of the anti-Jewish persecution associated with the First Crusade, I suggested that, particularly in the area of Germany, the anti-Jewish preaching may have fallen on the fertile soil of social tensions between the burgher class and the Jews, whom the former perceived as both economic competitors and political allies of the overlords. Otto lends some additional support to this suggestion by describing Ralph as an agitator "who through the issue of the Jews was stirring repeated outbreaks of the people against their lords."[4]

Yet more striking is the valuable firsthand testimony of Rabbi Elazar ben Judah of Worms, who depicts the simultaneous emergence of reports of crusader losses in the East in late 1187, preparations for new crusading efforts, and anti-Jewish incitement. Rabbi Elazar shows us a Jewish community caught between pleasure at the catastrophe suffered by the hated crusaders and anxiety over the likelihood that anti-Jewish eruptions would ensue.

> While we were still involved in this incident, the entire world saw a sign in the sun. In 4947 [1187], on the eve of Rosh Hashanah, in the morning, we saw that the sun was as small as a half moon and was very dark. Afterwards the sun reddened, and the earth looked entirely green. At the end of a third part of the day, the sun was restored. After Sukkot and prior to Hanukah, we heard that the Muslims had gone out and conquered Acre, had killed all the inhabitants of

Acre, and had captured all the environs of Jerusalem—from Acre and Ekron to Jerusalem. On the eve of Rosh Hashanah, on the day when the sun was eclipsed, the Muslims had killed more than four thousand Frankish knights. They had also captured a relic upon which Jesus—may his bones be ground up—was crucified and brought it with them to their land. After Hanukah they captured the sepulcher and killed all the inhabitants of Jerusalem. They took out the tomb of the Crucified and destroyed the inside of the sepulcher. Afterwards the news reached all areas of Germany, and the Christians said to all the Jews: "Behold! The day which we have demanded has come—the day on which to kill all the Jews." This happened during the days of Lent. When we heard, a very great trembling seized us, and we took up the acts of our forefathers, decreeing fasting, weeping, and mourning.[5]

Despite the immediate outbreak of anti-Jewish sentiment and the obvious potential for large-scale anti-Jewish attacks, the major crusades of the twelfth century in fact saw very little serious persecution of European Jewry. Our key source that reports the fate of the Jews during the Second Crusade, the Hebrew chronicle of Rabbi Ephraim of Bonn, written for the express purpose of depicting Jewish suffering and martyrdom, does not present evidence that Jews lost their lives in significant numbers. We find Rabbi Ephraim indicating three costly disasters associated with the Second Crusade—the incidents at הם, סולי, and קרנטון.[6] The locales referred to are not clear, giving rise to a good deal of modern scholarly speculation. Ephaim's account of these incidents is sandwiched between his reports of a series of occurrences in Germany and his observations on events in France. These incidents may thus belong to the end of the German section or the beginning of the French section of his narrative.

More striking yet is the lack of detailed information on these incidents in Ephraim's account. He does offer substantial detail on attacks that claimed no Jewish lives, but he is apparently ignorant of the specifics of these serious outbreaks. He does know that the outburst at הם claimed approximately one hundred and fifty Jewish lives, but can only indicate that at סולי "many were killed" and at קרנטן "innumerable were killed." Dates are unknown, and the only specific actions reported are the heroic efforts at self-defense by two brothers at קרנטן. The lack of detail is curious, to say the least. The only major incident Ephraim described in detail, which took place at Wurzburg and cost the lives of twenty-two Jews, is reminiscent of the initial assault on Worms Jewry in 1096. An accusation of murder was raised against the Jews, moving the crusaders and the populace to attack Wurzburg Jewry. The bulk of these Jews were spared. They initially fled to sympathetic neighbors and then left the city for a fortified refuge, as most other communities in Germany had already done.[7]

The remaining incidents depicted by Ephraim of Bonn all involve isolated attacks on individual Jews. According to the categories I established for the First Crusade assaults, I thus conclude that, with the possible exception of the poorly reported incidents at הם, סולי, and קרנטן, there is no evidence for assaults perpetrated by roving crusader bands or for attacks planned and organized by large numbers of crusaders in a given town—the most devastating patterns of violence seen during the First Crusade. There is evidence for a spontaneous crusader-burgher outburst, occasioned by the murder accusation in Wurzburg. The bulk of the incidents reported involve incidental violence by crusaders or, in several instances, by burghers. Again it must be emphasized that Ephraim is quite interested in transmitting evidence of Jewish suffering and Jewish heroism. The paucity of information in his account must reflect a clear improvement in conditions for the Jews during the Second Crusade.

The Third Crusade shows essentially the same pattern. There was a potential for serious anti-Jewish violence but very little actually occurred. Effective preparedness on the part of German Jews and their overlord averted any damaging incidents in the Empire. Only in England were a few Jewish communities caught unawares, and casualties resulted. The level of violence, though lamentable, does not approach that of 1096

Surely the most significant factor in this improvement in the fate of the Jews during the great crusades of the twelfth century was the preparedness on the part of the sponsoring authority, the Church, and its determination to control these crusades more effectively than it had the first. As it did in many spheres of life during the twelfth and thirteenth centuries, the increasingly centralized and well-organized Roman Catholic Church strove to define and control crusading. This intention was proclaimed clearly and decisively during the Second Crusade, which was organized and directed by Pope Eugenius III and Saint Bernard of Clairvaux, the dominant spiritual figure of the period. For the duration of active crusading, the Church never relaxed its efforts at defining, initiating, and controlling the enterprise.

Because the institutionalization of crusading centered on the Second Crusade, it warrants detailed study. Fortunately there exists a series of valuable sources that illuminate Church efforts at stamping out anti-Jewish excesses like those that had been manifested during 1096. In fact the non-Jewish sources for Jewish fate during the Second Crusade are much better than those for the First Crusade. There is, first of all, the documentary evidence provided by the letters of Saint Bernard of Clairvaux. These include both a series of general letters of exhortation, which contain important passages concerning the Jews,[8] and a specific letter to the archbishop of Mainz concerning the dangerous preaching of the monk Ralph.[9] The chronicle of Odo of Deuil, which focuses on the army of Louis VII of France, says nothing of the anti-Jewish hostility evoked by the crusade, but in Otto of Freising's biography of Emperor Frederick I, the section devoted to the Second Crusade includes a useful passage on the anti-Jewish preaching of Ralph and the vigorous counterefforts of Bernard of Clairvaux.[10] The evidence from these Christian sources is nicely corroborated by the Hebrew chronicle of Rabbi Ephraim of Bonn. Ephraim's account shows broad familiarity with developments during the 1140s and indicates that the Jews were fully aware of the protracted efforts on the part of Church leadership to maintain effective control of the new crusade and to obviate any anti-Jewish outbursts.[11]

It is valuable, before undertaking to analyze Church activity on the Jewish issue, to establish a brief chronological framework of developments in western Europe. The call to the new crusade was issued by Pope Eugenius III in December 1145, although it had no immediate results. The Second Crusade really began at Vezelay on Easter Sunday 1146. There Saint Bernard first made his mark, arousing important French barons to follow the lead of King Louis VII. From Vézelay, Bernard embarked on a preaching campaign that took him north into areas of Flanders and Lorraine. In addition to his own preaching, Bernard delegated others to do likewise and also sent off a series of letters soliciting participation in the crusade. These letters were so widely circulated that they have been designated by Jean Leclerq, their great modern student, an encyclical. In his exhaustive textual and historical studies on these letters, Leclerq notes three essential versions, which he identifies as the short continental version (CB), the English version (A), the long continental version (CL). The overwhelming number of extant manuscripts fall into the latter two categories and include Saint Bernard's exhortation against harming the Jews.[12] Clearly the potential for anti-Jewish hostility developed quickly and widely.

The major identifiable figure in the anti-Jewish preaching, the monk Ralph, reached Cologne in August of 1146 and began to incite violence in the Rhineland cities where the worst excesses had taken place in 1096. This elicited from Bernard a general letter of exhortation and warning meant to obviate the danger, along with a specific reply to the missive of the archbishop of Mainz. By late 1146 Bernard went to the Rhineland area, in part to stem the preaching of the monk Ralph. While in the Rhineland he also persuaded Conrad to join the crusade. The two great crusading armies organized themselves during the spring of 1147, with the German troops departing eastward in May of 1147 and the French troops approximately a month later. Ephraim of Bonn reflects this departure when he notes that, by mid-July 1147, the situation had quieted to the point where the Jews felt safe in leaving their refuges to return home.[13]

Anti-Jewish animus, whether spontaneous or the result of specifically anti-Jewish preaching seems to have developed very quickly during the spring months of 1146. Bernard therefore included a statement condemning such tendencies in the general exhortation he issued[14] and in letters addressed directly to some of the affected cities.[15] These efforts are clearly reflected in the account of Otto of Freising as well.[16] The relevant passage in Bernard's letters reads as follows:

> Moreover, I warn you, brethren—indeed not only I but the apostle of God along with me—, not to believe every spirit. We have heard with great joy that the zeal of God burns in you. But it is necessary in all things that the restraint of knowledge not be absent. The Jews are not to be persecuted, killed, or even put to flight. Ask those who knows the Sacred Scriptures what prophecy is found in the psalm concerning the Jews. "God," says the Church, "will show me victory over my foes. Do not kill them, lest my people be unmindful."[17] They [the Jews] are for us living words, for they remind us always of the divine passion. They are dispersed into all areas so that, while they suffer the appropriate punishment for such a crime, they are everywhere the witnesses of our redemption. Hence the Church adds in the same psalm: "With your power make wanderers of them; bring them low, O our shield, the Lord."[18] And so it happened. They have been dispersed and brought low. Under Christian princes they endure a hard captivity. However, "they

will return towards evening"[19] and in time there will be a reconsideration of their part. Then, when the time is ripe, all Israel shall be saved, says the Apostle. But those who die before will remain in death. . . ."[20] If the Jews are utterly wiped out, what will become of the hope for their promised salvation, their eventual conversion? If the pagans were similarly subjugated to us, then, in my opinion, we should wait for them rather than seek them out with swords. But as they have now begun to attack us, it is necessary for those of us who carry a sword purposefully to repel them with force. It is an act of Christian piety both "to vanquish the proud" and also "to spare the subjected," especially those from whom we have a law and a promise, from whom we have our forefathers, and from whom we have Christ of the flesh, whose name be forever blessed above all.[21]

This statement shows the nature of Bernard's stand against anti-Jewish violence and deserves careful analysis. There are two foundations to Bernard's call for Jewish security: biblical authority and human reason. Biblical verses indicate two grounds upon which anti-Jewish violence is condemned. In the first place, the oft-cited verses from Psalms indicate the Jewish role as witnesses to the truth of Christianity. These verses note explicitly that the enemy is not to be killed but is to serve as testimony by virtue of its degradation. Likewise there is scriptural basis for eventual conversion and salvation of the Jews. This can obviously not take place, however, if the Jews are wiped out. In both these senses then, divine revelation requires the ongoing existence of the Jews. To this Bernard adds the argument that reason is a better weapon for dealing with the nonbeliever than force. Indeed, had the Muslims not allegedly set into motion the cycle of violence, they too could best be met with kindness. The Jews, who posed no physical threat to Christianity, should receive the traditional and sensible treatment of nonviolence. Indeed the

Jews have special claims to such treatment: from their ancestors came the laws and promises of the Old Testament period; from them came the early Christian community; indeed from them, in a physical sense, came Jesus himself. This last argument is quite positive: under normal circumstances all non-Christians should be treated with restraint, the Jews most of all. The earlier two arguments, while concluding that Jews should not be attacked, hardly enhance the prestige of the Jews. In fact both are demeaning, the first by emphasizing the significance of Jewish dispersion and degradation and the second by focusing on the point at which the Jews will cease to be Jews. Despite the negative aspects of some of his arguments, Bernard's rejection of anti-Jewish agitation and violence is unequivocal and resolute.[22]

Beyond these general exhortations, evidence is extant of direct communication between at least one of the prelates in the affected area and Saint Bernard. In reply to a letter from the archbishop of Mainz, complaining specifically of the preaching of the monk Ralph, Bernard excoriated the errant monk.[23] This letter involves somewhat different issues than the general letters. In this case, Bernard clearly addresses himself to a specific complaint. There was more at stake here than simply the issue of the Jews. Bernard found three things reprehensible in the preaching of Ralph, and two of them involve general ecclesiastical discipline. When he addresses himself to the issue of the Jews, Bernard uses essentially his third argument—the preference for reason over violence—and his second—the prediction that the Jews would eventually be converted, which would be impossible if they were wiped out. The broad stance here is more positive than that expressed in the general letters.

Written messages clearly were not sufficient to silence the monk Ralph, and Bernard set out for the Rhineland area. According to Otto of Freising, he did so "both that he might by the word of sacred exhortation stir the heart of the prince of the Romans to accept the cross and that he might silence Ralph."[24] According to Otto, Bernard confronted Ralph directly, finally silencing him by invoking monastic discipline.

The Hebrew report of Ephraim of Bonn gives a somewhat different version, emphasizing Bernard's counter-preaching:

> Then the Lord heard our cries, turning to us and having pity upon us in the fullness of his mercy and kindness. He sent after this wicked one [Ralph] a great and proper priest, head of all the priests, wise and understanding in their faith. His name was Bernard, the abbot of Clairvaux, the city in France, He likewise preached, as is their custom. Thus he said to them: "It is fitting that you go forth against the Muslims. But anyone who harms a Jew to kill him is the same as one who harms Jesus himself. Ralph my disciple who urged you to destroy the Jews spoke improperly. For concerning the Jews, it is written in the book of Psalms: 'Do not kill them lest my people be unmindful.'"[25]

In all probability both Otto and Ephraim are correct. That is to say, Bernard in all probability silenced Ralph directly and, at the same time, preached publicly against anti-Jewish violence.

Thus the Second Crusade reveals that the Roman Catholic Church was resolutely committed to closer control of crusading ideology and practice. The Jewish issue serves as a useful gauge of Church resolve. Anti-Jewish agitation along the same lines as the 1090s was met with clear theoretical rejection and strong action. The radical ideology that had developed during the First Crusade was countered by the traditional position that the Jews had the right to exist in preredemptive Christendom, a right grounded in both Scriptures and reason. In fact, Jewish existence was more than a right; it was a prerequisite for the onset of the Christian drama of redemption. There is in all this no theological innovation; this is simply established Church doctrine. What is striking is the readiness of the Church leadership to invoke this traditional argumentation and its firm resolution to exert control over the vast crusading enterprise. This determination characterizes the stance that the Church leadership would maintain during the subsequent crusades. It is surely a major factor in the relatively low level of anti-Jewish violence during the organized crusades of the twelfth and thirteenth centuries. To be sure, crusading always bore the potential for evoking anti-Jewish hostility, and where crusading efforts were popular and escaped ecclesiastical control, there were outbursts of violence against Jews.[26] Nonetheless, in the enterprises directed by the Church itself, the Church asserted effective control and suppressed the anti-Jewish violence that had marked the First Crusade.

RELATED ECONOMIC ISSUES

While the Church was both zealous and effective in affording the Jews physical safety during the subsequent organized crusades, there were economic issues related to crusading which called forth ecclesiastical involvement and the imposition of limitations upon the Jews. An important general issue in crusading involved the rights and privileges of the warriors who had committed themselves to the sacred mission.[27] From the outset of the First Crusade, though the need for certain basic protections for those taking on the rigors of crusading was recognized, the First Crusade itself produced no clear delineation of these protections. The first important papal bull on this topic was Pope Eugenius III's *Quantum praedecessores,* which inaugurated the Second Crusade. This key pronouncement promulgated basic safeguards for the property of those taking the cross.

> We decree that their wives and their sons, their goods also and their possessions, shall remain under the protection of the Holy Church and under our own protection and that of the archbishops, bishops, and other

prelates of the Church of God. Moreover we forbid, by apostolic authority, that any legal procedure be set in motion touching any property within their peaceful possession at the time when they accepted the cross, until there is sure knowledge concerning their return or their decease.[28]

Later in this important bull a clause concerning usury is added:

Moreover, all they that are burdened by debt and have, with pure heart, undertaken so holy a journey need not pay the interest past due, and, if they themselves or others for them have been bound by oath and pledge, by reason of such interest, by apostolic authority we absolve them.

This important clause is extremely vague. It would seem that the papal intention was to lighten the burden of debt carried by crusaders. Interest owed seems to have been remitted. There is no hint of any restitution of usury already exacted or of any provisions for repaying the sums owed. Most significant for our purposes is the lack of any specific reference to the Jews. Be that as it may, the inclusion of a clause protecting the crusader in debt was likely to have a significant impact on Europe's Jews, as they began to involve themselves increasingly in moneylending.

Many of the crusade-related twelfth-century bulls repeat the provision of *Quantum praedecessores* with regard to usury; none singles out the Jews. The bull *Audita tremendi*, occasioned by the terrible news from the East, alters the earlier language slightly, but seems to intend the same remission of interest.[29] As in so many other areas, the pontificate of Pope Innocent III introduced new clarity and new stances in the papal position on crusader debts. Early in his reign the new pope issued a call for renewal of crusading. This call included the following statement on debts.

Moreover, we take under the protection of St. Peter and of ourselves, as well as of the archbishops and all the prelates of the Church of God, the property of these men from the moment they take the cross. We decree that their property shall remain untouched and undisturbed until the death or the return be known with certainty. But if anyone dare to act in contrary fashion, he shall be restrained through ecclesiastical censure without appeal.

If any of those about to depart be held bound by an oath to pay usury, you, brother archbishops and bishops, shall force their creditors in your dioceses, by means of the same measure with no obstacle of appeal, completely to absolve the crusaders from their oath and to desist from any further exaction of usury. But if any of the creditors should compel them to pay usury, you shall, by similar punishment without appeal, force him to return it. We order that the Jews shall be forced by you, my sons and princes, and by the secular powers to remit the usury to them; and, until they remit it, we order that all contact with faithful Christians, whether in commerce or other ways, shall be denied the Jews by means of a sentence of excommunication.[30]

Innocent III repeats here the earlier papal call for remission of usury. What is new is that the Jews are specifically singled out, and that the enforcement techniques for securing compliance with the papal demands are indicated. In regard to the Jews two methods of enforcement are specified: the backing of the Jews' overlords and, failing that, pressure on the Jews by isolating them from the Christian populace. The second technique was extremely difficult to implement. A boycott of the Jews would be difficult to organize and enforce. That the activist Innocent III was unwilling to specify papal demands without defining procedures for enforcement, however cumbersome these might have been, indicates his determination.

Pope Innocent III hardened his demands on usury

owed to the Jews by crusaders twice during his pontificate. In October of 1208 he addressed King Philip Augustus of France, insisting not only upon remission of usury owed to Jews but also upon postponement of payment of the principal as well.[31] The fullest and most extreme stipulations concerning usury owed to Jews were enunciated during the Fourth Lateran Council of 1215.[32] This important edict involved three demands: (1) remission of usury; (2) moratorium on collection of the principal; (3) reckoning of the income derived from the gage into the amount ultimately to be repaid. All this represents an effort to afford extensive protection to the crusaders by infringing heavily on the interests of the creditor class. It is not surprising that the position elaborated during the Fourth Lateran Council became the Church's normative stance in the thirteenth century. The demand for remission of usury and for a moratorium on the repayment of the debt was sounded repeatedly during the rest of the thirteenth century.[33]

I have focused thus far on ecclesiastical policy. However, even the Church's own documents indicate that the key to fulfilling Church demands was the cooperation of the political authorities to whom the Jews were subservient. Rabbi Ephraim of Bonn records a striking report of secular compliance with papal demands by the most important political figure associated with the Second Crusade, King Louis VII of France. After detailing isolated attacks against French Jewry, Ephraim adds:

> In the rest of the communities of France we have not heard of anyone killed or forcibly converted. But the Jews did lose a great deal of their wealth. For the king of France commanded: "Anyone who has volunteered to journey to Jerusalem shall have his debt forgiven, if he is obligated to the Jews." Since most of the debts of the Jews of France are by charter, they therefore lost their money.[34]

Ephraim's statement, which reveals inter alia the widespread use of sophisticated lending techniques in France, depicts a royal stance that went much farther than the papal position on the subject. While Pope Eugenius III had ordered remission of usury owed to the creditor, the king enforced a total remission of debts. The difference, to both creditor and debtor, is enormous. To be sure, Ephraim also leaves the impression that the French monarch had singled out the Jews as objects of this radical legislation. In this sense, the royal move goes beyond protection of the crusader in the direction of financing the crusade and recruiting for it. In any case, there is no other evidence that supports Ephraim's account of this radical action by Louis VII.

More extensive and more trustworthy evidence for royal policy on debts owed the Jews by crusaders is afforded by Rigord's report of the elaborate arrangements made by King Philip Augustus before his departure on the Third Crusade. Unlike his father, the young monarch was far from supportive of the Church's demands.

> With the advice of the archbishops and barons of his lands, the lord Philip, king of the French, decrees that the bishops and prelates and the clergy of the assembled churches and the soldiers who have taken the cross shall be granted alleviation in the repayment of debts which they owed either to Jews or Christians before the king took the cross. [This is to extend] from the next All Saint's Day after the departure of the lord king for two years. Thus, the creditors shall have one third of the debt on the next All Saints' Day, and another third of the debt on All Saints' Day following, and the last third of the debt on the third All Saints' Day. Moreover, interest shall not accrue upon any of the debts previously contracted from the day upon which the debtor took the cross.[35]

This set of procedures is far more explicit than that outlined in the earlier papal missives. It mentions the Jews specifically—an indication in all probability of the increasingly important role which they were playing in moneylending. Close scrutiny of these provisions reveals that they actually offered far less benefit for crusaders in debt than did the broad papal stipulations. There is no forgiving of interest, merely a suspension of interest from the point when the individual joined the crusade. While helpful and protective of crusader interests, these measures fall far short of what the popes had called for. As noted before, the vague papal edicts had made no specifications concerning repayment of debts. The elaborate arrangements established by Philip Augustus very much favor the creditor. With the suspension of interest, the loan becomes profitless for the lender; indeed it becomes burdensome, tying up needed capital. The royal provision for repayment thus worked largely for the benefit of the creditor. The royal pronouncement then is clearly a compromise. It represents an effort to aid the crusader by suspending interest and by allowing an extended period for repayment of loans. At the same time there is protection for the creditor as well. Viewed against the backdrop of earlier papal legislation, the Jewish lenders can only have applauded the amelioration in the royal pronouncement.

Pope Innocent III was unswayed by the stance taken by King Philip Augustus. He repeated the traditional papal position early in his reign, in 1198, adding provisions for enforcement. King Philip Augustus, however, was equally determined. In his first major legislation concerning moneylending by Jews, enacted in 1206 in concert with Blanche of Champagne and Guy of Dampierre, the king addressed in a minor clause the issue of debts owed by crusaders, indicating that they were to run at the legally permitted rate of two pennies per pound per week.[36] This afforded the crusaders only minimal protection, saving them from the burden of compounded interest. Clearly this is a retreat from the earlier position of Philip Augustus, in which he had ordered all usury to cease upon the taking of the cross. The edict of 1206 is even farther from the demands of the Church.

The distance between the positions of Innocent III and Philip Augustus caused a series of minor skirmishes during the early years of the thirteenth century. In an interesting letter, the duke of Burgundy objected to ecclesiastical pressures related to crusaders and urged Philip Augustus to stand firmly against them.[37] A number of documents indicate friction over the specific issue of crusader debts between the countess of Champagne and the chief prelates of her domain. One papal letter focuses entirely on the matter of debts owed by crusaders to Jews.

> Our dear daughter in Christ, the noblewoman Blanche, countess of Champagne, proved to us that, while it was specifically decreed in the General Council that Jews should be compelled by secular lords to remit usury to crusaders, nevertheless, certain archbishops and other prelates of the Church, usurping undue jurisdiction over the Jews in the lands of the said countess, by new devices and under pretext of ecclesiastical freedom, not content with the decrees promulgated by this council, greatly harass and disturb the land of this countess and her Jews, in contravention of the decrees of the council mentioned above. Wishing, therefore, to preserve the complete rights of this countess, we, through apostolic letters, order you that by our authority you shall expressly prohibit these archbishops and other prelates from exceeding the regulation of the said council with regard to the above-named matters. If any should disobey, you shall restore to its proper status whatever you find to have been done in these matters contrary to the regulation of the said council. If there are any opponents or rebels, after giving them warning, you will restrain them by whatever punishment is proper, without appeal.[38]

It would of course be interesting to know what additional demands were imposed by the prelates of Champagne. In any case, the pope, in this letter, sided with the secular authorities in limiting unwarranted restrictions. An earlier letter concerning the general friction between Blanche of Champagne and the prelates of her domain mentions again the issue of debts owed by crusaders. This letter notes the accusation that these prelates "refuse to permit her the very same privileges with regard to crusaders and the Jews who live in the territory of this countess which they permitted to Philip, king of the French, with regard to the Jews who live in his domain."[39] This may be simply the same general complaint against ecclesiastical excesses, or it may reflect some kind of compromise between Philip and the Church on this issue; the former is more likely.

In sum, the growing body of detailed legislation indicates that the Church was committed to maintaining control of the crusading enterprise. The effort to protect crusaders and to specify their prerogatives included provisions for safeguarding those who took the cross from the economic pressures flowing from debt. As time went on, these stipulations identified the Jews directly as an important group of creditors and attempted to extend the protections granted to the debtors. In this process, conflict was engendered with the baronial overlords of the Jews, who would be adversely affected by any serious decline in Jewish wealth. From the Jewish perspective, these issues were surely not a matter of life and death. Nonetheless, in certain periods, Jews with fortunes might have seen them significantly eroded through enforcement of papal decree or augmented by execution of baronial legislation. Such an impact was a secondary, but not insignificant, effect of the crusades for European Jewry.

The notion of crusader protection was clear and circumscribed. There was a looser, more general, and more dangerous ramification of the economic nexus between the Jews and the crusades: this involved the idea that the Jewish "enemy," although not to be attacked as part of crusading, should at least be made to defray some of the costs of the sacred struggle. Nowhere during the First Crusade was such a view articulated and defended, although we have seen a number of instances in which Jewish wealth was tapped for crusading purposes. Whether these instances reflect sheer extortion or an ideologically grounded appeal—or both—cannot be known.

An explicit statement of the view that Jewish goods should properly be used toward recovery of the Holy Land was articulated by Peter the Venerable, on the eve of the Second Crusade.[40] The notion of the Jews as the most virulent enemies of Christendom is carefully expressed in the first section of his epistle and then reinforced throughout. It was of course precisely this notion that served as the basis for the ideologically inspired assaults of 1096. To be sure, Peter the Venerable is too aware of cumulative Church tradition to push his premise to the radical conclusion of authorizing anti-Jewish violence. He makes it clear that Jews are not to be killed, but the reason for sparing the lives of Jews is more negative than any I presented here. It lies not in the sense that conversion must be voluntary, nor that the Jews must survive for eventual redemption, nor even in the notion that Jewish degradation serves as a useful indication of the truth of Christianity; in Peter's view the basis for nonviolence toward the Jews lies rather in the sense that they have been consigned to a fate worse than death, along the lines of the fratricide Cain. The Jews must be preserved because the degradation of their fate is in itself fitting punishment for the act of fratricide and deicide they committed.

At this point in his epistle the abbot of Cluny addresses the issue of the crusade. He suggests that a suitable part of the ongoing punishment deserved by the Jews would be to use their goods for the benefit of the forthcoming crusade. This suggestion seems to Peter doubly appropriate, first as part of the general pattern of punishment, and second as a justified reaction to the improper ways in which Jews were believed to have amassed their wealth.

No major echo of Peter's radical view can be discerned among documents from ecclesiastical circles. However Peter's call did possibly influence the recipient of his letter, King Louis VII of France. I have noted Ephraim of Bonn's statement that "the king of France commanded: 'Anyone who has volunteered to journey to Jerusalem shall have his debt forgiven, if he is obligated to the Jews.'"[41] I pointed out earlier that this report depicts the king as singling out the Jews and that in it he goes far beyond the papal demand for remission of interest. In fact, if Ephraim's account is accurate, the royal edict was much closer to the position of Peter the Venerable than to the demands of Pope Eugenius III. The king allegedly turned over to the crusaders the money that had been lent by the Jews and was in effect Jewish property. Again reservations concerning Ephraim's report are warranted. That Peter the Venerable's admonitions and this alleged royal action are possibly connected should not be ruled out.

Confiscations of Jewish goods accompanied several major thirteenth-century crusades, particularly those of Saint Louis. These confiscations, while tangentially related to crusading, do not reflect doctrinal stance such as that enunciated by Peter the Venerable. The confiscations of 1234, 1246–47, and 1268 all seem to involve efforts to exact retribution for usury by Jews, specifically to afford a large sum of money from which Christian lenders might regain sums that they had earlier paid out as usury.[42] Saint Louis's biographer, William of Chartres, describes the purpose of the confiscation during the 1240s in the following terms: "He caused the Jews and their goods to be taken, not indeed with the intention of retaining them, but rather so that the goods might be restored to those from whom the Jews had extorted them through usurious viciousness— when legitimate proofs had been given."[43] There is no mention here of crusading, and the only possible nexus is the heightened religious fervor associated with taking the cross. It is well known that part of Louis's preparation for his two crusading efforts involved spiritual cleansing of his realm, and the assault on Jewish usury was simply part of this effort. There is no evidence to support the thesis that what were thought of as ill-gotten Jewish gains should be appropriated for the crusade. To be sure, when efforts to identify those who had paid out the usury failed, the standard procedure was to use the remaining funds for what were designated as pious purposes. To the extent that these purposes involved crusading the connection was fortuitous. No case can be made for a priori intentions to fuel Louis's crusades with Jewish wealth.[44]

While Peter the Venerable's views were apparently not echoed in ecclesiastical circles or among secular political leaders, with the possible exception of King Louis VII of France, there were significant popular expressions of this attitude. These popular views are revealed in England, where Jewish moneylending was well developed, during the agitation engendered by the accession of Richard to the throne, which was followed almost immediately by his departure for the crusade. Our most important source for the anti-Jewish violence during this period, William of Newburgh, indicates clearly that crusading was but one factor among many in the anti-Jewish outbursts. Thus the assaults in London, Lynn, and Lincoln were said by William to stem from general tensions.[45] In connection with the violence at Stamford, William does specify that crusaders were involved.

> After these events, the fury of a new storm against the Jews developed at Stamford. At that place fairs were held during the solemnities of Lent. A multitude of young men from different areas, who had accepted the sign of the Lord and were about to set out for Jerusalem arrived there. They were indignant that the enemies of the cross of Christ who lived there should possess so much, while they themselves had so little for the expenses of so great a journey. They thought they would extort from the Jews, as unjust possessors, that which they could apply to the needs of the pilgrimage which they had undertaken. Thinking therefore that they would render service to Christ by attacking his enemies, whose goods they desired to possess, they violently attacked them. None of the inhabitants of the place or those who had come to the fairs opposed such efforts; some even cooperated with them. Several of the Jews were killed, and the rest, who escaped with

difficulty, were received within the castle. Their houses, however, were plundered, and a great quantity of money was seized. The plunderers left with the reward of their labor; and no one was questioned on account of this affair, out of a concern for public order.[46]

The views of these crusaders is quite close to the doctrine expoused by Peter the Venerable, although there is no evidence indicating a causal relationship.

The York massacre, described in detail and at length by William of Newburgh, reflected similar thinking. Once again William de-emphasizes the role of crusading but, among the crusaders, a doctrine of legitimate exploitation of the Jews was in fact expressed in practice:

Now the king, after the tumult at London, had enacted a law for the peace of the Jews and had acted in good faith towards the rest of the Jews throughout England, according to the ancient custom. Yet, when the king was afterwards resident in areas beyond the sea, many in the county of York took an oath together against the Jews, being unable to bear their opulence while they themselves were in want. Without any scruple of Christian conscience, they thirsted for their perfidious blood, aroused by desire of plunder. Those who urged them on to dare these measures were certain persons of higher rank, who were indebted for large sums to those impious usurers. Some of these, who had pledged their estates to them for sums received, were overwhelmed by great poverty. Others, who were obligated by their own bonds, were pressured by the tax-gatherers to satisfy the royal usurers. Some also of those who had accepted the sign of the Lord and were now in readiness to set out for Jerusalem could more easily be impelled to aid the expenses of a journey undertaken for the Lord out of the plunder of his enemies, because they had very little reason to fear that any question would arise on this account after they had begun their journey.[47]

It does seem that a notion of "legitimate" exploitation of the Jews did develop recurrently among certain crusading circles.

In sum, crusading had economic implications for European Jewry. Several interpretations of these implications are possible, but it can be stated with certainty that the papacy strove continually to carefully define its economic policies and to enforce them rigorously. The institutionalization of crusading ideals and behaviors I have outlined was clearly reinforced in the sphere of economic issues as well. Once again, there was occasional distortion of normative doctrine, which served to legitimate popular despoliation of the Jews.

VII

Glances Backward and Forward

REFLECTIONS OF THE LATE ELEVENTH CENTURY

The events of 1096, the developments that led up to them, and their aftermath provide a rare and valuable glimpse into a turbulent and creative epoch in the history of Europe and the Jews. Since sources for Jewish history during this important period are sparse, the preceding analyses provide significant insights.

For the general medievalist, the events of 1096 provide an additional and unusual perspective on the broad crusading experience. To be sure, sources for crusading history are copious, and modern researchers have intensively investigated most of the important aspects of the crusades. This analysis of Jewish fate does not break any new ground in understanding the First Crusade and its successors. Nonetheless, looking back over the results of this study, we find a series of useful corroborations for recent work in crusading historiography. Chief among these is the sense of the anarchic nature of the First Crusade and the potential for radical doctrinal distortion produced by the combination of extreme exhilaration and loss of central control. We have seen that the major attacks on the Jews of northern Europe were not the result of individual or group depravity or cupidity but reflect rather a radical and unwarranted extension of some of the underlying themes of the crusade. The central motifs of the crusade—holy war and pilgrimage—generated a powerful anti-Jewish animus in certain quarters that were far removed from the control and guidance of the initiators of the vast enterprise. Our understanding of the crusade has been enriched not only by an awareness of the anti-Jewish motifs but also by an investigation into what I have called the Jewish "countercrusade" mentality. In the behavior of the Jewish martyrs we have seen a mirror image of many of the themes of crusading martyrdom: the sense of cosmic confrontation, the conviction of the absolute validity of one's own religious heritage, the emphasis on profound self-sacrifice, the certainty of eternal reward for the commitment of the martyrs, the unshakable belief in the ultimate victory and vindication of one's own community and its religious vision. Finally, this study of the Jewish communities of northern Europe has shown the protracted efforts of the Church's leadership to reassert its control over the crusading enterprise. Anti-Jewish violence, which represented a major theoretical and practical distortion during the First Crusade, became an issue that the leaders of the Second Crusade sought seriously to define and control. With assistance from other elements in the European establishment and from the Jews themselves, the papacy was in fact quite successful in this effort, and nearly eliminated major anti-Jewish violence in the ensuing great crusades of the twelfth and thirteenth centuries.

The implications of this study for the history of early Ashkenazic Jewry are far wider and deeper. Perhaps most important is the extent of Jewish involvement in the life and culture of the general Christian society of the period. Here the findings of this study afford an important corrective to prior views of the relationship of early Ashkenazic Jewry to the non-Jewish world that surrounded it.

Both general medievalists and specialists in Jewish history have tended to see the nascent Jewish communities of northern Europe as highly segregated—at least socially and spiritually—from their Christian counterparts. General medievalists have, over the past century, depicted these Jews essentially as economic entrepreneurs or as victims of majority animosity and persecution. What they have not done, however, is to examine how the internal life of this nascent Jewry reflected the general spiritual and intellectual climate of the period. One striking index of this failure can be noted here. In 1977, on the fiftieth anniversary of the publication of Charles Homer Haskins's *The Renaissance of the Twelfth Century,* a conference was held in Cambridge, Massachusetts, under the joint sponsorship of the University of California, Los Angeles and Harvard University, in cooperation with the Mediaeval Academy of America. The conference and the ensuing volume, titled *Renaissance and Renewal in the Twelfth Century,* represent the fruit of half a century of enormous advances in the investigation of that crucial epoch.[1] Yet not a single paper or article was devoted to aspects of Jewish "renaissance and renewal" during this period; indeed the term "Jew" does not even appear in the index of the important volume generated by this great conference. It is as though these Jews did not exist on the cultural and spiritual plane.[2]

To be sure, the insularity is as strong or even stronger on the "Jewish" side. For example, the two most significant studies of eleventh- and twelfth-century rabbinic creativity, Abraham Grossman's *Ḥakhmei Ashkenaz ha-Rishonim* and E. E. Urbach's *Ba'alei ha-Tosafot,* both outstanding works of scholarship, treat this fecund cultural moment in utter isolation from the general intellectual trends of the period. This view of early Ashkenazic Jewry was best expressed by the late and great Jewish historian Yitzhak Baer. Baer, whose area of prime interest was medieval Spanish Jewry, often drew sharp contrasts between southern European Jewry, upon which his own work concentrated and which he found deeply immersed in and influenced by the larger world around it, and the Ashkenazic Jews of the north, who, he felt, drew more profoundly on the original wellsprings of Jewish tradition. Let us note one formulation of this point of view, in Baer's introduction to a major collection of northern European Hebrew chronicles and dirges:

> In contrast to the Jews of southern Europe and the lands of the East, who were influenced more than is

proper by the rationalist culture of Islam, the Ashkenazim seem to return to the sources of the life of the
nation, which had been opened during the days of the
Second Temple.[3]

While Baer's own view was in fact more complex than it
would seem from this,[4] this sense of Ashkenazic Jewry as
essentially isolated has long dominated modern Jewish
historical thinking. Close analysis of the events of 1096
leads us to a much firmer sense of the integration of early
Ashkenazic Jewry in its late eleventh- and early twelfth-
century milieu.

My analysis of the events of 1096 has revealed a set of
Jewish communities socially integrated into the environment around them. The Jews had, in many instances,
strong and positive ties to the political overlords of the
area and to their urban neighbors. Alongside acts of callousness and cruelty on the part of crusaders and burghers, we also find evidence of warmth and generosity on
the part of churchmen, statesmen, and some members of
the burgher class. Clearly, when many of the Jews, in the
earliest stages of the assaults, turned to their Christian
neighbors for assistance, they did so because they felt
certain that their neighbors had the desire and capacity to
provide the needed aid. All this suggests that these small
Jewish communities were enmeshed in the life of the society around them. In the wake of the catastrophe, some of
the survivors came to doubt whether their neighbors and
overlords had been sincere. Such questioning notwithstanding, it seems clear that the Jews originally believed
that they could count on the Christians to provide genuine
care and concern and that, after the crisis had passed, their
confidence in the protection extended by overlords and
neighbors reemerged anew.

The most striking index of this Jewish involvement in
the life of northern Europe comes not from the political
realm, but from the spiritual and intellectual. One of the
most interesting and important conclusions I reached in
this study concerns the extent to which the phenomenon

of Jewish martyrdom reflects much of the general atmosphere of the turbulent last decade of the eleventh century.
The themes of activist Jewish martyrdom which we have
encountered are remarkably parallel to the martyrological
emphases in crusading circles of the period. The behavior
of the besieged Jews, the spiritual ideals and motifs which
sustained and stimulated them, and the literary forms in
which their heroism was enshrined all reflect a deep Jewish
sharing in the intense zeitgeist of late eleventh-century
northern European civilization.

Indeed the events of 1096 reflect more than the immediate crusading milieu; equally apparent is the broader
set of developments often labeled "the twelfth-century renaissance." The behavior and attitudes of Jews during the
1096 crisis mirror many of the major characteristics of
this creative epoch in European history. In this sense, the
1096 period affords us valuable insight into the emergence
of a new style of Jewish life, that generally designated
"Ashkenazic." For if the term *Ashkenazic* be taken to mean
something more than simply a geographic locus or biological continuity, then the life-style that one associates with
it found important, early expression in the events of 1096.
Some of the same new energy and creativity that would
refashion European societies and push them to the fore-
front of Western civilization makes its appearance in the
Jewish communities of this dynamic era as well, and the
1096 episodes and their enshrinement in the Hebrew
chronicles afford us a striking glimpse of this emerging
Ashkenazic élan, and the style of life and culture associated with it.

In this sense the events of 1096 are—or should be—
once again of interest to the general medievalist. The
aspects of Jewish behavior and thinking revealed here
reinforce a series of recent conclusions regarding the central characteristics of the late eleventh- and early twelfth-
century "renaissance" or "renewal." Again my findings do
not really break new ground in explaining this creative
period; they do afford, however, a valuable additional
perspective from a minority community long neglected in

the study of this decisive epoch. The late eleventh and early twelfth century, a period of remarkable intensity and creativity, has left its mark both on subsequent European civilization and on the character of later Ashkenazic Jewry. Out of the turbulent creativity of the period emerged a series of striking characteristics that became the hallmarks of European society and of the Ashkenazic Jewish experience.

1096 AS A WATERSHED

It is appropriate at this juncture to widen our horizons and examine the place of 1096 in the broader context of the medieval Jewish experience. Most recent specialists in the history of the Jews concur that 1096 marks a dramatic and decisive watershed in medieval Jewish history. Prior to that date, according to the prevalent view, positive growth and development can be discerned; the violent attacks associated with the First Crusade ushered in a long and steady decline for medieval Jewry. Haim Hillel Ben-Sasson, for example, suggests that a new epoch in Jewish history

> begins with the First Crusade in 1096, the massacres perpetrated by the crusaders in the Rhine Valley and beyond and the readiness of Jews to incur martyrdom for the glory of God—events that had a major impact on Jewish history. The changes that followed in the twelfth century were considerable in many respects. The phenomenon of large-scale martyrdom and the mentality that it signified left their mark on the Ashkenazi Jews living in Europe north and east of the Alps and influenced the thinking of the Sephardi (Spanish) Jews. A far-reaching transformation also occurred in Jewish economic life, legal status, and sense of well-being among the Christian population of Europe.[5]

Ben-Zion Dinur, the mentor of Ben-Sasson and of a generation of Jewish historians, makes an even sharper formulation. In the introduction to the second volume of his monumental collection of documents illustrating diaspora Jewish history—a volume that covers the period from 1096 to 1348—Dinur identifies 1096 as a

> turning point for a new period in Jewish history. These persecutions shook the civil and legal framework and the social and cultural framework within which the Jews lived in those lands. They affected these Jews radically and for generations to come. The entire climate of the Jewish world changed fundamentally.
>
> The historical significance of these persecutions resulted from the combination of five essential characteristics that distinguished them from the harassment of the preceding generations. These five characteristics are: (1) the broad territorial scope of these persecutions; (2) the two fundamental elements in their development: the aggressive religious element and the social revolutionary element; (3) their cruel and murderous nature; (4) the martyrdom, sublime in its awesomeness, of entire communities; (5) the political authorities as the sole faction that protected the Jews and attempted to save them during the persecutions.[6]

Perhaps most striking is the way in which 1096 has been taken as a turning point in organizing twentieth-century analyses of medieval Jewish experience. Most comprehensive Jewish histories accord 1096 a major function in their periodization of the medieval Jewish experience,[7] and most studies of early medieval European Jewish history choose 1096 as a natural cut-off point.[8] 1096 is viewed as a major turning point for almost all important recent studies of medieval Jewish history.[9]

While the widespread notion of 1096 as a decisive turning point in European Jewish history has not in fact been carefully analyzed or argued, implicit in this view are at least three key assumptions: (1) There was significant change in the immediate wake of 1096. Jewish life in the twelfth century is supposed to differ substantially from pre-1096 Jewish existence. (2) It is agreed by all that the change was deleterious. 1096 ushered in a period of radical decline in major aspects of Jewish life. (3) The events of 1096 somehow or other "caused" the changes that can be discerned. The precise dimensions of the causative role of the events of 1096 are never fully spelled out. I would argue that such a view of 1096 as a turning point, first of all, is not supported by the data, and, second, reflects a seriously flawed understanding of the historical process.

What would have made the First Crusade the occasion of major change in European Jewish history? There are two possibilities: (1) A major shift occurred in the basic features of the larger environment in which the Jewish minority lived, resulting in fundamental change in the situation of the Jewish minority. Such broad change did take place, for example, in the Roman Empire during the third century, in the Muslim world during the twelfth and thirteenth centuries, and in western European society during the eighteenth century. In all these instances the Jewish minority was deeply affected. (2) An event or set of events occurred involving the Jews directly and of such magnitude that subsequent Jewish fate was altered. An example of such an event would be the expulsions of the 1490s from the Iberian Peninsula. While one might wish to argue that late fourteenth- and fifteenth-century Spanish history showed significant change, which had already begun to undermine Jewish life, the sudden expulsions constitute a clear and well-defined terminus to the history of still-vital Jewish communities.[10]

Obviously the first question to pose is whether to view 1096 as a point of major change in western Christendom at large. The answer is resoundingly negative. General histories of medieval Europe do not take 1096 as a point of reference in the periodization of the Middle Ages. They rarely attribute to the events of 1096 any major impact on the subsequent growth and development of medieval European society. For most present-day medievalists, the First Crusade reveals the essential dynamics of the new European civilization; it did not, however, significantly alter or shape the course of that civilization.[11] The call at Clermont galvanized a society that had experienced remarkable development during the preceding century and that, even before 1095, had shown signs of aggressive expansionism. After the 1090s these tendencies intensified. These efforts were least successful in the eastern Mediterranean, the conquest of which was of course the goal of the First Crusade. In practical terms the most that can be claimed for the First Crusade is that it served as a catalyst, intensifying political and economic tendencies already well under way. It was not the opening move in the papal strategy to assert greater authority in western Christendom, but it did speed up the efforts. It did not inaugurate Mediterranean trade, but it did intensify it. It is not valid to treat 1096 as a turning point in general medieval history which brought in its wake a decisive change in the situation of the Jewish minority.

It is of course still possible that the events associated with the First Crusade might have been drastic enough in impact to affect decisively the subsequent development of Jewish life. Was this in fact the case? My analysis has shown that the actual impact of crusader violence in 1096 was quite restricted. The medieval Hebrew chronicles were anxious to fuse all the incidents and thereby to enhance the broad sense of tragedy, while I have made an effort to analyze and differentiate, noting that total wholesale destruction was limited to the major Jewish centers of Worms, Mainz, and Cologne. As important as these centers were, the destruction was limited: there were the few instances of wholesale slaughter noted and a number of additional cases of incidental violence, while the vast majority of western European Jewish communities escaped damage. This limited physical loss, as lamentable as it might be, hardly constitutes the material basis for a major turning point in the condition of European Jews. The more wide-ranging disasters of 1348–49 and 1648–49 contrast sharply with the limited impact of the assaults of 1096.

It thus seems prima facie unlikely that 1096 would

signal the beginning of a new stage in the experience of medieval Jewry. Nonetheless, central aspects of subsequent European Jewish life must be examined.

First it is necessary to recall the major distinction between southern and northern European Jewish experience, that is, the distinction between Sephardic and Ashkenazic Jewries. As we have seen, the Iberian peninsula was hardly a central staging ground for the popular armies of the First Crusade and no significant reports of anti-Jewish violence emerged from the period. The critical juncture in the development of medieval Sephardic Jewry was the transfer of power on the Iberian Peninsula from Muslim to Christian hands. Thus, the Sephardic sphere needs no further consideration in this study. It was Ashkenazic Jewry that suffered during 1096 and it is in regard to Ashkenazic Jewry that claims concerning the impact of 1096 have been advanced. I shall attempt to briefly review Ashkenazic history[*] following the violence that overcame these Jewish settlements during the spring months of 1096. At the same time I will examine critically a number of aspects of Ashkenazic experience in the effort to determine whether sudden and deleterious change actually occurred.

It is quite clear that 1096 in no way marked the beginning of a period of rapid demographic decline for Ashkenazic Jewry. To the contrary, the demographic curve rose more steeply during the twelfth century. Though hard data are lacking, the conclusions of Salo Baron represent the consensus of students of the period.[12] The first and simplest is that 1096 represents no demographic watershed. The First Crusade was preceded and succeeded by periods of Jewish demographic growth, with the clear pattern of development only intensifying during the twelfth century. It has long been known that even the centers that experienced destruction—Worms, Mainz, and Cologne—were quickly rebuilt and repopulated, adding weight to the argument that vigorous Jewish population growth was taking place. Beyond this, Baron argues—and most other Jewish historians concur—that much of this population growth resulted from enhanced immigration from the other centers of Jewish settlement. This would imply that the economic and political realities can hardly have deteriorated in the wake of 1096. The decision of Jews to move into western Christendom surely implies that they perceived relative economic opportunity and relative political stability there. Finally, Baron argues that the First Crusade may well have intensified in certain ways the process of Jewish population growth through immigration. By accelerating the development—already under way—of travel and communication through the Mediterranean basin, the crusade, once more operating as a catalyst, enhanced the development of Jewish migration.

The economic sphere presents a very similar picture. It is widely agreed that the budding Jewish communities of western Christendom had developed economically as well as demographically during the eleventh century. Local trade in all likelihood formed the foundation of Jewish economic life, and primitive banking transactions flowed very naturally from business affairs. In both spheres Jews were useful to and supported by the progressive elements in the political hierarchies. Again 1096 represents nothing like a sharp turn. Neither the external circumstances nor internal realities in these communities changed sufficiently to represent a downward turn in Jewish economic affairs. To the contrary, the broad (though unprovable) consensus is that the Jews of northwestern Christendom simply flourished during the twelfth century. Moneylending increased, bringing in its wake a dramatic business boom, particularly for those Jews in the more westerly areas of England and France.[13] The crusades, to the extent that they had an impact, were primarily beneficial. As the most ambitious military efforts of the times, the crusades necessitated large sums of capital, affording an increasingly important role to those who made their livelihood from supplying capital. Again there seems to have been no dramatic turn for the worse; rather there is evidence for accelerated processes that entailed, among other things, enhanced opportunities for the Jews of north-western Christendom.

While few have argued that 1096 constituted a demo-graphic or economic watershed in the history of medieval European Jewry, it has often been suggested that the First Crusade did initiate a period of increasing insecurity for Europe's Jews. New slanders against the Jews circulated and reports indicate that Jews were killed at a growing rate. A stark contrast is occasionally drawn between the serene and secure years that preceded 1096 and the stormy ones that followed.

There are, however, many problems with this facile contrast. As indicated in chapter one, the eleventh century was far from serene for northern European Jewry. The violence endemic to northern-European society in general did not spare the Jews of that area. They were victims of the anarchic conditions of rapid expansion and growth in much the same way as were their Christian neighbors. It is highly likely that, as an exposed and vulnerable minority community, the Jews may well have suffered dispropor-tionately. In some instances we have noted specifically anti-Jewish outbreaks, predicated on perceptions of spe-cific problems and dangers associated with the Jews.

Conversely, 1096 did not usher in a period of unrelent-ing insecurity for Jewish life. When the violence of the spring months subsided, much of Jewish life returned to the status quo ante. As we have seen, the Second Crusade brought with it little actual violence against European Jewry. The slanders of the twelfth century occasioned anxiety and fear, but little bloodshed. Protracted and devastating violence did not occur until the end of the thirteenth century and the beginning of the fourteenth, under a new set of circumstances, far different from those that had spawned the outbreaks of 1096.

Perhaps the best gauge of the ongoing security of post-1096 Jewish existence is the continued population growth, including the movement of southern European Jews into the northern regions. Such movement would obviously

not have taken place if northern Christendom were perceived as teetering precariously on the brink of chaos and
prone to anti-Jewish outbreaks. The economic growth of
the twelfth and thirteenth centuries adds further weight
to the argument for relative stability and security. Overall
the picture of post-1096 Jewish life in northern Europe
hardly conveys a sense of rapid deterioration of Jewish
safety and security.

Although it has long been recognized that the eleventh
century saw the beginning of significant Jewish intellectual
creativity in western Christendom, it has rarely been
suggested that this nascent creativity was choked by the
violence of 1096. Those attacks did decimate the great
centers of the developing intellectual life of northwestern
European Jewry. Worms, Mainz, and Cologne were, for
reasons that are not altogether clear, the focal point of this
creative vitality, and were acknowledged as such at the
time; this is reflected in the elegiac pronouncements of
both S and L. At the outset of the description of the assault
on Mainz Jewry, S laments:

> It came to pass on the third of the month of Sivan, on
> that very day when Moses said: "Be ready for the third
> day." On that very day the crown of Israel fell. Then
> the students of Torah fell and the scholars disap-
> peared. The honor of the Torah fell. "He threw down
> from heaven to earth the glory of Israel." Fear of sin
> and humility came to an end. Men of deeds, the luster
> of wisdom and purity, those who turn back [evil]
> decrees and the anger of their Creator disappeared.
> The givers of charity in secret diminished. Truth was
> eclipsed; the preachers disappeared; the revered fell
> and the arrogant multiplied.[14]

In this broad elegy, the central loss mourned is the loss of
the Torah: "the students of Torah fell, the schools ceased,
the glory of the Torah came to an end." I have already
indicated that the serious outbursts of violence were limited to a few important Jewish communities. In view of

the fact that these were precisely the centers of pre-1096 Jewish intellectual life, one may imagine that in demographic, economic, and political terms northern European Jewry might have continued to grow, while the promising intellectual developments of the eleventh century would have been cut off. Yet even this did not happen. Despite the disproportionably heavy blow suffered by the spiritual centers, intellectual growth continued, indeed at an accelerated pace.[15]

In every area of Jewish culture, important groundwork was laid during the eleventh century, with enhanced creative activity proceeding into the twelfth. In the central field of medieval Jewish intellectual endeavor—the study and expansion of Jewish law—this was clearly the case. While the academies of the Rhineland had established important foundations for the study of Jewish law prior to 1096, these efforts bore fruit during the century and a half following the First Crusade. The comprehensive and influential commentary of Rabbi Solomon ben Isaac of Troyes (Rashi) spans the First Crusade period. Educated himself in the Rhineland academies, Rashi wrote before, during, and after the tumultuous events of 1096. One might argue that his efforts yet represent the culmination of pre-1096 Rhineland Jewish scholarly activity. The same cannot, however, be said for his successors, particularly the strikingly new school of the Tosafists.[16] It is widely acknowledged that the Tosafists represent a significant new phenomenon in the unfolding pattern of analysis of Jewish law, one destined to have a rich and protracted impact on subsequent Jewish intellectual life. Although much remains to be done in analyzing the methodological innovations of the Tosafists, it seems highly likely that these innovations represented a blending of traditional forms of Jewish study with the newly developing emphasis on the use of dialectics in both law and philosophy in twelfth-century France. The Tosafists represent the most obvious refutation of the thesis that the destruction of the Jewish communities of Worms, Mainz, and Cologne stemmed the creativity of northern European Jewry.

The advances in the field of Jewish law are, however, but one index of the ongoing vitality of twelfth- and early thirteenth-century European Jewry. The field of Bible study shows much the same pattern. Again, there was significant creativity before 1096, little evidence of which has survived; Rashi, who studied at the Rhineland academies, reached new heights of achievement before, during, and after 1096, and his efforts set the stage for impressive further developments during the twelfth century. Here, too, much methodological analysis remains to be done and the impact of the broad cultural environment upon patterns of Jewish exegesis (and vice versa) still needs to be explored. There can be no doubt, however, as to the accelerating productivity of the post-1096 period.[17]

There is one area of Jewish creative endeavor in which we encounter explicit claims for the impact of 1096 upon subsequent achievements, that is, among the Pietists. This claim is advanced by Rabbi Elazar ben Judah of the late twelfth and early thirteenth century whose report on the Third Crusade I have already addressed. In the course of his description of the chain of oral tradition through which the mystical secrets of prayer had been passed down to him, Rabbi Elazar makes the following statement:

> They received the mystical lore associated with prayer and other mystical lore—teacher from teacher, back to Abu Aaron, the son of R. Samuel the *nasi*, who came from Babylonia because of a certain incident. He was forced to wander about, coming to Lombardy and a city called Lucca. There he found R. Moses who composed the poem "The Awe of Your Majesty" and passed on to him all his mystical lore. This was R. Moses the son of R. Kalonymous the son of R. Judah. He was the first who left Lombardy, he and his sons, R. Kalonymous and R. Yekutiel, and his relative R. Itiel and other important figures. King Charles brought them with him from Lombardy and settled them in Mainz. There they produced and multiplied and increased mightily, until the Lord visited his anger

there upon the sacred communities in the year 1096.
There we were cut down and destroyed. All of us were
destroyed, except a few who remained from the family
of our grandfather. He transmitted to R. Elazar the
hazan from Speyer, as we have written above. R. Elazar
the *hazan* transmitted to R. Samuel the *hasid* and
R. Samuel the *hasid* transmitted to R. Judah the *hasid*
and from him I the insignificant have received the
mystical lore or prayer and other mystical lore.[18]

In this depiction the disruptive effects of 1096 are clearly
indicated. It must be noted, however, that the description
is associated only with mystical lore passed on orally from
generation to generation and said to center in the Mainz
community. Furthermore, the chain of mystical tradition,
though endangered, was not severed. It did survive the
catastrophe to reach Rabbi Elazar of Worms himself. Finally, one may raise doubts concerning the entire statement. It reflects an assertion common in conservative mystical circles, that the great era of creativity lay in the past,
while the present proponents of the movement are merely
the weak and insignificant transmitters of past insights.
Rarely are such protests accurate; often they mask a highly
creative and innovative spirit. In terms of available literary
material, at least, the late twelfth and thirteenth centuries
seem to mark the apogee of medieval German-Jewish
Pietism, casting further doubt on the accuracy of Rabbi
Elazar ben Judah's statement. The great names of this
mystical and pietistic group are twelfth- and early thirteenth-century figures. It was not until the latter half of
the twelfth century and in the thirteeth century that the
Pietists began to exert influence over a number of Jewish
intellectual leaders who worked in a variety of literary
genres. While the claims of decline cannot be utterly dismissed, they seem dubious. Once more, there seems to
have been slow and steady advance, beginning before the
First Crusade and reaching fruition well afterward.[19]

There is one further refinement that might be made in
the argument that 1096 forms an intellectual watershed for

medieval Ashkenazic Jewry. It might be suggested that, while Ashkenazic Jewry in general continued to develop, German Jewry, where the earliest intellectual progress had taken place, declined in the wake of 1096. According to this view, the First Crusade would constitute a turning point at least in the intellectual vitality of German Jewry.[20] In assessing this argument, it must be noted at the outset that the notion of a transfer in the center of Ashkenazic spiritual life from Germany to France is surely borne out. It is clear that the focus of eleventh-century Jewish intellectual activity was in the Rhineland, while the major role in twelfth- and early thirteenth-century creativity was played by French Jewry. It is also clear that the events of 1096 played a role in the speed of the shift in intellectual leadership. It was as a result of the devastation of the old intellectual centers in the Rhineland that the new creativity of French Jewry became so immediately noticeable. This does not mean that the events of 1096 wholly caused the shift. Even without the violence that struck Rhineland Jewry, French Jewish intellectual life certainly would have advanced the way it did. The factors that gave rise to this creativity, particularly the broad flourishing of the French Jewish community and the positive impact of the general French intellectual vigor of the twelfth century, operated totally independent of the events of 1096. Less certain is the course of German Jewish intellectual vitality: did it decline irreversibly after 1096? The response to this question is not completely clear. It is obvious that German Jewish spiritual life was immediately impeded and retarded by the losses suffered in Worms, Mainz, and Cologne. Was it impaired over the long run as well? Although the issue is debatable, the answer seems to be no. German Jewry did revive itself and produced significant works in such areas as Jewish law, mysticism and pietism, liturgical poetry, and exegesis. Taken by itself, German Jewish intellectual life seems to have bent, but not broken in the wake of 1096. By the middle of the twelfth century, active intellectual creativity was well under way once again. The growing gap between this German Jewish community and its French counterpart is less a function of the retarding influence of 1096 than of the remarkable, unrelated upsurge in France.

As in the areas of demography and economics, the First Crusade was positively related to the healthy developments that took place in Jewish intellectual life during the twelfth and thirteenth centuries. Progress was a reflection of the maturing European society of the twelfth century. More important, the contacts with older centers of civilization that resulted from the armed expedition of 1096 were destined to have a profound impact on the so-called renaissance of the twelfth century and thus indirectly upon the efflorescence of Jewish creativity in a variety of disciplines.

The following conclusions are evident: (1) The First Crusade scarcely represented a major shift in the underlying conditions of European life and can in this sense hardly be claimed to have served as the occasion for fundamental changes in Jewish existence. (2) The damage wrought upon European Jewry by the events of 1096 was not significant enough to alter the historic course of this Jewry. Although leading communities were wiped out, the vast majority of European Jewry survived intact. (3) No sharp changes can be identified in the wake of 1096. Rather, there seems to have been continued development in pre-1096 directions. These tendencies, which had begun prior to the First Crusade and continued subsequent to it, were not entirely negative. Demographically, economically, and intellectually achievement continued unabated. To be sure, not all was positive: the possibilities of rejection that had manifested themselves before and during 1096 intensified during the course of the twelfth and thirteenth centuries. (4) These changes—both for the better and for the worse—were clearly not "caused" by the First Crusade; at the same time they were not unrelated to it. The First Crusade can be viewed as a symptom of developments that had begun to take place during the eleventh century and as a catalyst for the intensification of these tendencies.

In sum, my investigation would reject the prevailing

view of 1096 as a watershed in European Jewish life. The
year was an important and disastrous time; it did not,
however, inaugurate rapid change and certainly did not
"cause" such change. European Jewish life from the
eleventh through the twelfth and on into the early thirteenth century evolved in a relatively steady fashion. Significant and deleterious changes came long after 1096 and
resulted from a complex set of developments in European
life. Neither 1096 nor any other specific incident can suitably explain the thirteenth- and fourteenth-century deterioration in European Jewish history.

1096 AS A "PORTENT OF THINGS TO COME"

I suggested in the preceding section that to present 1096
as a sharp turning point in the medieval Jewish experience
would represent both a misinterpretation of the data and
a flawed understanding of the historical process. The reg-
nant view of historical change in the period under discussion is provided nicely for us by R. W. Southern. His
observations reinforce the conclusions of the preceding
section and point to the real significance of the events of
1096 for subsequent Jewish history:

> This silence in the great changes of history is some-
> thing which meets us everywhere as we go through
> these centuries. The slow emergence of a knightly aris-
> tocracy which set the social tone of Europe for hun-
> dreds of years contains no dramatic events or clearly
> decisive moments such as those which have marked
> the course of other great social revolutions. The eco-
> nomic face of Europe and its position in the world was
> transformed in this period, but this revolution was
> occasioned by no conspicuous discoveries or inven-
> tions which focus our attention. There were of course
> resounding events: the capture of Jerusalem by the
> Crusaders in 1099, and of Constantinople by their suc-
> cessors in 1204, are great moments for good or ill, but

their greatness lies less in their practical consequences than in their indication of the forces at work in the world. Indeed it is characteristic of the period that the importance of events is to be measured less by the decisions which they enforce than by their symbolic value as revelations of change or as potents of things to come.[21]

I would likewise argue that, in the history of medieval Ashkenazic Jewry, 1096 serves not as a decisive watershed, but rather as "an indication of the forces at work in the world," in both a negative and positive sense.

The eventual decline of European Jewry is a complex and intriguing issue. Any effort to identify a central causal factor in this decline is, I believe, doomed to failure. The decline of medieval European Jewry is the result of the interaction of a variety of factors—economic, political, and cultural-spiritual. The events of 1096 contribute little of significance to our understanding of developments in the economic and political spheres; they do show us early signs of the emergence of an exclusivist mentality fated to add its force to the eventual weakening of the Jewish position in Europe.

The First Crusade expressed clearly a growing sense of cohesion in western Christendom and an enhanced awareness of the distinction between Christendom and those outside it, who were increasingly perceived as enemies. Indeed, the successes of the First Crusade heightened this distinction. Such a magnificent undertaking and achievement was sure to engender feelings of intense pride, and subsequent threats to the crusader states carved out in the Near East aroused the fury of European society. In 1096 and afterward, a major ramification of the sense of solidarity expressed in and enhanced by crusading was an increased awareness of internal non-Christians, who all too often were seen as enemies and in most cases were Jews. Such views were extremely dangerous to the Jewish minority in western Christendom.

The perception of the Jew as enemy so sharply reflected in the popular assaults of 1096 finds its continuation in the set of slanders that began to proliferate in northern European society during the twelfth century. The central element in these slanders is the notion that there exists powerful animosity on the part of Jews to Christianity and Christendom. This alleged hostility was said to be expressed in varied ways.[22] Perhaps the simplest was the charge of malicious murder, the allegation that out of their hatred for Christianity Jews took every opportunity to kill unsuspecting Christians. Because of the realities of Christian power and Jewish powerlessness and because of imputed Jewish shiftiness as well, these crimes were supposed to have been committed furtively, with the victims often the weak and defenseless, particularly young children. As the twelfth century proceeded, this basic theme was expanded, developing into allegations that Jews did away with their neighbors in ritually significant modes. One such ritually meaningful form of murder was crucifixion. A number of Christian children were supposedly crucified by the Jews out of a perverse compulsion to reenact what Christians saw as the historic Jewish crime of deicide. Young children are highlighted in this allegation not only for their weakness and defenselessness but for their purity and innocence as well. Another variation in this same motif is the thirteenth-century claim that Jews murder Christian youngsters and utilize the blood of these victims in the Passover ritual. The crucifixion slander and the blood libel are clearly related; they not only derive from the same basic theme of Jewish hostility but revolve around the Christian and Jewish festivals of the spring season, which often coincide. Obviously the allegation of host desecration is yet another closely related derivative of the basic charge of Jewish animosity. All these slanders found a growing number of adherents during the twelfth and thirteenth centuries.

Increasingly prominent during the fourteenth century was the charge that Jews attempted to wipe out large segments of Christian society wholesale, by such means as well poisoning. To be sure, this charge had surfaced, as I have noted, during the First Crusade.[23] The initial attack in Worms was triggered by the parading of a Christian corpse through the town, with the charge that the Jews had boiled the body and introduced the contaminated waters into the wells of Worms in order to wipe out the Christian populace. While such allegations were old, they achieved enhanced credibility during the fourteenth century, as European society was visited by a number of uncontrollable catastrophes. Particularly during the gruesome plague years of 1348 and 1349, the allegation that Jews poisoned wells received widespread attention and credence.

How then is the proliferation of these slanders related to the First Crusade? It is tempting to suggest that the basic crusader perception of the Jews as enemies of Christendom was the foundation for the efflorescence of anti-Jewish mythology during the subsequent centuries. My analysis of crusader slogans has indicated that the view of the Jews as enemies was central to the anti-Jewish violence of 1096. Indeed it would seem that the Jews had reinforced this perception by their resolute refusal to save themselves by baptism. Their rejection of Christianity, even at the pain of death, certainly might have been interpreted as proof of Jewish enmity to Christianity. In fact there is more: recall the horror with which Albert of Aix described Jewish mothers slaughtering their young children. Jewish rejection of Christianity is seen as a sentiment, which, by its intensity, leads to the shattering of normal moral and ethical constraints. One might easily hypothesize a connection between the 1096 reality of Jewish parents willing to take the lives of their own children rather than submit to conversion and the subsequent image of Jews capable of taking the lives of Christian youngsters out of implacable hostility to the Christian faith.

While linkage of the twelfth- and thirteenth-century slanders with the events of 1096 is intellectually appealing, serious questions must be posed: first, was the pattern of Jewish behavior in 1096 in fact widely known in Christian society? The answer seems to be no. As noted earlier, the major chroniclers of the First Crusade were oblivious to both the attacks on European Jewry and the Jewish responses. There were thus few channels available for the dissemination of this information and Christian literature and art of the twelfth and thirteenth centuries show almost no familiarity with these incidents.[24] Given this dearth of information, the proposals for linking the later anti-Jewish slanders with patterns of Jewish behavior elicited by the crisis of 1096 are untenable. Rather it seems far more likely that the stereotypes that gave rise to the heightened images of Jewish enmity in 1096 continued to operate during the twelfth and thirteenth centuries, producing the variety of anti-Jewish motifs noted. The fundamental Christian view of the Jew as negator and malefactor emerged during the exhilaration of 1096. It sparked the massacres perpetrated by the fringe crusading bands and broke forth once more during the imaginative twelfth century in the form of elaborate visions of Jewish malevolence and cruelty. In this unfortunate sense the radical 1096 notions of Jewish hostility and enmity do serve as a "portent of things to come." This perception of the Jew as enemy, discernible both in 1096 and in the slanders of the twelfth and thirteenth centuries, is one of the significant factors in the eventual decline of medieval European Jewry. The sentiments that exploded in the persecutions of 1096 are a revealing gauge of this newly emerging factor in Jewish fate in medieval western Christendom.

When we look into the pattern of Ashkenazic Jewish life itself, we find once more the events of 1096 functioning as a harbinger of things to come, albeit in a much more positive fashion. The very term *Ashkenazic Jewry* indicates an awareness that a new pattern of Jewish living emerged in the dynamically developing areas of medieval northern Europe. Thus far, unfortunately, few serious attempts have been made to analyze the underlying characteristics of this new Ashkenazic Jewish style. The recent studies of Haym Soloveitchik and Ivan G. Marcus of the German-Jewish Pietists, it seems to me, have significant far beyond the phenomenon of Pietism itself.[25] According to Soloveitchik,

> Underlying the movement of *Haside Ashkenaz* was the recent discovery of man and his hitherto unsuspected capacities. In the first fresh look at human nature since the Midrash, the Pietists uncovered a creature who (among other qualities) possessed infinite resourcefulness, restless energy, and was capable of heroic exertion in achieving his own ends, and they insisted that religion demand of man the equivalent mobilization of his abilities for the divine service. The traditional requirements touched only a fraction of his capacities, and he who contented himself with this was no true worshiper of God. This discovery of man and his potentialities was not an opening to humanism, as in several strands of Christian thought of the time, but a summons to an infinitely more comprehensive submission to the heavenly yoke.[26]

The suggestion of "a first fresh look at human nature since the Midrash" has far-ranging implications. Soloveitchik draws some tentative parallels between the enterprise of the Pietists and that of the Tosafists, observing that both reflect a profound new sense of the complexity of the world as God's creation and the capacity of human beings to plumb the depths of this complexity. Thus these Jews share deeply in the restless energies and startlingly new insights that characterize late eleventh- and twelfth-century northern Europe civilization. It seems fair to suggest that in this creative outburst the essence of early Ashkenazic Jewry may be found.

The patterns of Jewish behavior in 1096 affords us clear and early evidence of these important new tendencies. Among the martyrs of 1096 and those who chronicled their heroism there is an overwhelming sense of the Divine Will, as it forced upon Rhineland Jewry an awesome test and challenge. References to and reflections upon God's will abound. The Jewish martyrs of 1096 see themselves as, above all else, fulfilling the extreme demands imposed by the Divine Will.

> Ultimately one must not question the ways of the Holy One, blessed be he and blessed be his Name, who gave us his Torah and commanded us to put to death and to kill ourselves for the unity of his holy Name.[27]

The behavior of the Rhineland Jews in 1096 reflects unusual perspectives on the varied and complex demands imposed by the Divine Will. Most striking of course is the extreme demand for martyrdom. These Jews fulfill the halachic injunction regarding forced acceptance of idolatry; they exhibit willingness to be killed rather than to transgress. Quite clearly, however, they went far beyond the simple dictates of the halachah, going so far as to take the lives of others in order to protect them from the possibility of conversion.[28] Most striking is the extensive sacrifice of children to preserve them from what these Jews saw as the pollution of idolatry. All this represents an expansion of the normal directives of halachah in a manner parallel to the later *Hasidut Ashkenaz*. It is not only the act of martyrdom itself that shows such parallels; they are further reflected in the style and manner of the martyrdom as well. Established rituals are adapted in novel ways: the implements Jews used to kill themselves or others were carefully examined in accordance with the requirements of ritual slaughtering of animals for food, according to halachah; the horrible act is accompanied by intonation of a benediction; the speech of Rabbi Moses the *Cohen*, quoted above, began and ended with the normal grace after meal, refashioned into a prelude to martyrdom.[29] In all this there is novel expansion of halachic dictate in precisely the manner that became so central to the fully mature *Hasidut Ashkenaz*.

Underlying these remarkable behaviors was the conviction that human beings had the capacity to fathom God's will and to muster the incredible strength necessary to fulfill its dictates. Embodied here is the new sense of the heroic capacities of human beings described by Soloveitchik. The martyrs of 1096 certainly exhibited "infinite resourcefulness, restless energy, and . . . heroic exertion." As I have argued, the Hebrew narratives are essentially histories of this heroism; they focus neither on the persecution inflicted upon these Jews nor on the resultant losses. Instead they are devoted to recounting the achievements of the Rhineland martyrs who reached the highest possible levels of human heroism, a heroism that even exceeded that of the giants of the Jewish past.[30] Indeed the martyrs themselves view their own actions as emulations of the most extraordinary deeds of Jewish history.[31] The willingness on the part of pious and traditional Jews to compare themselves to the great figures of the past, including the patriarchs themselves, bespeaks a bold new sense of human capacity. The audacity to see themselves as exceeding the heroism and virtue of these revered ancestors is yet more striking.

Just as the heroism of the crusading Christians provides a glimpse into the newly discovered capacities of human beings, so too the militant Jewish response to crusading persecution reveals the same new human vigor within the Jewish community and provides a useful index of the subsequent creativity that would mark Ashkenazic Jewish life during the twelfth and thirteenth centuries. The unusual behavior pattern elicited by the assaults of 1096 will rarely be repeated, but the restless energy and human strength reflected in the martyrdoms of 1096 lay at the core of the creative upsurge that distinguishes Ashkenazic Jewry of the centuries that followed.

New-Style Persecution and New-Style Martyrdom

I have argued thus far that the events of 1096 do not constitute a watershed or turning point in medieval Jewish history or even in the evolution of medieval Ashkenazic

Jewry, but that they do reveal important new developments, both negative and positive, that would be felt more intensely over the ensuing centuries. It is now appropriate to step back even farther to view the events of 1096 from an even broader perspective. From this broader perspective, I wish to suggest that the most enduring significance of the events that have been carefully analyzed in this study lies in their introducing into the history of the Jewish people a new style of physical persecution and a strikingly new style of Jewish martyrdom.

Early Jewish history shows anti-Jewish violence that is either political or socioeconomic in origin. The Assyrian, Babylonian, Seleucid, and Roman assaults on Palestinian Jewry and its religious institutions all flowed from political tensions. Empires that generally espoused a doctrine of tolerating minority communities and faiths broke with that general policy when they perceived the Jews as politically rebellious and threatening. Even the two instances of decrees outlawing Jewish religious practice—the Antiochene decrees of the 160s B.C.E. and the Hadrianic decrees of the 130s C.E.—do not reflect an ideological commitment to the extirpation of Judaism on the part of the Seleucid and Roman authorities; rather they bespeak a desire to suppress political rebellion by striking at its religious roots.[32] There are likewise instances of violence flowing from socioeconomic tensions, such as the anti-Jewish rioting in first-century Alexandria and the anti-Jewish outbursts that accompanied the rebellion against Rome in the 60s. Ideologically motivated violence, however, is not in evidence.

With the emergence of Christianity and its rise to power in the Roman Empire, the stage was set for a new threat to Jewish existence. Committed to an exclusivist monotheistic vision, Christianity (and later Islam) negated the ultimate validity of all other religious faiths. While this might well have led to a practical program of extirpation of Judaism (along with all other non-Christian faiths), in fact a preredemptive modus vivendi was established. Judaism was accorded a temporary legitimacy, with a set of conditions prescribed for acceptable Jewish behavior.

Indeed the continued existence of the Jews was seen, in some senses, as necessary and useful in the preredemptive scheme of things. To be sure, this in no way diminished the desirability of converting the individual Jew to Christianity. The continued existence of Jews also allowed for the possibility of punishing perceived Jewish transgression of the conditions imposed as a prerequisite for toleration in Christendom. The most extreme form of punishment would be expulsion of the offending Jews from a given territory, and in fact such expulsions occurred many times. In all of this, however, the basic policy of toleration remains and the notion of liquidation of the Jews and Judaism makes no appearance.

During the eleventh century, a new aggressiveness developed in western Christendom and expressed itself in a new potential for persecution of the Jews.[33] This new-style persecution, as I have already shown, involves the notion of the total destruction of Jewishness and the Jews. Conversion of individual Jews is not the desideratum nor is expulsion of allegedly offending Jews from a given area; the goal is rather a removal of Judaism from the world, preferably by mass conversion or, failing that, by slaughter. The general bellicosity of certain segments of the Christian populace expressed itself in a new and clearly nonnormative view of the Jews and the treatment appropriate for them. As my analysis has shown, these views were restricted to small and marginal groups of popular crusaders. In the subsequent organized crusades, the Church leadership went to great lengths to repudiate this unorthodox stand. Nonetheless this radical posture does constitute a new-style persecution of European Jewry. The impact of this radical thinking in later periods is a question that is both significant and almost impossible to answer. It has recently been argued that the thirteenth century saw the alteration of the traditional Church theory of the legitimacy of Jewish existence in Christendom,[34] while it has long been recognized that some leading Protestant thinkers repudiated the accepted Catholic doctrine of the Jewish place in Christian society. Finally, the twentieth century has witnessed a massive effort to eliminate the Jews and Judaism. The extent to which lines of influence can be drawn between these later developments and the eruption of radical anti-Jewishness in 1096 is uncertain. What is clear, however, is that the bellicosity of the First Crusade period spawned a new-style threat to the existence of Judaism, a threat founded on the ideological negation of the legitimate place of the Jews in the Christian world. The precedent it set was a dolorous one.

This new-style threat serves as the backdrop for the reaffirmation of old styles of Jewish resistance to persecution and for the emergence of a distinctly new style of Jewish martyrdom.[35] In my analysis of Jewish martyrdom in 1096, I have shown that the eleventh-century Rhineland Jews were heirs to a rich and diverse legacy of martyrological thought and attitudes. In fact, however, a more-or-less normative stance on the issue of martyrdom had developed in earlier Jewish history, expressed in halachic injunction and in historical precedent. This normative stance called for adamant but passive resistance to external pressure, culminating in the requirement of accepting death at the hands of persecutors under specified conditions. This resistance was limited to acceptance of death; self-destruction and the killing of others lay beyond the limits of halachic discussion. This normative halachic view was reinforced by known historical precedent. For the Rhineland Jews the major precedents available were the heroes of the book of Daniel, those who resisted Seleucid oppression, and the martyrs of the Hadrianic period. In all these instances, the model behavior involved an acceptance of death at the hands of the enemy. There is no normative historical legacy of activism beyond this; indeed the major instance of more radical behavior—the self-destruction of some of the anti-Roman rebels culminating in the mass suicide at Masada—was deliberately omitted from the historical tradition of rabbinic Judaism.

Many of the Rhineland Jews of 1096 followed in remarkable fashion the normative tradition of the sacrifice of one's life in resistance to external pressures and persecution. Large numbers of pious and respected Jews gave up their lives in the face of the new-style Christian persecution I have described. Confronted with the halachically defined choice of conversion or death, they chose to be put to death, thus emulating Hananiah, Mishael, and Azariah; the aged priest and the mother and her seven sons; and the great Rabbi Akiba and Rabbi Haninah ben Teradion. These martyrs added an intense new element to the normative Jewish tradition of martyrdom—the frenzied vilification of the persecuting enemy and the enemy's faith. A remarkable chapter was added to the history of normative-style Jewish martyrdom.

There was, however, more. The intense atmosphere of 1096 activated a series of less normative Jewish images and thereby produced a striking break with earlier patterns of Jewish martyrdom. The ritualized acts of Jewish self-sacrifice made a profound impression. As we have seen, these acts were viewed by the Jewish chroniclers as sublime and by their Christian counterparts as barbaric. From a more dispassionate perspective they are surely new and innovative. A radical new form of *kiddush ha-Shem* was introduced into Jewish history. The extreme actions of these pious Rhineland Jews of 1096 added a potent new element to the saga of Jewish martyrdom. Unlike the martyrs of the rebellion against Rome, they could not be dismissed as brigands and outlaws. Men, women, and children at the very core of Ashkenazic Jewry chose to take their own lives and the lives of their neighbors in acts of radical religiosity. To be sure, the extremity of these Jewish behaviors inspired both pride and a measure of concern. As we have seen, there was a subsequent tendency to efface some of the radicality and to buttress the more traditional and more conservative postures. The actions of the martyrs of 1096 were toned down in much of the memorialization, but they could not be effaced. A significant new dimension had been added in 1096 to the legacy of *kiddush ha-Shem*.

Viewed then from the broad perspective of Jewish history, the events of 1096 are significant in introducing into that history a new-style persecution and a new-style martyrdom. The new-style persecution was by and large repudiated by the Roman Catholic Church; the new-style martyrdom served to intensify and deepen traditional Jewish attitudes and norms, while losing along the way much of its innovative and radical force. For all these considerations, the sanguinary and heroic deeds of 1096 merit analysis and recollection.

Appendix
The Hebrew First-Crusade
Chronicles

INTRODUCTORY REMARKS

Translating the two original Hebrew First-Crusade chronicles is no easy task. The fundamental problem is the dolorous state of the two unique manuscripts. Each is replete with erasures, omissions, and blatant errors. N&S is quite faithful and accurate in its transcription of the Hebrew text; Habermann often includes corrections and revisions and must therefore be used with care. For the purposes of this translation, I have used the text presented in N&S. At numerous points microfilm copies of the manuscripts have been consulted, in order to verify—where possible—the precise reading.

A few brief observations concerning the style of these two chronicles are in order. These Hebrew texts are studded with biblical citations and references. One does not find a belabored effort to introduce such citations; one finds, rather, that the usage is comfortable, that the Hebrew idiom is suffused thoroughly and naturally with biblical terminology. In order to highlight the appearance of biblical citations and references, I have placed them in quotation marks and identified their sources in the notes. In this effort, I have been greatly aided by the extensive notes in the German translation found in N&S. In addition, I have augmented substantially the number of identified biblical citations, although I am certain that a more discerning eye than mine would uncover even more instances. Where verses are consciously quoted by the authors, I have identified the quotations even when they recur. When clauses or phrases are cited in passing, I have noted them by quotation marks each time they appear, but have identified the sources only for the first appearance of the clause or phrase. I have treated each text separately, beginning the process of identification afresh for each. In translating the biblical clauses or phrases cited, I have used the new translation published by the Jewish Publication Society of America. In many instances, it has been necessary to depart from this translation in order to present the meaning of the biblical text as perceived by the medieval author.

Two further characteristics of these Hebrew chronicles might be noted: the tendency toward long and complex sentences and frequent ambiguity of pronoun reference. I have tried to achieve clarity by breaking the lengthy Hebrew sentences into shorter English units and by specifying in brackets the referents of ambiguous pronouns. In general, it has been my intention to provide as literal a translation as possible. I am fully aware that my English rendition often pales in comparison to the rich and evocative language of the original. The Hebrew of these dramatic accounts possesses a power and impact, based often on association and cadence, that no translation can hope to capture.

S

I shall begin the account of the former persecution. May the Lord protect us and all Israel from persecution.[1]

It came to pass in the year one thousand twenty-eight after the destruction of the Temple[2] that this evil befell Israel. There first arose the princes and nobles and common folk in France, who took counsel and set plans to ascend and "to rise up like eagles"[3] and to do battle and "to clear a way"[4] for journeying to Jerusalem,[5] the Holy City, and for reaching the sepulcher of the Crucified, "a trampled corpse"[6] "who cannot profit and cannot save for he is worthless."[7] They said to one another: "Behold we travel to a distant land to do battle with the kings of that land. 'We take our souls in our hands'[8] in order to kill and to subjugate[9] all those kingdoms that do not believe in the Crucified. How much more so [should we kill and subjugate] the Jews, who killed and crucified him." They taunted us from every direction. They took counsel, ordering that either we turn to their abominable faith or they would destroy us "from infant to suckling."[10] They—both princes and common folk—placed an evil sign upon their garments, a cross, and helmets upon their heads.

When the [Jewish] communities in France heard, they were seized by consternation, fear, and trembling[11] . . . [12] They wrote letters and sent emissaries to all the [Jewish] communities along the Rhine River, [asking that they] fast and deprive themselves and seek mercy from [God "who dwells on high,"[13] so that he deliver them [the Jews] from their [the crusaders'] hands. When the letters reached the saintly ones who were in that land, they—those men of God, "the pillars of the universe,"[14] who were in Mainz— wrote in reply to France. Thus was it written in them [their letters]: "All the [Jewish] communities have decreed a fast. We have done our part. May God save us and save you from 'all distress and hardship.'[15] We are greatly fearful for you. We, however, have less reason to fear [for ourselves], for we have heard not even a rumor [of such developments]." Indeed we did not hear that a decree had been issued and that "a sword was to afflict us mortally."[16]

When the crusaders[17] began to reach this land, they sought funds with which to purchase bread. We gave them, considering ourselves to be fulfilling the verse: "Serve the king of Babylon, and live."[18] All this, however, was of no avail, for our sins brought it about that the burghers in every city to which the crusaders came were hostile to us, for their [the burghers'] hands were also with them [the crusaders] to destroy vine and stock all along the way to Jerusalem.

It came to pass that, when the crusaders came, battalion after battalion, like the army of Sennacherib,[19] some of the princes in the empire said: "Why do we sit thus? Let us also go with them. For every man who sets forth on this journey and undertakes to ascend to the impure sepulcher dedicated to the Crucified will be assured paradise."[20] Then the crusaders along with them [the princes] gathered from all the provinces until they became as numerous "as the sands of the sea,"[21] including both princes and common folk. They circulated a report . . .[22] "Anyone who kills a single Jew will have all his sins absolved." Indeed there was a certain nobleman, Ditmar by name, who announced that he would not depart from this empire until he would kill one Jew—then he would depart. Now when the holy community in Mainz heard this, they decreed a fast. "They cried out mightily to the Lord"[23] and they passed night and day in fasting. Likewise they recited dirges both morning and evening, both small and great. Nonetheless our God "did not turn away from his awesome wrath"[24] against us. For the crusaders with their insignia came, with their standards before our houses. When they saw one of us, they ran after him and pierced him with a spear, to the point that we were afraid even to cross our thresholds.

It came to pass on the eighth of the month of Iyyar,[25] on the Sabbath, the measure of justice began to manifest itself against us. The crusaders and burghers arose first against the saintly ones, the pious of the Almighty in Speyer. They took counsel against them, [planning] to seize them together in the synagogue. But it was revealed to them and they arose [early] on the Sabbath morning and prayed rapidly and left the synagogue. When they [the crusaders and burghers] saw that their plan for seizing them together was foiled, they rose against them [the Jews] and killed eleven of them. From there the decree began, to fulfill that which is said: "Begin at my sanctuary."[26] When Bishop John heard, he came with a large force and helped the [Jewish] community wholeheartedly and brought them indoors and saved them from their [the crusaders' and burghers'] hands. He seized some of the burghers and "cut off their hands."[27] He was a pious one among the nations. Indeed God brought about well-being and salvation through him. R. Moses ben Yekutiel the parnas[28] "stood on the breach"[29] and extended himself on their behalf. Through him all those forcibly converted who remained "here and there"[30] in the empire of Henry returned [to Judaism].[31] Through the emperor, Bishop John removed the remnant of the community of Speyer to his fortified towns, and the Lord turned to them, for the sake of his great Name. The bishop hid them until the enemies of the Lord passed. They [the Jews] remained there, fasting and weeping and mourning. "They despaired deeply,"[32] for every day the crusaders and the gentiles and Emicho— may his bones be ground up—and the common folk gathered against them, to seize them and to destroy them. Through R. Moses the parnas, Bishop John saved them, for the Lord inclined his heart to save them without bribery. This was from the Lord, in order to give us there "a remnant and a residue"[33] through him.

It came to pass that, when the sad report that some of
the community of Speyer had been killed reached Worms,
they [the Jews of Worms] cried out to the Lord and wept
loudly and bitterly, for they saw that a decree had been
issued from heaven and that there was no place to flee,
neither forward nor backward. Then the community divided itself into two groups. Some of them fled to the
bishop in his towers; some of them remained in their
homes, for the burghers promised them vainly and cun-
ningly. They are "splintered reeds,"[34] for evil and not for
good, for their hand was with the crusaders in order to
destroy our name and remnant. They gave us vain and
meaningless encouragement, [saying]: "Do not fear them,
for anyone who kills one of you—'his life will be forfeit
for yours.'"[35] They [the burghers] did not give them [the
Jews] anywhere to flee, for [the members of] the community deposited all their money in their [the burghers']
hands. Therefore they surrendered them.

It came to pass on the tenth of Iyyar, on Sunday,[36]
"they plotted craftily against them."[37] They took "a trampled corpse" of theirs, that had been buried thirty days
previously and carried it through the city, saying: "Behold
what the Jews have done to our comrade. They took a
gentile and boiled him in water. They then poured the
water into our wells in order to kill us."[38] When the crusaders and burghers heard this, they cried out and gathered—
all who bore and unsheathed [a sword], from great to
small—saying: "Behold the time has come to avenge him
who was crucified, whom their ancestors slew. Now let
not 'a remnant or a residue' escape, even 'an infant or a
suckling' in the cradle." They then came and struck those
who had remained in their houses—comely young men
and comely and lovely young women along with elders.
All of them stretched forth their necks. Even manumitted
servingmen and servingwomen were killed along with
them for the sanctification of the Name which is awesome
and sublime, . . .[39] who rules above and below, who was
and will be. Indeed the Lord of Hosts is his Name. He is
crowned with the splendor of seventy-two names;[40] he

created the Torah nine hundred and seventy-four generations prior to the creation of the world.[41] There were
twenty-six generations from the creation of the world to
Moses, the father of the prophets, through whom [God]
gave the holy Torah. Moses came and wrote in it: "The
Lord has affirmed this day that you are, as he promised
you, his treasured people which shall observe all his commandments."[42] For him and his Torah they were killed like
oxen and were dragged through the market places and
streets "like sheep to the slaughter"[43] and lay naked, for
they [the attackers] stripped them and left them naked.

It came to pass that, when those who remained saw
their brethren naked and the modest daughters of Israel
naked, they then acceded to them [the attackers] under
great duress, for the crusaders intended to leave not "a
remnant or a residue." There were those of them who said:
"Let us do their will for the time being, and let us go and
bury our brethren and save our children from them." For
they had seized the children that remained, "a small
number,"[44] saying that perhaps they would remain in their
pseudo-faith. They [the Jews who converted] did not desert their Creator, nor did their hearts incline after the
Crucified. Rather they cleaved to the God on high. Moreover, the rest of the community, those who remained in
the chambers of the bishop, sent garments with which to
clothe those who had been killed through those who had
been saved. For they were charitable. Indeed the heads of
the community remained there [in the bishop's chambers]
and most of the community was saved during the first
incident. They sent to those forcibly converted messages
of consolation: "Fear not and do not take to heart that
which you have done. For if the Holy One, blessed be he,
saves us from the hands of our enemies, then we shall be
with you 'for both death and life.'[45] 'However do not desert
the Lord.'"[46]

It came to pass on the twenty-fifth of Iyyar[47] that the
crusaders and the burghers said: "Behold those who remain in the courtyard of the bishop and in his chambers.
Let us take vengeance on them as well." They gathered

from all the villages in the vicinity, along with the crusaders and the burghers; they beseiged them [the Jews]; and they did battle against them. There took place a very great battle, one side against the other, until they seized the chambers in which the children of the sacred covenant were. When they saw the battle raging to and fro, the decree of the King of kings, then they accepted divine judgment and expressed faith in their Creator and "offered up true sacrifices."[48] They took their children and slaughtered them unreservedly for the unity of the revered and awesome Name. There were killed the notables of the community.

There was a certain young man, named R. Meshullam ben R. Isaac. He called out loudly to all those standing there and to Zipporah his helpmate: "Listen to me both great and small. This son God gave me. My wife Zipporah bore him in her old age and his name is Isaac. Now I shall offer him up as did our ancestor Abraham with his son Isaac."[49] Zipporah replied: "My lord, my lord. Wait a bit. Do not stretch forth your hand against the lad[50] whom I have raised and brought up and whom I bore in my old age. Slaughter me first, so that I not witness the death of the child."[51] He then replied: "I shall not delay even a moment. He who gave him to us will take him as his portion. He will place him in the bosom of Abraham our ancestor." He then bound Isaac his son and took in his hand the knife[52] with which to slaughter his son and made the benediction for slaughtering. The lad answered amen. He then slaughtered the lad. He took his screaming wife. The two of them departed together from the chamber and the crusaders killed them. "At such things will you restrain yourself, O Lord?"[53] Nevertheless "he did not turn away from his great wrath"[54] against us.

There was a certain young man, named Isaac ben Daniel. They asked him, saying: "Do you wish to exchange your God for 'a wretched idol?'"[55] He said: "Heaven forfend that I deny him; in him shall I trust. Thus shall I commend to him my soul." They put a rope around his neck and dragged him throughout the entire city, through the mud of the streets, up to the place of their idolatry. His soul was still bound up in his body. They said to him: "You may still be saved. Do you wish to convert?" He signaled with his finger—for he was unable to utter a word with his mouth, for he had been strangled—saying: "Cut off my head!" and they severed his neck.

There was still another young man, named R. Simhah the *cohen* son of our teacher R. Isaac the *cohen*. They sought to sully him with their fetid waters. They said to him: "Behold, all of them have already been killed and they lie naked." Then the young man answered them cleverly: "I shall fulfill all your desires, but take me with you to the bishop." They took him and led him to the chamber of the bishop. The nephew of the bishop was there with them. They began designating him with the name of "the loathsome offshoot,"[56] leaving him in the chamber of the bishop. Then the young man took out his knife and "gnashed his teeth"[57] in anger against the prince, the relative of the bishop, as does the lion over its prey. He . . .[58] and sank the knife in his belly, and he fell and died. He turned and stabbed two more until the knife broke in his hand. They all fled "to and fro." But when they saw that the knife had broken, they assaulted him and killed him. There was killed the young man who sanctified the [Divine] Name and who did what the rest of the community did not do, for he killed three of the uncircumcised with his knife. The rest had devoted themselves and had fasted daily. Previously they had wept, each for his family and friends, to the point where their strength dissipated. They were unable to do battle against them [the enemy]; rather they said: "It is the decree of the King. 'Let us fall into the hands of the Lord.'[59] Then we shall come and see the great light." There they all fell for the unity of the [Divine] Name.

There was also a respected woman there, named Minna, hidden in a house underground, outside the city. All the men of the city gathered and said to her: "Behold you are 'a capable woman.'[60] Know and see that God does not wish to save you, for 'they lie naked at the corner of

every street,"[61] unburied. Sully yourself [with the waters
of baptism]." They fell before her to the ground, for they
did not wish to kill her. Her reputation was known widely,
for all the notables of the city and the princes of the land
were found in her circle. She responded and said: "Heaven
forfend that I deny the God on high. For him and his holy
Torah kill me and do not tarry any longer." There the woman "whose praises were sung at the gates"[62] was killed.
All of them were killed and sanctified the Divine Name
unreservedly and willingly. All of them slaughtered one
another together—young men and young women, old
men and old women, even infants slaughtered themselves
for the sanctification of the [Divine] Name. Those who
have been designated by name did so; the rest who have
not been designated by name did so all the more. They
behaved in a way never seen by the human eye.[63] With
regard to them and those like them it is said: "[Rescue me
from the wicked with your sword,] from men, O Lord, by
your hand, from men whose share in life is fleeting. [But
as to your treasured ones, fill their bellies. Their sons too
shall be satisfied, and have something left over for their
young.]"[64] "[Such things have never been heard or noted.]
No eye has seen [them], O God, but you, who act for those
who trust in you."[65] They all fell by the hand of the Lord
and returned[66] to their rest, to the great light in paradise.
Behold their souls are bound up in the bond of life, with
the God who created them, to the end of days.

It came to pass that, when the saintly ones, the pious
of the Almighty, the holy community in Mainz, heard that
some of the community of Speyer had been killed and the
community of Worms [had been attacked] twice, then their
spirit collapsed and "their hearts melted and turned to
water."[67] They cried out to the Lord and said: "'Ah Lord
God of Israel! Are you wiping out the remnant of Israel?'[68]
'Where are all your wondrous deeds about which our ancestors told us, saying: "Truly the Lord brought you up
from Egypt." But now you have abandoned us, delivering
us into the hands of the gentiles for destruction.'"[69] Then
all the leaders of Israel gathered from the community and

came to the archbishop and his ministers and servants and said to them: "What are we to do with regard to the report which we have heard concerning our brethren in Speyer and Worms who have been killed?" They said to them: "Heed our advice and bring all your moneys into our treasury and into the treasury of the archbishop. Then you and your wives and your children and all your retinue bring into the courtyard of the archbishop. Thus will you be able to be saved from the crusaders." They contrived and gave this counsel in order to surrender us and to gather us up and to seize us "like fish enmeshed in a fatal net."[70] In addition, the archbishop gathered his ministers and servants—exalted ministers, nobles and grandees—in order to assist us and to save us from the crusaders. For at the outset it was his desire to save us, but ultimately he failed.

It came to pass on a certain day that a gentile woman came and brought with her a goose that she had raised since it was a gosling. This goose went everywhere that the gentile woman went. She said to all passersby: "Behold this goose understands that I intend to go on the crusade and wishes to go with me."[71] Then the crusaders and burghers gathered against us, saying to us: "Where is your source of trust?[72] How will you be saved? Behold the wonders[73] that the Crucified does for us!" Then all of them came with swords and spears to destroy us. Some of the burghers came and would not allow them [to do so]. At that time they stood . . .[74] and killed along the Rhine River, until they killed one of the crusaders. Then they said: "All these things the Jews have caused." Then they almost gathered [against us]. When the saintly ones saw all these things, their hearts melted. They [the Christians] spoke harshly with them, [threatening] to assault and attack us. When they [the Jews] heard their words, they said—from great to small: "If only we might die by the hand of the Lord,'[75] rather than die at the hands of the enemies of the Lord. For he is a merciful God, the only king in his universe."

They left their houses empty and came to the synagogue only on the sabbath, that last sabbath prior to our disaster,[76] when "a few" entered to pray. R. Judah ben R. Isaac entered there to pray on that Sabbath. They wept copiously, to the point of exhaustion, for they saw that this was the decree of the King of kings. There was a venerable scholar, R. Baruch ben R. Isaac, and he said to us: "Know that a decree has truly and surely been enacted against us, and we will not be able to be saved. For tonight we—I and my son-in-law Judah—heard[77] the souls praying here loudly, [with a sound] like weeping. When we heard the sound, we thought that perhaps they [those praying] came from the courtyard of the archbishop and that some of the community had returned to pray in the synagogue at midnight out of pain and anguish. We ran to the door of the synagogue, but it was closed. We heard the sound, but we comprehended nothing. We returned home shaken, for our house was close to the synagogue." When we heard these words, we fell on our faces and said: "'Ah Lord God! Are you wiping out the remnant of Israel?'"[78] They went and recounted these incidents to their brethren in the courtyard of the burgrave and in the courtyard of the archbishop. They likewise wept copiously.

It came to pass on the new moon of Sivan[79] that the wicked Emicho—may his bones be ground up on iron millstones—came with a large army outside the city, with crusaders and common folk. For he also said: "It is my desire to go on the crusade." He was our chief persecutor. He had no mercy on the elderly, on young men and young women, on infants and sucklings, nor on the ill. He made the people of the Lord "like dust to be trampled."[80] "Their young men he put to the sword and their pregnant women he ripped open."[81] They camped outside the city for two days. Then the heads of the [Jewish] community said: "Let us send him money, along with our letters, so that the [Jewish] communities along the way will honor him. Perhaps the Lord will treat us with his great loving-kindness." For previously they had liberally spent their moneys, giving the archbishop and the burgrave and their ministers and their servants and the burghers approximately four hundred marks, so that they might aid them. It availed them nothing. We were unlike Sodom and Gomorrah, for in their case ten [righteous] were sought in order to save them.[82] For us neither twenty nor ten were sought.

It came to pass on the third of the month of Sivan,[83] on that very day when Moses said: "Be ready for the third day."[84] On that very day the crown of Israel fell. Then the students of Torah fell and the scholars disappeared. The honor of the Torah fell. "He threw down from heaven to earth the glory of Israel."[85] Fear of sin[86] and humility came to an end. Men of deeds, the luster of wisdom and purity, those who turn back [evil] decrees and the anger of their Creator disappeared. The givers of charity in secret diminished. Truth was eclipsed; the preachers disappeared; the revered fell and the arrogant multiplied. Woe for all these! From the day that the Second Temple was destroyed, there have been none like them; after them there will be no more. For they sanctified the [Divine] Name "with all their hearts and with all their souls and with all their might."[87] They are blessed.

It came to pass at midday that the wicked Emicho—may his bones be ground up—he and all his army—came, and the burghers opened up to him the gates. Then the enemies of the Lord said one to another: "Behold the gates have been opened by themselves. All this the Crucified has done for us, so that we might avenge his blood on the Jews." They came with their standards to the archbishop's gate, where the children of the sacred covenant were—an army as numerous "as the sands on the seashore."[88] When the saintly and God-fearing saw the huge multitude, they trusted in and cleaved to their Creator. They donned armor and strapped on weapons—great and small—with R. Kalonymous ben Meshullam at their head.

There was a pious one, one of the great men of the generation, Rabbi Menahem ben Rabbi David the *levi*. He said: "All the congregation, sanctify the revered and awesome Name unreservedly." They all replied: . . . [He said]:[89] "All of you must do as did the sons of our ancestor Jacob when he sought to reveal to them the time of redemption, at which point the Divine Presence left him. [Jacob said]: 'Perhaps I too am sullied as was my grandfather Abraham [from whom proceeded Ishmael] or like my father Isaac [from whom proceeded Esau.'] [His sons said to him: 'Hear O Israel! The Lord is our God; the Lord is one.']⁹⁰ [Do] as did our ancestors when they answered and said, as they received the Torah at this very time on Mount Sinai: 'We shall do and hear.'"⁹¹ They⁹² then called out loudly: "Hear O Israel! The Lord is our God, the Lord is one."⁹³ They all then drew near to the gate to do battle with the crusaders and with the burghers. They did battle one with another around the gate. Our sins brought it about that the enemy overcame them and captured the gate. The men of the archbishop, who had promised to assist, fled immediately, in order to turn them over to the enemy, for they are "splintered reeds." Then the enemy came into the courtyard and found R. Isaac ben R. Moses [and others and struck them]⁹⁴ a mortal sword blow. Not so for the fifty-three souls who fled with R. Kalonymous through the chambers of the archbishop, exiting into a long room called . . .⁹⁵ and remaining there.

The enemy entered the courtyard on the third of Sivan,⁹⁶ on the third day of the week, "a day of darkness and gloom, a day of densest clouds."⁹⁷ May darkness and day gloom reclaim it."⁹⁸ "May God above have no concern for it; may light never shine upon it."⁹⁹ O sun and moon! Why did you not hide your light? And you stars, to whom Israel has been compared,¹⁰⁰ and you twelve constellations, like the number of the tribes of Israel, the sons of Jacob, how was it that your light not cease to provide illumination to the enemy who intended to blot out the name of Israel? Ask and see—was there ever so numerous a set of sacrifices from the days of Adam?

When the children of the sacred covenant saw that the decree had been issued and that the enemy had overcome them, they all cried out—young men and old men, young women and children, menservants and maidservants— and wept for themselves and their lives. They said: "We shall suffer the yoke of awe of the sacred. For the moment

the enemy will kill us with the easiest of the four deaths—
by the sword.[101] But we shall remain alive; our souls [will
repose] in paradise, in the radiance of the great light,
forever." They all said acceptingly and willingly: "Ultimately one must not question the ways of the Holy One
blessed be he and blessed be his Name, who gave us his
Torah and commanded us to put to death and to kill
ourselves for the unity of his holy Name. Blessed are we
if we do his will and blessed are all those who are killed
and slaughtered and who die for the unity of his Name.
Not only are they privileged to enter the world to come
and sit in the circle of the saintly, 'the pillars of the universe.' What is more, they exchange a world of darkness
for a world of light, a world of pain for a world of happiness, a transitory world for a world that is eternal and
everlasting." They all cried out loudly and in unison: "Ultimately we must not tarry. For the enemy has come
upon us suddenly. Let us offer ourselves up before our
Father in heaven. Anyone who has a knife should come
and slaughter us for the sanctification of the unique Name
[of God] who lives forever. Subsequently let him pierce
himself with his sword either in his throat or in his belly
or let him slaughter himself." They all stood—men and
women—and slaughtered one another. The young women
and the brides and bridegrooms looked through the windows and cried out loudly and said: "Look and see, God,
what we do for the sanctification of your great Name,
rather than to abandon your divinity for a crucified one,
a trampled and wretched and abominable offshoot . . . ,[102]
a bastard and a child of menstruation and lust." They were
all slaughtered. The blood of this slaughter flowed through
the chambers in which the children of the sacred covenant
were. They lay in slaughtered rows—the infant with the
elderly. . . .[103] [making sounds] like those made by
slaughtered sheep. "At such things will you restrain yourself, O Lord; will you stand idly by and let us suffer so
heavily?"[104] Avenge the blood of your servants that has
been spilled. Behold, has such a thing ever happened
before? For they jostled one another, saying: "I shall

sanctify first the Name of the King of kings." The pious women threw money outside, in order to deter them [the enemy] a bit, until they might slaughter their children, in order to fulfill the will of the Creator. . . .[105]

It came to pass that, when the enemy came to the chambers and broke down the doors and found them convulsing, still writhing in their blood, they took their money and stripped them naked. They struck those remaining and left not "a remnant or a residue." Thus they did in all the chambers where there were children of Israel, [children of] the sacred covenant, with the exception of one chamber which was too strong. The enemy did battle against it till evening. When the saintly ones [in that chamber] saw that the enemy was mightier than they were, the men and the women rose up and slaughtered the children. Subsequently, they slaughtered one another. Some fell on their swords or knives. The saintly women threw rocks through the windows. The enemy in turn struck them with rocks.[106] They [the Jewish women] endured all these rocks, until their flesh and faces became shredded. They cursed and blasphemed the crusaders in the name of the Crucified, the profane and despised, the son of lust: "Upon whom do you rely? 'Upon a trampled corpse!'" Then the crusaders advanced to break down the door.

There was a notable lady, Rachel the daughter of R. Isaac ben R. Asher. She said to her companions: "I have four children. On them as well have no mercy, lest these uncircumcised come and seize them and they remain in their pseudo-faith. With them as well you must sanctify the holy Name." One of her companions came and took the knife. When she saw the knife, she cried loudly and bitterly. She beat her face, crying and saying: "'Where is your steadfast love, O Lord?'"[107] She took Isaac her small son—indeed he was very lovely—and slaughtered him. She . . . [108] said to her companions: "Wait! Do not slaughter Isaac before Aaron." But the lad Aaron, when he saw that his brother had been slaughtered, cried out: "Mother, Mother, do not slaughter me!" He then went and hid himself under a bureau. She took her two daughters, Bella and Matrona, and sacrificed them to the Lord God of Hosts, who commanded us not to abandon pure awe of him and to remain loyal to him. When the saintly one finished sacrificing her three children before our Creator, she then lifted her voice and called out to her son: "Aaron, Aaron, where are you? I shall not have pity or mercy on you either." She pulled him by the leg from under the bureau, where he had hidden, and sacrificed him before the sublime and exalted God. She then put them under her two sleeves, two on one side and two on the other, near her heart. They convulsed near her, until the crusaders seized the chamber. They found her sitting and mourning them. They said to her: "Show us the money which you have under your sleeves." When they saw the slaughtered children, they smote her and killed her. With regard to them and to her it is said: "Mother and babes were dashed to death together."[109] She died with them, as did the [earlier] saintly one with her seven sons.[110] With regard to her it is said: "The mother of the child is happy."[111] The crusaders killed all those in the chamber and stripped them naked. They were still writhing and convulsing in their blood, as they stripped them. "See, O Lord, and behold, how abject I have become."[112]

Subsequently they threw them from the chambers through the windows naked, heap upon heap and mound upon mound, until they formed a high heap. Many of the children of the sacred covenant, as they were thrown, still had life and would signal with their fingers: "Give us water that we might drink." When the crusaders saw this, they would ask them: "Do you wish to sully yourselves [with the waters of the baptism]?" They would shake their heads and would look at their Father in heaven as a means of saying no and would point with their fingers to the Holy One blessed be he. The crusaders then killed them.

All these things were done by those whom we have designated by name. The rest of the community all the more proclaimed the unity of the sacred Name, and all fell in the hands of the Lord.

Then the crusaders began to exult in the name of the

Crucified. They lifted their standards and came to the remnant of the community, to the courtyard of the bur-grave. They besieged them as well and did battle against them and seized the entranceway to the courtyard and smote them also.

There was a certain man, named Moses ben Helbo. He called to his sons and said to them: "My sons Simon and Helbo. At this moment hell and paradise are open [before you].[113] Into which do you wish to enter?" They answered him and said: "Bring us[114] into paradise." They stretched forth their necks. The enemy smote them, the father along with the sons.

There was a Torah scroll there in the chamber. The crusaders came into the chamber, found it, and tore it to shreds. When the saintly and pure daughters of royalty [the Jewish women] saw that the Torah had been torn, they called out loudly to their husbands: "Behold, behold the holy Torah. The enemy is tearing it." Then they all, the men and the women, said together: "Woe for the holy Torah, 'perfect in beauty,'[115] 'the delight of our eyes.'[116] We used to bow before it in the synagogue; we used to kiss it; we used to honor it. How has it now fallen into the hands of the unclean and uncircumcised." When the men heard the words of the saintly women, "they became exceedingly zealous"[117] for the Lord our God and for the holy and beloved Torah. There was there a young man named R. David ben Rabbi Menahem. He said to them: "My brethren, rend your garments over the honor of the Torah." They rent their garments as our teacher commanded. They then found a crusader in a chamber and they all—both men and women—rose up and stoned him. He fell and died. Now when the burghers and crusaders saw that he had died, they did battle against them. They went up on the roof over the place where the children of the covenant were, broke the roof, shot at them with arrows, and pierced them with spears.

There was a certain man named Jacob ben Sullam. He was not from a family of notables. Indeed his mother was not Jewish. He called out loudly to all standing near him:

"All the days of my life till now, you have despised me.
Now I shall slaughter myself." He slaughtered himself for
the Name which is most sublime, which is the Name of
the Lord of Hosts.

There was, in addition, a certain man named Samuel
the elder ben R. Mordechai. He also sanctified the [Divine]
Name. He took his knife and plunged it into his belly,
spilling his innards upon the ground. He called to all
standing near him and said to them: "Behold my brethren
what I do for the sanctification of the Eternal." There the
elder fell for the unity of the [Divine] Name and sanctified
his awesome God.

The crusaders and burghers turned from there and
came to the center of the city, to a certain courtyard. There
was hidden David the *gabbai*[118] ben R. Nathaniel—he, his
wife, his children, and all the members of his household—
in the courtyard of a certain priest. The priest said to him:
"Behold there remains in the courtyard of the archbishop
and in the courtyard of the burgrave 'neither a remnant
nor a residue.' They have all been killed, cast out, and
trampled in the streets, with the exception of a few whom
they baptized. Do likewise and you will be able to be
saved—you and your wealth and all the members of your
household—from the hands of the crusaders." The God-
fearing man replied: "Indeed go to the crusaders and to
the burghers and tell them to come to me." When the
priest heard the words of David the *gabbai*, he was very
happy over his words, for he thought: "This distinguished
Jew has agreed to heed us." He ran to meet them and told
them the words of the saintly one. They likewise were
very happy. They gathered around the house by the
thousands and the ten thousands. When the saintly one
saw them, he trusted in his Creator and called to them
saying: "Lo you are the children of lust. You believe in one
who was born of lust. But I believe in the God who lives
forever, who dwells in the highest heaven. In him have I
trusted to this day, to the point of death.[119] If you kill me,
my soul will repose in paradise, in the light of life. But
'you will descend to the nethermost pit,'[120] 'to everlasting

abhorrence,'[121] to hell, where you will be judged along with your deity, who was a child of lust and was crucified." When they heard the pious one, they were enraged. They raised their standards and camped about the house and began to call and shout in the name of the Crucified. They assaulted him and killed him and his saintly wife and his children and his son-in-law and all the members of his household and his maidservant. All were killed there for the sanctification of the [Divine] Name. There fell the saintly one and the members of his household.

They turned and came to the house of R. Samuel ben R. Naaman. He likewise sanctified the [Divine] Name. They gathered around his house, for he alone of all the community had remained in his house. They asked him and sought to baptise him with fetid and impure waters. He put his trust in his Creator—he and all those with him. They [the Jews] did not heed them [the crusaders and burghers]. They killed all of them and threw them all from the windows.

All these things were done by those whom we have singled out by name. The rest of the community and the notables of the congregation—what they did for the unity of the Name of the King of kings, the Holy One blessed be he and blessed be his Name, like R. Akiba and his associates. . . .[122]

I know not how much is missing here. May God save us from this exile. The end of the former persecutions.[123]

L

Now I shall recount the development of the persecution in the rest of the [Jewish] communities that were killed for the sake of his unique Name and how they cleaved to the Lord God of their ancestors and declared his unity unto death itself.[1]

It came to pass in the year 4856,[2] the year 1028 of our exile,[3] in the eleventh year of the two hundred and fifty-sixth cycle,[4] during which we had hoped for salvation and comfort according to the prophecy of the prophet Jeremiah: "Cry out in joy for Jacob, shout at the crossroads of the nations!"[5] Instead it was turned into "agony and sighing,"[6] weeping and crying. Many evils designated in all the [passages of] rebuke—written[7] and unwritten[8]—passed over us. For then rose up initially the arrogant, "the barbaric,"[9] "a fierce and impetuous people,"[10] both French and German. They set their hearts to journey to the Holy City, which had been defiled by "a ruffian people,"[11] in order to seek there the sepulcher of the crucified bastard and to drive out the Muslims who dwell in the land and to conquer the land. "They put on their insignia"[12] and placed an idolatrous sign on their clothing—the cross—all the men and women whose hearts impelled them to undertake the pilgrimage[13] to the sepulcher of their messiah, to the point where they exceeded the locusts on the land—men, women, and children. With regard to them it is said: "The locusts have no king."[14]

It came to pass that, when they traversed towns where there were Jews, they said to one another: "Behold we

243

journey a long way to seek the idolatrous shrine and to take vengeance upon the Muslims. But here are the Jews dwelling among us, whose ancestors killed him and crucified him groundlessly. Let us take vengeance first upon them. 'Let us wipe them out as a nation; Israel's name will be mentioned no more.'[15] Or else let them be like us and acknowledge the son born of menstruation."

Now when the [Jewish] communities heard their words, they reverted to the arts of our ancestors—repentance, prayer, and charity.[16] The hands of the holy people fell weak and their hearts melted and their strength flagged. They hid themselves in innermost chambers before "the ever turning sword."[17] They afflicted themselves with fasting. They fasted three consecutive days—both night and day,[18] in addition to daily fasts, until "their skin shriveled on their bones and became dry as wood."[19] They cried out and gave forth a loud and bitter shriek. But their Father did not answer them. "He shut out their prayer"[20] and "screened himself off with a cloud, that no prayer might pass through."[21] "The tent [of prayer] was rejected"[22] and he banished them from his presence."[23] For a decree had been enacted before him from [the time when God had spoken] of a day of accounting,[24] and this generation had been chosen as his portion, for they had the strength and valor to stand in his sanctuary and to fulfill his command and to sanctify his great Name in his world. Concerning them David said: "Bless the Lord, O his messengers, mighty men who do his bidding, ever obedient to his bidding."[25]

That year Passover fell on Thursday[26] and the new moon of Iyyar on Friday.[27] On the eighth of Iyyar,[28] on the Sabbath, the enemy arose against the [Jewish] community of Speyer and killed eleven saintly souls who sanctified their Creator on the holy Sabbath day and refused to be baptized. There was a notable and pious woman who slaughtered herself for the sanctification of the [Divine] Name. She was the first of those who slaughtered themselves in all the communities. The rest were saved by the bishop without baptism, as has been written above.[29]

On the twenty-third of Iyyar,[30] they rose up against the [Jewish] community of Worms. The community divided into two groups. Some stayed in their homes and some fled to the bishop. Then "the wolves of the steppes"[31] rose up against those that were in their homes and pillaged them—men, women, and children; young and old. They tore down the stairways and destroyed the houses. They plundered and ravaged. They took the Torah and trampled it in the mud and tore it and burned it. "They devoured Israel with a greedy mouth."[32]

Seven days later, on the new moon of Sivan,[33] the day of the arrival of Israel at Sinai in order to receive the Torah, those who still remained in the chambers of the bishop were subjected to terror. The enemy assaulted them, as they had done to the earlier group, and put them to the sword. They [the Jews] held firm to the example of their brethren and were killed and sanctified the [Divine] Name publicly. They stretched forth their necks, so that their heads might be cut off for the Name of their Creator. There were some of them that took their own lives. They fulfilled the verse: "Mothers and babes were dashed together."[34] Indeed fathers also fell with their children, for they were slaughtered together.[35] They slaughtered brethren, relatives, wives, and children. Bridegrooms [slaughtered] their intended and merciful mothers their only children. All of them accepted the heavenly decree unreservedly. As they commended their souls to their Creator, they cried out: "Hear O Israel! The Lord is our God; the Lord is one."[36] The enemy stripped them and dragged them about. There remained only "a small number"[37] whom they converted forcibly and baptized against their will in their baptismal waters. Approximately eight hundred was the number killed, who were killed on these two days. All of them were buried naked. With regard to them Jeremiah laments: "Those who were reared in purple have embraced refuse heaps."[38] I have mentioned their names above.[39] May God recall them beneficently.

When the saintly ones, the pious of the Almighty, the holy community in Mainz—"a shield and buckler"[40] for

all the [Jewish] communities, whose reputation spread
throughout all the provinces—heard that some of the community in Speyer had been killed and that the community
in Worms [had been attacked] twice and that the sword
had reached them, their hands fell weak and "their hearts
melted and turned to water."[41] They cried out to the Lord
with all their heart and said: "'Lord God of Israel, are you
wiping out the remnant of Israel?'[42] 'Where are all your
awesome wonders about which our ancestors told us, saying, "Truly the Lord brought you up from Egypt and from
Babylonia?"'[43] How many times have you saved us? How
have you now abandoned and forsaken us, O Lord, leaving us in the hands of wicked Christendom that they might
destroy us? 'Do not distance yourself from us, for tragedy
is near and there is none to aid us.'"[44]

The notables of Israel gathered together to give them
good counsel, so that they might be able to be saved. They
said to one another: "Let us choose of our elders and let
us decide what we shall do, for this great evil will swallow
us up." They agreed on the counsel of redeeming their
souls by spending their moneys and bribing the princes
and officers and bishops and burghers. The leaders of the
community, notable in the eyes of the archbishop, then
rose and came to the archbishop and to his ministers and
servants to speak with them. They said to them: "What
shall we do about the report which we have heard concerning our brethren in Speyer and in Worms who have been
killed?" They said to them: "Listen to our advice and bring
all your moneys to our treasury. Then you, your wives,
your sons and daughters, and all that you have bring into
the chamber of the archbishop until these bands pass by.
Thus will you be able to be saved from the crusaders."
They contrived and gave this counsel in order to gather
us and to surrender us into their hands and to seize us
"like fish enmeshed in a fatal net"[45] and to take our
moneys, as they ultimately did. The end result proves the
original intention.[46] In addition, the archbishop gathered
his ministers and servants—exalted ministers, nobles—in
order to assist us. For at the outset it was his desire to save

us with all his strength. Indeed we gave him great bribes
to this end, along with his ministers and servants, since
they intended to save us. Ultimately all the bribery and all
the diplomacy did not avail in protecting us "on the day
of wrath"[47] from catastrophe.

At that time a duke arose, Godfrey by name—may
his bones be ground up—harsh in spirit. "A fickle spirit
moved him"[48] to go with those journeying to their idolatrous shrine. He swore wickedly that he would not depart
on his journey without avenging the blood of the Crucified
with the blood of Israel and that he would not leave "a
remnant or residue"[49] among those bearing the name Jew.
His anger waxed against us. To be sure, "a protector"[50]
arose—the exemplar of the generation, the God-fearing,
offered up on the innermost altar, R. Kalonymous the
parnas[51] of the community of Mainz—who immediately
sent an emissary to Emperor Henry in the kingdom of
Apulia, where he had tarried for nine years.[52] He told him
of all these events. Then the anger of the emperor was
aroused, and he sent letters throughout all the provinces
of his empire,[53] to the princes and bishops, to the nobles
and to Duke Godfrey—messages of peace and [orders]
with regard to the Jews that they protect them so that no
one harm them physically and that they provide aid and
refuge to them. The wicked duke swore that it had never
occurred to him to do them any harm. Nonetheless we
bribed him in Cologne with five hundred silver *zekukim*.
They likewise bribed him in Mainz. He swore on his staff
to behave peacefully toward them. But [God] "who truly
makes peace"[54] turned away from them and hid his eyes
from his people and consigned them to the sword. No
prophet or seer nor any man of wisdom or understanding
can fathom the essential issue—how could the sin of "the
innumerable people"[55] be so heavy and how could the
souls of these saintly communities be so destructive, as
though shedding blood. Except that surely [God] is "a just
judge"[56] and we bear the shortcomings.

Then "the seething waters"[57] gathered. "They heaped
up unfounded charges"[58] against the people of God. They

said: "You are the descendants of those who killed our deity and crucified him. Indeed he said: 'A day will surely arrive when my children will come and avenge my blood.' We are his children and it is our responsibility to avenge him upon you, for you are the ones who rebelled and transgressed against him. Indeed your God was never pleased with you. While he sought to do well by you, you did evil before him. Therefore he has forgotten you and no longer desires you, for you have been "stiff-necked"[59] with him. He has separated himself from you and has shown favor to us and has taken us as his portion." When we heard this, "our hearts quaked and were distressed."[60] "We were struck silent."[61] We sat in darkness "like those long dead,"[62] until "the Lord might look down and see from heaven."[63]

"Then Satan also came"[64]—the pope of wicked Rome— and circulated a pronouncement along all the gentiles who believe in the offshoot of adultery, the children of Seir, that they congregate together and ascend to Jerusalem and conquer the city "on a way built up"[65] for pilgrims and that they go to the sepulcher . . . [66] whom they accepted as a deity over them. Satan came and mingled among the nations. They all gathered as one man to fulfill the commandment. They came "as the sand on the seashore,"[67] with a noise like the rumbling of "a storm or a tempest."[68] It came to pass that, when the embittered and poor had gathered, they took evil counsel against the people of God. They said: "Why are they occupied with doing battle against the Muslims in the vicinity of Jerusalem? Indeed among them is a people which does not acknowledge their deity. What is more, their ancestors crucified their god. Why should we let them live? Why should they dwell among us? Let our swords begin with their heads. After that we shall go on the way of our pilgrimage." "The hearts of the people of God went numb"[69] and "their spirits departed"[70] . . . [71]

They came and pressed their entreaty before the Lord. They fasted and diminished their blood and flesh. "The hearts of Israel melted inside them."[72] Indeed "God did as he had said, for we sinned before him."[73] He forsook "the tabernacle of Shiloh,"[74] "the diminished sanctuary,"[75] which he had placed among his people in the midst of the nations. His anger waxed against them and "he unsheathed the sword against them,"[76] until "what was left of them was like a mast on a hilltop, like a pole upon a mountain."[77] "He let his might go into captivity"[78] and trampled it underfoot. "Look O Lord, and behold, to whom have you done thus?"[79] Is not Israel, "a people plundered and despoiled,"[80] your special portion? Why have you lifted the shield before his enemies? Why have they become mighty? "They hear how I sigh."[81] All those who hear about me . . . "both their ears will tingle."[82] "Alas the strong rod is broken, the lordly staff,"[83] the saintly congregation "valued as gold,"[84] the community of Mainz. For there was a divine edict in order to test those who fear him, that they suffer the yoke of his pure awe.

It came to pass on a certain day that a gentile woman came and brought with her a goose that she had raised since it was a gosling. This goose went everywhere that the gentile woman went. She said to all passersby: "Behold this goose understands that I intend to go on the crusade and wishes to go with me."[85] Then the crusaders and burghers and common folk gathered against us, saying to us: "Where is your source of trust? How will you be saved? Behold the signs that the Crucified does for them publicly in order to take vengeance on their enemies." Then all ot them came with swords to destroy us. Some of the high-ranking burghers came and stood opposite and would not allow them to harm us. At that moment the crusaders stood united against the burghers and one side smote the other until they killed one of the crusaders. Then they said: "All these things the Jews have caused." Then they almost gathered against us. They spoke harshly, [threatening] to assault and attack us. When the saintly ones saw all these things, their hearts melted. When they heard their words, they said, both great and small: "'If only we might die by the hand of the Lord,'[86] rather than die by the hands of the enemies of the Lord. For he is a merciful God, unique in his universe."

They left their houses empty and came to the synagogue only on the Sabbath before the new moon of Sivan,[87]
the last Sabbath prior to our destruction, when "a few"[88]
entered to pray. R. Judah ben R. Isaac entered there to
pray as part of that quorum. They wept copiously, to the
point of exhaustion, for they saw that this was the decree
of the King of all kings and that no one might annul
it. There was there a venerable scholar, R. Baruch ben
R. Isaac, and he said to us: "Know truly and surely that a
decree has been enacted against us from heaven and we
will not be able to be saved. For tonight we—I and my
son-in-law Judah—heard the souls which were praying at
night in the synagogue loudly, like a cry. When we heard
the sound, we thought that perhaps some of the community came from the courtyard of the archbishop to pray in
the synagogue at midnight, in anguish and bitterness. We
ran to the door of the synagogue to see who was praying.
The door was closed. We heard the sound and the loud
wail, but we could comprehend nothing of what they were
saying. We returned home shaken, for our house was
close to the synagogue." When we heard these words, we
fell on our faces and said: "You, O Lord God—are you
wiping out the remnant of Israel?"[89] They went and recounted these events to their brethren in the courtyard of
the burgrave and in the chambers of the archbishop. They
too knew that a decree had been issued by the Lord and
they wept copiously and accepted divine judgment and
said: "You are righteous, O Lord, and your rulings are
just."[90]

It came to pass on the new moon of Sivan[91] that Count
Emicho, the persecutor of all the Jews—may his bones be
ground up between iron millstones—came with a large
army outside the city, with crusaders and common folk in
tents. The gates of the city were locked before him. He
also had said: "It is my desire to go on the crusade." He
became head of the bands and concocted the story that an
emissary of the Crucified had come to him and had given
him a sign in his flesh indicating that, when he would
reach Byzantium,[92] then he [Jesus] would come to him

[Emicho] himself and crown him with royal diadem and that he would overcome his enemies. He was our chief persecutor. He had no mercy on the elderly or on young women; he had no pity on the infant and the suckling and the sickly. He made the people of the Lord "like dust to be trampled."[93] "Their young men he put to the sword and their pregnant women he ripped open."[94] They camped outside the city for two days.

At the time when the wicked one came to Mainz on his way to Jerusalem, the elders of the people came to their archbishop, Ruthard, and bribed him with two hundred silver *zekukim*. It had been his intention to go to the villages which belonged to the archbishops. But the [Jewish] community came, when they bribed him, and begged him, so that he stayed with them in Mainz. He brought all the community into his inner chambers and said: "I have agreed to aid you. Likewise the burgrave has said that he wishes to remain here for your sakes, to assist you. You must therefore supply all our needs until the crusaders pass through." The [Jewish] community agreed to do so. The two—the archbishop and the burgrave—agreed and said: "We shall either die with you or live with you." Then the community said: "Since those who are our neighbors and acquaintances have agreed to save us, let us also send to the wicked Emicho our moneys and our letters, so that the [Jewish] communities along the way will honor him. Perhaps the Lord will behave in accord with his great loving-kindness and will relent against us. For this purpose we have disbursed our moneys, giving the archbishop and his ministers and his servants and the burghers approximately four hundred silver *zekukim*." We gave the wicked Emicho seven gold pounds so that he might assist us. It was of no avail, and to this point no balm has been given for our affliction. For we were unlike Sodom and Gomorrah. For them ten [righteous] were sought in order to save them.[95] For us neither twenty nor ten were sought.

It came to pass on the third day of Sivan,[96] which had been a day of sanctity and setting apart for Israel at the time of the giving of the Torah—on that day when Moses

our teacher, may his memory be blessed, said: "Be ready
for the third day"[97]—on that day the [Jewish] community
of Mainz, the pious of the Almighty, were set apart in
holiness and purity and were sanctified to ascend to God
all together. "Cherished in life, in death they were not
parted."[98] For all of them were in the courtyard of the
archbishop. The wrath of the Lord was kindled against his
people and he fulfilled the counsel of the crusaders and
they were successful. All wealth was unavailing, along
with fasting, self-affliction, wailing, and charity. There was
no one "to stand in the breach"[99]—neither a teacher nor a
prince. Even the holy Torah did not protect those who
study it. "Gone from Zion are all that were her glory,"[100]
namely Mainz. The sound of "the lords of the flock"[101]
ceased, along with the sound of "the valorous who repel
attacks,"[102] "who lead the many to righteousness."[103] "The
glorious city, the citadel of joy,"[104] which had distributed
untold sums to the poor. One could not write with "an
iron stylus"[105] on a whole book the multitude of good
deeds that were done in it of yore. In one place [were
found] Torah and power and wealth and honor and wisdom and humility and good deeds, taking innumerable
precautions against transgression. But now their wisdom
had been swallowed up and turned into destruction, like
the children of Jerusalem in their destruction.

It came to pass at midday that the wicked Emicho,
persecutor of the Jews, came—he and all his army—to
the gate. The burghers opened the gate to him. Then the
enemies of the Lord said to one another: "Behold the
gate has been opened before us. Now let us avenge
the blood of the Crucified." When the children of the holy
covenant—the saintly ones, the God-fearing—who were
there saw the huge multitude, the army as large "as the
sand on the seashore," they cleaved to their Creator.
They donned armor and strapped on weapons—great and
small—with R. Kalonymous ben R. Meshullam the *parnas*
at their head. But from their great anguish and from
the many fasts undertaken, they did not have sufficient
strength to stand up before the enemy. They then came

in battalions and companies, sweeping down like a river, until Mainz was filled completely. The enemy Emicho made an announcement to the citizenry that they surrender and remove the enemy [the Jews] from the city. "A great panic from the Lord fell upon them."[106] The men of Israel strapped on their weapons in the innermost courtyard of the archbishop and all of them approached the gate [of the courtyard] to do battle with the crusaders and the burghers. They did battle against one another at the gate. Our sins brought it about that the enemy overcame them and captured the gate. "The hand of the Lord lay heavy"[107] upon his people. Then all the gentiles gathered against the Jews in the courtyard, in order to destroy them totally. The hands of our people wavered, when they saw that the hand of wicked Edom had overcome them. Indeed the men of the archbishop, who had promised to help them, fled immediately, in order to turn them over to their enemies, for they were "splintered reeds."[108] Even the archbishop himself fled from his church, for they intended to kill him as well, since he had spoken up on behalf of Israel.

The enemy entered the courtyard on the third of Sivan, on the third day of the week,[109] "a day of darkness and gloom, a day of densest clouds."[110] "May darkness and day gloom reclaim it";[111] "may God above have no concern for it; may light never shine upon it."[112] Woe for the day when we saw the anguish of our souls. Stars, why did you not cover your light—was not Israel compared to the stars?[113] The twelve constellations, like the number of the tribes of Jacob, why did you not extinguish your light from shining on the enemy that intended to blot out the name of Israel?

When the children of the sacred covenant saw that the decree had been enacted and that the enemy had overcome them, they entered the courtyard and all cried out together—elders, young men and young women, children, menservants and maidservants—to their Father in heaven. They wept for themselves and their lives. They accepted upon themselves the judgment of heaven. They said to one another: "Let us be strong and suffer the yoke of the sacred awe. For the moment the enemy will kill us, but the easiest of the four deaths is by sword.[114] We shall, however, remain alive; our souls [shall be] in paradise, in the radiance of the great light forever." They said unreservedly and willingly: "Ultimately one must not question the ways of the Holy One, blessed be he and blessed be his Name, who gave us his Torah and the commandment to put to death and to kill ourselves for the unity of his holy Name. Blessed are we if we do his will. Blessed are all those who are killed and slaughtered and die for the unity of his name. They are destined for the world to come and shall sit in the circle of the righteous, R. Akiba and his associates, "the pillars of the universe," who were killed for his Name. What is more, a world of darkness will be exchanged for a world of light, a world of pain for a world of happiness, a transitory world for a world that is eternal and everlasting." Then they all cried out loudly, saying in unison: "Now let us tarry no longer, for the enemy has already come upon us. Let us go quickly and sacrifice ourselves before the Lord. Anyone who has a knife should inspect it, that it not be defective. Then he should come and slaughter us for the sanctification of the unique [God] who lives forever. Subsequently he should slaughter himself by his throat or should thrust the knife into his belly.

The enemy, immediately upon entering the courtyard, found there some of the perfectly pious with Rabbi Isaac ben R. Moses the dialectician. He stretched out his neck and they cut off his head immediately. They had clothed themselves in their fringed garments and had seated themselves in the midst of the courtyard in order to do speedily the will of their Creator. They did not wish to flee to the chambers in order to go on living briefly. Rather, with love they accepted upon themselves the judgment of heaven. The enemy rained stones and arrows upon them, but they did not deign to flee. They struck down all those whom they found there, with "blows of sword, death, and destruction."[115]

Those in the chambers, when they saw this behavior on the part of those saintly ones and that the enemy had come upon them, all cried out: "There is nothing better than to offer ourselves as a sacrifice." There women girded themselves with strength and slaughtered their sons and daughters, along with themselves. Many men likewise gathered strength and slaughtered their wives and their children and their little ones. "The tenderest and daintiest"[116] slaughtered "their beloved children."[117] They all stood—men and women—and slaughtered one another. The young women and the brides and the bridegrooms gazed through the windows and cried out loudly: "Behold and see, our God, what we do for the sanctification of your holy Name, rather than deny you for a crucified one, a trampled and wretched and abominable offshoot, a bastard and a child of menstruation and lust."[118] "The precious children of Zion,"[119] the children of Mainz, were tested ten times, like our ancestor Abraham[120] and like Hananiah, Mishael, and Azariah.[121] They offered up their children as did Abraham with his son Isaac.[122] They accepted upon themselves the yoke of the fear of heaven, of the King of kings, the Holy One, blessed be he, willingly. They did not wish to deny the awe of our King or to exchange it for [that of] "a loathsome offshoot,"[123] a bastard born of menstruation and lust. They stretched forth their necks for the slaughter and commended their pure souls to their Father in heaven. The saintly and pious women stretched forth their necks one to another, to be sacrificed for the unity of the [Divine] Name. Likewise men to their children and brothers, brothers to sisters, women to their sons and daughters, and neighbor to neighbor and friend, bridegroom to bride, and betrothed to his betrothed. They sacrificed each other until the blood flowed together. The blood of husbands mingled with that of their wives, the blood of parents with that of their children, the blood of brothers with that of their sisters, the blood of teachers with that of their students, the blood of bridegrooms with that of their brides, the blood of cantors with that of their scribes, the blood of infants and sucklings with that of their mothers. They were killed and slaughtered for the unity of the revered and awesome Name. At such re-

ports "the ears of those who hear must surely tingle." "For
who has heard the like? Who has ever witnessed such
events?"[124] "Ask and see."[125] Were there ever so many
sacrifices like these from the days of Adam? Were there
ever a thousand one hundred sacrifices on one day, all of
them like the sacrifice of Isaac the son of Abraham? For
one the world shook, when he was offered up on Mount
Moriah, as is said: "Hark! The angels cried aloud!"[126] The
heavens darkened. What has been done [this time]? "Why
did the heavens not darken? Why did the stars not with-
draw their brightness?"[127] . . . [128] and light—"why did they
not darken in their cloud cover,"[129] when one thousand
one hundred holy souls were killed and slaughtered on
one day, on the third day of Sivan, a Tuesday—infants
and sucklings who never transgressed and never sinned
and poor and innocent souls? "At such things will you
restrain yourself, O Lord?"[130] "For your sake they were
killed"[131]—innumerable souls. "Avenge the blood of your
servants that has been spilled"[132] in our days and before
our eyes speedily. Amen.

That day the crown of Israel fell. Then the students of
Torah fell and the scholars disappeared. The honor of the
Torah fell, as is written: "He threw down from heaven to
earth the glory of Israel."[133] Those who fear sin ceased.
Men of good deeds disappeared, along with the splendor
of wisdom and purity and abstinence and the splendor of
the priesthood and men of trust and "those who repair the
breach"[134] and those who turn back evil decrees and the
anger of their Creator. Those who give charity in secret
diminished. "Truth was absent"[135] and preachers ceased,
along with the revered and the luster of old age. [Woe
for][136] the day upon which many troubles befell us.[137]
"There was nowhere to turn, either right or left,"[138] "because of the rage of the oppressor."[139] For from the day
that the Second Temple was destroyed there were none
like them in Israel and after them there will be no more.
For they sanctified and declared the unity of the [Divine]
Name with all their heart and with all their soul and with
all their might. Blessed are they and blessed is their por-

tion, for all of them are destined for the life of the world to come. May my portion be with them.

"He has increased within fair Judah mourning and moaning."[140] The enemy arose against them and killed youngsters and women, lads and elders on one day. "They showed no regard for the priests, no favor to elders."[141] They had no pity on infants or on sucklings nor on pregnant women. They left no remnant, like a date, like "two or three berries."[142] For all of them wished to sanctify the Name of their Creator. Indeed when the enemy came upon them, they all cried out loudly with one heart and mouth: "Hear O Israel! The Lord is our God; the Lord is one."[143]

There was a pious and righteous man—one of the great men of the generation—Rabbi Menahem ben R. Judah. He spoke to the people and expounded before them. [He said: "All of you must do as did the son of our ancestor Jacob][144] when he sought to reveal to them the time of redemption, at which point the Divine Presence left him. He said: 'Perhaps just as unworthiness proceeded from Isaac our father, so too am I sullied with unworthiness.' They [his sons] answered and said: 'Hear O Israel! The Lord is our God; the Lord is one.'[145] [Do also] as did our ancestors on Mount Sinai, at this very time, when they said: 'We shall do and hear.'[146] They said loudly: 'Hear O Israel! The Lord is our God; the Lord is one.'[147] You likewise must do so today." They declared his unity wholeheartedly and did as the leader of the land said. They called out with one mouth and heart: "Hear O Israel! The Lord is our God; the Lord is one." Rabbi Isaac ben R. Moses and the rest of the rabbis and notables were with him. They sat in the courtyard of the archbishop and wept, with their necks stretched out. They said: "When will the ravager come, so that we may accept upon ourselves the judgment of heaven. We have already set forth the sacrifice and constructed the altar for his Name."

Now I shall recount and tell the great wonders that were done that day by these saintly ones. Behold has such a thing ever happened before, from the earliest days? For they jostled one another saying: "I shall sanctify first the

Name of the King of kings, the Holy One, blessed be he."
The pious women, the daughters of kings, threw coins
and silver out the windows at the enemy, so that they be
occupied with gathering the money, in order to impede
them slightly until they might finish slaughtering their
sons and daughters. The hands of merciful mothers
slaughtered their children, in order to do the will of their
Creator.

When the enemy came to the chambers and broke
down the doors and found them still convulsing and
writhing in blood, they took their money and stripped
them naked and smote those who remained. They did not
leave "a remnant or a residue."[148] Thus they did in all the
chambers where the children of the holy covenant were,
with the exception of one chamber that was somewhat
stronger. The enemy did battle against them till evening.
When the saintly ones saw that the enemy was stronger
than they and that they would would be unable to withstand them any longer, they bestirred themselves and rose
up—men and women—and slaughtered the children first.
Subsequently the saintly women threw stones through
the windows against the enemy. The enemy threw stones
against them. They took the stones, until their flesh and
faces became shredded. They cursed and blasphemed the
crusaders in the name of the Crucified, the impure and
foul, the son of lust: "Upon whom do you trust? Upon a
rotting corpse!" The crusaders advanced to break down
the door.

"Who has seen anything like this; who has heard anything" like that which the saintly and pious woman, Rachel
daughter of R. Isaac ben R. Asher, wife of R. Judah, did?
She said to her companions: "I have four children. On
them as well have no mercy, lest these uncircumcised
come and seize them alive and they remain in their
pseudofaith. With them as well you must sanctify the
Name of the holy God." One of her companions came and
took the knife to slaughter her son. When the mother of
the children saw the knife, she shouted loudly and bitterly
and smote her face and breast and said: "Where is your

steadfast love, O Lord?"[149] Then the woman said to her companions in her bitterness: "Do not slaughter Isaac before his brother Aaron, so that he not see the death of his brother and take flight." The women took the lad and slaughtered him—he was small and exceedingly comely. The mother spread her sleeve to receive the blood; she received the blood in her sleeves instead of in the [Temple] vessel for blood. The lad Aaron, when he saw that his brother had been slaughtered, cried out: "Mother, do not slaughter me!" He went and hid under a bureau. She still had two daughters, Bella and Matrona, comely and beautiful young women, the daughters of R. Judah her husband. The girls took the knife and sharpened it, so that it not be defective. They stretched forth their necks and she sacrificed them to the Lord God of Hosts, who commanded us not to renounce pure awe of him and to remain faithful to him, as it is written: "You must be wholehearted with the Lord your God."[150] When the saintly one completed sacrificing her three children before the Creator, then she raised her voice and called to her son: "Aaron, Aaron, where are you? I shall not have mercy nor pity on you as well." She pulled him by the leg from under the bureau where he was hidden and she sacrificed him before the sublime and exalted God. She placed them under her two sleeves, two on each side, near her heart. They convulsed near her, until the enemy seized the chamber and found her sitting and mourning them. They said to her: "Show us the moneys which you have in your sleeves." When they saw the children and saw that they were slaughtered, they smote her and killed her along with them. With regard to her it is said: "Mothers and babes were dashed to death together."[151] She [died] with her four children as did the saintly woman with her seven sons.[152] With regard to them it is said: "The mother of the children is happy."[153] The father wailed and cried out when he saw the death of his four children, "comely and beautiful."[154] He went and threw himself on the sword in his hand. His innards flowed forth and he writhed in blood on the roadway along with those who had been killed, who had been

convulsing and writhing in their blood. The enemy killed
all those that remained in the chamber and stripped them
naked. "See, O Lord, and behold, how abject I have
become."[155]

Then the crusaders began to exult in the name of the
crucified, for they had done their will upon all those found
in the chambers of the archbishop, and there remained not
a remnant. They raised their standards and came "with
their tumult"[156] against the rest of the community, before
the courtyard of the burgrave. They besieged them as
well, until they seized the entrance to the gate of the
courtyard and smote those found there. There was a pious
man named Moses ben R. Helbo. He had two sons. He
called to his sons and said to them: "My sons, Helbo and
Simon. At this moment hell and paradise are open [before
you][157]. Into which of them do you wish to enter now?"
They answered and said to him: "We wish to enter
paradise." They stretched forth their necks and the enemy
smote them, father along with sons. May their souls reside
in paradise, in the light of life.

There was a Torah scroll there in the chamber. The
crusaders came into the chamber, found it, and tore it to
shreds. When the saintly and pious women, the daughters
of kings, saw that the Torah had been torn, they called
out loudly to their husbands: "Behold, behold the holy
Torah, for the enemy is tearing it." The women said all
together: "Woe for the holy Torah, 'perfect in beauty,'[158]
'the delight of our eyes.'[159] We would bow down to it in
the synagogue and our little children kissed it. We honored
it, yet how has it now fallen into the hands of these uncircumcised and impure." When the men heard the words
of the saintly women, "they became exceedingly zealous"[160] for the Lord our God and for his holy and beloved
Torah. There was there a lad named R. David ben Rabbi
Menachem. He said to them: "My brethren, rend your
garments over the honor of the Torah." They rent their
garments. They found in the chamber a crusader and they
all—men and women—arose and stoned him and he died.
When the burghers and the crusaders saw that the

crusader had died, they did battle with them. They went up on the roof [over the place] where children of the sacred covenant were and shot arrows at them and threw stones at them and pierced them, until they destroyed them.

There was there a very fine man, named Jacob ben R. Sullam. He did not come from a family of notables. Indeed his mother was not Jewish. He called out loudly to all those standing near him: "All the days of my life till now, you have despised me. Now I shall slaughter myself." He slaughtered himself for the Name which is most sublime, which is the Name of the Lord of Hosts.

There was, in addition, a certain man named Samuel the elder ben R. Mordechai. He also sanctified the [Divine] Name. He took his knife and plunged it into his belly, spilling his innards upon the ground. He called to all standing near him and said to them: "Behold my brethren what I do for the sanctification of the Eternal." There the elder fell for the unity of the [Divine] Name and sanctified his awesome God.

The crusaders and burghers turned from there and came to the center of the city, to a certain courtyard. There was hidden David the *gabbai*[161] ben R. Nathaniel—he, his wife, his children, and all the members of his household— in the courtyard of a certain priest. The priest said to him: "Behold there remains in the courtyard of the archbishop and in the courtyard of the burgrave 'neither a remnant nor a residue.' They have all been killed, cast out, and trampled in the dust of the street, except for a few of them whom they baptized and who turned to their faith. You do likewise and thus you will be able to be saved—you and your moneys and all the members of your house- hold—from the hands of the crusaders." The God-fearing one replied: "You go out to the crusaders and to the bur- ghers and tell them in my name that they should all come to me." When the priest heard the words of the pious David the *gabbai*, he was very happy over his words, for he said: "This important Jew has already agreed to heed us." He ran out to meet the folk and told them the words of the saintly one who had sent him. They likewise were very happy. They gathered around the house by the thousands and the ten thousands. When the saintly one saw them, he trusted in the God of his ancestors and called out to them and said: "You are the children of lust. You believe in a deity who was a bastard and was crucified. But I believe in the God who lives forever, who resides in the highest heavens. In him have I trusted to this very day and thus shall I continue to do unto death. I know the truth. If you kill me, my soul will reside in paradise, in the light of life. But 'you will descend to the nethermost pit,'[162] 'to everlasting abhorrence.'[163] In hell you shall be judged along with your deity and in boiling excrement, for he is the son of a harlot." When they heard the words of the pious one, they were enraged that he had blasphemed and had revealed to them their shame. They raised their standards and camped about the house. They began to call and shout in the name of the Crucified. They assaulted him and killed him and his saintly wife and his son and his daughter and his son-in-law and all the members of his household and his maidservant. All of them were killed for the sanctification of the [Divine] Name. There the saintly one fell along with the members of his household. They threw him through the windows into the street.

The burghers and crusaders turned from there to a certain house, the house of R. Samuel ben R. Naaman. He also sanctified the holy Name. They gathered around his house, for he had remained, of all the community, in his house, and a few others remained with him. They asked him and requested him to be baptized with their foul waters. They reposed their trust in the Creator—he and all those with him. They did not heed to him or do their will. They killed them all and trampled them underfoot.

"For these do I weep, my eyes flow tears"[164]—for the burning of the sanctuary of our God and the burning of Isaac ben R. David the *parnas* who was burned to death in his house. Now I shall recount and inform all how this occurred. It came to pass on the fifth day of Sivan,[165] on the eve of Shavuot, that the pious ones, Isaac the saintly son of David the *parnas* and Uri ben R. Joseph, came and met their Creator and sanctified the Name of their Maker exceedingly. For on Tuesday, when the community had been killed, on that day these two pious ones had been saved for hell, as the enemy baptized them against their will. Therefore they accepted upon themselves a death not written in any of the [passages of] retribution. Isaac the pious came to the house of his ancestors to check the treasures which had been hidden there from the days of his ancestors. He came to the cellar and found them, for the enemy had not touched them. He said to himself: "Of what value is all this money to me now, since the enemy 'fulfilled their purposes,'[166] in order to distance me from the Lord and to cause me to rebel against the Torah of our holy God. Moreover a certain priest requested me to recover with him. Will I find any further merit in this money? Neither silver nor gold accompanies a man to the grave— only repentance and good deeds." He thought: "I shall do penitence and 'be faithful and perfect with the Lord God' of Israel, to the point where I commend to him my soul. In his hand shall I fall. Perhaps he will do according to his loving-kindness and I shall still join my comrades and come with them to their circle, to the great light. It is revealed and known before the examiner of the heart that I did not accede to the enemy except in order to save my children from the hands of the wicked and so that they not remain in their pseudofaith. For they are young and cannot distinguish between good and evil." He went to the house of his ancestors and hired workers. They restored the doors of the house which the enemy had broken down. When they finished restoring the doors, on Thursday, the eve of Shavuot, he came to his mother and told her what he intended to do. He said to her: "Woe my mother, my lady! I have decided to offer a sin-offering to the God on high, so that I may thus find atonement." When his mother heard the words of her son and that he feared the Lord, she adjured him not to do this thing, for "her mercies toward him had been aroused."[167] Indeed he alone remained of all her beloved ones. His saintly wife had been killed—Scholaster—who was the daughter of R. Samuel the great. His mother herself was confined to bed, for the enemy struck her a number of blows. This son of hers, Isaac, saved her from death without baptism after he had already been baptized. Isaac the pious, her son, did not attend to her words and did not listen to her. He came and closed the doors of the house upon himself and his children and his mother from all sides. The pious one asked his children: "Do you wish that I sacrifice you to our God?" They said: "Do what you will with us." The saintly one responded and said: "My children, my children, our God is the true God and there is no other." Isaac the saintly one took his two children, his son and his daughter, and led them through the courtyard at midnight and brought them to the synagogue, before the holy ark, and slaughtered them there for the sanctification of the great Name, the sublime and exalted God, who commanded us never to deny his awe . . . [168] and to cleave to his holy Torah with all our heart and with all our soul. He spilled their blood on the pillars of the holy ark, so that it would come as a memorial before the unique and everlasting King and before the throne of his glory. [He said:] "May this blood serve me as atonement for all my sins." The pious one returned through the courtyard to the house of his ancestors and set fire to the house at its four corners. His mother remained in the house and was consumed by fire for the sanctification of the [Divine] Name. The pious Isaac returned a second time to burn the synagogue. He lit the fire at all the entrances. The pious one went from corner to corner "with his palms spread heavenward,"[169] to his Father in heaven. He prayed to the Lord from the midst of the fire in a loud and lovely voice. The enemy called out to him through the windows: "Wicked man! Escape the fire! You can still be saved!" They extended to him a staff with which to pull him out of the fire, but the saintly one did not wish it. "The blameless, upright, God-fearing man"[170] was there consumed by fire. His soul is hidden in the portion of the saintly in paradise.

Uri had been party to the same plan to burn the synagogue, for they heard that the enemy and the burghers intended to make and build out of it a church or a mint. When Isaac set fire to his ancestral house and to the synagogue, Uri was in a different house. He wished to aid Isaac in burning the synagogue and to thus sanctify the [Divine] Name with his companion Isaac. But he could not reach him, for the enemy arose from their beds in the middle of the night when they sensed the fire. Before he [Uri] could reach him [Isaac], they killed Uri on the way before he reached the fire, while Isaac was being consumed by the fire. There the two of them fell together before the Lord, with one heart unreservedly, for his Name which is called [Lord of] Hosts. With regard to these and others like them it is said: "He who sacrifices a thank offering honors me."[171] There are some who say that those forcibly converted heard that they wished to make of the synagogue a mint and for this reason the pious one burned it and was consumed by fire in the synagogue. Others say that they heard that the enemy wanted to make of the synagogue a church, therefore they burned it.

One year prior to the coming of "the day of the Lord,"[172] before the disaster struck, most of the rabbis in most of the communities died, and the notables of Israel likewise passed away, to fulfill what is written: "Prior to the evil the righteous is taken away."[173] Thus R. Elazar passed away. There were many women who sanctified the Name of the Creator to the death and did not wish to exchange him for the crucified bastard. Rachel, the companion of the deceased Rabbi Elazar and the companion of R. Judah ben R. Isaac, the great guide, was killed for the sanctification of his Name. Likewise other saintly women who were with them sanctified the [Divine] Name. These pious ones were brought before the courtyard of the church and they entreated them to immerse themselves in the waters of baptism. When they reached the church, they did not wish to enter a shrine of idolatry and their feet were mired, against their will, on the threshhold. They did not wish to enter the shrine of idolatry and to smell the odors of. . . .[174] When the crusaders saw that they would not accept baptism—rather that they trusted mightily in the living God with all their heart, then the enemy leaped upon them and struck them with axes and blows. There the pious ones were killed for the sanctification of the [Divine] Name. There were in addition two pious women. One was Guta, the wife of Rabbi Isaac ben R. Moses, who had been killed at the outset, and the second was Scholaster, the wife of R. Isaac who was [subsequently] burned for the sanctification of the [Divine] Name. They likewise sanctified the sacred and unique Name, whose uniqueness is celebrated by all the living, at the time when the saintly ones were killed in the courtyard of the archbishop. They were in the courtyard of a certain burgher. The enemy forced him out of his house, and the crusaders and burghers gathered against them and urged them to be baptized with their evil waters. They put their trust in the Holy One of Israel and stretched forth their necks. The crusaders struck them without mercy. There the holy ones were killed for the sanctification of the awesome and unique Name.

Likewise Samuel ben R. Isaac ben R. Samuel also sanctified the [Divine] Name. He was hidden in a certain house. When they told him that the saintly ones had been killed, he ran outside the city, to flee along with the community of Speyer. The enemy seized him and asked him: "If you wish to sully yourself, good; if not, we shall cut your neck at this very place." Samuel was silent and did not utter a sound from his mouth. He accepted upon himself the judgment. He immediately stretched forth his neck and they severed it. There the pious one fell for the sanctification of the [Divine] Name and proclaimed the unity of the Name of our God, who is the holy God.

After the children of the holy covenant who were in the [archbishop's] chambers were killed, the crusaders came upon them, to strip the corpses and to remove them from the chambers. They threw them naked to the ground through the windows—heap upon heap, mound upon mound, until they formed a high heap. Many were still

alive as they threw them. Their souls were still attached
to their bodies and they still had a bit of life. They signaled
to them with their fingers: "Give us a bit of water that we
might drink." When the crusaders saw them, that there
was still life in them, they asked them: "Do you wish to
sully yourselves? Then we shall give you water to drink
and you will still be able to be saved." They shook their
heads and looked to their Father in heaven, saying: "No."
They pointed with their fingers to the Holy One blessed
be he, but could not utter a word from their mouths as a
result of the many wounds which had been inflicted upon
them. They continued to smite them mightily, beyond
those [earlier] blows, until they killed them a second time.

All these things were done by those whom we have
singled out by name. That which they did is . . . .[175] The
rest of the community and the notables of the congregation, for whom we have not detailed their activities and
their piety, they did all the more. The activities which they
undertook in order to proclaim the unity of the Name of
the King of all kings, the Holy One blessed be he, [were]
like those of R. Akiba and his associates, and they stood
the test like Hananiah, Mishael, and Azariah. A miracle
was done for them like that done for the slain of Betar, for
whom [the rabbis] instituted the recitation of [the blessing]
"he is good and does good"—"he is good," for they did
not rot, and "he does good," for they were given burial.[176]
These saintly and pious as well—these miracles were done
for them as well, for the burghers buried them with the
money that they had safeguarded with them. However
they were buried naked. They dug nine pits in the cemetery and buried there lads with elders, men with women,
fathers with sons, mothers with daughters, masters with
servants, maids with mistresses. All of them together were
thrown one with the other and buried there. May God on
high remember them and avenge them speedily in our
days. Concerning them it is said: "He works judgment
upon the nations, heaping up bodies, crushing heads far
and wide."[177] "The Lord is a God of vengeance; God of
vengeance, appear."[178] Those who killed [are destined] for

"everlasting abhorrence"; those who were killed for the sanctification of the holy Name of the sublime God [are destined] for the life of the world-to-come. Their souls will reside in paradise, bound up in the bond of life. Amen.

Now I shall tell of the killing of R. Kalonymous the pious, the *parnas,* and his band. May God avenge him speedily in our days. It came to pass on the day when the Lord had said to his people: "Be ready for the third day"[179]—on that very day "they prepared themselves" and stretched forth their necks and made their sacrifice "as a pleasing odor to the Lord."[180] There were killed on that day for his great Name, for he is unique in his universe and beside him there is no God, eleven hundred holy souls, with the exception of R. Kalonymous the saintly, the *parnas,* and with him some of the young men of Israel, fifty-three souls who were saved on that day. They fled through the chamber of the archbishop and come into the storehouse in the church, which is the treasury, which they call . . . [181] They remained there "in anguish and distress,"[182] because of the sword [poised] above their necks. The entrance to the storehouse was narrow and dark, and no one of the enemy was aware of them. They were silent. "The sun set and it was very dark."[183] They expressed anguish. "Their tongues cleaved to their palates from thirst."[184] They approached the window to speak to the priest appointed over the treasury that he give them water to revive their souls. He did not wish to do so, until they gave him ten silver denarii for a jug of water, to fulfill that which is said: "You shall serve your enemy in hunger and thirst."[185] When the jug reached the window, its opening was narrow, and the jug could not be brought through it, until he took a lead tube and transferred the water with it. They drank in moderation, not to satisfaction.

Now I shall tell how it happened that these saintly ones were killed. In the middle of the night the archbishop sent someone to the window of the storehouse, to R. Kalonymous the *parnas.* He called to him and said: "Listen to me, Kalonymous. Behold the archbishop has sent me to you to learn whether you are still alive. He

commanded me to save you and all those with you. Come
out to me. Behold with him are three hundred warriors,
armed with swords and dressed in armor. 'Our persons
are pledged for yours, even to death.'[186] If you do not
believe me, then I shall take an oath. For thus my lord the
archbishop commanded me. He is not in the city, for he
went to the village of Rüdesheim. He sent us here to save
the remnant of you that remains. He wishes to assist
you." They did not believe until he took an oath. Then
R. Kalonymous and his band went out to him. The minister placed them in boats and ferried them across the Rhine
River and brought them at night to the place where the
archbishop was, in the village of Rüdesheim. The archbishop was exceedingly happy over R. Kalonymous, that
he was still alive, and intended to save him and the men
that were with him. But the enemy "unsheathed their
swords"[187] after them, and "the Lord did not relent in his
anger"[188] against them—[the Lord] "in whose hands are
the streams of water and the hearts of kings"[189] and ministers. He inclined in their favor the heart of the archbishop
initially. Afterward, however, he changed his mind and
called to R. Kalonymous and said to him: "I cannot save
you. Your God has abandoned you; he does not wish to
leave you 'a remnant and a residue.' I no longer have
sufficient strength to save you or assist you henceforth.
Therefore know what you must do—you and your band
that stands with you. Either believe in our deity or bear
the sins of your ancestors." R. Kalonymous the pious
answered him and cried out in anguish: "It is true that our
God does not wish to save us. Therefore your words are
true and correct, that you no longer have the power to
assist. Now give me time till tomorrow to respond to your
words." Then R. Kalonymous returned to his comrades,
the pious ones, and told them the words of the archbishop.
They all arose together and made a benediction over their
sacrifice and accepted the judgment unanimously and
singleheartedly and accepted upon themselves the yoke of
the fear [of God]. First, before he returned to the archbishop, R. Kalonymous the pious took his son Joseph,

kissed him, and slaughtered him. When the archbishop heard that he had slaughtered his son, he was exceedingly angry. He said: "Now I certainly do not wish to assist you further." When the villagers heard what the archbishop had said, they gathered against them, along with the crusaders, to kill the Jews. Meanwhile R. Kalonymous on that day returned to the archbishop. On the way R. Kalonymous learned and heard what the archbishop had said. When he returned before him, he took a knife in his hand. He came before him and wished to kill him. But the archbishop's men, and indeed the archbishop himself, were aware of the fact. He ordered that he be removed from his presence. The servants of the archbishop arose against him and killed him with a wooden staff. There are those who say that he did not return a second time to the archbishop. Rather, as soon as he slaughtered his son, he took his sword, planted it in the ground, fell upon it, and pierced his belly. There are those who say that the enemy killed him on the way. In any case, the prince was killed for the unity of the Name of the King of all kings, the Holy One blessed be he, and "was pure and perfect with the Lord God" of Israel. There the saintly one fell and was killed with his band.

Also R. Judah ben Isaac and Isaac his uncle ben R. Asher—they likewise were killed. Similarly the Jewish women who were there were all killed and slaughtered for the unity of the Name of the God of Israel. These are some of those who were in this second group: Seigneur and R. Kalonymous ben R. Joseph the elder of Speyer and Isaac ben R. Samuel and Isaac ben R. Moses and R. Elazar ben R. Judah and Helbo ben R. Moses and many others with them. They also trusted in the Rock of Israel. R. Seigneur killed a certain gentile and the villagers gathered against him in the forest to which the archbishop had sent them. They stoned them with rocks and shot at them with arrows and pierced and killed them with swords until the mighty of Israel fell there in the hand of the Lord. "At such things will your restrain yourself, O Lord?"[190]

Also there were in that second group in a different

place in the forest: Abraham ben R. Asher and Samuel
ben R. Tamar and many others. They also sanctified the
sublime and great [God]. The enemy gathered against
Abraham ben R. Asher and urged him to be baptized with
evil waters, for he was a well-known and comely man.
[There gathered][191] about him some of his acquaintances.
He said to them: "Is there anyone here who knows if there
remains from all my household or my family even one?"
They said: "We do not know." They urged him intensely
to convert. He responded and said: "How long will you
tarry? By your lives, kill me. For I shall not heed you in
this matter. I shall trust in the living God and to him shall
I cleave, until I commend to him my soul." Thus also said
Samuel to Abraham: "I shall be with you in life and in
death." The enemy smote them, because they did not
wish to heed their words. They smote Abraham and he
fell to the ground and died. Samuel was also killed there
with him. They put their trust in the Holy One of Israel
and the two of them entered together his storehouse of
treasures, till the day when he remembers the spilled blood
of his servants. Then "he shall work judgment upon the
nations, heaping up bodies, crushing heads far and
wide."[192] It is further said: "O nations, acclaim his people!
For he will avenge the blood of his servants and wreak
vengeance upon his foes."[193]

Also R. Yekutiel ben R. Meshullam and his son-in-law
they killed on the road between Mainz and Rüdesheim,
as they returned from the place where R. Kalonymous his
brother, the *parnas*, had been killed. They intended to
return to the city of Mainz, so that the enemy might kill
them there and bury them there in the cemetery with their
brethren the pious and upright and perfect. They could
not reach the place that they intended. The crusaders encountered them and killed them on the way. Behold their
souls are bound up in the bond of life, with the Lord our
God.

He who spoke and the world came into being—he will
avenge the blood of his servants that has been spilled.
They said: "Let us take the meadows of God as our posses-

sion."[194] They said: "Let us wipe them out as a nation; Israel's name will be mentioned no more."[195] They said: "[The Lord] does not see it, the God of Jacob does not pay heed."[196] "The Lord is a God of vengeance; God of vengeance, appear."[197] "It is for your sake that we are slain all day long."[198] "They devoured us with greedy mouths."[199] "See, O Lord, and behold, to whom have you done this. Alas, women eat their own fruit, their newborn babes! [Alas, priest and prophet are slain in the sanctuary of the Lord!] Prostrate in the streets lie both young and old. My maidens and youths are fallen by the sword. They slaughtered on your day of wrath; they slew and had no pity upon us."[200] "Pay back our neighbors sevenfold for the abuse they have flung at you, O Lord."[201] "Rise up, judge of the earth, give the arrogant ones their deserts!"[202] With regard to their adversaries, kindle your anger and take vengeance upon them, as is said: "The Lord with the weapons of his wrath [is coming] to ravage all the earth."[203] Subsequently, "he will yell, he will roar aloud, he will charge upon his enemies."[204] "Pour your fury on the nations that do not know you, upon the kingdoms that do not invoke your Name."[205] "Pour out your wrath on them; may your blazing anger overtake them."[206] Seek of them the blood of your servants that has been given "upon a bare rock."[207] "Land—cover not their blood, and let there not be a place for our cries."[208] May he give us our vengeance in our hands. "Before our eyes let it be known among the nations that you avenge the spilled blood of your servants"[209] speedily, for your great Name by which we are called. Let all creatures know and understand their sin and their guilt for what they did to us. Requite their deeds upon them as they did to us. Then shall they know and understand and take to heart that for vanity they have thrown down our corpses to the ground and for foolishness they have killed our pious and for a foul corpse they have spilled the blood of saintly women and for the words of "an enticer and beguiler"[210] they have spilled the blood of infants and sucklings. It is vanity—they do [not][211] recognize the [God] who created them and do not go on a good and straight path. They have not understood or taken to heart who made the sea and the land. In all their actions they have been foolish; they have lost their wisdom. [In vanity][212] they have placed their trust. They have not recognized or recollected the Name of the living God, who is the King of the universe and who is everlasting. May the blood of his pious ones serve for us as merit and atonement for succeeding generations and for all our descendants forever, like the binding of our ancestor Isaac, when our ancestor Abraham bound him on the altar. These pious ones did not say one to another: "Have pity on yourselves." Rather they said: "Let us spill our blood on the ground like water, and let it be considered by God like the blood of 'the gazelle and the deer.'"[213] It is written in the Torah: "[No animal from the herd or from the flock] shall be slaughtered on the same day with its young."[214] But here the father and the son [were slaughtered] on one day—the mother and the daughter on one day. Let the reader of these reports not say that these alone whom we have indicted have sanctified the Name of God on high. Also those for whom we have not specified here their names and the deeds which they did at their deaths sanctified the holy and revered [Name]. Thus testified "those few" remaining who were forcibly converted, who heard with their ears and saw with their eyes that which these pious ones did when they killed them and what they said at the moment of their death,[215] slaughter, and killing. May their virtue and their saintliness and their piety and their purity and their sacrifice serve us as an intercessor and as an advocate before the Almighty. May he deliver us from this exile under wicked Edom speedily in our days. May our true messiah arrive. Amen—speedily in our days.

Now I shall recount that which the [Jewish] community of Cologne did and how they sanctified the unique and sublime Name. It came to pass on the fifth of Sivan,[216] on the eve of Shavuot, that the report reached the city of Cologne, a lovely city which had hosted the ingathered flock, in which had collected the ingathered flock.[217] "Merit is advanced by the worthy."[218] From there radiated life and sustenance and judgment to all our brethren scattered everywhere. They began killing among them from Shavuot[219] through the eighth of Tammuz.[220] When they heard that the [Jewish] communities had been killed, they all fled to gentile acquaintances. They remained there for the two days of Shavuot. "On the third day, as morning dawned, there were rumblings"[221] and the enemy rose up against them. They broke into the house, "taking spoil and seizing booty."[222] They destroyed the synagogue and took out the Torah scrolls and desecrated them. They gave them over to "trampling in the streets."[223] On the very day when it was given, when the earth had been shaken and "its pillars trembled,"[224] it was torn and burned and the evil and wicked trampled it and "ruffians invaded it and defiled it."[225] For such deeds will you not repay them? How long "will you stand by idle while the one in the wrong devours [the one in the right]?"[226] "See, O Lord, and behold, how abject I have become."[227]

On that day they found a pious man, named Isaac ben R. Eliakim, who left his house. The enemy seized him and brought him to the church. He spat before them and before their shrine and cursed and reviled them. They killed him for the sanctification of the [Divine] Name, since he did not wish to flee out of respect for the holiday and because he was happy to accept the judgment of heaven.

They also found a notable woman there, named Rebecca, as she left her house. The enemy accosted her laden down with objects of gold and silver in her sleeves. She wished to carry them to her husband, R. Solomon, for he had already left his house and was in the house of his gentile acquaintance. They took the money from her and killed her. There the saintly one died in sanctity.

There was yet another woman, Matrona. But the rest of the community was saved, remaining in the houses of their acquaintances, to which they had fled. They remained there until the archbishop went to his towns on the tenth of the month of Sivan.[228] He divided them up and placed them in seven of his towns, in order to save them. They were there until the new moon of the month of Tammuz, every day anticipating death. They fasted daily and also on the two days of the new moon of Tammuz,[229] on a Monday and Tuesday. Likewise on the morrow they fasted night and day. [They fasted] consecutively for three days.[230]

On Tuesday[231] those in the town of Neuss were killed and buried. It was a [Christian] festival[232] and all of them gathered there from the villages. There was there a pious one, Samuel ben R. Asher. They killed him on the bank of the Rhine River, along with his two sons. They buried him in the sand near the river. One of his sons they hung in the doorway of his house, as a sign of mockery. [There was also a pious one named R. Isaac the *levi*. They afflicted him with harsh tortures][233] and baptized him against his will, for because of the blows which they struck him he was unaware. When he regained his senses, he returned three days later and went to Cologne, entered his house, waited a bit—an hour—went to the Rhine River, and drowned himself in the river. Concerning him and others like him it is said: "I will return from Bashan; I will retrieve from the depths of the sea."[234] He floated in the water until he came to the town of Neuss. The waters threw him up there on the river bank and he was deposited alongside the pious Samuel who had been killed in Neuss. The two pious ones were buried there together on the river bank in the sand in one grave. They sanctified the Name of heaven there in broad daylight. Gedaliah was in the town of Bonn prior to the disaster, along with his wife and children. They also were killed there in the town of Neuss and sanctified the [Divine] Name exceedingly.

On that day, Tuesday,[235] the enemy—the enemy of the Lord—came to a certain town.[236] Toward evening they sanctified the [Divine] Name there exceedingly. Bridegrooms and beautiful brides, old men and old women, young men and young women stretched forth their necks and slaughtered one another and gave their souls for the sanctification of the [Divine] Name in the ponds which surrounded the town.

When the enemy came before the town, then some of the pious ones went and ascended the tower and threw themselves into the Rhine River[237] that flows around the town and drowned themselves in the river and all died. Only two young men did not die in the water—R. Samuel the bridegroom ben R. Gedaliah and Yehiel ben R. Samuel. "Cherished in life," for they loved each other exceedingly; "they were never parted in death."[238] When they decided to throw themselves into the water, they kissed one another and held one another and embraced one another by the shoulders and wept to one another and said: "Woe for our youth, for we have not been deemed worthy to see seed go forth from us or to reach old age. Nonetheless 'let us fall into the hands of the Lord.'[239] He is a steadfast and merciful God and King. Better to die here for his great Name and to stroll with the saintly ones in paradise than that these uncircumcised and unclean seize us and sully us against our will 'with their evil waters.'" Subsequently those [Jews] that remained in the town, who did not go up on the tower, came and saw the others who had drowned. They found there the two good friends, totally saintly, clasped together. When the pious Samuel saw his son Yehiel who had thrown himself in the water but had still not died—he was a comely young man, "as majestic as Lebanon"[240]—he cried out: "Yehiel, my son, my son! Stretch out your neck before your father and I shall offer you up as a sacrifice before the Lord . . . [241] I shall make the benediction for slaughtering and you shall respond amen." R. Samuel the pious did so and slaughtered his son with sword in the water. When R. Samuel the bridegroom ben R. Gedaliah heard that his friend Yehiel the saintly had acceded to his father, that he slaughter him in the water, then he decided to do the same. He called to Menachem who was the sexton in the synagogue of Cologne and said to him: "By your life, take your sharp sword and examine it carefully that it have no defect and slaughter me likewise, so that I shall not see the death of my friend. Make the benediction for slaughtering and I shall respond amen." These pious ones did thus. When they were slaughtered together, prior to death, they clasped one another by the hand and died together in the river. They fulfilled the verse: "They were never parted in death."[242] When R. Samuel the elder, the pious, the father of R. Yehiel, saw this act of sanctification which they had undertaken, he also said to Menachem the pious, the sexton: "Menachem, conquer your will like a warrior and slaughter me with the same sword with which I slaughtered my son Yehiel. I have examined it well and it has no defect that might void the slaughtering." Menachem took the sword in his hand, examined it carefully, and slaughtered R. Samuel the elder as he had slaughtered R. Samuel the bridegroom. He made the benediction for slaughtering and he answered after him amen. Menachem the pious of God on high fell on the sword and it pierced his belly and he died there. Thus these pious ones sanctified the holy Name of the zealous and avenging [God] in the water. Now come all inhabitants of the world and see! Was there ever anything like this, such a declaration of the unity of the [Divine] Name, from the days of Adam? How great was the strength of these saintly ones, who were all slaughtered by their swords! How great was the strength of the father, "whose mercies were not aroused" for his son!

There were many who behaved similarly. "Eyes saw and gave testimony; ears heard and confirmed it."[243] There were some of them who drowned themselves in the water. There remained only "three berries." There was also there an elder, named Elazar the *levi*, and his saintly wife. He was the father-in-law of R. Levi ben R. Solomon. The enemy tortured them with terrible tortures and wounded them repeatedly, so that they believe in their abomination. But they did not wish to believe in their abomination. The saintly woman died quickly of hunger and thirst. But her pious husband lived three days and cried loudly to God on high that he take his soul. The enemy came to him every hour, for the ponds that went out from there were close to the town,[244] and afflicted him with terrible tortures. When the enemy wished to feed them of their food,[245] they did not wish to eat. The two of them died of hunger and thirst and were buried there. "At such things will you restrain yourself, O Lord."[246] "The Lord goes forth like a warrior."[247] It is said: "O nations, acclaim his people, for he will avenge the blood of his servants.[248] There were many in those two towns whom I have forgotten and who were not written down. They were killed for the sanctification of his great Name. Of all these souls there remained only two young men and two infants.

On the third day of the month of Tammuz, on Wednesday,[249] the pious of the Almighty in . . . [250] were killed. They also sanctified exceedingly the Name of the unique [God]. There remained of them only a few.

On the fourth of the month of Tammuz, on Thursday,[251] the enemy gathered together against the saintly ones of . . . [252] in order to torture them with great and terrible tortures until they agree to baptism. The matter became known to the pious ones. They confessed before their Creator and they volunteered and chose for themselves five pious and saintly ones,[253] men of good heart and God-fearing, who would slaughter all the rest. There were there approximately three hundred souls, the aristocrats of the community of Cologne. They were all slaughtered and there remained no one, for all of them died in purity for the sanctification of the unique Name.

There was the *parnas*, the head of them all, the most outstanding of the aristocrats, the leading spokesman, Judah ben R. Abraham, the counselor and sage and respected one. When all the communities came to Cologne to the fairs three times a year, he was the one who spoke before them all in the synagogue, and they sat silently before him and listened to his words. When the heads of the communities began to speak their words, they would rebuke them all and admonish them to heed his words. They would say: "His words are true, sincere, and clever." He was of the tribe of Dan, "an upright man,"[254] the exemplar of the generation. He devoted himself to the plight of his neighbors. All his days, evil had never been caused to his associates through him. He was the beloved of heaven and the delight of mankind. The entire psalm David said of him: "A psalm of David. [Lord,] who may stay in your tent, [who may reside in your holy mountain? He who lives without blame, who does what is right. . . .]"[255] The women likewise greatly sanctified the [Divine] Name publicly. When Sarit the young lady, the bride, saw that they had killed themselves with their swords and had slaughtered one another—she was "beautiful and comely" and exceedingly lovely in the eyes of those who beheld her—she wished to flee, out of fear of what she saw through the window. When her father-in-law Judah ben R. Abraham the pious saw that this was the intention of his daughter-in-law, he called to her and said: "My daughter, since you were not permitted to be wed to my son Abraham, you will not be wed to any other, to the foreigners." He seized her and held her outside the window and kissed her on the mouth and raised his voice in weeping along with the lass. He cried out loudly and very bitterly and said to all those standing there: "Behold, all of you. This is the bridal canopy of my daughter, my bride, that I make this day." They all wept with great weeping and wailing and "mourning and moaning." The pious Judah said to her: "My daughter, come and lie in the bosom of Abraham our ancestor. For in one moment you shall acquire your future and shall enter the circle of thesaintly and pious." He took her and placed her in the bosom of his son Abraham, her betrothed, and cut her with his sharp sword into two pieces. Subsequently he also slaughtered his son. "Over these I weep and my heart laments."[256]

Since they had committed themselves to fasting three days, both night and day—young men and women, infant and suckling, along with the elderly—"their tongues cleaved to their palates from thirst." They [the infants] did not suck at the breasts of their mothers prior to their slaughter. On the third day they roused themselves and proceeded zealously to the commandment of their Creator. They loved him to the death. Indeed this man, the pious David ben[257] R. Isaac, afflicted himself with fasting, so that there remained only a quarter of blood.[258] When they slaughtered him, only a quarter of a quarter of blood flowed forth. Then his spirit left and returned to its God and his pure soul departed. Behold how they sanctified the holy Name and had no mercy on their children. At the end of the three days, when the enemies of the Lord departed and those Jews forcibly converted came, they had pity upon [the slain] and wished to bury them, for they served "as food for the birds of the sky and the beasts of the earth."[259] They found her [antecedent unclear in text] convulsing in blood. They washed the blood away and brought her to a certain house. She remained seven days without speaking. Food and drink did not enter her mouth. Subsequently her spirit was revived and they healed her. From that day further she fasted daily, eating only once a day, except for Sabbaths and holidays and new moons, till now, the year 4900 [1140 C.E.].[260] I Solomon ben Simson[261] wrote down this incident in Mainz. There I asked the elders about the entire episode. From their mouths I arranged each detail properly. They told me of this act of sanctification.

On Friday, the fifth of the month,[262] on the eve of the Sabbath, at dusk on the eve of rest, the enemy—the enemy of the Lord—came upon the pious ones at Xantes. The enemy rose up against them at the hour of sanctification of the [Sabbath] day. They had seated themselves to break bread. They had sanctified the [Sabbath] day with the prayer "Va-yechulu"[263] and had made the benediction over the bread. They then heard the sound of the oppressor. "The seething waters" came upon them. They had eaten only the [bread of] the benediction. Then the head of all of them rose and said: "You, the descendant of Aaron the priest—you are worthy of greatness." "Woe for those who have been lost and cannot be found."[264] "My harp has been tuned for a dirge, my flute to the voice of those who sleep."[265] All those who heard his voice as he prayed used to say: "This voice is like a harp and a flute, like a drum and a pipe." His prayer ascended to the heavens, to the chair [of glory], sweetness for the eternal. It became a crown and a diadem for the head of Almighty God, the King of all kings, the Holy One blessed be he. Nonetheless the edict was issued and a sort of copper plate was created between us and our Father in heaven. "He closed off our prayer."[266] We found not "one proper advocate out of a thousand."[267] Indeed God came to test the generation, to proclaim to all and in the heavenly retinue their love. Thus said King David: "Therefore they love you *alamot*"[268]—they love you to death. Likewise he said: "It is for your sake that we are slain all day long, that we are thought of as sheep to be slaughtered."[269]

Then the pious and faithful one—the priest who stood above his brethren—said to the congregation seated around him at the table: "Let us recite the grace to the living God and to our Father in heaven. For the table is set before us in place of the altar. Now let us rise up and ascend to the house of the Lord and do speedily the will of our Creator. For the enemy has come upon us today. We must slaughter on the Sabbath sons, daughters, and brothers, so that he bestow upon us this day a blessing.[270] Let no one have mercy—neither on himself or on his companions. The last one remaining shall slaughter himself by the throat with his knife or pierce his belly with his sword, so that the impure and the hand of evil ones not sully us with their abominations. Let us offer ourselves up as a sacrifice to the Lord, 'like a whole burnt offering'[271] to the Most High offered on the altar of the Lord. We shall exist in a world that is entirely daylight, in paradise, in the shining light. We shall see him eye to eye, in his glory and in his majesty. Each one shall receive a golden crown on his head, in which are set precious stones and pearls. We shall be seated there among 'the pillars of the universe' and shall eat as part of the society of the saintly in paradise. We shall be part of the company of R. Akiba and his associates. We shall be seated on a golden throne under the Tree of Life. Each of us shall point to him by finger and say: 'This is our God; we trusted in him [and he delivered us. This is the Lord, in whom we trusted;] let us rejoice and exult in his deliverance.'[272] There we shall

observe the Sabbath [properly], for here, in this world of
darkness, we cannot rest and observe it properly." They
all responded loudly, with one mouth and one heart:
"Amen. So may it be and so may it be his will." The pious
Rabbi Moses began to recite the grace, for he was a priest
of Almighty God. He intoned: "Let us bless our God
of whose bounty we have eaten."[273] They responded:
"Blessed is our God of whose bounty we have eaten."[273]
They responded: "Blessed is our God of whose bounty we
have eaten and through whose goodness we exist." He
intoned: "May the Merciful avenge during the days of
those who remain after us and in their sight the blood of
your servants which has been spilled and which is yet to
be spilled. May the Merciful save us from evil men and
from conversion and from idolatry and from the impurity
of the nations and from their abominations."[274] He further
intoned many benedictions related to the event at hand,
because of the edict hanging over them, as my ancestors
and the rest of the elders occupied with the labor have told
me. They saw the great deed. When they rose from the
table, the pious one said to them: "You are the children of
the living God. Recite loudly and in unison: 'Hear O Israel!
The Lord is our God; the Lord is one.'"[275] They did so. [He
continued:] "Now do not tarry any longer, for the time has
come to act, to offer up our souls as a sacrifice before him."
On the eve of the Sabbath, at dusk, they offered themselves up as a sacrifice before the Lord in place of the daily
offering of dusk; they made themselves like the daily offering of the morning. "As the finder of booty exults in his
booty and with the joy of a harvest"[276] did they delight and
exult in undertaking the service of our God and in sanctifying his great and holy Name. They all came happy and
rejoicing before the exalted and sublime God. With regard
to such as them it is said: "Like a groom coming forth from
the chamber, like a hero eager to run his course."[277] Similarly were they happy to run and enter into the innermost
chamber of paradise. Regarding them the prophet proph-
esied: "No eye has seen [them], O God, but you, who act
for those who trust in you."[278]

There was an upright man, R. Natronai ben R. Isaac. The priests, his acquaintances, came to him all the previous day and urged him to sully himself with their "seething waters," for he was a pleasant and comely young man. He mocked[279] them and said: "Heaven forfend that I deny the God of heaven. In him shall I trust to the death." He slaughtered his brother and afterward himself for the unity of the unique and holy Name.

There was, in addition, a servant of the Lord who was a true convert. He asked Rabbi Moses, the high priest, and said to him: "My lord, if I slaughter myself for the unity of his great Name, what will be my lot?" He said to him: "You shall sit with us in our circle, for you shall be a true convert and sit with the rest of the saintly true converts in their circle. You shall be with our ancestor Abraham who was the first of the converts." When the pious one heard this, he immediately took the knife and slaughtered himself. Indeed his soul is bound up in the bond of life, in paradise, in the light of the Lord.

In this sacrifice there remained no one except those who were wounded and writhing in blood among the dead. When the enemy seized the tower before they had all been slaughtered, they all fled at night from among the dead. All of them were accorded burial—praise to the Creator. May their merit and the merit of the others who were slaughtered and pierced and strangled and burned and drowned and stoned and buried alive—who accepted upon themselves with love and affection these seven deaths, like the seven days of the week, for the sake of the holy and pure awe [of God]—serve as an intercessor before Almighty God, that he might redeem us speedily from the exile of wicked Edom, speedily in our days, and rebuild for us the walls of Jerusalem[280] and gather the scattered of Judah and Israel "who have been scattered as with a winnowing fork throughout the gates of the earth,"[281] the remnant of a remnant that yet remains in captivity and privation, "in trial and tribulation," among the nations, for the sake of his great and mighty and awesome Name by which we are designated.

On Sunday, the seventh of the month of Tammuz,[282] the enemy of the Lord arose against the pious of the Lord [in Moers][283] to obliterate them from the world. They besieged the city—a multitude as large "as the sand on the seashore." The mayor of the city came and went out to meet them in a field and requested them to wait till dawn. Thus he said to them: "Perhaps I shall convince the Jews and they will listen to me out of fear and do my will." The suggestion was acceptable to them. The mayor returned to the city, to the Jews, immediately and ordered that they be called and brought before him. Thus he said to them: "In truth, at the outset I promised to protect you and to maintain you until there remain no Jew in the world. But I have fulfilled this condition. Henceforth I cannot save you from all these people. Now decide what you wish to do. Know that, if you do not do thus and so, then the city will surely be destroyed. It is better for me to turn you over to them, so that they not come upon us in siege and destroy the fortress." They all—from small to great—said in unison: "We are prepared and wish to stretch forth our necks for the fear of our Creator and for the unity of his Name." When the minister saw that he could not overcome them, he immediately made a different plan, in order to impose upon them the fear of the crusaders so that they do their will and be baptized—to lead them out of the city to a place where the crusaders were camped. All of this was unavailing, for they said: "We are not moved by fear of the crusaders." Thus they all responded. When they saw that what they had done was unavailing, they returned them to the city, seized them, and put them in custody, each one separately, till the morrow, so that they not harm themselves for they heard that the others had harmed themselves. . . . [284] On the morrow they seized them against their will and gave them to the crusaders. They [the Jews] left the town "in urgent haste."[285] They killed some of them. Those whom they left alive they baptized against their will. They did with them as they wished.

From there fled a pious one, named Shmaryahu—

he and his wife and his three children—that night. For the treasurer, the servant of the archbishop, had promised to take them along and to save them, in return for much money which he gave him. He led them through the forest till the ninth of Av.[286] He led them from place to place, wandering, until he sent to his children in Speyer, R. Nathan and R. Mordechai, for money. They sent him gold pieces. When he had seized the money, he immediately gave them up and led them to the village of. . . .[287] When he came there, they were exceedingly happy, for they recognized him. They agreed to wait for the morrow and to do all their will and desire. They immediately made a feast of joy, but they [the Jews] did not wish to eat with them of their abominations, but rather [to eat] in purity and in accord with the law and with a new knife. For they said: "While we still remain in our faith, we wish to do as we were accustomed up till now. Tomorrow we shall belong to another people. Tonight place us in one chamber, till the morrow, for we are tired and exhausted from the exertions of the journey. They did as the pious one said to them, in order to fulfill his desire. He rose during the night. He took in his hand the knife, girded himself with courage, and slaughtered his wife and three children. Subsequently he slaughtered himself. He lost consciousness, but was still not dead. On the morrow, when the enemy came upon him, they thought that he would come over to them as he had promised. They found him lying on the ground. They asked him: "Do you still wish to abandon your God and to turn to our faith? For you may still live." He responded and said to them: "Heaven forfend! I shall not deny the living God for a dead deity, 'a trampled corpse.'[288] Rather I shall be killed for the Name of the Holy One, blessed be he, and for his holy Torah. I shall come today with the saintly in their circle. For this day I have hoped all my life." They said: "We shall not kill you as you think. Behold we shall bury you alive in the grave, or else you must acknowledge our faith." He responded and said to them: "Let it be as you say. I accept all upon myself out of love." "The

insolent dug him a pit."[289] He entered the grave himself, R. Shmarya[hu] the pious. He took his three children
and set them at his left and his wife [at his right], with
himself in the middle. They threw dirt upon him from
above. He screamed and wept aloud, mourning himself
and his children and his wife who lay near him all that
day till the morrow. The enemies of the Lord came upon
him a second time and took him alive from the grave, so
that he reconsider and acknowledge their faith. They asked
him again: "Do you wish to exchange the great and revered
[God] for a despised being?" He remained steadfast till
death. They placed him a second time in the grave and
threw dirt upon him. There the pious one died for the
unity of the revered and awesome Name. He there stood
the test, like Abraham our ancestor. Blessed be he and
blessed is his portion. With regard to him and others like
him it is said: "May his friends be as the sun rising in
might."[290] What is the meaning "in might"? During the
season of Tammuz. Consider how much more glorious the
sun is during the season of Tammuz than during the rest
of the year. Just so much greater will be the saints than all
other people in the world-to-come. They shall be part of
that group beloved by him more than any other. They are
destined to sit and stand in the shadow of the Holy One,
blessed be he, standing by his right hand, as is said: "Light-
ning flashing at them from his right."[291] With regard to
them this verse is said: "In your presence is perfect joy;
delights are ever in your right hand."[292] Read not "perfect"
but "seven,"[293] referring to the seven bands of saintly, one
ranged above the other, with faces like the sun and the
moon. With regard to them it is said: "How abundant is
the good that you have in store for those who fear you,
that you do for those who take refuge in you."[294] They shall
forever exult. "Light is sown for the righteous, radiance
for the upright."[295] These saintly ones desired to sanctify
the revered and awesome Name with joy and cheer, like
a man going to a feast, and to declare his unity "like a hind
crying for water."[296]

Of all the seven towns into which the community of

Cologne was distributed, only those few who were in the town of Kerpen were saved.[297] They were not killed. However, the mayor of the town was exceedingly wicked in another respect. For he commanded his servants that they take the gravestones of the dead buried in Cologne and fashion him a building with these gravestones. They did so. When they raised the stones on the ramparts over the building to build the wall, it came to pass through the zealous and vengeful Lord that a stone fell on the head of the enemy, the mayor of the town, and split his skull and shattered his brain and he died. Subsequently his wife became crazed, his consort demented, and she died of that disease. Thus the zealous and vengeful God hinted to us that he had given vengeance for what they had done. Thus may he avenge speedily and in our days the blood of his servants which has been shed and is shed daily on his behalf.

As the enemy did their will upon those communities which we have described, likewise they did [their will] on other communities: in the city of Trier, Metz, Regensburg, Prague, . . . ,[298] and. . . . [299] All of them sanctified the great and awesome Name out of love and affection. All this took place in one year and at one time, for the Lord chose all that fine generation for himself as his portion, in order to provide merit through them for the generations coming after them. Thus may it be [divine] will before the exalted and sublime God that he repay their descendants after them the reward of the deeds of their predecessors. May their virtue and saintliness and piety and purity serve us forever, selah, bringing closer redemption and "leading us beyond death"[300] in the land of the living.

I have been told the incident of Trier. It came to pass on the fifteenth of the month of Nisan, on the first day of Passover,[301] there arrived an emissary to the crusaders from France, an emissary of Jesus, named Peter. He was a priest and was called Peter the prelate. When he arrived there in Trier—he and the very many men with him—on his pilgrimage to Jerusalem, he brought with him a letter from France, from the Jews, [indicating] that, in all places "where his foot would tread"[302] and he would encounter Jews, they should give him provisions for the way. He would then speak well on behalf of Israel, for he was a priest and his words were heeded. When he came here, our spirit departed and our hearts were broken and trembling seized us and our holiday was transformed into mourning. For, up to that point, the burghers had never intended to do any harm to the [Jewish] community, until those pseudo-saintly ones arrived. We gave [funds] to the priest Peter and they went on their way. Then our wicked neighbors, the burghers, came and were jealous of all the incidents that befell the rest of the [Jewish] communities in Lorraine. They heard what had befallen them and what had been decreed against them and the many disasters. They [the Jews] took their money and bribed the burghers, each one individually. All this was unavailing on the day of the Lord's anger, for there was an edict on the part of the Lord from heaven against all that generation which had been chosen by him as his portion, to fulfill his commandment.

At that time members of the community of Trier took their Torah scrolls and placed them in a strong house. When the enemy became aware of this, they went there on the very same day, broke the roof from above, and took all the cloth and silver that was around the wooden rollers, and threw the Torah scrolls to the ground. They tore them and trampled them under foot. The [Jewish] community had already fled to the bishop and was no longer there. They took with them the ministers of the bishop and his servants and endangered themselves with death and went there and found the Torah scrolls trampled under foot. They rent their garments and cried out in bitterness: "See, O Lord and behold my misery; for the enemy has done great harm."[303] They took the Torah scrolls and raised them from the ground and kissed them and brought them with them into the palace. During those days they fasted excessively. They undertook penitence and charity; they fasted six weeks, from day to day, from Passover to Shavuot.[304] At evening time, they distributed daily their money to the poor. They imposed a tax upon themselves—four times they gave a denarius per pound. This still did not suffice, because of the multitude of bribes, until they gave all their goods—even the cloak on their shoulders. In the end they intended to give the bishop—so that he might save them from the hands of the wicked ones—everything they possessed. This availed them nothing, for the Lord had turned them over to their enemies. His anger had been kindled against them and he had hidden his face from them on the day of this reckoning.

It came to pass on the Sunday of Pentecost.[305] There also took place on that day the fair [dedicated] to their abomination. They came there from the Rhine River to the fair. The pious and saintly ones fled to the palace of the bishop, which is called "the palace."[306] Then the murderers came and exulted in the killing and destruction which they had perpetrated against the people of the Lord, the holy communities. The bishop came to the Church of St. Simon[307] to protect the Jews. When the enemy heard the words of the bishop, that he mentioned the Jews, then they gathered together to smite the bishop. Then the bishop fled into the church, into a certain room, and remained there for a week. All the gentiles came to the palace, where the people of the sacred covenant were, to do battle against it, but they could not overcome it. When they [the Jews] saw them, "their hearts trembled as the trees of the forest sway before a wind."[308] They [the crusaders] saw that they would not be able to do battle against it, for it was very strong. The thickness of the walls was five cubits and it was as high as the eye could see. They therefore departed and intended to kill the bishop in the Church of St. Simon. The bishop was very frightened because he was a stranger in the city, without a relative or acquaintance. He did not have the requisite strength to save them. Then the bishop came to them with advice as to what to do. He asked them: "What do you wish to do? Indeed you see that from every side the Jews have already been killed. It was my desire and it was proper to keep my pledge to you, as I had promised you, up to that time which I had specified to you—until there remained no [Jewish] community in the kingdom of Lorraine. Behold now the crusaders have risen against me, to kill me. I am still fearful of them. Behold I have fled from them for a fortnight." The community answered and said: "Did you not specify a time in your pledge—that you would support us until the emperor arrived in the kingdom?" The bishop answered and said: "The emperor himself could not save you from the crusaders. Be converted or accept upon yourselves the judgment of heaven." They answered him and said: "Know that, if each of us had ten souls, we would give them all for the unity of his Name, before they would sully us." Then they stretched forth their necks and said: "Cut off our heads. We shall not deny our God." When the bishop saw this, he went with his ministers, and they found respite for four days, until the day of the giving of the Torah had passed. Thus the pious ones had requested of him. They made that holiday a day of mourning, for they knew and heard that the bishop and all his spokesmen were counseling evil against them groundlessly.

The day came and the bishop sent an emissary to them, [asking] what he should do and what counsel he should adopt, for everyone had risen against him to kill him. They then thought that he wished them to give him a bribe. They told the emissary to bribe him with all their money. The emissary answered and said: "The bishop does not wish these [moneys]." Then the hands of the pious wavered. The hearts of the bishop and his ministers turned against them. They decided together not to kill them [all], but only two or three in order to weaken the spirit of the rest of them. Perhaps they might turn to our pseudo-faith. The bishop sent and called to the important men of his city and his ministers. They stood before the gateway of his palace. In the gateway there was a door like the grate of a furnace. The enemy stood around the palace by the hundreds and thousands, grasping sharp swords. They stood ready to swallow them alive, body and flesh. Then the bishop's military officer and ministers entered the palace and said to them: "Thus said our lord the bishop. Convert or leave his palace. I do not wish to preserve you any longer, for many times they have risen against him to kill him on your account. You cannot be saved—your God does not wish to save you now as he did in earlier days. Behold this large crowd that stands before the gateway of the palace." When they saw that the pain was very great, the pious came and sat on the ground. They lifted their voices in weeping and wept greatly and bitterly—men, women, and children. They confessed their sins.

They then led outside Asher ben R. Joseph the *gabbai* to be killed, in order to spread fear and anxiety among the rest, so that they might acknowledge their pseudo-faith. Asher answered and said: "'Let anyone among you of the people of the Lord—may his God be with him—go up.'[309] Let anyone who wishes to receive the countenance of the Divine Presence [go up]. Behold a world full of bounty in a brief moment." One lad, named Meir ben R. Samuel, responded and said: "Wait for me! I wish to come with you into a world that is entirely light. I shall with you declare the unity of the unique, revered, and awesome Name unreservedly and willingly." When they left the gateway of the palace, the crusaders brought before them [an image] so that they might bow down before it. They mocked [the image].[310] Then they killed these two pious ones for the sanctification of the [Divine] Name.

There was Abraham ben R. Yom Tov, faithful and saintly and righteous and beloved of heaven. He would arrive early at and depart late from the house of prayer. He fell on his face and confessed his sins before the King of kings, the Holy One blessed be he. He raised his voice and wept, saying: "Woe, O Lord God! Why have you abandoned your people Israel to calumny, plunder, and shame, destroying us through the hands of a people as impure as the pig which they eat. [Why have you done this] to us, the people that you chose to be your special people among all peoples. You have raised them up from the earth to heaven and now 'you have thrown down from heaven to earth the glory of Israel.' You have multiplied our corpses." The pious one fell full length on his face to the ground publicly. They raised him up and led him outside. There he was killed for the sanctification of the [Divine] Name. There was a young lass, the scion of a fine family. She also sanctified the [Divine] Name in holiness.

After these were killed, the enemy saw those remaining in the palace—that they were as firm in their faith as at the outset and that their hands had not been weakened by what had been done to these first [martyrs]. They said to one another: "All this the women do—they incite their husbands, strengthening their hands to rebel. . . ."[311] Then all the ministers came and each grasped forcefully the hands of the women, smiting and wounding them, and led them to the church in order to baptize them. Afterward they sent and took forcefully children from the bosoms of their mothers and took them with them, to fulfill what is said: "Your sons and daughters shall be delivered to another people."[312] The women raised their voices and wept. Three days prior to informing them of this forced conversion, the ministers came to the palace and closed the pit in which water was held in the palace, for they feared lest they throw their children there to kill them. They did not permit them to ascend the wall, so that they not throw themselves from the wall. All night they guarded them that they not kill one another, until dawn. All this they planned because they did not wish to kill them—rather they labored to seize them and to forcibly convert them.

There was a young woman in front of the gateway of the palace. She stretched her neck outside and said: "Anyone who wishes to cut off my head for the fear of my Rock let him come and do so." The uncircumcised did not wish to touch her, because the young lady was comely and charming. But many times they wished to take her and carry her off with them. They intended [to do so] but could not, for she threw herself to the ground and made herself dead weight. Thus she remained in the palace. Then her aunt came and said to her: "Do you wish to die with me for the fear of our Rock?" She answered and said to her:

"Yes, gladly." They went and bribed the guard of the gate. They left and went to the bridge and threw themselves into the water out of fear of the eternal King. Thus also did two young girls from Cologne. With regard to them and others like them it is said: "The Lord said: 'I will retrieve from Bashan, I will retrieve from the depths of the sea.'"[313] Praise to the Lord that they were accorded burial. May the Avenger avenge in our days and before our eyes the blood of his servants that has been spilled. May their virtue and saintliness serve for our merit and protect us on a day of evil.

Now I shall tell of those in Metz. "Have you then rejected Israel? Have you spurned"[314] Metz, the sacred community? Why were they struck—they and all their seed? The pious of the Almighty were killed there—the revered of the land, the scholars, R. Samuel the *cohen* and *gabbai* and many others. Saintly heroes, the pillars of the land, were killed there. The number of slain in that place was twenty-two. Most of them were forcibly converted, with great sin and guilt, until the days of wrath passed. Afterwards they returned to the Lord with all their heart. May the Almighty accept their penitence and forgive the sins of his people.

The community in Regensburg was forcibly converted in its entirety, for they saw that they could not be saved. Indeed those who were in the city, when the crusaders and the common folk gathered against them, pressed them against their will and brought them into a certain river. They made the evil sign in the water, the cross, and baptized them all simultaneously in that river. . . . [315] They also returned immediately to the Lord after the enemies of the Lord passed through and greatly repented. For what they had done they had done under great duress. They could not stand up against the enemy and indeed the enemy did not wish to kill them. May our Rock forgive us our shortcomings.

When the crusaders came upon the people of the Lord, the holy ones who were in the city of . . . ,[316] they said: "Now understand our words and decide what you will do.

Either turn to our pseudo-faith or accept upon yourselves the judgment of death by sword, as have done your brethren who dwell in the land of Horites."[317] They exacted from the crusaders and their fellow townsmen three days' time and reported the matter to their lord by means of emissary. For those three days they declared a fast and beseeched the living God with fast and weeping and crying out. Their prayer was accepted and the merciful God saved them. The Lord strengthened their hand during the three-day period and sent them a duke and with him a thousand calvarymen, girded with sword, along with the Jews living in the city of . . . —five hundred young men, armed with swords and men of war, who never retreat before an enemy. They came upon the city confidently and smote greatly the crusaders and the townspeople. Of the Jews only six were killed. The Light of Israel saved the rest of the community and led all of them together to a town opposite the city of . . . , across the river. They remained there in peace and tranquility until the enemies of the Lord passed.

Now it is fitting to tell the praise of those forcibly converted. For all that they ate and drank they mortally endangered themselves. They slaughtered meat and removed from it the fat. They examined the meat according to the regulations of the sages. They did not drink wine of libation. They did not go to church except occasionally. Every time they went, they went out of great duress and fear. They went reluctantly. The gentiles themselves knew that they had not converted wholeheartedly, but only out of fear of the crusaders, and that they did not believe in their deity, but that rather they clung to the fear of the Lord and held fast to the sublime God, creator of heaven and earth. In the sight of the gentiles they observed the Sabbath properly and observed the Torah of the Lord secretly. Anyone who speaks ill of them insults the countenance of the Divine Presence.

It came to pass after these events, in which they did their desire and will, that they turned and went on the way of their pseudo-pilgrimage to Jerusalem. The first band was that of the priest from France, and with him a very great army. He came to the borders of the kingdom of Hungary. He sent emissaries to the king of Hungary, saying: "Let us pass through your land. We shall travel on the royal road. We shall eat and drink only [by purchase of goods] with money." The king gave permission to cross through his borders—he and all his army. However, they must travel peacefully and not harm his people in all the cities. They came to a fortified city, a large city, in which there were many people. They [the crusaders] were already seized with hunger pangs, and they bought a bit of bread for a denarius. One of the crusaders carried in his hand woolen leg wrappers in order to sell them in the market and to purchase with the proceeds bread. One of the townspeople came and mocked him. Satan came between them, to the point they rose up to kill each other. An evil spirit circulated among them. The crusaders arose and killed all the townspeople, "from infant to suckling." The report reached the king. The enemies of the Lord traveled from there and came to a certain river, named the Danube. The river was full on all its banks. There were no boats with which to cross the river. Near the river was a village. They came and destroyed the village and took the wood of the houses. They fashioned the wood and made with it a bridge and crossed the river. They came to a city fortified with "wall, gates, and bars."[318] The townspeople closed the gate in their faces and did not wish to allow them entry into the city, for the king was already aware and had commanded that they not allow entry into their fortifications, so that they not destroy the kingdom. They did so. The priest Peter saw that he could not enter the city. He sent messengers to the city—a certain priest. [He said]: "Since you do not permit us to enter the city, send us bread outside the city and we shall buy it." The townspeople did not wish to do so, for thus was the command of the king. He sent further messengers to the town ruler to sell them bread at a double price. They answered him, saying: "Even to avoid endangerment to your lives we shall not sell to you." That night the enemies of the Lord fasted and all came before the priest Peter and took counsel with him as to what they should do. They said:

"On the morrow let us take vengeance upon them." Peter answered them and said: "It is certainly true that there is nothing of substance in this people and in its faith, for they are lesser in faith than the Muslims. Indeed they are worthy of stoning, for they are openly unconcerned with sustaining us." He called to the people and said: "Surround the city."[319] The enemy came into the city, broke down the gates, and killed all those found in it. They remained in the city for three days and consumed everything in it. They plundered the city and went on their way. The king of Hungary heard what the crusaders had done—that they had made desolate two of his towns—and his heart melted. He gathered all his army to do battle with the crusaders—it was a very mighty army, a people "like the sand on the seashore." Then the king commanded his servants to tell the people that they should return to their homes and be prepared to come to the king at any time that he might command. On the morrow, the king called his ministers, nobles, and officials alone. They took counsel with the king to close the gates of the border at the periphery of the kingdom of Hungary, so that henceforth no more crusaders might enter. With regard to those who had already entered, they began "to cut down all the stragglers."[320] When they seized a hundred crusaders together, they would kill them. On the next day they would do likewise and on the next day likewise, until they killed them all—those traveling with the priest Peter. The Holy One blessed be he avenged the blood of his servants upon them. There remained of them not one man.[321]

The kingdom of Hungary "was shut up tight"[322] in the face of the enemy. Then came the Rhinelanders, the inhabitants of the Rhineland, a very mighty army, along with the army of Swabia and the army of France and the army of Austria—they are the children of Seir the Horite[323]—an army as numerous as the sand on the shore of the sea. The head of them all was the wicked Count Emicho of Leinigen, may his bones be ground up. They came to the perimeter of the kingdom of Hungary, to the city of. . . . [324] Around the walls were pits of clay. They proceeded against it to do battle and could not overcome it. Then the leaders and nobles agreed upon the counsel of sending to the king of Hungary that he behave generously on behalf of the Crucified and give them a place for crossing. They would put aside their weapons. They took four noblemen from among them and sent him [a message] in these terms. The king came and ordered that they be imprisoned for three days. On the third day the four noblemen swore to him that they would bring him the head of Count Emicho. He then dismissed them with booty. The matter was told to Emicho and he fled during the night. Those remaining fled and the army of the king of Hungary pursued them. They struck them a great blow. More died in "the slimy clay"[325] than were killed by sword. When one fled, he fell into the clay up to his knees and could not move from there till he died. The Greeks[326] pursued them from all sides up to the Danube River. They fled on the bridge which the priest Peter had made. They broke the bridges and there drowned in the Danube River more than a thousand thousands and ten thousand myriads, to the point where they walked on the back [of the drowned] as one walks on dry land. The remnant came. Our hearts heard and were gladdened, for the Lord showed us vengeance upon our enemies. On these days the sun was eclipsed.[327] On that day God "broke the proud glory"[328] of our enemies and their name was uprooted. But the enemy has not yet repented of their evil thoughts. Every day they set forth for Jerusalem. The Lord has consigned them to slaughter "like sheep to slaughter and has set them aside for a day of slaying."[329] "Pay back our neighbors sevenfold."[330] "Give them, O Lord, their deserts according to their deeds. Give them anguish of heart; your curse be upon them. Oh, pursue them in anger and destroy them from under the heavens of the Lord."[331] "For it is the Lord's day of retribution, the year of vindication for Zion's cause."[332] "But Israel has won through the Lord triumph everlasting. You shall not be ashamed or disgraced in all the ages to come."[333]

Abbreviations

Chazan   English translation of S and L, found above

Eidelberg   Shlomo Eidelberg (trans.), *The Jews and the Crusaders* (Madison, 1977)

Habermann   Abraham Habermann (ed.), *Sefer Gezerot Ashkenaz ve-Zarfat* (Jerusalem, 1945)

L   The lengthy Hebrew First-Crusade chronicle, found in N&S, 1–30; Habermann, 24–60; Eidelberg, 21–71; Chazan

MGH, Scrip.   *Monumenta Germaniae Historica, Scriptorum* (32 vols.; Hanover, 1826–1934)

N&S   Adolf Neubauer and Moritz Stern (eds.), *Hebräische Berichte über die Judenverfolgungen während der Kreuzzüge* (Berlin, 1892)

P   The Hebrew First-Crusade chronicle attributed to Rabbi Eliezer bar Nathan and embellished with poetic dirges, found in N&S, 36–46; Habermann, 72–82; Eidelberg, 79–93

PAAJR   *Proceedings of the American Academy for Jewish Research*

REJ   *Revue des études juives*

RHC, Occ.   *Recueil des historiens des croisades, historiens occidentaux* (5 vols.; Paris, 1844–1895)

S   The short and truncated Hebrew First-Crusade
                     chronicle, found in N&S 47–57; Habermann,
                     93–104; Eidelberg, 99–115; Chazan

Notes

INTRODUCTION

1. All the major recent studies of the First Crusade have included a section on these anti-Jewish assaults. This is true, e.g., for Sir Steven Runciman's *A History of the Crusades*, 3 vols. (Cambridge, 1951–1954), I:134–141; for the composite *A History of the Crusades*, ed. Kenneth M. Setton, 2d ed., 5 vols. (Madison, 1969–1984), I:262–265; and especially for Joshua Prawer's *Toldot Mamlekhet ha-Ẓalbanim be-Ereẓ Yisrael*, 3d ed., 2 vols. (Jerusalem, 1971), I: 93–104.

2. The broad histories of Heinrich Graetz, S. M. Dubnow, and Salo W. Baron have discussed in substantial detail the crisis of 1096 and northern European Jewry, see Graetz, *Geschichte der Juden*, var. eds., 11 vols., 1873–1900, 3d ed., VI:82–98; Dubnow, *Weltgeschichte des Judischen Volkes*, trans. A. Steinberg, 10 vols. (Berlin, 1925–1929), IV:275–286, or *Divrei Yeme Am Olam*, trans. B. Krupnick 2d ed., 10 vols. (Tel Aviv, 1958), IV:157–162; Baron, *A Social and Religious History of the Jews* 2d ed., 18 vols. (New York, 1952–1983), IV:94–106. The same is true for the more limited studies of the medieval Jewish experience by Georg Caro and James Parkes; see Caro, *Sozial- und Wirtschaftgeschichte der Juden im Mittelalter und der Neuzeit*, 2 vols., (Leipzig, 1908–1920), I:202–216; Parkes, *The Jew in the Medieval Community* (London, 1938), 61–89. In vol. III of *Saeculum*, (1952), 94–131, Ernst L. Dietrich presented a lengthy article on the First Crusade and European Jewry, titled "Das Judentum im Zeitalter der Kreuzzüge"; his study is hardly comprehensive, however, and breaks no new ground in the analysis of these bloody incidents. Adolph Waas's "Volk Gottes und Militia Christi—Juden und Kreuzfahrer," which appeared in vol. IV of the *Miscellanea Medievalia*

published by the University of Cologne (Berlin, 1966), 410–434, adds nothing to previous presentations. The one aspect of the period that has been carefully investigated is the relationships among the endangered Jews, their imperial overlord, and their more immediate episcopal protectors. This issue was well researched by Sarah Schiffman in her doctoral dissertation, *Heinrich IV und die Bischöfe in ihrem Verhalten zu den deutschen Juden zur Zeit des ersten Kreuzzuges* (Berlin, 1931), reprinted as two separate articles in the *Zeitschrift für die Geschichte der Juden in Deutschland*, III (1931), 39–58 and 233–250.

I. THE BACKGROUND

1. For those seeking an introduction to the general developments of this exciting period, the following works are most useful: Robert S. Lopez, *The Commercial Revolution of the Middle Ages, 950–1350* (Englewood Cliffs, N.J., 1971); Carlo M. Cippola, ed., *The Fontana Economic History of Europe: The Middle Ages* (London, 1972); Georges Duby, *The Early Growth of the European Economy*, trans. Howard B. Clarke (Ithaca, N.Y., 1974); Lynn White, Jr., *Medieval Technology and Social Change* (Oxford, 1962); some of the essays in Jacques Le Goff, *Time, Work, and Culture in The Middle Ages*, trans. Arthur Goldhammer (Chicago, 1980); Marc Bloch, *Feudal Society*, trans. L. A. Manyon (Chicago, 1961); Robert Boutruche, *Seigneurie et féodalité*, 2 vols. (Paris, 1968–1970); R. W. Southern, *The Making of the Middle Ages* (London, 1953); idem, *Medieval Humanism and Other Studies* (Oxford, 1970); André Vauchez, *La spiritualité du Moyen Age occidental* (Paris, 1975); M. D. Chenu, *Nature, Man, and Society in the Twelfth Century*, ed. and trans. Jerome Taylor and Lester K. Little (Chicago, 1968). Important perspectives on the enormous cultural and spiritual changes that took place during the late eleventh and early twelfth century (roughly 1060–1160) can be found in the essays collected in *Renaissance and Renewal in the Twelfth Century*, ed. Robert L. Benson and Giles Constable (Cambridge, Mass., 1982). For more detailed literature on the new spiritual tendencies of this period, see below, chap. 4.

2. See, e.g., Duby, *The Early Growth of the European Economy*, 134–135, for a summary statement on this urbanization; and, passim, on the place of the Jews in this process.

3. For a concise statement of this renewal, including the role

of the Jews, see Southern, *Medieval Humanism*, 11–12. For a variety of perspectives on this renewal see Benson and Constable, *Renaissance and Renewal* and the extensive bibliography provided there.

4. See Southern, *The Making of the Middle Ages*, and Benson and Constable, *Renaissance and Renewal*.

5. Two of the latest works in this area are Jeffrey Burton Russell, *Dissent and Reform in the Early Middle Ages* (Berkeley, 1965), and R. I. Moore, *The Origins of European Dissent* (New York, 1977).

6. Quoted from an extensive depiction of the violence of the period in Bloch, *Medieval Society*, 410–412.

7. The term *Ashkenaz*, which appears in Gen. 10:3, I Chron. 1:6, and Jer. 51:27, was appropriated by the medieval Jews as a designation for northern European Jewry in general and German Jewry more specifically. The basis for this utilization is still a puzzle. See Baron, *A Social and Religious History*, IV:3–4 and 236 n. 1, where the relevant literature is discussed.

8. On this eleventh-century revival see, inter alia, chaps. IX–XII in Cecil Roth, ed., *The Dark Ages* (Tel Aviv, 1966; The World History of the Jewish People); Ephraim E. Urbach, *Ba'alei ha-Tosafot*, 4th ed., 2 vols. (Jerusalem, 1980), chap. I; Abraham Grossman, *Ḥakhmei Ashkenaz ha-Rishonim* (Jerusalem, 1981); Samuel Poznanski, *Mavo 'al Ḥakhmei Ẓarfat Mefarshei ha-Mikra* (Warsaw, 1913), ix-xxxix.

9. Note, e.g., the modern collections of the responsa of Rabbi Gershom ben Judah of Mainz, ed. Shlomo Eidelberg (New York, 1955), and those of Rabbi Solomon ben Isaac of Troyes, ed., Israel Elfenbein (New York, 1943).

10. The most important of these was the extensive commentary of Rabbi Solomon ben Isaac of Troyes on the Babylonian Talmud, printed in all standard editions of the Talmud.

11. See e.g., Rabbi Judah ha-Cohen's *Sefer ha-Dinim*, ed. Abraham Grossman (Jerusalem, 1977).

12. A critical edition of this commentary on the Torah was prepared by Abraham Berliner (Frankfort, 1905). An English translation is available by M. Rosenbaum and A. M. Silvermann, 5 vols., (London, 1929–1934).

13. Note, e.g., the collected poems of Rabbi Simon ben Isaac, ed. Abraham Habermann (Berlin, 1938); those of Rabbi Gershom ben Judah of Mainz, ed. Abraham Habermann (Jerusalem, 1944); those of Rabbi Solomon ben Isaac of Troyes, edited by Abraham Habermann (Jerusalem, 1941).

14. Note, e.g., the Le Mans letter of 992, in Abraham Berliner, *Oẓar Tov*, 1878, 49–52, and Habermann, pp. 11–15; and the report on the activities of Jacob ben Yekutiel, in Berliner, *Oẓar Tov*, 46–48, and Habermann, 19–21.

15. Major recent treatments include Bernhard Blumenkranz, *Juifs et Chrétiens dans le monde occidental* (Paris, 1960); Lea Dasberg, *Untersuchungen über die Entwertung des Judenstatus im 11 Jahrhundert* (Paris, 1965); Roth, *The Dark Ages;* Irving A. Agus, *The Heroic Age of Franco-German Jewry* (New York, 1969).

16. See, e.g., *Teshuvot Maharam ben Baruch*, ed. Moshe Bloch (Budapest, 1895), 212a, no. 890, and *Maʿaseh ha-Geonim*, ed. Abraham Epstein (Berlin, 1909), 70.

17. See, e.g., *Teshuvot Maharam*, ed. Bloch, 131a–b, no. 935, and 124b, no. 904.

18. N & S, 20; Habermann, 47.

19. *Gislebert Crispini disputatio judei et christiani*, ed. Bernhard Blumenkranz (Utrecht, 1961).

20. See, inter alia, the discussion by Agus in Roth, *The Dark Ages*, pp. 215–219. For a full discussion of these eleventh-century intellectual centers see Grossman, *Ḥakhmei Ashkenaz ha-Rishonim*. On the general phenomenon of travel for business and scholarly purposes, see the important observations of Bloch, *Feudal Society*, 62.

21. Berliner, *Oẓar Tov*, 49–52; Habermann, 11–15. See Robert Chazan, "The Persecution of 992," *REJ* CXXIX (1970), 217–221.

22. Berliner, *Oẓar Tov*, 46–48; Habermann, 19–21. On this source see Robert Chazan, "1007–1012: Initial Crisis for Northern-European Jewry," *PAAJR* XXXVIII–XXXIX (1970–1), 103–106.

23. N & S, 31; Habermann, 59–60. On the structure of this community record see Robert Chazan, "A Twelfth-Century Communal History of Spires Jewry," *REJ* CXXVIII (1969), 253–257.

24. Alfred Hilgard, ed., *Urkunden zur Geschichte der Stadt Speyer* (Strasbourg, 1885), 11–12.

25. See the exhaustive study by Abraham Grossman in *Zion*, XL (1975), 154–185.

26. *Teshuvot Maharam*, ed. Bloch, 133, no. 941. Cf. the English translation provided in Irving A. Agus, *Urban Civilization in Pre-Crusade Europe*, 2 vols. (New York, 1968), II: 439–440.

27. See, e.g., *Teshuvot Ḥakhmei Ẓarfat ve-Lotir*, ed. Joel Muller (Vienna, 1881), 58b, no. 101.

28. Both Duncalf, in Setton, *A History of the Crusades*, I:263, and Runciman, *A History of the Crusades*, I:134–135 speak of the

heavy involvement of Jews in usury as a potent factor in crusader animosity toward the Jews. The evidence of the eleventh-century sources does not support this contention.

29. *Ma'aseh ha-Geonim*, 70.

30. Hilgard, *Urkunden zur Geschichte der Stadt Speyer*, 12.

31. The fullest description of the self-governing apparatus can be found in Agus, *The Heroic Age*, 185–276.

32. See the works above in n. 2.

33. See Grossman, *Hakhmei Ashkenaz ha-Rishonim*.

34. A major statement of the extensive Christian-Jewish contact in northern Europe at this period can be found in Jacob Katz, *Exclusiveness and Tolerance* (Oxford, 1961), 24–36.

35. *Teshuvot Rashi*, ed. Elfenbein, 142, no. 114.

36. *Ma'aseh ha-Geonim*, ed. Epstein, 76; *Teshuvot Rabbenu Gershom Me'or ha-Golah*, ed. Eidelberg, 171, no. 75.

37. Berliner, *Ozar Tov*, 50; Habermann, 12.

38. Constantine of Metz, "Vita Adalberonis," *MGH, Scrip.*, IV:661; Dietmar of Merseberg, "Chronicon," *ibid.*, III:827; "Vita maior Bardonis Moguntini," *ibid.*, XI:341.

39. See above.

40. See, e.g., the story of Vecelin in Albert of Metz, "De diversitate temporum" *MGH, Scrip.*, IV:704 and 720–723.

41. *Teshuvot Ba'alei ha-Tosafot*, ed. Irving A. Agus (New York, 1954), 45–46, no. 3.

42. On Rabbi Simon see Adolf Jellinek ed., *Bet ha-Midrash*, 2d ed., 6 vols. in 2 (Jerusalem, 1938), V:148–152, and VI:137–139. On Rabbi Gershom see Rabbi Isaac ben Moses, *Or Zaru'a*, 4 vols. in 2 (Zhitomir, 1862–1890), II:88b, no. 428. The latter case, to be sure, clearly involved coercion.

43. As we shall see in chapter VII, many modern scholars have viewed 1096 as a watershed in the history of European Jewry. This has generally resulted in the depiction of the period prior to 1096 as relatively calm and stable for Europe's Jews. Cecil Roth set out to challenge this view in his "European Jewry in the Dark Ages: A Revised Picture," *Hebrew Union College Annual* XXIII (1950–51), pt. II, 151–169. To be sure, Roth's examples of pre-1096 tension are drawn from a wide geographic area and are not always convincing. He could have made a strong case for pre-1096 violence within the orbit of Ashkenazic Jewry only. Baron, *A Social and Religious History*, IV:91–94, depicts pre-1096 insecurity, as does Agus, *The Heroic Age*, 56–57. The Hebrew poetry of the pre-1096 period recurrently bemoans persecution.

While it is impossible to reconstruct specific incidents from these poems and tempting to see them as stereotyped examples of the lachrymose, a broad sense of real instances of persecution and suffering lying behind the poetic facade emerges from these texts.

44. *Teshuvot Ḥakhmei Ẓarfat ve-Lotir*, 58b, no. 101. Cf. the English translation in Agus, *Urban Civilization*, I:99–100.

45. Berliner, *Oẓar Tov*, 50; Habermann, 12.

46. *Teshuvot Geonim Kadmonim*, ed. David Kassel (Berlin, 1851), 13b, no. 64.

47. See, inter alia, the discussion by Katz, *Exclusiveness and Tolerance*, 37–47.

48. See the study by Diethard Aschoff, "Zum Judenbild der Deutschen vor den Kreuzzugen: Erkenntnismoglichkeiten und Quellenprobleme," *Theokratia*, II (1970–72), 232–252. While the methodological observations are valuable, the lack of substantive conclusions is disappointing.

49. Berliner, *Oẓar Tov*, 50–51; Habermann, 13.

50. Berliner, *Oẓar Tov*, 52; Habermann, 15.

51. See Chazan, "1007–1012: Initial Crisis for Northern European Jewry."

52. See above.

II. The Sources and Their Reliability

1. For a brief overview of the major sources, see Setton, *A History of the Crusades*, I:220–221 and 253, and Runciman, *A History of the Crusades*, I:342–350. For a fuller list, see the extensive and invaluable bibliography of Hans Eberhard Mayer, *Bibliographie zur Geschichte der Kreuzzüge* (Hanover, 1960).

2. The best edition of the *Gesta Francorum* is that of Roger Mynors with translation by Rosalind Hill (London, 1962); of Fulcher's chronicle, that of Heinrich Hagenmeyer (Heidelberg, 1913); of Raymond's narrative, that of John and Laurita Hill (Paris, 1969).

3. For Ekkehard's chronicle, see *RHC, Occ.* V:7–40.

4. For Albert's chronicle, see ibid., IV:271–713.

5. Among the most useful local reports are those in the *Annales Wirziburgenses, MGH, Scrip.* II:246; in Bernold's *Chronicon*, ibid. V:464–465; in the *Annalista Saxo*, ibid., VI:729; in the *Gesta*

Treverorum, ibid. VIII:190–191; and in Cosmas of Prague's *Chronica Boemorum,* ed. Bertold Bretholz (Berlin, 1923), 164–165.

6. All three chronicles were published in N&S, reprinted in Habermann, and translated by Shlomo Eidelberg (Madison, 1977). From the inception of this study, prior to the publication of the Eidelberg translation, I decided to translate all texts utilized in the book myself. When the University of California Press suggested appending a translation of the two original Hebrew chronicles to my analysis of the events of 1096, the only reasonable course was to complete my own translation. Thus references will be made to N&S, Habermann, Eidelberg, and my own translation. References to my translation, which appears in the Appendix, specify simply S or L.

7. Recently Anna Sapir Abulafia has reopened the issue in her "The Interrelationship between the Hebrew Chronicles of the First Crusade," *Journal of Semitic Studies* XXVII (1982), 221–239.

8. See the convenient chart assembled by Abulafia, ibid., 239.

9. A look at the various views assembled by Abulafia indicates that a great deal of the earlier discussion of the relationships among the chronicles and the analysis of the individual chronicles as well focuses on introductory observations by later copyists.

10. See Robert Chazan, "The Hebrew First-Crusade Chronicles," *REJ* CXXXIII (1974), 235–254; idem, "The Hebrew First-Crusade Chronicles: Further Reflections," *AJS Review* III (1978), 79–98.

11. I have examined more fully the relationship between L and P in "The Deeds of the Jewish Community of Cologne," *Journal of Jewish Studies* XXXV (1084), 185–195.

12. For a full discussion of S, see my "The Hebrew First-Crusade Chronicles."

13. See idem, "A Twelfth-Century Communal History of Spires Jewry," *REJ* CXXVIII (1969), 253–257.

14. See idem, "The Hebrew First-Crusade Chronicles: Further Reflections," *AJS Review* III (1978), 79–98. In that study, I assumed a unified composition, of which I am no longer certain. It should be noted that the various components of L stem from differing points in time. On the one hand, the praise for the insincerity of the Jewish converts to Christianity must antedate

the imperial permission to return to Judaism of 1097; on the other, the Cologne unit is clearly quite a bit later, written in all likelihood in 1140. In my study, "The Deeds of Cologne Jewry," I noted also stylistic differences between the Cologne unit and the Speyer-Worms-Mainz unit, e.g. the former is cavalier toward the details related to the persecutions and the persecutors and concentrates its attention on martyrdom; the Cologne unit also shows a propensity for the miraculous. Note the story of the floating of the body of Isaac the *levi* from Cologne to Neuss, where it washed ashore next to the corpse of his close friend Samuel ben Asher and the story of the death of the mayor of Kerpen through divine intervention in N&S, 18 and 25; Habermann, 44 and 52; Eidelberg, 51 and 61; Chazan, L.

15. To pursue the two possibilities cited above, Rabbi Eliezer had at his disposal either the Speyer mélange or the unified composition. For a discussion of Rabbi Eliezer's alterations of L, see my "The Deeds of the Jewish Community of Cologne," 193–195.

16. N&S, 17; Habermann, 43; Eidelberg, 49; Chazan, L.

17. N&S, 21; Habermann, 48; Eidelberg, 55; Chazan, L. I think it likely that Solomon ben Simson was the author of only the Cologne unit of L.

18. N&S, 22; Habermann, 49; Eidelberg, p. 57; Chazan, L.

19. This is emphasized in Yitzhak Baer, "The Persecution of 1096" (Hebrew), *Sefer Assaf*, ed. M. D. Cassuto et al. (Jerusalem, 1953).

20. See below, chap. 5.

21. My friend and colleague, Ivan G. Marcus, has recently emphasized, in his "From Politics to Martyrdom: Shifting Paradigms in the Hebrew Narratives of the 1096 Crusading Riots," *Prooftexts* II (1982), 40–52, the ordering imposed by the Jewish chroniclers on the data available to them. Marcus makes a valid general observation: "What appears to be fact in a medieval chronological narrative, then, should be considered a highly edited version of 'the deeds' (*gesta*) which the narrator learned from traditional accounts, hearsay, or eyewitness reports. The events actually reported qualify only when they fit the narrator's preconceived religious and literary schema." While I agree of course that this is often the case in medieval (and modern) historiography, I believe that Marcus has overstated the case with regard to the Hebrew First-Crusade chronicles. He has reduced these chronicles to religious and literary schema that the Jewish authors themselves did not utilize. Thus, e.g., Marcus proposes

"a highly articulated five-part structure to the Hebrew narratives. . . . Each community's experience is structured, in effect, as a drama in which a liturgical prologue introduces the first act which then narrates the political events which took place when a particular community confronted the crusader threat; a liturgical entr'acte separates the political narrative in Act One from the list of martyrologies in Act Two. Finally, a liturgical epilogue concludes the action by addressing the ultimate meaning of the acts of martyrdom. By constructing each community account in this highly stylized way, the narrator affirms that a fundamental shift took place in the world view of the Jews he is describing: a shift from politics to martyrdom." There are two problems with the framework proposed: (1) It cannot be discerned in the narrative outside of the Mainz episode. There is no record in the accounts of Speyer, Worms, or Cologne of political negotiation and therefore no textual support for Marcus's contention that the editors constructed an interpretive framework that shifted from politics to martyrdom. (2) Rather than the imaginative scheme Marcus sees, the chroniclers simply reflect the realities: The Jews of Mainz (and probably other towns as well) attempted to secure political safeguards but took other steps when these efforts broke down. In a general way, I would argue once again that these texts are distinguished by their commitment to diversity, rather than by schematization. Further, I would argue that a respect for the concrete and individual was characteristic of the time.

22. Brian Stock, *The Implications of Literacy* (Princeton, 1983).

23. Bernard Guénée, *Histoire et culture historique dans l'occident médiéval* (Paris, 1980). Cf. other recent treatments of medieval historiography, including Amos Funkenstein, *Heilsplan und naturliche Entwicklung* (Munich, 1965); Beryl Smalley, *Historians in the Middle Ages* (London, 1974); the series of essays by R. W. Southern in the *Transactions of the Royal Historical Society* between 1970 and 1973; and the essay by Peter Classen in *Renaissance and Renewal*, ed. Benson and Constable, 387–417.

24. See N&S, 15; Habermann, 41; Eidelberg, 46; Chazan, L; N&S, 13; Habermann, 38; Eidelberg, 41; Chazan, L.

III. THE VIOLENCE OF 1096

1. That events in the eastern Mediterranean were of secondary significance in the call to the crusade is emphasized in Setton,

I:3–29 and 220–233; in Prawer, I:35–65; and in H. E. J. Cowdrey, "The Genesis of the Crusades: The Springs of Western Ideas of Holy War," *The Holy War*, ed. Thomas Patrick Murphy (Columbus, 1976), 9–32. Note Cowdrey's summary statement (p. 13): "All things considered, historians would, I think, now be pretty generally agreed that the First Crusade, the 'great stirring of the heart' in the West, was not, at root, caused by any pull of events in the East. On the contrary, knights like the author of the *Gesta* were impelled to go by constraints and shifts within western society itself—its social classes, its institutions, and its ideas."

2. See, inter alia, the classic study of Dana Munro, "The Speech of Pope Urban II at Clermont, 1095," *American Historical Review* XI (1906):231–242, and the recent analysis by H. E. J. Cowdrey, "Pope Urban II's Preaching of the First Crusade," *History* LV (1970):177–188.

3. Note, e.g., the sharp delineation in book III of Runciman I:83–118.

4. N&S, 3; Habermann, 26–27; Eidelberg, 24–25, Chazan, L. Cf. N&S, 48; Habermann, 94; Eidelberg, 100, Chazan, S.

5. The classic study of Peter the Hermit remains that of Heinrich Hagenmeyer (Leipzig, 1879).

6. N&S, 47; Habermann, 93; Eidelberg, 99; Chazan, S.

7. *Guibert de Nogent: Histoire de sa vie*, ed. Georges Bourgin (Paris, 1907), 118.

8. N&S, 48; Habermann, 94; Eidelberg, 100; Chazan, S.

9. N&S, 25; Habermann, 53; Eidelberg, 62; Chazan, L. For a general depiction of such exploitation, see N&S, 47; Habermann, 93–94; Eidelberg, 100; Chazan, S.

10. N&S, 51–52; Habermann, 98; Eidelberg, 106; Chazan, S. Cf. N&S, 4; Habermann, 28; Eidelberg, 27; Chazan, L.

11. N&S, 49; Habermann, 95; Eidelberg, 102; Chazan, S.

12. N&S, 48; Habermann, 94; Eidelberg, 100–101; Chazan, S.

13. N&S, 49–50; Habermann, 96; Eidelberg, 103; Chazan, S.

14. N&S, 53; Habermann, 99–100; Eidelberg, 108; Chazan, S. Cf. N&S, 6; Habermann, 30; Eidelberg, 30; Chazan, L.

15. N&S, 55; Habermann, 102; Eidelberg, 112; Chazan, S. Cf. N&S. 10; Habermann, 34–35; Eidelberg, 36; Chazan, L.

16. RHC, Occ., IV:292.

17. This crusading army, in all likelihood that of Emicho himself, assaulted on the first of Tammuz (June 24) those Jews gathered in Neuss and Wevelinghofen. This army then hunted down the further remnants of the Jewish community of Cologne.

For fuller detail see my "The Deeds of the Jewish Community of Cologne," 185–189.

18. N&S, 23; Habermann, 50; Eidelberg, 58; Chazan, L.

19. *RHC, Occ.,* V:20

20. Ibid., IV:292. The general remarks of much later observers, such as those found in the *Notitiae Duae Lemovincenses de Praedictione Crucis in Aquitania, RHC, Occ.,* V:351, do not merit serious consideration; they are simply part of the emergent mythology of the First Crusade.

21. N&S, 26; Habermann, 54; Eidelberg, 64; Chazan, L.

22. N&S, 23; Habermann, 50; Eidelberg, 59; Chazan, L.

23. Neither S nor L mentions the assault in Rouen, which was hardly, however, a major instance of anti-Jewish violence.

24. A few additional incidents are reflected in the literature and should be noted briefly: (1) L makes reference to an assault in the Jews of שלא, which was met by armed resistance on the part of a combined force of ducal troops and young Jewish men. Six Jewish warriors are said to have lost their lives, with the rest of the Jewish community saved. The place שלא has never been satisfactorily identified and the entire report seems questionable. See N&S, 28–29; Habermann, 57; Eidelberg, 67–68; Chazan, L. (2) Norman Golb, in his "New Light on the Persecution of French Jews at the Time of the First Crusade," *PAAJR,* XXXIV (1966), 1–63, proposed a crusader attack on the southern French town of Monieux. The text analyzed by Golb is brief and in a problematic state. Golb's reading of "Monieux" (pp. 8–9) has not been universally accepted. Indeed the key sentence, which speaks of the tribulations endured by a pious proselyte widow, merely notes that her late husband "fled with her to our place, until the Holy One decreed this persecution upon us, righteous is he and righteous [. . . The husband was killed] in the synagogue and the two children were taken captive" (pp. 60–61). Despite the ingenuity of Golb's reconstruction, this hardly constitutes firm evidence of a crusader assault in Monieux. (3) Many Jews, as is well known, lost their lives in the 1099 conquest of Jerusalem; this, however, had nothing to do with the European phenomenon or the anti-Jewish animus being examined in this study. The Jews who perished in Jerusalem in 1099 were victims of the general anti-Muslim hatred and ferocity that moved the maddened crusaders to kill all Jerusalemites indiscriminately—Muslims, Jews, and even their fellow Christians.

25. This statement is not intended to reflect callousness to

human suffering, but rather to distinguish between the events of 1096 and the truly wide-ranging assaults that occurred in the late thirteenth and early fourteenth century in Germany, in 1348–49 all across Europe, in 1391 in Spain, and in 1648–49 in Poland. In these latter cases, unlike 1096, literally hundreds of Jewish communities were attacked and destroyed.

26. This point was made also by Frederic Duncalf, "The Peasants' Crusade," *American Historical Review* XXVI (1921), 440–454.

27. This is the view of Runciman, *A History of the Crusades*, I:134–135, and of Duncalf, in Setton, *A History of the Crusades*, I:263. On this tendency, see Gavin I. Langmuir, "From Ambrose of Milan to Emicho of Leinigen: The Transformation of Hostility against Jews in Northern Christendom," *Settimane di studio del Centro italiano di studi sull 'alto medioevo* XXXVI (1980), 313–314. It seems clear that the anti-Jewish crusading violence in 1189–90 in England was rooted in cupidity masked as crusading fervor. One should not, however, read back from the latter set of events to the former.

28. Langmuir, in his study cited in the previous note, reviews the earlier treatments of crusader motivation (pp. 313–316) and proceeds to attempt an explanation of the eruptions of 1096 in sociological terms. This is certainly the most ambitious effort to analyze the factors that brought about the anti-Jewish assaults. I feel unequal to the sociological analysis proposed by Langmuir and have restricted myself to observations on the lack of discipline within the popular bands, the general tendency of the period to invest old symbols and doctrines with new meanings, and the specific crusade themes that lent themselves to anti-Jewish distortions. I am aware that more needs to be said but am uncertain as to how far the meager sources allow us to proceed. In noting the disparity between Langmuir's approach and my own, I have been struck by the current debate raging among Holocaust historians between the "intentionalist" school and the "functionalist" school. For a valuable survey of this dispute, see Saul Friedländer's introduction to Gerald Fleming, *Hitler and the Final Solution* (Berkeley, 1984). To be sure, Langmuir's analysis and mine are not mutually exclusive; they can complement each other nicely.

29. There has been new interest of late in popular religious expression during the Middle Ages. The two most comprehensive works are Raoul Manselli, *La religion populaire au moyen âge* (Montreal, 1975) and Rosalind and Christopher Brooke, *Popular*

Religion in the Middle Ages (London, 1984). There are very serious problems in this area of research. The sources are meager, and even defining the topic is problematic.

30. *RHC, Occ.*, V:20.

31. Ibid., IV:292.

32. N&S, 5; Habermann, 29; Eidelberg, 28; Chazan, L.

33. *RHC, Occ.*, IV:292.

34. Ibid., V:20.

35. N&S, 47; Habermann, 93; Eidelberg, 99; Chazan, S.

36. N&S, 1; Habermann, 24; Eidelberg, 21; Chazan, L.

37. N&S, 4; Habermann, 27; Eidelberg, 26; Chazan L.

38. This is noted in passing by Caro, *Sozial- und Wirtschafts- geschichte*, I:210–214. For sources which reflect the general crusader commitment to expansion of Christendom, see Paul Rousset, *Les origines et les caractères de la première croisade*, (Neuchatel, 1945) 100–107.

39. N&S, 1; Habermann, 24; Eidelberg, 21; Chazan, L. Because the development of Christianity as a separate religion involved the abrogation of Jewish law, several criticisms of Jesus became standard among medieval Jews. Among them was the suggestion that he was conceived during Mary's menstrual period, a time during which sexual relations are prohibited according to Jewish law. Implied within this negative view, of course, is the denial of the Christian notion of the Virgin Birth. The Jews not only were denying the virginity of Mary, but implying that Jesus was conceived in contravention of law and decency.

40. N&S, 49; Habermann, 95; Eidelberg, 102; Chazan, S.

41. N&S, 52; Habermann, 99; Eidelberg, 107; Chazan, S. Cf. N&S, 5; Habermann, 29; Eidelberg, 28; Chazan, L.

42. *RHC, Occ.*, IV:292.

43. *RHC, Occ.*, IV:292–293.

44. The *Annalista Saxo* notes briefly the same tendency toward total destruction. It describes the slaughter in Mainz as follows: "Unde etiam in civitatae Mogontia interfecerunt circiter 900 de Judeis, *non parcentes omnino vel mulieribus vel parvulis*," MGH, *Scrip.*, VI:729.

45. For a full discussion of these Jewish responses see below, chap. 4.

46. N&S, 14; Habermann, 39; Eidelberg, 43; Chazan, L.

47. N&S, 20; Habermann, 46; Eidelberg, 53; Chazan, L.

48. Ibid.

49. N&S, 20; Habermann, 46–47; Eidelberg, 53; Chazan, L. The problems of two sites designated אילנא is addressed by Rabbi Eliezer bar Nathan who adds: "One is the town of אילא near Julich, and the other is the town of אילנא, somewhere in the vicinity," N&S, 45; Habermann, 80; Eidelberg, 91.

50. N&S, 22; Habermann, 50; Eidelberg, 58; Chazan, L.

51. N&S, 23; Habermann, 51; Eidelberg, 59; Chazan, L.

52. N&S, 24; Habermann, 52; Eidelberg, 61; Chazan, L.

53. N&S, 56; Habermann, 103; Eidelberg, 114; Chazan, S; cf. N&S, 11; Habermann, 35–36; Eidelberg, 38; Chazan, L. It is in this light that the speech of the mayor of Moers and the general observations of Ekkehard of Aura and Albert of Aix on total destruction of the Jews should be understood.

54. It is striking to note the appearance of this same ideology and behavior in the *chansons de geste*. One of the most famous passages in the *Chanson de Roland* depicts the victorious Christian assault on Saragossa.

> The day wears on, the night has gathered now, the
> moon shines bright, the stars are all ablaze, the
> Emperor has taken Saragossa.
> He sends a thousand French to search the city, the
> synagogues, the mosques of Mahumet; with iron mauls
> and hatchets in their hands, they break the images,
> shatter all idols:
> there shall be no more magic and no more fraud.
> The King believes in God, he has one will:
> to serve the Lord; and his bishops bless the
> waters, lead the pagans to the baptismal font;
> if there is one who now refuses Charles,
> he has that man struck dead, or hanged, or burned;
> and they baptized more than a hundred thousand
> true Christians all, but not Queen Bramimunde:
> she will be led, a captive, to sweet France:
> the King wants her led to conversion by love.

The Song of Roland, trans. Frederic Goldin (New York, 1978), 153.

55. N&S, 1; Habermann, 24; Eidelberg, 22; Chazan, L., Cf. the indication of these same alternatives in the *Annales Wirziburgenses:* "Iudeos baptizari compulit, rennuentes immensa cede profligavit" *MGH, Scrip.,* II:246; in the *Gesta Treverorum:* "et

cogere illos the Jews aut dominum Ihesum Christum credere, aut sub ipsa hora vitae periculis subiacere," ibid., VIII:190; and in Cosmas of Prague: "et eos invitos baptizabant, contradicentes vero trucidabant," *Chronica Boemorum*, ed. Bretholz, 164.

56. In his article, "The First Crusade and the Idea of 'Conversion,'" *The Muslim World* LVIII (1968), 57–71 and 155—164, Allan Cutler argues for a conversionist element in the First Crusade. See the response by James Waltz, ibid., LXI (1971), 170–186. My analysis of the attacks on European Jewry indicates that the efforts to convert the Jews do not represent a truly conversionist impulse; they are rather one of the ways—indeed from the Christian perspective the "best" way—to eliminate rapidly and totally Judaism and the Jews. For a full discussion of the place of missionizing in the First Crusade, see the superb study by B. Z. Kedar, *Crusade and Mission* (Princeton, 1984), 57–59 and 61–65. For an unusual instance of the choice of conversion or death being imposed upon Muslims, see *Gesta Francorum*, 73.

57. N&S, 56; Habermann, 103; Eidelberg, 114; Chazan, S. Cf. N&S, 11; Habermann, 36; Eidelberg, 38; Chazan, L.

58. N&S, 23; Habermann, 50–51; Eidelberg, 58–59; Chazan, L. Cf. the report on Trier N&S, 26–28; Habermann, 54–56; Eidelberg, 64–66; Chazan, L.

59. One of the excellences of the Kedar study, *Crusade and Mission*, is the sense it conveys of the fluidity of crusading ideals and principles. If in establishment circles there could develop a wide variety of interpretations of crusading, then the potential for divergent—and in some cases radical—views of crusading in the popular bands is hardly surprising.

60. The major works on the ideological elements in the First Crusade include Carl Erdmann, *The Origin of the Idea of Crusade*, trans. Marshall W. Baldwin and Walter Groffart (Princeton, 1977); Rousset, *Les origines et les caractères de la première croisade*, particularly valuable for its extensive citation and analysis of primary sources; Paul Alphandéry, *La Chrétienté et l'idée de croisade*, 2 vols. (Paris, 1954–1959); E. O. Blake, "The Formation of the 'Crusade Idea,'" *Journal of Ecclesiastical History* xxi (1970), 11–31; Bernard McGinn, "*Iter sancti Sepulchri*: The Piety of the First Crusaders," *Essays on Medieval Civilization*, ed. Bede Karl Lackner and Kenneth Roy Philip (Austin, 1978), 33–71. The centrality of the twin notions of holy war and pilgrimage and their impact on the fate of European Jewry is noted by Hans Liebes-

chütz, "The Crusading Movement in Its Bearing upon the Christian Attitude towards Jewry," *Journal of Jewish Studies* X (1959), 97–111.

61. Note, e.g., the reflection of anti-Jewish animus among the southern French crusaders in *Le "Liber" de Raymond d'Aguilers*, ed. Hill and Hill, 115.

62. *Guibert de Nogent*, ed. Bourgin, 118.

63. N&S, 4; Habermann, 27; Eidelberg, 26; Chazan, L.

64. N&S, 47; Habermann, 93; Eidelberg, 99; Chazan, S.

65. N&S, 1; Habermann, 24; Eidelberg, 22; Chazan, L.

66. It will be recalled that Peter the Hermit preached in Cologne on Easter Sunday. The coincidence of this call to the crusade in the Rhineland occurring precisely on Easter Sunday, with its evocation of the theme of Jewish deicide, deepened the sense of Jewish culpability for the actions that created the Holy Sepulcher as a shrine.

67. N&S, 49; Habermann, 95; Eidelberg, 102; Chazan, S.

68. N&S, 49; Habermann, 96; Eidelberg, 103; Chazan, S.

69. N&S, 53; Habermann, 99; Eidelberg, 108; Chazan, S. Cf. N&S, 6; Habermann, 30; Eidelberg, 30; Chazan, L. Cf. the report in the *Annalista Saxo* concerning crusader intentions: "Hic siquidem habebant in professione ut vellent ulcisci Christum in gentilibus vel Iudeis," *MGH, Scrip.*, VI:729. It is striking that, in the *Gesta Treverorum* report of the conversionist appeal of the bishop of Trier, reference is made to the role of the Jews in the crucifixion of Jesus, with the citation of the inflammatory verse from Matthew 27:26, "His blood be on us, and on our children." This is a further reflection of the centrality of this motif in the thinking of the period.

70. *Gesta Francorum*, ed. Hill, 91–92.

71. N&S, 47–48; Habermann, 94; Eidelberg, 100; Chazan, S.

72. See below, chap. IV.

73. For the violence in the cities of German, see, e.g., the incidents in Cologne in 1074: Arnold Stelzmann, *Geschichte der Stadt Köln*, 3d ed. (Cologne, 1962), 77–78, and Paul Strait, *Cologne in the Twelfth Century* (Gainseville, 1974), 25–30. For an incident in Mainz in 1077: Ludwig Falck, *Mainz im Fruhen und Hohen Mittelalter* (Dusseldorf, 1972), 122–123.

74. On these political realities see Schiffman, *Heinrich IV und die Bischöfe* or the two separate articles in the *Zeitschrift für die Geschicte der Juden in Deutschland*, vol. III, in which the original study was republished.

75. N&S, 3; Habermann, 26–27; Eidelberg, 25; Chazan, L.

76. N&S, 26; Habermann, 54; Eidelberg, 64; Chazan, L.

IV. The Patterns of Response

1. N&S, 47, Habermann, 93–94; Eidelberg, 100; Chazan S.

2. See below, chap. VI.

3. N&S, 25; Habermann, 53; Eidelberg, 62; Chazan, L.

4. S: N&S, 48, Habermann, 94; Eidelberg, p. 100, Chazan, S. L: N&S, 3; Habermann, 26–27; Eidelberg, 24–25; Chazan, L.

5. N&S, 5, Habermann, 29; Eidelberg, 29; Chazan, L.

6. N&S, 48–49; Habermann, 95; Eidelberg, 101–102; Chazan, S.

7. N&S, 17; Habermann, 43–44; Eidelberg, 49; Chazan, L.

8. This line of defense was carefully analyzed by Sarah Schiffman in *Heinrich IV und die Bischöfe* cited above. This study includes a number of useful observations on the political realities of late eleventh-century Germany. It would have benefited from a clearer analysis of the precise sources of danger and destruction associated with the First Crusade.

9. N&S, 3; Habermann, 27; Eidelberg, 25; Chazan, L.

10. N&S, 26, Habermann, 54; Eidelberg, 64; Chazan, L.

11. *RHC, Occ.* IV:292.

12. N&S, 3; Habermann, 26; Eidelberg, 24; Chazan, L. Cf. N&S, 51; Habermann, 98; Eidelberg, 106; Chazan, S.

13. N&S, 48; Habermann, 95; Eidelberg, 101; Chazan, S.

14. N&S, 48; Habermann, 94; Eidelberg, 101; Chazan, S.

15. N&S, 3; Habermann, 26; Eidelberg, 24; Chazan, L.

16. N&S, 15; Habermann, 40–41; Eidelberg, 45; Chazan, L.

17. Mainz: N&S, 52 and 5; Habermann, 99 and 29; Eidelberg, 107 & 28; Chazan, S & L; Moers: N&S, 23; Habermann, 50; Eidelberg, 58; Chazan, L.

18. N&S, 48; Habermann, 94; Eidelberg, 101; Chazan, S.

19. N&S, 18–25; Habermann, 44–52; Eidelberg, 50–61; Chazan, L. The somewhat suspect report in L on the Jews in שלא also mentions this strategy: "Of the Jews only six were killed. The Light of Israel saved the rest of the community and led all of them together to a town opposite the city of . . . , across the river," N&S, 29; Habermann, 57; Eidelberg, 68; Chazan, L.

20. *RHC, Occ.*, IV:292.

21. N&S, 15; Habermann, 41; Eidelberg, 45; Chazan, L.

22. N&S, 26 and 23; Habermann, 54 and 52; Eidelberg, 64 and 59; Chazan L.

23. *MGH, Scrip.*, VIII:190–191.

24. N&S, 27–28; Habermann, 55–56; Eidelberg, 66; Chazan, L. It is of course not surprising that the Christian source describes the conversion as the result of episcopal exhortation, while the Jewish source sees it as forced.

25. N&S, 28; Habermann, 56; Eidelberg, 67; Chazan, L.

26. N&S, 23; Habermann, 50–51; Eidelberg, 59; Chazan, L.

27. N&S, 49; Habermann, 96; Eidelberg, 103; Chazan, S.

28. N&S, 53; Habermann, 99–100; Eidelberg, 108; Chazan, S. Cf. N&S, 6; Habermann, 30; Eidelberg, 30; Chazan, L.

29. N&S, 28–29, Habermann, 57; Eidelberg, 67–68; Chazan, L.

30. See above, chap. III.

31. *RHC, Occ.*, IV:293.

32. N&S, 29; Habermann, 57; Eidelberg, 68; Chazan, L.

33. Cf. the awareness of such insincerity in the *Annales Wirziburgenses, MGH, Scrip.*, II:246; in the *Gesta Treverorum*, ibid., VIII:191; and in Cosmas of Prague's *Chronica Boemorum*, ed. Bretholz, 164–165. Note the specially harsh formulation of Ekkehard in his *Chronicon*, where he describes these relapsing Jews in the following terms: "plurimi, sicut canes ad vomitum, postea retro rediebant," *MGH, Scrip.*, VI:208.

34. N&S, 23; Habermann, 51; Eidelberg, 59; Chazan, L.

35. N&S, 28; Habermann, 56; Eidelberg, 67; Chazan, L.

36. See above, chap. III.

37. N&S, 50–51; Habermann, 97; Eidelberg, 105; Chazan, S.

38. *MGH, Scrip.*, VIII:190.

39. N&S, 49; Habermann, 95–96; Eidelberg, 103; Chazan, S.

40. Note again the notion of conversion in order to aid others.

41. N&S, 12–13; Habermann, 37–38; Eidelberg, 40–41; Chazan, L.

42. See chap. V.

43. *RHC, Occ.*, IV:293. Note further awareness of the Jewish tendency toward self-sacrifice in Bernold's *Chronicon, MGH, Scrip.*, V:465, and in the *Gesta Treverorum, ibid.*, VIII:190.

44. On the martyrdoms of 1096, see Katz, *Exclusiveness and Tolerance*, 82–92; idem, "Martyrdom in the Middle Ages and in 1648–9" (Hebrew), *Sefer Yovel le-Yitzḥak Baer*, ed. Samuel Ettinger et al. (Jerusalem, 1961), 318–337; Moshe Shulvass, "Crusaders,

Martyrs, and the Marranos of Ashkenaz," *Between the Rhine and the Bosphorus* (Chicago, 1964), 1–14.

In my earlier discussion of the reliability of the Hebrew chronicles, I have made allowance for some exaggeration in the description of Jewish heroism; I argued that there was, however, no fabrication of patterns of Jewish behavior or thought.

45. N&S, 18; Habermann, 44; Eidelberg, 50; Chazan, L.

46. N&S, 7; Habermann, 31; Eidelberg, 31–32; Chazan, L. Cf. N&S, 53; Habermann, 100; Eidelberg, 109; Chazan, S.

47. N&S, 56; Habermann, 103–104; Eidelberg, 114; Chazan, S. Cf. N&S, 11; Habermann, 36; Eidelberg, 38; Chazan, L.

48. In thirteenth-century missionizing efforts. Church spokesmen often espoused the notion of missionizing among the Muslims through overtly challenging Islam in its own territories and thereby bringing on a martyr's death. For a useful description of this missionizing style, see E. Randolph Daniel, *The Franciscan Concept of Missionizing in the High Middle Ages* (Lexington, 1975), 39–45. Later Jewish sources occasionally reflect a sense of the relationship of martyrdom to interfaith rivalry. See, for example, the passage in the thirteenth-century *Sefer Niẓaḥon Yashan* in David Berger, *The Jewish-Christian Debate in the High Middle Ages* (Philadelphia, 1979), 151–153 (Hebrew text), 216–218 (English translation), and 334–335 (notes).

49. N&S, 18–19; Habermann, 45; Eidelberg, 51; Chazan, L. Cf. the *Gesta Treverorum, MGH, Scrip.*, VIII:190.

50. N&S, 27–28; Habermann, 56; Eidelberg, 66; Chazan, L.

51. N&S, 20; Habermann, 46; Eidelberg, 53; Chazan, L.

52. N&S, 19; Habermann, 45; Eidelberg, pp. 51–52; Chazan, L.

53. A later Ashkenazic legal source focuses on the issue of the taking of children's lives. It speaks of "children who cannot distinguish between good and evil," concluding that it is better that such children perish in the innocence of their childhood, rather than later in the guilt of an assumed Christianity. See below, chap. IV, for a fuller analysis of subsequent halachic rationalization.

54. Cf. the *Gesta Treverorum, MGH, Scrip.*, VIII:190.

55. N&S, 9–10; Habermann, 34; Eidelberg, 35–36; Chazan, L. Cf. N&S, 54–55; Habermann, 101–102; Eidelberg, 111–112; Chazan, S.

56. N&S, 53; Habermann, 100; Eidelberg, 109; Chazan, S. Cf. N&S. 6; Habermann, 31; Eidelberg, 31; Chazan, L.

57. An interesting passage in *Sefer Ḥasidim*, ed. Judah Wis-tinetzki (2d ed.; Frankfort, 1924), 449, no. 1862 (for a translation of much of the passage, see below, chap. V) suggests that nor-mally there are gradations in readiness for martyrdom—the old and the poor are seen as having less to lose and being therefore willing for self-sacrifice, while the young and the wealthy are depicted as more hesitant to part with their lives.

58. N&S, 56; Habermann, 103; Eidelberg, 113; Chazan, S. Cf. N&S, 10; Habermann, 35; Eidelberg, 37; Chazan, L.

59. N&S, 54; Habermann, 101; Eidelberg, 110; Chazan, S. Cf. N&S, 7; Habermann, 31; Eidelberg, 32; Chazan, L.

60. N&S, 19; Habermann, 45; Eidelberg, 51; Chazan, L.

61. Note, e.g., the story of Moses ben Helbo and his sons—N&S, 55, 10; Habermann, 102, 35; Eidelberg, 112, 37; Chazan, S, L.

62. N&S, 20; Habermann, 47; Eidelberg, 53–54; Chazan, L.

63. Grossman, *Ḥakhmei Ashkenaz ha-Rishonim*, 436–440.

64. The most important analyses of the thinking of the mar-tyrs are those by Katz, *Exclusiveness and Tolerance*, and Cohen, "Messianic Postures of Ashkenazim and Sephardim," *Studies of the Leo Black Institute*, ed. Max Kreutzberger (New York, 1967), 117–156.

65. For further observations on these soliloquies, see below, chap. V.

66. There is, unfortunately, no comprehensive study of Jewish martyrdom available. On aspects of this important is-sue, see, inter alia, W. H. C. Frend, *Martyrdom and Persecution in the Early Church* (Oxford, 1965), 22–57; David Flusser, "Jewish Sources of Christian Martyrdom and Their Influence on Its Fun-damental Concepts" (Hebrew), *Milḥemet Kodesh u-Martirologiah* (Jerusalem, 1968), 61–71; Gerson D. Cohen, "Hannah and Her Seven Sons in Hebrew Literature" (Hebrew), *Sefer ha-Yovel le-Khevod M. M. Kaplan*, ed. Moshe Davis (New York, 1953), 109–122; M. D. Heer, "Martyrdom and Its Background in the Second Century" (Hebrew), *Milḥemet Kodesh u-Martirologiah*, 73–92; Saul Lieberman, "Persecution of the Jewish Religion" (Hebrew), *Salo Wittmayer Baron Jubilee Volume*, ed. Saul Lieberman, 3 vols. (New York, 1974), Heb. vol., 213–245. In the wake of the emergence of Masada in the 1960s as a major new symbol of Jewish martyr-dom, there was a spate of studies devoted to the martyrs of Masada. Of these the most useful by far is that of Dov. I. Frimer, "Masada in the Light of Halachah," *Tradition* XII, no. 1 (1971),

27–43. Extremely valuable is the magisterial study of the binding of Isaac motif—and much more—by Shalom Spiegel, *The Last Trial*, trans. Judah Goldin (Philadelphia, 1967).

67. T.B., Sanhedrin, 73a–74b.

68. According to medieval Jewish halachists, Christianity was to be considered in the category of idolatry. On this see Katz, *Exclusiveness and Tolerance*, passim. In some senses, conversion to Christianity might have been seen as less offensive than acceptance of outright idolatry. Under the circumstances of 1096, however, it is clear that conversion to Christianity was viewed as intensely offensive. In any case, whatever the differences between Christianity and the idolatries of the Talmudic period, the decision at Lod was surely seen as applicable and binding.

69. Deut. 6:5.

70. Exod. 7:28.

71. T.B., Pesaḥim, 53b.

72. For a full study of this tale, see Cohen, "Hannah and Her Seven Sons in Hebrew Literature."

73. Exod. 20:2 and Deut. 5:6.

74. Exod. 20:3 and Deut. 5:7.

75. Exod. 22:19.

76. Exod. 34:14.

77. Deut. 6:4.

78. Deut. 4:39.

79. Deut. 26:17–18.

80. The entire passage is found in T.B., Gittin, 57b.

81. T.B., Berakhot, 61b.

82. T.B., Avodah Zarah, 17b–18a.

83. N&S, 14; Habermann, 39; Eidelberg, 43; Chazan, L. R. Akiba is cited by the martyrs themselves in N&S, 7; Habermann, 31; Eidelberg, 31; Chazan, L.

84. N&S, 55; Habermann, 102; Eidelberg, 112; Chazan, S. Cf. N&S, 10; Habermann, 34; Eidelberg, 36; Chazan, L.

85. N&S, 53; Habermann, 100; Eidelberg, 109; Chazan, S. Cf. N&S, 8; Habermann, 33; Eidelberg, 34; Chazan, L.

86. N&S, 22; Habermann, 49; Eidelberg, 57; Chazan, L.

87. N&S, 50; Habermann, 96; Eidelberg, 104; Chazan, S.

88. N&S, 51; Habermann, 97; Eidelberg, 105; Chazan, S.

89. N&S, 54; Habermann, 101; Eidelberg, 110; Chazan, S. Cf. N&S, 7; Habermann, 31; Eidelberg, 32; Chazan, L.

90. N&S, 54; Habermann, 101; Eidelberg, 110; Chazan, S. Cf. N&S, 9; Habermann, 33; Eidelberg, 34; Chazan, L.

91. Psalms 68:23.

92. Psalms 44:23. Entire passage in T.B., Gittin, 57b.

93. In a brief paper delivered at Dropsie University and soon to be published in the *Jewish Quarterly Review*, I have suggested that this creative adaptation of old symbols reflects the early stages of a proto-*Ḥasidut-Ashkenaz*, an embryonic version of the later German-Jewish Pietism.

94. N&S, 21–22; Habermann, 48–49; Eidelberg, 56–57; Chazan, L. Cf. the extraordinary speech of the Mainz martyrs in N&S, 53–54 and 6–7; Habermann, 100–101 and 31; Eidelberg, 109–110 and 31; Chazan, S and L.

95. Emphasized by Cohen, "Messianic Postures of Ashkenazim and Sephardim," 35–38; Marcus, "From Politics to Martyrdom;" Alan Mintz, *Ḥurban: Responses to Catastrophe in Hebrew Literature* (New York, 1984), 93–98.

96. *Gesta Francorum*, ed. Hill, 1–2.

97. See below, chap. V.

98. See the aforecited study of Spiegel, *The Last Trial*.

99. N&S, 50; Habermann, 96; Eidelberg, 103–104; Chazan, S.

100. The material available to us from 1096 is far too limited to permit any sort of psychological speculation. It might be noted, however, that modern persecution has given rise to a rich psychological literature, in which the phenomenon of identification with forebears plays a central role. As indicative of this phenomenon in modern literature we might note the following from *Generations of the Holocaust*, ed. Martin S. Bergman and Milton E. Jacoby (New York, 1982), 148–148.

> Adaptation to reality [by Rachel] was characterized by the simultaneous living in her present and in the past of her father. It is not sufficient to speak of her identification with the father as he was in the past and he was currently, nor to speak of an identification with the mother as the rescuer of the father. The mechanism goes beyond identification. I have called it "transposition" into the world of the past, similar—but not identical—to the spiritualist's journey into the world of the dead. Living in the past, Rachel was not only enacting the role of her grandmother but was also active on her own behalf, bringing order into the Holocaust chaos, providing for food and rationing it, letting people come in and out of confinement and watching over them, yet killing them as the Nazis had and then resurrecting them. Playing

> all roles in the historical drama into which she wandered, she was her own father, his mother, herself, people in the ghettoes and camps, their persecutors and their rescuers. . . . Throughout she was Rachel, the American college girl, an artist, and her grandmother Rosa-Margit as well.

While our evidence for the Middle Ages is too skimpy to permit much speculation, the notion that such a "transposition" might have occurred among the martyrs of 1096 is intriguing.

101. Again I have suggested such ritual embellishment as reflective of a proto-*Ḥasidut-Ashkenaz* mentality.

102. There is unfortunately no comprehensive study of medieval Jewish polemics currently available. The best introduction to this important topic can be found in the valuable general observations of David Berger in his *The Jewish-Christian Debate in the High Middle Ages*. For an effort to analyze the major themes in one rich and important polemical work, see my "Polemical Themes in the *Milḥemet Miẓvah*," *Les Juifs au regard de l'histoire*, ed. Gilbert Dahan (Paris, 1984), 169–184.

103. See Berger, *The Jewish-Christian Debate*, 350–354, and Chazan, "Polemical Themes in the *Milḥemet Mizvah*," 177–179.

104. N&S, 54; Habermann, 101; Eidelberg, 110; Chazan, S. Cf. N&S, 7; Habermann, 31; Eidelberg, 32; Chazan, L.

105. Emphasized by Katz, *Exclusiveness and Tolerance*, 86–87, and by Cohen, "Messianic Postures of Ashkenazim and Sephardim," 36–37. In the Talmudic stories of martyrdom, there are fleeting references to the rewards of afterlife. These notions of reward are reflected more fully in the *Book of Josippon* and in the *chansons de geste*, both of which influenced both the martyrs of 1096 and the chroniclers.

106. N&S, 22; Habermann, 48–49; Eidelberg, 56; Chazan, L. The recently published and highly stimulating study of Jacques Le Goff, *The Birth of Purgatory*, trans. Arthur Goldhammer (Chicago, 1981), raises interesting issues of the medieval development of Jewish thinking with regard to personal afterlife. I have consciously decided not to pursue these issues here, but to reserve them for separate, subsequent treatment.

107. N&S, 53–54; Habermann, 100; Eidelberg, 109–110; Chazan, S. Cf. N&S, 7; Habermann, 31; Eidelberg, 31; Chazan, L.

108. N&S, 56; Habermann, 104; Eidelberg, 114; Chazan, S. Cf. N&S, 11; Habermann, 36; Eidelberg, 38; Chazan, L.

109. The only one to suggest—if only in a partial way—the

decisive impact of the Christian milieu on Jewish martyrdom in 1096 was the late Yitzhak Baer. Curiously, in his major study of the Hebrew chronicles, "The Persecution of 1096," published in 1953, Baer does not explore seriously such influence, which he had earlier pointed to briefly in his "The Religious and Social Tendency of *Sefer Ḥasidim*" (Hebrew), *Ẓion* III (1938), 3–5. In general the complex views of Baer concerning medieval Ashkenazic Jewry deserve careful analysis.

Eleventh- and twelfth-century Ashkenazic Jewry has often been treated as a Jewry radically isolated from its general milieu—except with regard to its economic activities. The suggestion advanced here alters that picture considerably. For evidence from a different cultural domain of significant Jewish-Christian interaction, see the forthcoming study by David Berger, "Mission to the Jews and Jewish-Christian Contacts in the Polemical Literature of the High Middle Ages." For further observations on this issue, see below, chap. VII.

The term "counter-crusade" has been used of late in studies of the slowly developing Muslim reaction to the onset of the crusades. See in particular the fine study of Emmanuel Sivan, *L'Islam et la croisade* (Paris, 1968), and the literature cited there, 5–6.

110. See especially Southern. *The Making of the Middle Ages;* the essays collected in Robert L. Benson and Giles Constable (eds.), *Renaissance and Renewal in the Twelfth Century* (Cambridge, Mass., 1982); Caroline Walker Bynum, *Jesus as Mother: Studies in the Spirituality of the High Middle Ages* (Berkeley, 1982).

111. Southern, *The Making of the Middle Ages.*

112. See, e.g., Lynn White, Jr., "Science and the Sense of Self: The Medieval Background of a Modern Confrontation," *Daedalus* CVII, no. 2 (Spring, 1978), 47–59; Charles M. Radding, "Superstition to Science: Nature, Fortune, and the Passing of the Medieval Ordeal," *American Historical Review* LXXXIV (1979), 945–969; and especially Bynum, *Jesus as Mother,* 82–109.

113. Bynum, *Jesus as Mother,* 86.

114. N&S, 12; Habermann, 37; Eidelberg, 40; Chazan, L.

115. N&S, 55; Habermann, 102; Eidelberg, 112; Chazan, S. Cf. N&S, 10; Habermann, 35; Eidelberg, 37; Chazan, L.

116. Bynum, *Jesus as Mother,* 107–108.

117. The impact of the symbolism created by these Rhineland Jews can be clearly discerned in the broad studies of Mintz, *Ḥurban,* and David G. Roskies, *Against the Apocalypse: Responses*

to Catastrophe in Modern Jewish Literature (Cambridge, Mass., 1984).

V. Subsequent Jewish Reactions

1. For fuller consideration of these matters, see below, chap. VII.

2. N&S, 48; Habermann, 94; Eidelberg, 101; Chazan, S; *MGH, Scrip.*, V:208. The securing of permission for those forcibly converted to return to the Jewish fold must be seen as an index of the relative immaturity of the Church at this juncture. Striking contrast is provided by the resolute rejection of this course in the wake of the forced conversions of 1391 in Spain, thereby creating the massive New-Christian problem.

3. This is emphasized by Haim Hillel Ben-Sasson, "The Goals of Jewish Chronography during the Middle Ages and Its Problematics" (Hebrew), *Historyonim ve-Askolot Historyot* (Jerusalem, 1963), 29–49.

4. See below, chap. VI.

5. N&S. 60; Habermann, 117; Eidelberg, 123–124.

6. N&S, 76–77; Habermann, 161–162.

7. N&S, 77; Habermann, 162.

8. For a fuller analysis of these events see my "Emperor Frederick I, the Third Crusade, and the Jews," *Viator* VIII (1970), 83–93.

9. The manuscript is slightly deficient at this point.

10. N&S, 78; Habermann, 163.

11. N&S, 78; Habermann, 164.

12. *Baron, A Social and Religious History of the Jews*, IV:89.

13. The important twelfth-century history of the Sephardic Abraham ibn Daud, *Sefer ha-Qabbalah*, does not mention 1096. Most of the sixteenth-century Jewish historians, who are largely Sephardic, make brief reference to 1096, although Samuel Usque does not. Even the Ashkenazic David Gans does not accord excessive attention to 1096 in his *Zemah David*.

14. In his study, "The Problem of *Kiddush ha-Shem* in the Speculative Teaching of the German Ḥasidim," *Milḥement Kodesh u-Martirologiah*, 121–129, Joseph Dan notes the lack of specific reference to *kiddush ha-Shem* in this literature. He suggests that the ongoing crisis of Ashkenazic Jewry is reflected in the gener-

ally pessimistic tone that pervades this literature. For our purposes it is significant that Dan found so few references to persecution and martyrdom. In his recent study on German-Jewish Pietism, Ivan G. Marcus examines at some length the suggestion that the persecution of 1096 was a key factor in shaping the pietistic movement, concluding that "the data do not permit us to recover the causal nexus in which Qalonimide [Kalonymide] Pietism was created." Even more important to our purposes in Marcus's corroborative observation that persecution and martyrdom are not "a major theme in *Sefer Ḥasidim* and the other pietistic texts." See *Piety and Society: The Jewish Pietists of Medieval Germany* (Leiden, 1981), 150–151, n. 57.

15. *Sefer Ḥasidim*, ed. Judah Wistinetzki, 2d ed., (Frankfort, 1924), 449, no. 1862.

16. Rabbi Abraham ben Azriel, *Sefer 'Arugat ha-Bosem*, ed. Ephraim E. Urbach, 4 vols. (Jerusalem, 1939–1963) IV:49.

17. II Sam. 1:23.

18. Deut. 32:43.

19. Joel 4:21. The translation has been modified to fit the usage.

20. Psalms 79:10.

21. Ibid., 9:13.

22. Ibid., 110:6–7. The entire passage can be found in S. Baer (ed.), *Seder 'Avodat Yisra'el* (Redelheim, 1848), 233.

23. Katz, *Exclusiveness and Tolerance*, 83–84.

24. See, e.g., Rabbi Moses of Coucy's discussion of the commandments of *ahavat ha-Shem* (love of God) and *kiddush ha-Shem* in his *Sefer Miẓvot Gadol* and Rabbi Isaac of Corbeil's treatment of these same two commandments in his *Sefer Miẓvot Katan*.

25. Judges 7:17.

26. *Sefer Ḥasidim*, ed. Wistinetzki, 465, no. 1922.

27. Ibid., 428, no. 1798.

28. Given the existence of independent local reports and the fact that S and L had separate editors, the likelihood of individual genius inventing a radically new historiographic style is negligible.

29. Indeed the martyrs of 1096 are seen as exceeding the heroism of their biblical predecessors. For interesting and valuable perspectives on the historical perceptions of both the Bible and the Hebrew First-Crusade chronicles—and more—see Yosef Hayim Yerushalmi, *Zakhor* (Seattle, 1982). See also Mintz, *Ḥur-*

ban, and Roskies, *Against the Apocalypse*, for studies of changing patterns of Jewish response to catastrophe. Because these three studies focus on long-range patterns of Jewish thinking, they rely heavily on the poems of commemoration, which became part of the mainstream of Jewish literature. Since my interest is rather with the immediate and innovative, I stress the less popular prose compositions, which, I believe, better reflect the immediate milieu of the late eleventh and early twelfth century.

30. For this material, synthetically arranged, see Louis Ginzberg, *The Legends of the Jews*, 7 vols. (Philadelphia, 1909–1938). It is precisely this organizational structure that the material lacks in its original setting.

31. See the edition of David Flusser, 2 vols. (Jerusalem, 1978–1980). The second volume consists of a lengthy study of this important work.

32. See Flusser, *Sefer Josippon*, II:3–10 and 63–74.

33. The martyrs of Masada did not directly influence the thinking of the Rhineland martyrs nor did they figure in the subsequent efforts to justify the extreme behaviors of 1096. However, I believe that the account of Masada in the widely read *Book of Josippon* may have some impact on the narrative style of the First Crusade Chronicles.

34. On the *chansons de geste*, see, inter alia, W. T. H. Jackson, *The Literature of the Middle Ages* (New York, 1960), 60–174; Urban Tigner Holmes, Jr., *A History of Old French Literature* (New York, 1962), 66–122; Jessie Crosland, *The Old French Epic* (Oxford, 1951). There are sporadic indications of Jewish familiarity with this literature. See especially the quote in the Tosafot to Tractate Shabbat, 116b, which prohibits the reading on the Sabbath of "war tales written in the vernacular."

35. Yitzhak Baer, in his study of the Hebrew chronicles in *Sefer Assaf*, 127–130, claims Jewish knowledge of the Latin sources and vice versa. His case, however, is far from persuasive. His argument involves simply the appearance of such stock phrases as "resting in the bosom of Abraham" in both Hebrew and Latin records; he suggests that the Christian authors appropriated these images from their Jewish counterparts. However, the imagery Baer notes was widely and independently used in both Jewish and Christian circles. On the symbolism of "the bosom of Abraham" in twelfth-century Christian sources, for example, see Le Goff, *The Birth of Purgatory*, 150–158. Rather than assume

direct contact, I would propose instead that both Jewish and Christian authors were reacting to the same events and were guided in their history writing by parallel creative influences.

36. Fulcher of Chartres, 115–118. Cf. the brief introductory observations in Raymond of Aguilers and the lack of any such remarks in the *Gestas Francorum*.

37. In saying that there is no sense of divine intervention, here I do not mean to imply that these people had a view of history that removes any celestial element. As I shall show, the Jewish chronicles express an absolutely firm conviction that God controls history and that he will intervene in the future to avenge the defeat and suffering inflicted upon his people.

38. Note the introduction to the Cologne segment of L, N&S, 17; Habermann, 43; Eidelberg, 49; Chazan, L. The designation "The Account of the Former Persecution," appended to S as a title by a medieval copyist, is a poor one, not at all consonant with the spirit of the chronicle.

39. See especially Bruce A. Rosenberg, *Custer and the Epic of Defeat* (University Park, 1974), and Yael Zerubavel, *The Last Stand: On the Transformation of Symbols in Modern Israeli Culture*, unpub. doct. diss., (Philadelphia, 1980). See also the interesting observation of Southern, *The Making of the Middle Ages*, 12.

40. For an analysis of these characteristics, see Rosenberg, *Custer and the Epic of Defeat*, 1–4.

41. N&S, 1; Habermann, 24; Eidelberg, 21; Chazan, L.

42. Much has been written on the emergence of the individual in the literature of the late eleventh and twelfth century. See especially Peter Dronke, *Poetic Individuality in the Middle Ages* (Oxford, 1970), and Robert W. Hanning, *The Individual in Twelfth-Century Romance* (New Haven, 1977). Again I believe that the literature of the Jews reflects the general ambiance. In terms of the phrase coined by R. W. Southern, "from epic to romance," the Jewish chronicles, it seems to me, move somewhere along the line between the two. They are more individuated than the epic, but do not reach the level of absorption with the individual psyche that we find in the twelfth-century romance. See my earlier remarks at the end of chap. IV and the literature there cited.

43. See, e.g., the poems collected in Habermann, 61–71.

44. Cf. the *chansons de geste*.

45. I Sam. 31:4–6; T.B., Gittin, 57b; T. B., Avodah Zarah, 18a.

46. *Da'at Zekanim me-Rabbenu Ba'lei ha-Tosafot*, ed. I. J. Nunez-Vaes (Livorno, 1783), to Gen. 9:5, s.v. *ve-akh*.

47. Tosafot to Avodah Zarah, 18a, s.v. *ve-al yehabel 'azmo*.

48. *Tosafot 'al Massekhet 'Avodah Zarah le-Rabbenu Elhanan*, ed. David Fränkel (Husatyn, 1901), to Avodah Zarah, 18a, s.v. *mutav sheyitlenu*.

49. Rabbi Meir ben Baruch of Rothenburg, *Teshuvot, Pesakim, u-Minhagim*, ed. I. Z. Cahana 3 vols. (Jerusalem, 1957–1962), II: 54.

50. *Da'at Zekanim*, to Gen. 9:5, s.v. *ve-akh*.

51. *Ha-Semak mi-Zurich*, ed. Isaac Rosenberg (Jerusalem, 1973), 58.

52. Rabbi Meir ben Baruch of Rothenberg, *Teshuvot, Pesakim, u-Minhagim*, II, 54.

53. David Berger, "Study of the Rabbinate of Early Ashkenaz" (Hebrew), *Tarbiz* LIII (1984), 484, n. 6.

54. This translation is that of Judah Goldin in Spiegel, *The Last Trial*, 148–149.

55. N&S, 51; Habermann, 97; Eidelberg, 105; Chazan, S.

56. N&S, 15; Habermann, 41; Eidelberg, 45; Chazan, L.

57. N&S, 51; Habermann, 98; Eidelberg, 105; Chazan, S. Cf. N&S, 2; Habermann, 26; Eidelberg, 24; Chazan, L.

58. N&S, 27; Habermann, 55; Eidelberg, 65; Chazan L.

59. In his study "From Politics to Martyrdom," *Prooftexts*, Ivan G. Marcus emphasizes the theological perspectives of the Hebrew chronicles. While I agree that these theological perspectives are central concern of the chronicles, I think it important to emphasize that the theological views are superimposed upon the historical recital and do not distort the narrative.

60. N&S, 48; Habermann, 94; Eidelberg, 100; Chazan, S.

61. N&S, 53; Habermann, 100; Eidelberg, 109; Chazan, S. Cf. N&S, 6; Habermann, 30; Eidelberg, 30; Chazan, L.

62. N&S, 4; Habermann, 27; Eidelberg, 26; Chazan, L.

63. N&S, 3; Habermann, 26; Eidelberg, 25; Chazan, L.

64. There appears once in the Hebrew narratives an alternative to the simple sin-punishment paradigm. Early in L we find: "But their Father did not answer them. He shut out their prayer and screened himself off with a cloud, that no prayer might pass through. The tent [of prayer] was rejected and he banished them from his presence. For a decree had been enacted before him from [the time when God has spoken] of a day of accounting."

(N&S, 1–2; Habermann, 25; Eidelberg, 22; Chazan, L). The reference is to Exodus, chapter 32, and the sin of the golden calf. Moses pleads on behalf of his people for divine forgiveness. The incident concludes when God tells Moses to resume leadership of the Israelites, but notes that there will eventually be a reckoning for the sin of the golden calf. L suggests that the persecutions of 1096 may have been such a reckoning, thus making the Rhineland martyrs bear the burden not of their own sin, but that of earlier Israel. The notion appears only in this single passage. It is interesting to note that L juxtaposes to this passage a statement that interprets the persecutions as a divine test, a view to be discussed in detail shortly.

65. N&S, 6; Habermann, 30; Eidelberg, 29–30; Chazan, L. Cf. N&S. 8 and 52; Habermann, 32 and 99; Eidelberg, 33 and 108; Chazan, L and S.

66. N&S, 7–8; Habermann, 31–32; Eidelberg, 32–33; Chazan, L.

67. N&S, 8; Habermann, 32; Eidelberg, 33; Chazan, L. See again Spiegel's brilliant analysis of the Abraham incident as reflected in subsequent Jewish history and literature, *The Last Trial*. On 1096, see in particular pp. 17–27.

68. On similar feelings among the Crusaders, see Rousset, *Les origines et les caractères de la première croisade*, 183–189. The epic of defeat, as described by Rosenberg, generally carries the same conviction.

69. N&S, 8; Habermann, 32; Eidelberg, 33; Chazan, L.

70. Gen. 22:16–18.

71. N&S, 17; Habermann, 43; Eidelberg, 48–49; Chazan, L.

VI. The Church, the Jews, and the Later Crusades

1. I shall emphasize the two great crusades of the twelfth century, and shall refer only occasionally to the organized crusades of the thirteenth century and to the popular crusading movements.

2. N&S, 58; Habermann, 115; Eidelberg, 121.

3. Otto of Freising, *Gesta Friderici I imperatoris*, ed. B. de Simson (Hanover, 1912), 58.

4. Ibid.

5. N&S, 78; Habermann, 161.

6. N&S, 63; Habermann, 120; Eidelberg, 128–129. For the literature on these locales, see Baron, *A Social and Religious History*, IV:300, n. 39.

7. N&S, 62; Habermann, 119; Eidelberg, 127–128.

8. All prior editions of this important missive are now superceded by the exhaustive work embodied in the new *Sancti Bernardi opera*, ed. J. Leclercq and H. M. Rochais, 8 vols. (Rome, 1957–1977), VIII:311–317. All previous studies are superceded by Jean Leclercq, "L'encyclique de saint Bernard en faveur de la croisade," *Revue bénédictine*, LXXXI (1971), 282–308, and idem, "Pour l 'histoire de l 'encyclique de saint Bernard sur la croisade," *Mélanges E.-R. Labande* (Poitiers, 1974), 479–490.

9. *Sancti Bernardi opera*, VIII:320–322.

10. Odo of Deuil, *De profectione Ludovici VII in orientem*, ed. and trans. Virginia Gingerich Berry (New York, 1948); Otto of Freising, *Gesta Friderici imperatoris*, ed. de Simson.

11. N&S, 58–66; Habermann, 115–123; Eidelberg, 121–133. On this chronicle see my "R. Ephraim of Bonn's *Sefer Zechirah*, *REJ* CXXXII (1973), 119–126.

12. See the two full studies cited above in note 8.

13. N&S, 65; Habermann, 122; Eidelberg, 131.

14. Note the letters addressed: "Ad peregrinantes;" "Ad archiepiscopos orientalis Francie et Bavarie;" "Ad gentem Anglorum," Leclercq, "L'encyclique de saint Bernard en faveur de la croisade," 293.

15. Note the letter addressed specifically to the archbishop of Cologne and the bishop of Speyer, ibid.

16. Otto of Freising, *Gesta Friderici*, 58–59.

17. Psalms 59:11–12.

18. Ibid., 59:12.

19. Ibid., 59:16.

20. The deleted passage, which breaks the thought, includes a gratuitously negative reference to Jewish moneylending.

21. *Sancti Bernardi opera*, VIII:316.

22. See David Berger's study of Bernard's general attitudes toward Jews, "The Attitude of St. Bernard of Clairvaux Toward the Jews," *PAAJR* XL (1972), 89–108. Berger notes the divergent elements in Bernard's stance toward the Jews—traditional protection on the one hand and damaging negative stereotypes on the other. He concludes by pointing out the contradictory results of these divergent attitudes: "The great Christian protector of

twelfth-century Jewry sowed seeds which would claim the life of many a Jewish martyr."

23. *Sancti Bernardi opera*, VIII:320–322.

24. Otto of Freising, *Gesta Friderici*, 59.

25. Psalms 59:12. The entire passage can be found in N&S, 59; Habermann, 116; Eidelberg, 122.

26. For evidence of violence associated with the popular crusades, see inter alia, Adolphe Cheruel, *Normanniae nova chronica* (Caen, 1850), 23–24—1251; *MGH, Scrip.*, X:412—1309; Gustave Mollat (ed.), *Vitae paparum Avinoniensium*, 4 vols. (Paris, 1914–1927), I:129–130 and 161–163—1320; Jean Duvernoy, ed., *Le registre d'inquisition de Jacques Fournier*, 3 vols. (Toulouse, 1965), I:177–180—1320.

27. See, inter alia, Michel Villey, *La croisade: essai sur la formation d'une théorie juridique* (Paris, 1942), 151–158, and James Brundage, *Medieval Canon Law and the Crusader* (Madison, 1969), 159–190.

28. Otto of Freising, *Gesta Friderici*, 57.

29. J. P. Migne ed., *Patrologiae cursus completus, series Latina*, 217 vols. (Paris, 1844–1855), CCII:1539–1542.

30. Ibid., CCXIV:311–312, no. 366. Cf. a similar demand on Dec. 31, 1199, *ibid.*, CCXIV, 831–832, no. 270.

31. See *ibid*, CCXV:1470–1471, no. 159. Cf. the similar papal demand of November 11, 1209, ibid., CCXVI:158–159, no. 136.

32. J. D. Mansi et al., *Sacrorum conciliorum nova et amplissima collectio*, 53 vols. in 58 (Florence and Paris, 1759–1927), XXII:1063.

33. For subsequent papal repetitions of these demands, see the convenient collection of Solomon Grayzel, *The Church and the Jews in the XIIIth Century*, 2d ed. (New York, 1965), 180, no. 58; 216, no. 77; 218, no. 80; 280, no. 121; 290, no. 129; 290, no. 130. For an interesting Jewish complaint on this issue, see *Milḥemet Miẓvah*, Biblioteca Palatina Parma, MS. 2749, folio 72b; and my "A Jewish Plaint to Saint Louis," *HUCA*, XLV (1974), 294.

34. N&S, 64; Habermann, 121; Eidelberg, 131.

35. *Ouevres de Rigord et de Guillaume le Breton*, ed. H.-Francois Delaborde, 2 vols. (Paris, 1882–1885), I:85.

36. H.-Francois Delaborde ed., *Recueil des actes de Philippe Auguste*, 3 vols. (Paris, 1916–1966), II:550–551, no. 955.

37. Alexandre Teulet et al., eds., *Layettes du Tresor des Chartes*, 5 vols. (Paris, 1863–1909), I:292–293, no. 768.

38. Petrus Pressutti ed., *Regesta Honorii Papae III*, 2 vols. (Rome, 1888–1895), I:no. 3120.

39. Pressutti, *Regesta Honoris Papae III*, I:no. 288.

40. Giles Constable ed., *The Letters of Peter the Venerable*, 2 vols. (Cambridge, Mass., 1967), I:328–330, no. 130.

41. N&S, 64; Habermann, 121; Eidelberg, 13.

42. See my *Medieval Jewry in Northern France* (Baltimore, 1973), 110–111, 119–123, 148.

43. Martin Bouquet et al., eds., *Recueil des historiens des Gaules et de la France*, 24 vols. (Paris, 1737–1904), XX:34.

44. In his fine study of St. Louis and his crusading ventures, William Chester Jordan suggests that Louis IX did adopt a policy of confiscation of Jewish usury for the Holy War; see *Louis IX and the Challenge of the Crusade* (Princeton, 1979), 84–86 and 98–100. While I agree that, after the fact, confiscated debts owed to Jews were used for crusading, I would argue that the original confiscation was ordered to provide funds with which to reimburse debtors who had earlier paid out usury—illegal under ecclesiastical law—to the Jews.

45. *Chronicles of the Reign of Stephen, Henry II, and Richard I*, ed. Richard Howlett, 4 vols. (London, 1884–1889), I:294–312.

46. Ibid., 310–311.

47. *Ibid.*, 313–314. See further the excellent monograph by R. B. Dobson, *The Jews of Medieval York and the Massacre of March 1190* (York, 1974).

VII. Glances Backward and Forward

1. The period, according to most of the contributors to Benson and Constable, *Renaissance and Renewal in the Twelfth Century*, extended roughly from 1060 to 1160.

2. It is interesting that Charles Homer Haskins himself was aware of and took serious interest in developments in Jewish cultural life during the twelfth century.

3. Habermann, 1.

4. In his extremely important study of German-Jewish Pietism, published in *Zion* III (1937–38), Baer made some penetrating observations on the spiritual interaction between early Ashkenazic Jewry and its host environment. There have been two studies of Baer's historiography: Isaiah Sonne, "On Baer and His Philosophy of Jewish History," *Jewish Social Studies* IX (1947), 61–80; and Pinchas E. Rosenbluth, "Yitzhak Baer: A Reappraisal

of Jewish History," *Yearbook of the Leo Baeck Institute* XXII (1977), 175–188. The issues raised by Baer's historiography are exceedingly complex and, given the richness and influence of his oeuvre, deserve extensive treatment.

5. Haim Hillel Ben-Sasson (ed.), *A History of the Jewish People*, English translation (Cambridge, Mass., 1976), 386. The incomprehensible English of the closing sentence has been corrected on the basis of the Hebrew original.

6. Ben-Zion Dinur (ed.), *Yisraʾel ba-Golah*, 2d ed., 2 vols. in 8 (Tel Aviv, 1958–1972), II: bk. 1:1.

7. See, e.g., Dubnow, *Weltgeschichte des Judischen Volkes* or *Divrei Yemei Am Olam*; Roth, *The Dark Ages*; Caro, *Sozial-und Wirtschaftsgeschichte der Juden im Mittelalter und der Neuzeit*; Leon Poliakov, *A History of Anti-Semitism*, trans. Richard Howard, 3 vols. (New York, 1965–1975).

8. Bernhard Blumenkranz, *Les auteurs chrétiens latins du moyen âge sur les Juifs et le Judaïsme* (Paris, 1963); idem, *Juifs et Chrétiens dans le monde occidental*; Agus, *Urban Civilization in Pre-Crusade Europe*; idem, *The Heroic Age of Franco-German Jewry*; Dasberg, *Untersuchung über die Entwertung des Judenstatus im 11 Jahrhundert*.

9. For a valuable survey of nineteenth- and twentieth-century views of the critical turning point in medieval Jewish experience, see the first chapter in the doctoral dissertation of Jeremy Cohen, *Mendicants, The Medieval Church, and the Jews* (Cornell University, 1978).

10. This is not to suggest that Sephardic Jewish history comes to an end in 1492. It is meant simply to note the radical physical changes which take place.

11. See, e.g., E. J. Passant, "The Effects of the Crusades Upon Western Europe," *Cambridge Medieval History*, ed. J. B. Bury et al., 8 vols. in 9 (Cambridge, 1911–1936), V:320–333 and Southern, *The Making of the Middle Ages*, 13.

12. Baron, *A Social and Religious History*, IV:90–91. It is noteworthy that Baron, unlike most modern Jewish historians, does not use 1096 as a dividing line in his periodization of medieval Jewish history.

13. See, inter alia, Chazan, *Medieval Jewry in Northern France*; H. G. Richardson, *The English Jewry under Angevin Kings* (London, 1960); Cecil Roth, *A History of the Jews in England*, 3d ed. (Oxford, 1964), chaps. 1–4.

14. N&S, 52; Habermann, 99; Eidelberg, 108; Chazan, S. Cf. N&S, 8; Habermann, 32; Eidelberg, 33; Chazan, L.

15. At the conclusion of his *Ḥakhmei Ashkenaz ha-Rishonim*, Avraham Grossman notes carefully the devastating impact of the assaults of 1096 on the scholarly elites of Worms and Mainz. While suggesting that some time was required for rebuilding the intellectual life of these formerly great centers, Grossman does not make exaggerated claims for the overall impact of the catastrophe on medieval Ashkenazic intellectual life.

16. See Urbach, *Ba'alei ha-Tosafot*.

17. See Poznanski, *Mavo al Ḥakhmei Ẓarfat Mefarshei ha-Mikra*.

18. Text taken from Joseph Dan, *Torat ha-Sod shel Ḥasidut Ashkenaz* (Jerusalem, 1968), 16.

19. See the aforecited study by Dan and Ivan G. Marcus, *Piety and Society*.

20. Again the careful Grossman study does not suggest permanent disruption of German Jewish intellectual life, let alone of all Ashkenazic creativity.

21. Southern, *The Making of the Middle Ages*, 13.

22. Important studies have been published recently in this area by Gavin I. Langmuir. See especially "Thomas of Monmouth: Detector of Ritual Murder," *Speculum* LIX (1984), 820–846; "The Knight's Tale of Young Hugh of Lincoln," *Speculum* XLVII (1972), 459–482; "L'absence d'accusation de meurtre rituel à l'ouest du Rhône," *Juifs et judaisme de Languedoc*, ed. M.-H. Vicaire and Bernhard Blumenkranz (Toulouse, 1977), 235–249. See also Langmuir's more general studies: "Prolegomena to Any Present Analysis of Hostility against Jews," *Social Science Information* XV (1976), 689–727; "Medieval Anti-Semitism," *The Holocaust: Ideology, Bureaucracy, and Genocide*, ed. Henry Friedlander and Sybil Milton (Millwood, 1980), 27–36.

23. See above, chap. III.

24. Bernhard Blumenkranz's *Le Juif médiéval au miroir de l'art chrétien* (Paris, 1966) shows no trace of artistic depiction of crusading attacks upon the Jews.

25. Haym Soloveitchik, "Three Themes in *Sefer Ḥasidim*," *AJS Review* I (1976), 311–357; Marcus, *Piety and Society*.

26. Soloveitchik, "Three Themes," 317.

27. N&S, p. 53; Habermann, 100, Eidelberg, 109; Chazan, S. Cf. N&S, 7; Habermann, 31; Eidelberg, 31; Chazan, L.

28. See above, chap. IV.

29. Ibid.

30. See above, chap. V.

31. See above, chap. IV.

32. On the problematic Antiochene decrees, see in particular Victor Tcherikover, *Hellenistic Civilization and the Jews*, trans. S. Applebaum (Philadelphia, 1959), 175–203; on the Hadrianic decrees, see especially Lieberman, "Persecution of the Jewish Religion."

33. See Langmuir, "From Ambrose of Milan to Emicho of Leiningen: The Transformation of Hostility against Jews in Northern Christendom," in which sociological categories are used to highlight the novelty of the persecution of 1096.

34. Jeremy Cohen, *The Friars and the Jews* (Ithaca, 1982). I have growing doubts with regard to this view and hope to address the matter at length shortly.

35. The innovation in patterns of Jewish response to persecution is emphasized by both Mintz, *Hurban*, and Roskies, *Against the Apocalypse*.

APPENDIX:
THE HEBREW FIRST-CRUSADE CHRONICLES

S

1. This is an introductory statement by the copyist. In the manuscript each word has a line above it, e.g. אתחיל.

2. Ashkenazic Jews reckoned the destruction of the Second Temple in the year 68 C.E., thus giving the date of 1096 C.E.

3. Obad. 1:4.

4. Isa. 40:3, 57:14, 62:10.

5. The Hebrew reads ולפנות דרך ללכת דרך ירושלים ; the second דרך is probably superfluous.

6. Isa. 14:19.

7. I Sam. 12:21.

8. Jud. 12:3; I Sam. 28:21; Job 13:14.

9. The reading in N&S is ולשבר. As noted in footnote d, the manuscript reads ולשעבר , which is better.

10. I Sam. 15:3. The implication is total destruction.

11. Influenced by Ps. 48:7.

12. The text includes two additional words, which are unintelligible and have not been translated.

13. Isa. 33:5.

14. Prov. 10:25.

15. Isa. 30:6; Prov. 1:27.

16. Jer. 4:10.

17. The Hebrew term תועים has the connotation of erring; it is a derogatory term for the crusaders and is widely used throughout the Hebrew chronicles.

18. Jer. 27:17.

19. Depicted in II Kings 18–19 and II Chron. 32.

20. Again a derogatory term is used in the Hebrew, תופתה, a reference to the site where human sacrifices were offered. See e.g., II Kings 23:10.

21. Gen. 32:13 and 41:49; Isa. 10:22; Hos. 2:1.

22. The Hebrew is וברנקי. Baer translated this into German as "einen Ausruf der Freiheitserklarung;" Eidelberg omitted the word in his translation.

23. Influenced by Jon. 3:8.

24. II Kings 23:26.

25. The manuscript has אדר, which is clearly in error. I have followed the N&S emendation in the translation. The date is May 3, 1096.

26. Ezek. 9:6 and T. B., Sabb., 55a.

27. II Sam. 4:12.

28. A designation for the leader of the Jewish community.

29. Ps. 106:23.

30. Josh. 8:20.

31. This is of course a subsequent activity.

32. Gen. 27:46.

33. II Kings 19:31; Isa 37:32; Ezra 9:14.

34. II Kings 18:21; Isa. 36:6.

35. Exod. 21:23.

36. The tenth of Iyyar in 1096 was a Monday, corresponding to May 5, 1096. Note that L assigns a different date to this catastrophe. Joseph Hacker, "About the Persecutions during the First Crusade" (Hebrew), *Zion* XXI (1966):227–229, notes that L's date is the one subsequently recognized by Ashkenazic Jewry and suggests, on that basis, a late provenance for S. If, however, an accepted date were widely recognized in later Ashkenazic Jewry, a late author would have no reason to provide an alterna-

tive. The problem of divergence in dating is an interesting one but contributes nothing to the dating of S.

37. Ps. 83:4.

38. H. Bresslau, in his introductory observations to N&S, p. xiv, suggests that the accusation of well poisoning, which became common in the fourteenth century, indicates late provenance for S. This is a weak argument for late dating. The spread of this accusation in the fourteenth century does not negate its occurrence earlier.

39. The manuscript contains an extra word, which I have not translated.

40. See the comments of Rashi and the Tosafists on the words אני והו, T.B., Sukk., 45a.

41. On the notion of 974 generations, see Louis Ginzberg, *The Legends of the Jews*, 7 vols. (Philadelphia, 1909–1938), vol. V, 3–4, n. 5.

42. Deut. 26:18.

43. Jer. 12:3.

44. Deut. 26:5 and 28:62.

45. Influenced by II Sam. 15:21.

46. II Kings 18:6; II Chron. 25:27 and 34:33.

47. May 20, 1096. Again L gives a different date.

48. Deut. 33:19.

49. This entire passage is heavily influenced by the biblical account of the binding of Isaac, Gen. 22:1–19.

50. An allusion to Gen. 22:12.

51. An allusion to Gen. 21:16.

52. The key words ויעקד and מאכלת from Gen. 22 are central here.

53. Isa. 64:11.

54. II Kings 23:26.

55. Jer. 22:28.

56. Isa. 14:19. The term נצר is meant to evoke recollections of Isa. 11:1 and of נוצרי, the Hebrew designation for Christian. All of this is made derogatory through the combination נצר נתעב.

57. Job 16:9; Ps. 37:12.

58. I have left untranslated the unintelligible וידין עליו.

59. II Sam. 24:14.

60. Prov. 12:4 and 31:10.

61. Isa. 51:20.

62. Prov. 31:31.

63. The manuscript is unclear. I have emended the reading to עין ארם.

64. Ps. 17:13–14. I have filled in the complete text in the translation.

65. Isa. 64:3. I have again filled in the complete text.

66. The manuscript reads וישם, which I have emended to ושבו.

67. Josh. 7:5.

68. Ezek. 11:13.

69. Jud. 6:13.

70. Ecc. 9:13.

71. Albert of Aix, in his closing pejorative note on the popular crusading bands, cites the veneration of a goose which was seen as inspired by the Holy Spirit, along with a goat similarly viewed. See *RHC, Hist. Occ.*, IV:295.

72. The emendation in N&S has been used.

73. Again the emendation in N&S has been used.

74. The words בלב אחד have not been translated.

75. Exod. 16:3. This quotation is somewhat curious. It cites a statement by the rebellious Israelites longing to return to Egypt, a somewhat strange paradigm for the pious Rhineland Jews committing themselves to martyrdom.

76. May 24, 1096.

77. The emendation in N&S has been utilized.

78. Ezek. 11:13.

79. May 25, 1096.

80. I have read כעפר לדוש, as is found in L. See II Kings 13:7.

81. II Kings 8:12.

82. Gen. 18:23–32.

83. May 27, 1096.

84. Exod. 19:15.

85. Lam. 2:1.

86. I have emended the text to read יראת חטא.

87. Deut. 6:5.

88. Gen. 22:17; I Kings 5:9.

89. The group's reply and the introduction to Rabbi Menahem's next statement are missing.

90. Deut. 6:4. The entire passage is taken from T.B., Pes., 56a. I have quoted the story in its entirety, for the sake of clarity. The point of the story is that the Jews should immediately recite the statement of Jewish faith normally made prior to death.

91. Exod. 24:7.

92. The manuscript reads ויקרא, but I have emended to ויקראו for better sense.

93. Deut. 6:4.

94. The manuscript is deficient.

95. The manuscript reads שיניר. Baer suggested "Secretarium"; Eidelberg suggested "sacristy"; I have chosen to leave the term untranslated.

96. May 27, 1096.

97. Zeph. 1:15.

98. Job 3:5.

99. Job 3:4.

100. Gen. 22:17.

101. The four modes of capital punishment in Jewish law are by stoning, burning, strangulation, and sword.

102. I have not translated the unintelligible word סרור.

103. I have not translated the words ומכר נשים.

104. Isa. 64:11.

105. I have not translated the closing six words, which are unintelligible.

106. The manuscript reads לסקלם, which I have emended to סקלם.

107. Ps. 89:50.

108. I have not translated seven words here which seem misplaced.

109. Hos. 10:14.

110. A reference to the woman of II Macc., 7, widely celebrated in subsequent Jewish literature. See Cohen, "Hannah and Her Seven Sons in Hebrew Literature."

111. Ps. 113:9.

112. Lam. 1:11.

113. T.B., Ber. 28b.

114. I have emended the text to read הוליכינו.

115. Lam. 2:15.

116. I Kings 20:6; Ezek. 24:16, 21, 25.

117. Zach. 1:14 and 8:2.

118. The term denotes leadership in the synagogue.

119. The manuscript reads יום, which I have emended to אם.

120. Ps. 55:24.

121. Dan. 12:3.

122. The text is abruptly cut off.

123. Again this is the copyist's notation. Once more there are lines over each word.

L

1. This seems to be an introductory statement by an editor who gathered diverse materials. On the possible identification of this editor, see above, chap. II.

2. The spring months of 1096.

3. Ashkenazic Jews dated the destruction of the Second Temple to the year 68 C.E.

4. Recurrent cycles of nineteen years each.

5. Jer. 31:6. The first word of the verse is רני, the numerical value of which is 256.

6. Isa. 35:10 and 51:11.

7. Deut. 28:16–68.

8. Note the reference in Deut. 28:61.

9. Ps. 114:1.

10. Hab. 1:6.

11. Ezek. 7:22.

12. Ps. 74:4.

13. The term תעות denotes error, as does the term used for the crusaders.

14. Prov. 30:27.

15. Ps. 83:5. The psalm beseeches God to visit many forms of retribution on those who make such statements.

16. This is the tripartite formula which plays a central role in the liturgy of the Day of Atonement.

17. Gen. 3:24.

18. Esth. 4:16.

19. Lam. 4:8.

20. Lam. 3:8.

21. Lam. 3:44.

22. Ps. 78:67.

23. II Kings 17:18.

24. Exod. 32:34.

25. Ps. 103:20.

26. April 10, 1096.

27. April 25–26, 1096.

28. May 3, 1096.

29. This seems to be the editor's inserted remark.

30. May 18, 1096. This date differs from that given in S.

31. Jer. 5:6; Zeph. 3:3.
32. Isa. 9:11.
33. May 25, 1096.
34. Hos. 10:14.
35. The Hebrew כי נשחט עליהם is not clear.
36. Deut. 6:4.
37. Isa. 10:25, 16:14, and 29:17.
38. Lam. 4:5.
39. Again apparently the editor's note.
40. Ezek. 38:4 and 39:9.
41. Josh. 7:5.
42. Ezek. 11:13.
43. Jud. 6:13.
44. Ps. 22:12.
45. Ecc. 9:12.
46. T.B., B.B., 138a.
47. Prov. 11:4.
48. Hos. 4:12.
49. Josh. 8:22; Jer. 42:17.
50. Isa. 58:12.
51. A designation for the leader of the community.
52. This is not quite correct. Emperor Henry IV spent the period between 1090 and 1097 in northern Italy.
53. Esth. 1:22.
54. Isa. 45:7.
55. Num. 23:10.
56. Jer. 11:20.
57. Ps. 124:5.
58. II Kings 17:9.
59. Exod. 32:9, 33:3 and 5, 34:9; Deut. 9:6 and 13.
60. Job 37:1.
61. Ps. 39:3.
62. Ps. 143:4; Lam. 3:6.
63. Lam. 3:50.
64. Job 2:1.
65. Isa. 57:14.
66. Words are missing in the manuscript.
67. Gen. 22:17; I Kings 5:9.
68. Isa. 29:6.
69. Gen. 45:26.
70. Josh. 2:11.

71. There are seven words in the manuscript that are unintelligible.

72. Isa. 19:1.

73. Jer. 40:3.

74. Ps. 78:60.

75. Ezek. 11:16 and T.B., Meg., 29a.

76. Lev. 26:33.

77. Isa. 30:17.

78. Ps. 78:61.

79. Lam. 2:20.

80. Isa. 42:22.

81. Lam. 1:21.

82. II Kings 21:12.

83. Jer. 48:17.

84. Lam. 4:2.

85. Albert of Aix, in his closing pejorative note on the popular crusading bands, cites the veneration of a goose that was seen as inspired by the Holy Spirit, along with a goat similarly viewed. See *RHC, Hist. Occ.,* IV:295.

86. Exod. 16:3. This is a somewhat strange citation in that these words, in their original context, are uttered by the rebellious Israelites seeking to return to Egypt.

87. May 24, 1096.

88. Deut. 26:5 and 28:62.

89. Ezek. 11:13.

90. Ps. 119:137.

91. May 25, 1096.

92. The Hebrew, איטליא של יון, is not entirely clear.

93. II Kings 13:7.

94. II Kings 8:12.

95. Gen. 18:23–32.

96. May 27, 1096.

97. Exod. 19:15.

98. II Sam. 1:23.

99. Ps. 106:23.

100. Lam. 1:6.

101. Jer. 25:34.

102. Isa. 28:6.

103. Dan. 12:3.

104. Jer. 49:25.

105. Jer. 17:1; Job 19:24.

106. Zach. 14:13.

107. I Sam. 5:6.

108. II Kings 18:21; Isa. 36:6.

109. May 27, 1096.

110. Zeph. 1:15.

111. Job 3:5.

112. Job 3:4.

113. Gen. 22:17.

114. The four modes of capital punishment in Jewish law are by stoning, burning, strangulation, and sword.

115. Esth. 9:5.

116. Deut. 28:56.

117. Jer. 31:20.

118. I have used the reading suggested in N&S.

119. Lam. 4:2.

120. M. Avot 5:3. See Ginzberg, *The Legends of the Jews*, V:218, n. 52.

121. Dan. 3.

122. Gen. 22:1–19.

123. Isa. 14:19. The term נצר is meant to evoke recollections of Isa. 11:1 and of נוצרי, a Hebrew designation for Christian. All of this is made derogatory through the combination נצר נתעב.

124. Isa. 66:8.

125. Jer. 30:6.

126. Isa. 33:7.

127. Joel 2:10.

128. I have not translated וצר.

129. Isa. 5:30.

130. Isa. 64:11.

131. Ps. 44:23.

132. Ps. 79:10.

133. Lam. 2:1.

134. Isa. 58:12.

135. Isa. 59:15.

136. The manuscript is deficient at this point.

137. An allusion to Deut. 31:17.

138. Num. 22:26.

139. Isa. 51:13.

140. Lam. 2:5.

141. Lam. 4:16.

142. The manuscript may be defective here. See Isa. 17:6.

143. Deut. 6:4.

144. The manuscript is defective here.
145. Deut. 6:4. The story of Jacob and his sons is found in T.B., Pes., 56a. The point is to arouse the Jews of Mainz to pronounce the declaration of faith in preparation for martyrdom.
146. Exod. 24:7.
147. Deut. 6:4. This sentence may well be superfluous.
148. II Kings 19:31; Isa. 37:32; Ezra 9:14.
149. Ps. 89:50.
150. Deut. 18:13.
151. Hos. 10:14.
152. II Macc. 7. This pious woman is widely celebrated in Jewish literature.
153. Ps. 113:9.
154. Gen. 39:6.
155. Lam. 1:11.
156. Isa. 13:4 and 66:6.
157. T.B., Ber. 28b.
158. Lam. 2:15.
159. II Kings 20:6; Ezek. 24:16, 21, and 25.
160. Zach. 1:14 and 8:2.
161. The term denotes leadership in the synagogue.
162. Ps. 55:24.
163. Dan. 12:3.
164. Lam. 1:16.
165. May 29, 1096.
166. Jer. 23:20 and 30:24.
167. Gen. 43:30; I Kings 3:26.
168. I have not translated התורה.
169. I Kings 8:54.
170. Job 1:1.
171. Ps. 50:23.
172. Mal. 3:23.
173. Isa. 57:1.
174. I have not translated the words עורות התועבה.
175. I have not translated the words צידה לדרך.
176. T.B., Ber., 48b.
177. Ps. 110:6.
178. Ps. 74:1.
179. Exod. 19:15.
180. Exod. 29:18 et al.
181. Baer translated the term as "Secretarium"; Eidelberg translated it as "sacristy"; I have chosen to leave it untranslated.

182. Ps. 119:143.
183. Gen. 15:17.
184. Lam. 4:4.
185. Deut. 28:48.
186. Joah. 2:14.
187. Exod. 15:9.
188. Deut. 13:18; Josh. 7:26.
189. Prov. 21:1.
190. Isa. 64:11.
191. The manuscript is defective. I have accepted N&S's suggestion, in note a, of reading ויתקבצו.
192. Ps. 110:6.
193. Deut. 32:43.
194. Ps. 83:13.
195. Ps. 83:5.
196. Ps. 94:7.
197. Ps. 94:1.
198. Ps. 44:23.
199. Isa. 9:11.
200. Lam. 2:20–21.
201. Ps. 79:12.
202. Ps. 94:2.
203. Isa. 13:5.
204. Isa. 42:13.
205. Ps. 79:6.
206. Ps. 69:25.
207. Ezek. 24:7.
208. Job 16:18.
209. Ps. 79:10.
210. Deut. 13:7–12.
211. The manuscript is defective here.
212. The manuscript is defective here. I have read: בהבל.
213. Deut. 12:15 and 15:22.
214. Lev. 22:28.
215. The manuscript has the word סיתתן which is omitted in N&S.
216. May 29, 1096.
217. The text seems defective.
218. T.B., Taan., 29a.
219. May 30–31, 1096.
220. July 1, 1096.

221. Exod. 19:16.
222. Isa. 10:6; Ezek. 38:12.
223. After Isa. 10:6 and Micah 7:10.
224. Job 9:6.
225. Ezek. 7:22.
226. Habb. 1:13.
227. Lam. 1:11.
228. June 3, 1096.
229. June 23–24, 1096.
230. Esth. 4:16.
231. June 24, which is the Feast of St. John. Both Baer and Eidelberg translate וביום השלישי "on the third day," i.e. the third of the days mentioned in the previous sentence, which means the second of Tammuz or Wednesday, June 25.
232. P, which often supplements or corrects the account in L, notes specifically the Feast of St. John.
233. I have accepted the emendation in N&S, which is based on P.
234. Ps. 68:23; T.B., Gitt., 57b.
235. June 24, 1096. P places this attack on the next day.
236. P identifies the town as Wevelinghofen.
237. The river that runs past Wevelinghofen is in fact a tributary of the Rhine, the Erft River.
238. II Sam. 1:23.
239. II Sam. 24:14.
240. S. of S. 5:15.
241. I have not translated the words נפש בני.
242. II Sam. 1:23.
243. Job 29:11.
244. The point of this is unclear.
245. Dan. 1:15.
246. Isa. 64:11.
247. Isa. 42:13.
248. Deut. 32:43.
249. The third of Tammuz, June 26, fell on a Thursday. P simply identifies the date as the third of Tammuz.
250. The site indicated here is uncertain. Baer identifies it as Altenahr; Eidelberg suggested Eller; Abulafia argues for Ellen, see "The Interrelationship between the Hebrew Chronicles of the First Crusade," 227 n. 25. In my article, "The Deeds of the Jewish Community of Cologne," I accepted Altenahr on geographic

grounds; it is closest to Cologne and is near Julich, as noted in P. Here I have decided to be more cautious and refrain from making a problematic identification.

251. The fourth of Tammuz fell on Friday, June 27. P rectifies L's report, making it Friday, the fourth of Tammuz.

252. See note 249 above.

253. The manuscript has a number of extra words, not noted in N&S. I have followed the reading in N&S, which is a sensible one.

254. Prov. 20:6.

255. Ps. 15.

256. Lam. 1:16.

257. The manuscript lacks the designation for "ben" or "son of."

258. T.B., Sabb., 31b.

259. Jer. 7:33, 16:4, 19:7, 34:20.

260. This is an important point. I have followed the suggestion of Ismar Elbogen, "Zu den hebräischen Berichten über die Judenverfolgungen im Jahre 1096," *Beiträge zur Geschichte der deutschen Juden* (Leipzig, 1916), 20–22, for this translation.

261. Solomon ben Simson may have been the editor of the entire collection, the author of the entire Cologne unit, or the author of the report on Xantes only. I would suggest tentatively the middle possibility.

262. Again the fifth of Tammuz fell on Saturday, June 28. The story makes it clear that the group at Xantes was attacked late on Friday. P eliminates the problem by placing the incident on the fourth of Tammuz.

263. This passage opens the *kiddush*, which marks the inception of the Sabbath.

264. T.B., San., 111a.

265. Job 30:31.

266. Lam. 3:8.

267. Job 33:23.

268. S. of S. 1:3. The simple translation of the biblical verse is: "Therefore do maidens love you." I have translated the verse in this odd fashion in order to clarify the author's midrashic understanding of it.

269. Ps. 44:23.

270. Exod. 32:29.

271. I Sam. 7:9.

272. Ps. 25:9.

273. The opening of the grace after meal.

274. The grace after meal (birkat ha-mazon) includes a series of standard petitions which begin: "May the Merciful . . . " These special petitions were appended to the standard prayer formulae.

275. Deut. 6:4.

276. Isa. 9:2.

277. Ps. 19:6.

278. Isa. 64:3.

279. An allusion to Ezek. 8:17.

280. Isa. 29:1.

281. Jer. 15:7.

282. The manuscript reads: באחר בשבת בשבע לחורש תמח, giving this translation. Again this is problematic in that the seventh of Tammuz, June 30, fell on Monday. P avoids the problem by not specifying the day of the week.

283. The name of the town is missing in the manuscript. N&S supplied it from P.

284. The manuscript includes two additional words that make no sense in context and which I have not translated.

285. Esth. 8:14.

286. July 31, 1096. This is the fast day which commemorates the destruction of the temples in Jerusalem.

287. Baer—and Eidelberg after him—identifies this place as Dortmund. I have left the site unidentified.

288. I have accepted the reading suggested in N&S.

289. Ps. 119:85.

290. Judges 5:31.

291. Deut. 33:2.

292. Ps. 16:11.

293. Read שֶבֶע instead of שֶבַע.

294. Ps. 31:20.

295. Ps. 97:11.

296. Ps. 42:2.

297. The four identified towns in which Jews were assaulted—Neuss, Wevelinghofen, Moers, and Xantes—are all north of Cologne. Kerpen is southwest of Cologne, perhaps explaining its happy fate.

298. Baer left this site unidentified; Eidelberg suggested Wesseli. For various identifications, see Baron, *A Social and Religious History of the Jews*, IV:291, n. 17. Samuel Steinherz, "Kreuzfahrer und Juden in Prag (1096)," *Jahrbuch der Gesellschaft für die Geschichte der Juden in der Cechoslowakischen Republik*, I, (1929) 1–32,

discusses at some length the report on successful Jewish military resistance in a fourteenth-century Czech chronicle. There are serious problems associated with this late report and Steinherz's efforts to find the "grain of historical truth" in it and in L's account of events in שלא are far from convincing. It is interesting that P omits reference to this site.

299. Baer suggests Pappenheim; Eidelberg suggests Bohemia. Again P omits.

300. Ps. 48:15. The author clearly intended the juxtaposition of על מות, understood as "beyond death," with ארץ חיים "the land of the living."

301. April 10, 1096.

302. Deut. 11:24; Josh. 1:3.

303. Lam. 1:9.

304. This is a period of seven weeks, not six.

305. June 8, 1096.

306. As happens occasionally, the vernacular term is indicated in Hebrew letters.

307. The Hebrew is סימון. Eidelberg suggests that this may be a derogatory term for St. Simon. There is indeed a monastery of St. Simon in Trier, and it would be significant that the bishop was obliged to find refuge there and not in the cathedral.

308. Isa. 7:2.

309. II Chron. 36:23; Ezra 1:3.

310. The manuscript is defective at this point.

311. The manuscript is defective at this point.

312. Deut. 28:32.

313. Ps. 68:23 and T.B., Gitt., 57b.

314. Jer. 14:19.

315. There are four words in the manuscript that are unintelligible and have not been translated.

316. See above, note 296.

317. The Horites are described in Gen. 36:20–29. The precise meaning of the term here is unclear.

318. Deut. 3:5.

319. An allusion to Josh. 6:7.

320. Deut. 25:18.

321. This concluding observation, like much of the account, is incorrect. The great rout of Peter's forces took place at Civetot, beyond the Byzantine border. Even there the entire force was far from wiped out.

322. Josh 6:1.

323. See above, note 315.
324. The manuscript has מיזנבורק.
325. Ps. 40:3.
326. I.e. the Hungarians.
327. There was no eclipse of the sun at this time. See Theodor
Ritter von Oppolzer, *Canon of Eclipses*, trans. Owen Gingerich
(New York, 1962), charts 110–112.
328. Lev. 26:19.
329. Jer. 12:3.
330. Ps. 79:12.
331. Lam. 3:64–66.
332. Isa. 34:8.
333. Isa. 45:17.

Glossary

Aggadah (adj. aggadic)	The body of Jewish lore outside the realm of halachah, including history, folklore, ethical teachings, and theological speculation.
Ashkenaz (adj. Ashkenazic)	A medieval Hebrew term sometimes used to designate Germany and sometimes used to designate northern Europe in general.
Aquedah	The binding and near-sacrifice of Isaac, the son of Abraham, as depicted in Genesis 22:1–19 and embellished in subsequent Jewish lore.
Cohen (pl. *cohanim*)	A descendant of the priestly family of biblical times.
Gabbai	An honorific designation for a leader in synagogue and community.
German-Jewish Pietism	See *Ḥasidut Ashkenaz*.
Halachah	The set of regulations, consisting of both negative commandments and positive commandments, which governs Jewish individual and corporate behavior and thinking.
Ḥasid	Sometimes used to indicate an adherent of *Ḥasidut Ashkenaz*; sometimes used simply as a designation for a pious Jew.

Ḥasidut Ashkenaz	German-Jewish Pietism, a religious orientation that developed in twelfth-century German Jewry.
Ḥazan	A synagogue functionary, whose precise responsibilities during the period under consideration are uncertain.
Kiddush ha-Shem	Broadly used to designate any action that sanctifies the Divine Name; more narrowly used to designate acts of martyrdom.
Levi	A descendant of the tribe of Levi; members of this tribe in biblical times assisted the priests (*cohanim*) in carrying out temple rituals.
Memorbuch (pl. *Memorbuchen)*	A book that lists, by date of death, deceased members of the community to ensure appropriate memorialization.
Midrash	Rabbinic exegesis of biblical texts for both halachic and aggadic purposes.
Mishnah	The first authoritative code of rabbinic law, compiled ca. 200 C. E.
Mizvah	A commandment, one of the complex of commandments that constitutes halachah.
Nasi	An honorific designation for a highly respected Jewish leader, used rarely in Ashkenazic circles.
Parnas	A leader of the Jewish community.
R.	In S and L, a designation, perhaps akin to present-day "Mr."; in the body of the text, this designation has been omitted.
Rabbi	A person recognized for expertise in Jewish law. The precise training and accreditation

implied when the term was applied at this early stage of Ashkenazic Jewry is unknown.

Talmud   The Babylonian Talmud is the body of exegetical material on the Mishnah, compiled in the Babylonian academies during the fifth and sixth centuries C. E.; the Palestinian Talmud, a parallel collection of materials, was drawn up in the Palestinian academies at a slightly earlier date. (The Babylonian Talmud is cited in the notes as T. B.)

Tosafists   A school of commentators on the Talmud, which developed in twelfth-century France.

Tosafot   The commentaries on the Talmud by the Tosafists.

Bibliography

PRIMARY SOURCES

Abraham ben Azriel. *Sefer ʿArugat ha-Bosem*. Ed. Ephraim E. Urbach. 4 vols. Jerusalem, 1939–1963.

Abraham ibn Daud. *Sefer ha-Qabbalah*. Ed. Gerson D. Cohen. Philadelphia, 1967.

Albert of Aix. *Liber Christianae expeditionis*. In *Recueil des historiens des croisades, historiens occidentaux*. Vol. IV.

Annales Wirziburgenses. In *Monumenta Germaniae Historica, Scriptorum*. Vol. II.

Annalista Saxo. In *Monumenta Germaniae Historica, Scriptorum*. Vol. VI.

Bernard of Clairvaux. *Sancti Bernardi opera*. Ed. J. Leclercq and H. M. Rochais. 8 vols. Rome, 1955–1977.

Bernold. *Chronicon*. In *Monumenta Germaniae Historica, Scriptorum*. Vol. V.

Bouquet, Martin et al., ed. *Recueil des historiens des Gaules et de la France*. 24 vols. Paris, 1737–1904.

Chanson de Roland. Eng. trans. by Frederick Goldin. *The Song of Roland*. New York, 1978.

Constantine of Metz. *Vita Adalberonis*. In *Monumenta Germaniae Historica, Scriptorum*. Vol. IV.

Cosmas of Prague. *Chronica Boemorum*. Ed. Bertold Bretholz. Berlin, 1923.

Crispin, Gilbert. *Gislebert Crispini disputatio judei et christiani*. Ed. Bernhard Blumenkranz. Utrecht, 1961.

Daʿat Zekanim me-Ba ʿalei ha-Tosafot. Ed. I. J. Nunez-Vaes. Livorno, 1783.

Delaborde, H.-Francois, ed. *Recueil des actes de Philippe Auguste*. 3 vols. Paris, 1916–1966.

Duvernoy, Jean, ed. *Le registre d'inquisition de Jacques Fournier.* 3 vols. Toulouse, 1965.

Eidelberg, Shlomo, trans. *The Jews and the Crusaders.* Madison, 1977.

Ekkehard of Aura. *Hierosolymita.* In *Recueil des historiens des croisades, historiens occidentaux.* Vol. V.

Elhanan ben Isaac. *Tosafot ʿal Massekhet ʿAvodah Zarah le-Rabbenu Elḥanan.* Ed. David Frankel. Husatyn, 1901.

Ephraim ben Jacob of Bonn. *Sefer Zechirah.* In *Hebräische Berichte über die Judenverfolgungen während der Kreuzzüge* and in *Sefer Gezerot Ashkenaz ve-Zarfat.*

Fulcher of Chartres. *Historia Hierosolymitana.* Ed. Heinrich Hagenmeyer. Heidelberg, 1913.

Gans, David. *Zemaḥ David.* Jerusalem, 1966.

Gershom ben Judah of Mainz. *Seliḥot u. Fizmonim.* Ed. Abraham Habermann. Jerusalem, 1944.

———. *Teshuvot Rabbenu Gershom Me'or ha-Golah.* Ed. Shlomo Eidelberg. New York, 1959.

Gesta Francorum. Ed. Roger Mynors. Trans. Rosalind Hill. London, 1962.

Gesta Treverorum. In *Monumenta Germaniae Historica, Scriptorum.* Vol. VIII.

Guibert of Nogent. *Guibert de Nogent: Histoire de sa vie.* Ed. Georges Bourgin. Paris, 1907.

Habermann, Abraham, ed. *Sefer Gezerot Ashkenaz ve-Zarfat.* Jerusalem, 1945.

Ha-Semak mi-Zurich. Ed. Isaac Rosenberg. Jerusalem, 1973.

Howlett, Richard, ed. *Chronicles of the Reign of Stephen, Henry II, and Richard I.* 4 vols. London, 1884–1889.

Hilgard, Alfred. ed. *Urkunden zur Geschichte der Stadt Speyer.* Strasbourg, 1885.

Isaac ben Moses. *Or Zaruʿa.* 4 vols. in 2. Zhitomir, 1862–1890.

Isaac ben Joseph of Corbeil. *Sefer Miẓvot Katan.* Ladi, 1805.

Judah ha-Cohen. *Sefer ha-Dinim.* Ed. Abraham Grossman. Jerusalem, 1977.

L. In *Hebräische Berichte über die Judenverfolgungen während der Kreuzzüge* and in *Sefer Gezerot Ashkenaz ve-Zarfat.*

Ma'aseh ha-Geonim. Ed. Abraham Epstein. Berlin, 1909.

Mansi, J. D., et al., eds. *Sacrorum conciliorum nova et amplissima collectio.* 53 vols. in 58. Florence and Paris, 1759–1927.

Meir ben Baruch of Rothenburg. *Teshuvot, Pesakim, u-Minhagim.* Ed. I. Z. Cahana. 3 vols. Jerusalem, 1957–1962.

Migne, J. P. ed. *Patrologiae cursus completus, series Latina.* 217 vols. Paris, 1844–1855.

Milḥemet Miẓvah. Biblioteca Palatina Parma, MS. 2749.

Monumenta Germaniae Historica, Scriptorum. 32 vols. Hanover, 1826–1934.

Moses ben Jacob of Coucy. *Sefer Miẓvot Gadol.* Munkacs, 1905.

Neubauer, Adolf, and Moritz Stern, eds. *Hebräische Berichte über die Judenverfolgungen während der Kreuzzüge.* Berlin, 1892.

Normanniae nova chronica. Ed. Adolphe Cheruel. Caen, 1850.

Notitiae Duae Lemovincenses de Praedictione Crucis in Aquitania. In *Recueil des historiens des croisades, historiens occidentaux,* vol. V.

Odo of Deuil. *De profectione Ludovici VII in orientem.* Ed. and trans. Virginia Gingerich Berry. New York, 1948.

Oeuvres de Rigord et de Guillaume le Breton. Ed. H.-Francois Delaborde. Paris, 1882–1885.

Otto of Freising. *Gesta Friderici I imperatoris.* Ed. B. de Simson. Hanover, 1912.

P. In *Hebräische Berichte über die Judenverfolgungen während der Kreuzzüge* and in *Sefer Gezerot Ashkenaz ve-Ẓarfat.*

Peter the Venerable. *The Letters of Peter the Venerable.* Ed. Giles Constable. 2 vols. Cambridge, Mass., 1967.

Pressutti, Petrus, ed. *Regesta Honorii Papae III.* 2 vols. Rome, 1885–1895.

Rashi. *See* Solomon ben Isaac of Troyes.

Raymond of Aguiliers. *Le "Liber" de Raymond d'Aguiliers.* Ed. John Hill and Laurita Hill. Paris, 1969.

Recueil des historiens des croisades, historiens occidentaux. 5 vols. Paris, 1844–1895.

S. In *Hebräische Berichte über die Judenverfolgungen während der Kreuzzüge* and in *Sefer Gezerot Ashkenaz ve-Ẓarfat.*

Seder Avodat Yisra'el. Ed. S. Baer. Redelheim, 1848.

Sefer Ḥasidim. Ed. Judah Wistinetzki. 2d ed. Frankfort, 1924.

Sefer Josippon. Ed. David Flusser. 2 vols. Jerusalem, 1978–1980.

Simon ben Isaac. *Piyyutim.* Ed. Abraham Habermann. Berlin, 1938.

Solomon b. Isaac of Troyes (Rashi). *Piyyutei Rashi.* Ed. Abraham Habermann. Jerusalem, 1941.

———. *Commentary on the Torah.* Ed. Abraham Berliner. Frankfort, 1905. Eng. trans. by M. Rosenbaum and A. M. Silverman. 5 vols. London, 1929–1934.

———. *Commentary on the Talmud.* Printed in all standard editions of Talmud.

———. *Teshuvot Rashi.* Ed. Israel Elfenbein. New York, 1943.
Teshuvot Ba'alei ha-Tosafot. Ed. Irving A. Agus. New York, 1954.
Teshuvot Geonim Kadmonim. Ed. David Kassel. Berlin, 1851.
Teshuvot Ḥakhmei Ẓarfat ve-Lotir. Ed. Joel Muller. Vienna, 1881.
Teshuvot Maharam ben Baruch. Ed. Moshe Bloch. Budapest, 1895.
Teulet, Alexandre, et al., eds. *Layettes du Trésor des Chartes.* 5 vols. Paris, 1863–1909.
Tosafists. *Commentary on the Talmud.* Printed in all standard editions of Talmud.
Vitae paparum Avinoniensium. 4 vols. Paris, 1914–1927.

SECONDARY SOURCES

Abulafia, Anna Sapir. "The Interrelationship between the Hebrew Chronicles of the First Crusade." *Journal of Semitic Studies* XXVII (1982), 221–239.
Agus, Irving A. *The Heroic Age of Franco-German Jewry.* New York, 1969.
———. *Urban Civilization in Pre-Crusade Europe.* 2 vols. New York, 1968.
Alphandéry, Paul. *La Chrétienté et l'idée de croisade.* 2 vols. Paris, 1954–1959.
Aschoff, Diethard. "Zum Judenbild der Deutschen vor den Kreuzzugen: Erkenntnismoglichkeiten und Quellenprobleme." *Theokratia* II (1970–1972), 232–252.
Baer, Yitzhak. "The Persecution of 1096" (Hebrew). *Sefer Assaf,* ed. M. D. Cassuto et al., 126–140. Jerusalem, 1953.
———. "The Religious and Social Tendency of *Sefer Ḥasidim.*" (Hebrew). *Ẓion* III (1938), 1–50.
Baron, Salo W. *A Social and Religious History of the Jews.* 18 vols. 2d ed. New York, 1952–1983.
Ben-Sasson, Haim Hillel, ed. *A History of the Jewish People.* English trans. Cambridge, Mass., 1976.
———. "The Goals of Jewish Chronography during the Middle Ages and Its Problematics" (Hebrew). *Historyonim ve-Askolot Historyot,* 29–49. Jerusalem, 1963.
Benson, Robert L., and Constable, Giles, eds. *Renaissance and Renewal in the Twelfth Century.* Cambridge, Mass., 1982.
Berger, David. "The Attitude of St. Bernard of Clairvaux Toward the Jews." *Proceedings of the American Academy for Jewish Research* XL (1972), 89–108.

————. *The Jewish-Christian Debate in the High Middle Ages.* Philadelphia, 1979.

————. "Mission to the Jews and Jewish-Christian Contacts in the Polemical Literature of the High Middle Ages."

————. "Study of the Rabbinate in Early Ashkenaz" (Hebrew), *Tarbiz* LIII (1984), 479–487.

Bergman, Martin S., and Jacoby, Milton E., eds. *Generations of the Holocaust.* New York, 1982.

Blake, E. O. "The Formation of the 'Crusade Idea.'" *Journal of Ecclesiastical History* XXI (1970), 11–31.

Bloch, Marc. *Feudal Society.* Trans. L. A. Manyon. Chicago, 1961.

Blumenkranz, Bernhard. *Juifs et Chrétiens dans le monde occidental.* Paris, 1960.

————. *Le Juif médiéval au miroir de l'art chrétien.* Paris, 1966.

————. *Les auteurs chrétiens latins du moyen âge sur les Juifs et le Judaïsme.* Paris, 1963.

Boutruche, Robert. *Seigneurie et féodalité.* 2 vols. Paris, 1968–1970.

Brooke, Rosalind, and Brooke, Christopher. *Popular Religion in the Middle Ages.* London, 1984.

Brundage, James. *Medieval Canon Law and the Crusader.* Madison, 1969.

Bynum, Caroline Walker. *Jesus as Mother: Studies in the Spirituality of the High Middle Ages.* Berkeley, 1982.

Caro, Georg. *Sozial- und Wirtschaftsgeschichte der Juden im Mittelalter und der Neuzeit.* 2 vols. Leipzig, 1908–1920.

Chazan, Robert. "A Jewish Plaint to Saint Louis," *Hebrew Union College Annual* XLV (1974), 287–305.

————. "A Twelfth-Century Communal History of Spires Jewry." *Revue des études juives* CXXVIII (1969), 253–257.

————. "Emperor Frederick I, the Third Crusade, and the Jews. *Viator* VIII (1970), 83–93.

————. *Medieval Jewry in Northern France.* Baltimore, 1973.

————. "Polemical Themes in the *Milḥemet Miẓvah.*" In *Les Juifs au regard de l'histoire,* ed. Gilbert Dahan, 169–184. Paris, 1984.

————. "R. Ephraim of Bonn's *Sefer Zechirah.*" *Revue des études juives* CXXXII (1973), 119–126.

————. "1007–1012: Initial Crisis for Northern-European Jewry." *Proceedings of the American Academy for Jewish Research* XXXVIII-XXXIX (1970–1971), 101–117.

————. "The Deeds of the Jewish Community of Cologne." *Journal of Jewish Studies* XXXV (1984), 185–195.

————. "The Early Development of Ḥasidut Ashkenaz." *Jewish Quarterly Review,* in press.

———. "The Hebrew First-Crusade Chronicles." *Review des études juives* CXXXIII (1974), 235–254.

———. "The Hebrew First-Crusade Chronicles: Further Reflections." *AJS Review* III (1978), 79–98.

———. "The Persecution of 992." *Revue des études juives* CXXIX (1970), 217–221.

Chenu, M. D. *Nature, Man, and Society in the Twelfth Century.* Ed. and trans. Jerome Taylor and Lester K. Little. Chicago, 1968.

Cippola, Carlo M., ed. *The Fontana Economic History of Europe: The Middle Ages.* London, 1972.

Classen, Peter. "*Res gestae,* Universal History, Apocalypse: Visions of Past and Future." In *Renaissance and Renewal,* ed. Robert L. Benson and Giles Constable, 387–417. Cambridge, Mass., 1982.

Cohen, Gerson D. "Hannah and Her Seven Sons in Hebrew Literature" (Hebrew). In *Sefer ha-Yovel le-Khevod M. M. Kaplan,* ed. Moshe Davis, 109–122. New York, 1953.

———. "Messianic Postures of Ashkenazim and Sephardim." In *Studies of the Leo Barck Institute,* ed. Max Kreutzberger, 117–156. New York, 1967.

Cohen, Jeremy. "Mendicants, the Medieval Church, and the Jews." Ph.D. dissertation, Cornell University, 1978.

———. *The Friars and the Jews.* Ithaca, N.Y., 1982.

Cowdrey, H. E. J. "Pope Urban II's Preaching of the First Crusade." *History* LV (1970), 177–188.

———. "The Genesis of the Crusades: The Springs of Western Ideas of Holy War." In *The Holy War,* ed. Thomas Patrick Murphy, 9–32. Columbus, 1976.

Crosland, Jessie. *The Old French Epic.* Oxford, 1951.

Cutler, Allan. "The First Crusade and the Idea of 'Conversion.'" *Muslim World* LVIII (1968), 57–61 and 155–164.

Dan, Joseph. "The Problem of *Kiddush ha-Shem* in the Speculative Teaching of the German Ḥasidim" (Hebrew). In *Milḥemet Kodesh u-Martirologiah,* 121–129. Jerusalem, 1968.

———. *Torat ha-Sod shel Ḥasidut Ashkenaz.* Jerusalem, 1968.

Daniel, E. Randolph. *The Franciscan Concept of Missionizing in the High Middle Ages.* Lexington, 1975.

Dasberg, Lea. *Untersuchungen über die Entwertung des Judenstatus im 11 Jahrhundert.* Paris, 1965.

Dietrich, Ernst L. "Das Judentum im Zeitalter der Kreuzzüge." *Saeculum* III (1952), 94–131.

Dinur, Ben-Zion, ed. *Yisra'el ba-Golah.* 2 vols. in 8. 2d ed. Tel Aviv, 1958–1972.

Dobson, R. B. *The Jews of Medieval York and the Massacre of March 1190*. York, 1974.

Dronke, Peter. *Poetic Individuality in the Middle Ages*. Oxford, 1970.

Dubnow, Simon. *Divrei Yeme Am Olam*. Trans. B. Krupnick. 10 vols. 2d ed. Tel Aviv, 1958.

———. *Weltgeschichte des Judischen Volkes*. Trans. A. Steinberg. 10 vols. Berlin, 1925–1929.

Duby, George. *The Early Growth of the European Economy*. Trans. Howard B. Clarke. Ithaca, N.Y., 1974.

Duncalf, Frederic. "The Peasants' Crusade." *American Historical Review* XXVI (1921), 440–454.

———. "The First Crusade: Clermont to Constantinople." In *A History of the Crusades*, ed. Kenneth M. Setton, I:253–279. 5 vols. 2d ed. Madison, 1969–1984.

Elbogen, Ismar. "Zu den hebräischen Berichten über die Judenverfolgungen im Jahre 1096." *Beiträge zur Geschichte der deutschen Juden*. Leipzig, 1916.

Erdmann, Carl. *The Origin of the Idea of Crusade*. Trans. Marshall W. Baldwin and Walter Groffart. Princeton, 1977.

Falck, Ludwig. *Mainz im Fruhen und Hohen Mittelalter*. Dusseldorf, 1972.

Fleming, Gerald. *Hitler and the Final Solution*. Berkeley, 1984.

Flusser, David. "Jewish Sources of Christian Martyrdom and Their Influence on Its Fundamental Concepts" (Hebrew). *Milḥemet Kodesh u-Martirologiah*, 61–71 (Jerusalem, 1968).

Frend, W. H. C. *Martyrdom and Persecution in the Early Church*. Oxford, 1965.

Frimer, Dov. I. "Masada in the Light of Halachah." *Tradition* XII, no. 1 (1971), 27–43.

Funkenstein, Amos. *Heilsplan und naturliche Entwicklung*. Munich, 1965.

Ginzberg, Louis. *The Legends of the Jews*. 7 vols. Philadelphia, 1909–1938.

Golb, Norman. "New Light on the Persecution of French Jews at the Time of the First Crusade." *Proceedings of the American Academy for Jewish Research* XXXIV (1966), 1–63.

Graetz, Heinrich. *Geschichte der Juden*. 11 vols. Various places, 1873–1900.

Grayzel, Solomon. *The Church and the Jews in the XIIIth Century*. 2d ed. New York, 1965.

Grossman, Abraham. *Ḥakhmei Ashkenaz ha-Rishonim*. Jerusalem, 1981.

Guénée, Bernard. *Histoire et culture historique dans l'occident médiéval*. Paris, 1980.

Hagenmayer, Heinrich. *Peter der Eremite*. Leipzig, 1879.

Hanning, Robert W. *The Individual in Twelfth-Century Romance*. New Haven, 1977.

Haskins, Charles Homer. *The Renaissance of the Twelfth Century*. Cambridge, Mass., 1927.

Heer, M. D. "Martyrdom and Its Background in the Second Century" (Hebrew). In *Milḥemet Kodesh u-Martirologiah*, 73–92. Jerusalem, 1968.

Holmes, Urban Tigner, Jr. *A History of Old French Literature*. New York, 1962.

Jackson, W. T. H. *The Literature of the Middle Ages*. New York, 1960.

Jellinek, Adolf, ed. *Bet ha-Midrash*. 6 vols. in 2. 2d ed. Jerusalem, 1938.

Jordan, William Chester. *Louis IX and the Challenge of the Crusade*. Princeton, 1979.

Katz, Jacob. *Exclusiveness and Tolerance*. Oxford, 1961.

————. "Martyrdom in the Middle Ages and in 1648–9" (Hebrew). In *Sefer Yovel le-Yitzhak Baer*, ed. Samuel Ettinger et al., 318–337. Jerusalem, 1961.

Kedar, B. Z. *Crusade and Mission*. Princeton, 1984.

Langmuir, Gavin I. "From Ambrose of Milan to Emicho of Leiningen: The Transformation of Hostility against Jews in Northern Christendom." *Settimane di studio del Centro italiano di studi sull'alto medioevo* XXXVI (1980), 313–368.

————. "L'absence d'accusation de meutre rituel à l'ouest du Rhone." In *Juifs et judäisme de Languedoc*, ed. M.-H. Vicaire and Bernhard Blumenkranz, 235–249. Toulouse, 1977.

————. "Medieval Anti-Semitism." In *The Holocaust: Ideology, Bureaucracy, and Genocide*, ed. Henry Friedlander and Sybil Milton, 27–36. Millwood, N.J., 1980.

————. "Prolegomena to Any Present Analysis of Hostility against Jews." *Social Science Information* XV (1976), 689–727.

————. "The Knight's Tale of Young Hugh of Lincoln." *Speculum* XLVII (1972), 459–482.

————. "Thomas of Monmouth: Detector of Ritual Murder." *Speculum* LIX (1984), 820–846.

Leclercq, Jean. "L'encyclique de saint Bernard en faveur de la croisade." *Revue bénédictine* LXXXI (1971), 282–308.

————. "Pour l'histoire de l'encyclique de saint Bernard sur la croisade." In *Melanges E.-R. Labande*, 479–490. Poitiers, 1974.

Le Goff, Jacques. *The Birth of Purgatory.* Trans. Arthur Gold-hammer.

———. *Time, Work, and Culture in the Middle Ages.* Trans. Arthur Goldhammer. Chicago, 1980.

Lieberman, Saul. "Persecution of the Jewish Religion" (Hebrew). In *Salo Wittmayer Baron Jubilee Volume,* ed. Saul Lieberman, Heb. vol., 213–245. 3 vols. New York, 1974.

Liebeschütz, Hans. "The Crusading Movement in Its Bearing upon the Christian Attitude towards Jewry." *Journal of Jewish Studies* X (1959), 97–111.

Lopez, Robert S. *The Commercial Revolution of the Middle Ages, 950–1350.* Englewood Cliffs, N.J., 1971.

McGinn, Bernard. "*Iter sancti Sepulchri:* The Piety of the First Crusaders." In *Essays on Medieval Civilization,* ed. Bede Karl Lackner and Kenneth Roy Philip, 33–71. Austin, 1978.

Manselli, Raoul. *La religion populaire au moyen âge.* Montreal, 1975.

Marcus, Ivan G. "From Politics to Martyrdom: Shifting Paradigms in the Hebrew Narratives of the 1096 Crusading Riots." *Prooftexts* II (1982), 40–52.

———. *Piety and Society: The Jewish Pietists of Medieval Germany.* Leiden, 1981.

Mayer, Hans Eberhard. *Bibliographie zur Geschichte der Kreuzzüge.* Hanover, 1960.

Mintz, Alan. *Ḥurban: Responses to Catastrophe in Hebrew Literature.* New York, 1984.

Moore, R. I. *The Origins of European Dissent.* New York, 1977.

Munro, Dana. "The Speech of Pope Urban II at Clermont, 1095." *American Historical Review* XI (1906), 231–242.

Ritter von Oppolzer, Theodor. *Canon of Eclipses.* Trans. Owen Gingerrich. New York, 1962.

Parkes, James. *The Jew in the Medieval Community.* London, 1938.

Passant, E. J. "The Effects of the Crusades upon Western Europe." In *Cambridge Medieval History,* ed. J. B. Bury et al., vol. V, 320–333. 8 vols. in 9. Cambridge, 1911–1936.

Poliakov, Leon. *A History of Anti-Semitism.* Trans. Richard Howard. 3 vols. New York, 1965–1975.

Poznanski, Samuel. *Mavo ʿal Ḥakhmei Ẓarfat Mefarshei ha-Mikra.* Warsaw, 1913.

Prawer, Joshua. *Toldot Mamlekhet ha-Ẓalbanim be-Ereẓ Yisrael.* 2 vols. 3d ed. Jerusalem, 1971.

Radding, Charles M. "Superstition to Science: Nature, Fortune, and the Passing of the Medieval Ordeal." *American Historical Review* LXXXIV (1979), 945–969.

Richardson, H. G. *The English Jewry under Angevin Kings.* London, 1960.

Rosenberg, Bruce A. *Custer and the Epic of Defeat.* University Park, Pa., 1974.

Rosenbluth, Pinchas E. "Yitzhak Baer: A Reappraisal of Jewish History." *Yearbook of the Leo Baeck Institute* XXII (1977), 175–188.

Roskies, David G. *Against the Apocalypse: Responses to Catastrophe in Modern Jewish Literature.* Cambridge, Mass., 1984.

Roth, Cecil. *A History of the Jews in England.* 3d ed. Oxford, 1964.

———. "European Jewry in the Dark Ages: A Revised Picture." *Hebrew Union College Annual* XXIII (1950–1951), pt. II, 151–169.

———. ed. *The Dark Ages.* The World History of the Jewish People. Tel Aviv, 1966.

Rousset, Paul. *Les origines et les caractères de la première croisade.* Neuchâtel, 1945.

Runciman, Steven. *A History of the Crusades.* 3 vols. Cambridge, 1951–1954.

Russell, Jeffrey Burton. *Dissent and Reform in the Early Middle Ages.* Berkeley, 1965.

Schiffman, Sarah. *Heinrich IV und die Bischöfe in ihrem Verhalten zu den deutschen Juden zur Zeit des ersten Kreuzzuges.* Berlin, 1931.

Setton, Kenneth M., ed. *A History of the Crusades.* 5 vols. 2d ed. Madison, 1969–1984.

Shulvass, Moshe. "Crusaders, Martyrs, and the Marranos of Ashkenaz." In *Between the Rhine and the Bosphorus,* 1–14. Chicago, 1964.

Sivan, Emmanuel. *L'Islam et la croisade.* Paris, 1968.

Smalley, Beryl. *Historians in the Middle Ages.* London, 1974.

Soloveitchik, Haym. "Three Themes in *Sefer Ḥasidim.*" *AJS Review* I (1976), 311–357.

Sonne, Isaiah. "On Baer and His Philosophy of Jewish History." *Jewish Social Studies* IX (1947), 61–80.

Southern, R. W. *Medieval Humanism and Other Studies.* Oxford, 1970.

———. *The Making of the Middle Ages.* London, 1953.

Spiegel, Shalom. *The Last Trial.* Trans. Judah Goldin. Philadelphia, 1967.

Steinherz, Samuel. "Kreuzfahrer und Juden in Prag (1096)." *Jahrbuch der Gesellschaft fur die Geschichte der Juden in der Cechoslowakischen Republik* I (1929), 1–32.

Stelzmann, Arnold. *Geschichte der Stadt Köln*. 3d ed. Cologne, 1962.

Stock, Brian. *The Implications of Literacy*. Princeton, 1983.

Strait, Paul. *Cologne in the Twelfth Century*. Gainesville, 1974.

Tcherikover, Victor. *Hellenistic Civilization and the Jews*. Trans. S. Applebaum. Philadelphia, 1959.

Urbach, Ephraim. *Baʿalei ha-Tosafot*. 2 vols. 4th ed. Jerusalem, 1980.

Vauchez, Andre. *La spiritualité du Moyen Age occidental*. Paris, 1975.

Villey, Michel. *La croisade: essai sur la formation d'une theorie juridique*. Paris, 1942.

Waas, Adolph. "Volk Gottes und Militia Christi—Juden und Kreuzfahrer." *Miscellanea Medievalia*, vol. IV, 410–434. Berlin, 1966.

Waltz, James. "Historical Perspectives on 'Early Missions' to Muslims." *Muslim World* LXI (1971), 170–186.

White, Lynn, Jr. *Medieval Technology and Social Change*. Oxford, 1962.

———. "Science and the Sense of Self: The Medieval Background of a Modern Confrontation." *Daedalus* CVII, no. 2 (Spring 1978), 47–59.

Yerushalmi, Yosef Hayim. *Zakhor*. Seattle, 1982.

Zerubavel, Yael. "The Last Stand: On the Transformation of Symbols in Modern Israeli Culture." Doctoral dissertation, University of Pennsylvania, 1980.

Index

Abelard, 134
Abraham ben Yom Tov, 160
Abraham-Isaac imagery, 127, 158–159, 165; testing theme and, 163–164.
Adhemar, Bishop, 51
Afterlife, reward for martyrdom in, 130–131, 165, 166
Aggadah, 120, 123–124; biblical commandments underlying, 121–122; on suicide, 155
Akiba, Rabbi, 119–120, 121, 163, 221
Albert of Aix, 53, 59–60, 61, 62, 65, 213; on Bishop Ruthard, 94; on Cologne massacre, 69–70; on conversions, 100, 101; on responses of Mainz Jewry, 70, 89, 101, 106, 111; on zeal of German crusaders, 65–66
Alexandria, 218
Anonymity, personal, 135
Anti-Jewish ideology/sentiments, 8, 30–32, 33–37, 99; call to crusade and, 66–68, 77–84; Church doctrine and, 28–29; in fourteenth century, 212–213; Jewish behavior in First Crusade and, 213; Jewish perception of, 152; key motifs, 170; Le Mans incident, 34–35;

of Peter the Hermit's forces, 55; in Second Crusade, 169–170, 175; in Third Crusade, 141–142; in thirteenth century, 212; in twelfth century, 212; usury as factor in, 188, 304–305 n. 28. See also Violence against Jews
Ashkenazic Jewry, 2; business as primary occupation of, 21, 23; codes, 146; creativity of, 8, 27, 215; derivation of term, 303 n. 7; development of new lifestyle, 196, 197, 214; early development of, 5; effects of martyrdom on, 197; emergence as cohesive force, 5; after First Crusade events, 8–9, 137–147, 197, 203–209; growth and development before First Crusade, 16–37; intellectual vigor of, 13, 14, 17, 25–26, 27, 114, 195–196; literary traditions, 17, 148–150; norms of resistance, 146, 147; origins, 20–21; perceptions of, 138–139, 142–143; population growth, 16–27, 201–202; relationship to non-Jewish world, 193; self-rule, 25; thirteenth-century decline of, 8; transfer

369